The Creative Brain
by Ned Herrmann

PUBLICATION INFORMATION

ISBN: 0-944850-01-4 Hardback edition—Includes brain dominance profile insert

ISBN: 0-944850-02-2 Paperback edition—Same text as harbound without brain dominance profile insert

Library of Congress Catalog Card Number: 87-072980

First Edition published in 1988.

Second Edition published in 1989, second printing, 1990, third printing, 1993.

Second Edition printed in paperback in 1990 and 1992.

Printed in the United States of America by Arcata Graphics, Kingsport, Tennessee.

A Brain Books imprint distributed by The Ned Herrmann Group.

CREDITS

Cartoon on page 124 is reprinted with permission from the artist, Joseph Farris, © 1981 AMA and Joseph Farris

The Decision-Making Model on page 128 has been reproduced and adapted with permission from Ted Coulson and Alison Strickland, © ACLS

ILLUSTRATORS

Ron Bell, Marilyn Meeks, Roger D. Merrill, Allan Olsen, Angelo Renaldi and Minaco Sakai

PHOTOGRAPHERS

Ned Herrmann, M.A. Nehdi, Bob Samples

COVER ILLUSTRATOR

James Noel Smith

The Ned Herrmann Group
2075 Buffalo Creek Road, Lake Lure, North Carolina 28746
Telephone: (704) 625-9153   Fax: (704) 625-2198

DEDICATION

This book is dedicated to all those who have expressed interest in my work. No matter what their age, role, position, wealth, or power, their interest in what I am doing has provided and will continue to provide access to my ideas. Interest in the human brain is the common denominator of all those I consider colleagues and associates. My door is always open for those who want to share in that interest.

Ned Herrmann

CONTENTS

I. BACKGROUND

II WHAT THE BRAIN QUADRANTS MEAN TO US ALL

III. THE CREATIVE LIFE AND HOW TO ENHANCE IT

ILLUSTRATION LIST

PREFACE

A personal note for those who are searching for a clearer understanding of self.

The urge to experience and define personal identity must be genetic, woven into the human DNA, because it is a driving force that has motivated people throughout all history. In the search for some understanding of themselves, some sense of who they are in their universe, human beings repeatedly ask, Who am I? Why am I the way I am? Who can I become? In what direction should I go? How can I change? Why am I here?

The search for the answers, which is a life-long process, takes many forms and these vary from one individual to another. For example, many of us, as we mature, want to learn more about our roots, not just concerning our mother and father and their parents, but going way back into family genealogy. Who came before them? and How did that influence us? are questions we want answered. However, as those who have traced their ancestry can attest, knowing our biological roots is only a small part of knowing who *we* are. For most of us this knowledge derives not from our family tree, but from our unique inner mental, emotional, and spiritual experiences. Most of these experiences are usually invisible to an observer. They're internal, private, largely non-verbal, and often a mystery even to ourselves.

For this reason, the quest for a sense of self is a very personal one. No other human being can give any one of us "The Answers." We need to find those answers for ourselves, and they seldom come fast, simple, or tidy (except maybe in retrospect). We are always "piecing it together," as long as we live.

In my own search for my place and work, I made some remarkable discoveries about the human brain, and these have changed my life enormously. What I found was an explanation of the double existence I'd been leading for most of my long life—with one foot in the world of big business, the other planted just as solidly in the world of art and music. The insights into the brain acted as a mirror that showed me who I was and why I behaved the way I did. What follows is the story of that discovery and of many other discoveries that have followed since. I wrote this book as a very personal story for several reasons: First, it's more interesting that way, both to read and to write. Second, the ideas will be more real and believable when you see how they worked for me. Finally, I hope that you'll see in the story some parallels to your own life that will serve to confirm and strengthen you in your own search.

Thank you for your interest. I wish you an exciting journey through *The Creative Brain.*

For those you who are seeking a fuller understanding of self, I encourage you to complete the Herrmann Participant Survey Form before reading further and send it to our office for free scoring.

Having your own personal profile data before you will enable you to more readily apply the concepts presented in this book. You will find the survey form inserted at the beginning of Chapter 3 (p.43) and printed on colored stock so you may locate it quickly.

Ned Herrmann

INTRODUCTION

The Creative Brain tells the story of what I consider my life's work: learning and teaching in very practical ways how understanding the brain can enhance our creativity, education, competence, communication, relationships, parenting, management style, productivity, and self-understanding, to name just a few.

Although it was only recently that I learned the term *brain dominance*, I've been actively thinking about the subject for over 50 years, through an unusually varied set of overlapping life experiences: 35 years with General Electric in a wide variety of staff and line management positions, 12 of those years in designing and teaching management education programs; 30 years as an active singer/actor; 24 years as a practicing professional artist; and, most recently, 8 years as head of my own company.

Based on my own experience and that of many others, I know that the lessons this book offers on creativity and the brain apply equally to all fields of human endeavor. Most of the examples are from the business and artistic worlds because that's what I know best. But successful applications of my work can be found in more than 30 fields outside of my own personal areas of concentration, and if my experience had been in public education, government service, communications, or any other occupation, equally relevant examples would have been just as easy to come by. So you can safely and freely translate my examples to suit your own areas of interest.

I have tried to be creative in writing about creativity and the human brain. The resulting book therefore differs in format, content, and approach from other books on the same general subject. In particular, it does things that the many other works don't do:

- Includes the Herrmann Brain Dominance Instrument (HBDI), which entitles you to a complete report on your personal brain dominance profile. This report alone, which normally costs as much as this book, has been of inestimable value for many thousands of people.

- It traces the historical development of my theory of how the specialized brain works.

- It clearly explains the four-quadrant metaphoric model of brain dominance and its derivation, and includes extensive studies validating it.

- It offers insights into how brain dominance affects human behavior. Based on over half a million completed surveys, and hundreds of workshop experiences, these insights have relevance for every person in every setting—individual, in groups, in families, in business, and in a wide variety of human endeavors.

- It lays out a proven creative problem-solving process, expressed in terms of brain quadrants and based on decades of experience.

- It defines issues of innovation, motivation, and productivity—in business—in a way that points clearly toward a solution.

- It establishes the source of creativity, demonstrates that creativity is well within the reach of anyone with a sound mind and a desire to be creative, and offers a rich array of options for increasing your own creativity.

- It provides a new basis for the understanding of self and offers a new definition of normal.

Had I written the book ten years ago, when the Aha! of the brain dominance concept first exploded in my own brain, the story line would have been simpler and more contained—less complicated by the myriad applications that have resulted. That early audience would have been limited to those who were interested in new information on brain specialization and in the psychometric validation studies.

But now, because so many lives have been touched by this new knowledge of brain function, today's audience has been broadened to include much of the general public. And that's a dilemma! How to put a technical subject into lay terms for such diverse audiences, each with varied interests. Friends, colleagues, and editors counseled me to limit my audience. But who was I going to leave out? Parents looking for ways to understand their kids? Educators looking for ways to revitalize tired classrooms? Artists struggling to manage the business side of art? Business executives looking for ways to make their company more creative? Managers seeking to make work more rewarding? Individuals searching for themselves? I couldn't make such choices, so I chose to talk to you all.

Partly for that reason, I encourage you, in reading this book, to start with what interests you the most, just as I did in writing it. There are, of course, advantages to reading the book straight through. Chief among them is that you'll learn from my experience. You'll get a sense of how creativity can evolve in a person's life and see the creative process at work in all its stages.

To help you decide how to read the book, here is a brief outline. The first three chapters establish the physiological premise upon which the metaphoric model is based. The latter chapters expand on that premise with examples and specific applications. The book is divided into three main sections, with a wrap-up chapter, as follows:

I. *Background* tells how I developed my concept of brain dominance, devised a paper-and-pencil instrument to measure it, and developed the metaphoric four-quadrant model of brain dominance. Here are the chapters:

1. *Duality and Beyond: The Journey to Wholeness Begins* describes my early awareness of duality and sketches the process I went through in discovering more about brain dominance.

2. *Brain 101: A Short Course on Brain Basics* is for those who are interested in the evolution of my thinking, and want to understand how the left brain/right brain theory and the triune brain theory contributed to the development of the four-quadrant model of brain dominance.

3. *From Duality to Quadrality: How the HBDI Was Born* describes, step-by-step, how I developed the Participant Survey Form, the Consolidated Scoresheet, and the Brain Dominance Profile, which together comprise the Herrmann Brain Dominance Instrument (HBDI). It also explains how early learnings about brain dominance were applied to improve the design of GE's management education courses.

II. *What the Brain Quadrants Mean to Us All* describes the fascinating insights gained as a result of having studied tens of thousands of brain dominance profiles and having correlated them with observations of human behavior.

4. *Discoveries About Brain Dominance Profiles and You* describes each quadrant and the major types of profiles in terms of individual behavior in specific areas such as time, dress, and occupation. It also discusses organizational and family group behavior patterns that are based on dominance profiles.

5. *What Does the Brain Have To Do with Management, Anyway?* explains the concept of whole-brain management, and how that concept can help fill our critical need to: (a) revive the creative potency of our corporations, and (b) reverse the productivity declines that have plagued our established companies.

6. *War or Peace? Communication Across Mental Boundaries* surveys the various verbal and nonverbal dialects associated with each brain quadrant; takes a look at quadrant-related humor; and then examines communication mismatches in business.

III. *The Creative Life and How To Enhance It* explains what creativity is and offers a wide array of options for increasing your experience of it.

7. *Zigzag Lightning: Creativity and the Whole Brain* debunks the myth that you need to be a genius to be creative, defines creativity in whole-brain terms, explains what hinders creativity, and offers four sure ways to reclaim one's creative passion.

8. *ACT I: Breakthrough to Creativity* presents a sample of what breakthrough means and then explains how our flagship workshop, Applied Creative Thinking I, works so you can develop ideas for your own creative expansion.

9. *After ACT—Into Action* tells how you can apply what you've learned about yourself to becoming a more balanced and creative individual. It also gives tips for excelling in various stages of the creative process.

10. *Building Your Creative Environment: Both Inside and Out* gives practical examples of how to nurture the creative process by transforming our mental, physical, emotional, and spiritual surroundings into creative space that can be claimed and then owned.

In the final chapter, *Messages of Hope for the Future*, I respond to some of the major issues raised by my work. These concern: (1) the way we define normalcy; (2) how we look at differences, especially between men and women; (3) "going creative" as a better way to manage change; (4) how we define "gifted" and the resulting choices we make of education and careers; (5) the immense productivity gains we can tap through matching jobs and mental preferences; and, finally, (6) how working in composite whole-brain groups can teach us to operate in a community.

In addition, the book includes a glossary of terms, a bibliography for references and further reading, and several major appendices containing sample profiles, validation studies on the instrument, and valuable exercises.

I. Background

DUALITY AND BEYOND: THE JOURNEY TO WHOLENESS BEGINS

Have you ever felt like you're missing the mark? I have. In fact, if the life lived fully and well were a bull's eye, then for a number of years, most of my arrows seemed to be hitting around the edge of the target rather than its center. Even though I was considered to be successful, many of my arrows never hit the target at all. Then virtually overnight, I discovered that the brain is the center of who I am. The target grew easier to see and my aim improved dramatically. I gained new confidence and my inner self became more visible, not just in parts, but in toto. The result was hitting more bull's eyes: at work, at home, as a husband, a father, an artist, an educator, a manager, and beyond roles—as a person. How that happened is the foundation of this book and the good news I want to share with you. My hope is that the ideas and the concepts I have put together will do for you what they have done for me and thousands of others—that is, help you to hit your own bull's eyes; to feel unique, normal, and confident in your new understanding of self and, thereby, increase your success in learning, competence, work, communication, management, productivity, leadership, fulfillment, marriage, family relationships, and creativity.

In brief, here is what my insight was about. I had always thought of myself as normal, but I wasn't like most people I knew. There's a part in all of us that wonders if we are completely normal. In my own case, why did people say things to me like: "Ned, you're too sensitive," "Ned, you've got the right answers, but you used the wrong method," "Ned, you're too different to be successful and happy here." These comments shook my carefully constructed sense of "okayness"—not enough for me to change very much, but definitely enough for me to wonder uncomfortably: "Am I really okay?" Then one day, an intuitive lightning strike of understanding about the brain allowed me to remain unique and still feel normal.

That initial insight was followed by many others that opened up a whole new dimension of intellectual and creative functioning. The brain, I learned, is specialized—not just physically, but mentally as well. Its specialized modes can be organized into four separate and distinct quadrants—each with its own language, perception, values, gifts, and ways of knowing and being. We are all unique composites of those differing modes according to our particular mix of mental preferences and avoidances.

The behavioral differences resulting from our mental preferences are, like handedness, just perfectly normal expressions of human dominance. Each of us is dominant mentally as well as physically, and our mental dominances ultimately affect our behavior. With the four-quadrant model as an organizing principle, we can array the many

Figure 1-1. Bull's Eye (opposite)

$O_2 = C_6H_{12}O_6 + H_2O$

Figure 1-2. High School Years—Pondering Which Path to Take

varieties of thinking preferences into a sensible whole. This then provides a basis of understanding of the brain's role in human behavior.

I expect that many of you have wondered who you are, why you do the things you do, who you could become. If I asked you now to go back to the first moments when such thoughts occurred to you, it would likely be some years ago when you were a young person. This is also where my story starts. For it was as a young person that the first aspects of my own inner struggle became visible to me.

SCHOOL YEARS: MY FIRST LOOK AT DUALITY

Like most young people, I starred in some subjects, did okay in others, and bombed in a few that I couldn't get through my head. At any particular time, I might be grinding a telescope mirror, playing chess, participating in a debate, conducting a science experiment, singing, or performing in a variety show. School was fun and I loved the adventure of it. I was energized and motivated.

By the time I reached my sophomore year in high school, it became clear that my interests fell into two distinct and divergent areas. While I found math and science easy, I was also a natural in singing and acting and was very active in the Glee Club and Drama Society. People in these two areas didn't cross paths often. Those who did well in mathematics and science, as I did, tended to choose certain activities after school. Those who did well in music and the performing arts seemed to do poorly in mathematics and science, and chose different activities. This diversity meant I had two sets of friends—my math and science buddies and my acting and singing friends.

This duality was no problem for me. In fact, I liked living in my two favorite worlds. I not only got to do most of what I wanted, but also derived satisfaction from being able to perform well in either one. The duality of activities meant double the adventure and fun and double the rewards. It was great!

In college, however, the expectations were different. One was expected to *specialize*. It was time to think about a career, after all. In my heart of hearts, I wanted to study physics, but instead of asserting my personal preference, I fell into the trap so many of us fall into—selecting a career path because someone else did. My father, brother, and uncles were all chemists, so although I wasn't all that interested in the field, I elected to major in chemical engineering.

Having chosen to study engineering, I continued to pursue my musical interests outside of class, but for the first time the sense of personal integration I had enjoyed in high school was rapidly drifting away. In fact, because my musical interests so far outweighed my interest in chemical engineering, I was quite unable to balance these two divergent drives. The net result was a disaster. I failed miserably. In high school, I had felt smart enough to enjoy learning and so I did well. In college, I felt too dumb to ever get involved in the learning that was offered and did poorly in those first few years.

Ultimately, I got back on track after returning from military service in World War II. I dropped chemical engineering and graduated in physics and music. It turned out that I was "smart" in physics and "dumb" in chemistry. This double major of physics and music both enriched my education and left me wondering even more, not only

"The strongest principle of growth lies in human choice."

George Eliot

Out of the night that covers me,
Black as the pit from pole to pole,
I thank whatever gods that be
For my unconquerable soul.

In the fell clutch of circumstance
I have not winced or cried aloud,
Under the bludgenings of chance
My head is bloody but unbowed.

Beyond this place of wrath and tears
Looms but the horror of the shade,
And yet the menace of the years
Finds, and shall find me unafraid.

It matters not how straight the gate,
How charged with punishments the scroll,
I am the master of my fate,
I am the captain of my soul.

'Invictus' William Ernest Henley

Figure 1-3. Spring Pathway (*by the author, gouache*)

Figure 1-4. Peacham Barn (*by the author, oil on canvas*)

about my own duality, but also about the duality in the worlds around me. One world, the engineering and scientific schools of Cornell University, was populated by students who were primarily male, had crew cuts, and were equipped with slide rules. They attended classes in institutional-type buildings—some of stone and others of glass, plastic panels, and steel; some temporary gray-painted wooden barracks, others made of regulation slabs of concrete. The faculty members wore white shirts, ties, and three-piece suits.

It seemed fitting that to get from Cornell's College of Engineering to the Music Department I had to cross not only a mental bridge but an actual physical bridge as well. On the other side, across the gorge, the buildings were all quite different. Typically old Victorian houses that had been converted into teaching spaces, they were homey and informal, set into a wooded area surrounded by lawns and meandering paths. Here there was an equal number of men and women, and the teachers were much less formal in their dress and manner.

The contrast between these two areas was striking, but no more so than the pieces of my own life. My senior thesis concerned the origins of the craters of the moon; while I was writing it, I tried out for the Metropolitan Opera. Good fortune had already given me the chance to solo in both Carnegie Halls (Pittsburgh and New York).

Eventually, I had to make a choice between music and science for my professional life. The rigors of war, the maturity of age, and the prospect of supporting a family had tilted me toward the serious business of becoming a scientist and had subordinated both my desire and capability to be a professional opera singer. I look back on this period of integration as the last time for many years that

I could enjoy the freedom to incorporate all my interests into my daily worklife.

GE AND THE RETURN TO THE CREATIVE

After receiving my bachelor's degree, I finally—after much cogitation—made my major career choice and joined the General Electric Company. When the employment recruiters arrived on campus in the spring of my graduation year, GE announced interviews for engineers interested in joining the "Test" program. I was not an engineer, but I had some technical background and I wanted to work for the company, so I signed up for the interview and told my story to Maynard Boring, the company's chief recruiter. When I explained my view of the differences between engineering and physics, he seemed to experience a very visible Aha! I was amazed at what happened next. Then and there, he decided to create a Physics Program as a new entry-level training program for General Electric and invited me to be the first member. Later on, he told me that the key words for this spontaneous decision had been, "Engineering taught me facts, physics taught me how to think."

Impressed as he may have been, GE was still a company dominated by engineers and I was treated as one by my first boss. In my first job, the head of the General Engineering Laboratory insisted that I was an engineer, because everyone else was. Fortunately, it would be only one year before I could shift out of the engineering mode. I would then proceed through managerial positions in a variety of functions, including sales, marketing, employee relations, and human resources, finally finding my niche as corporate manager of management education.

For most of my long career, however, I would find it impossible to express my personal duality in my professional life. Instead, like so many of us, I lived two lives, pursuing my interests in music and drama only as an off-hours avocation.

Then suddenly in 1963, my singing was cut short by the onset of a mysterious and debilitating illness. Abruptly and with no warning, I would black out for periods of a second or two up to several minutes. These attacks, initially brought on most frequently by the act of singing, came in increasing frequency until I could neither drive, perform in public, nor travel. In fact, I went from work to bed on weekdays, and spent the entire weekend in bed for many months. All I felt able to do was work on my business papers or sleep. I was frustrated and unhappy without an outlet for my artistic urges.

I would never have imagined then that the very condition that seemed to be killing my artistic life would eventually redirect me, not only to even more creative expression, but also to a way of reintegrating my two selves professionally as well. Here's how it happened.

One day, after a few months of this semi-invalid life, my wife, Margy, brought home an inexpensive set of oil paints for me. The painting that came out of that five dollar set amazed us all, but particularly me. That was the start of a second profession, simultaneous with the one I had at GE. In the 16 years that followed my return to health,* I produced over 600 paintings and 100 sculptures,

*For the curious, my condition was heartblock (not epilepsy as major clinics had diagnosed), a malfunction of the mechanism that paces the heart in response to changing needs. The intermittent condition causing the blackouts was resolved in 1965 when the mechanism failed and my pulse dropped to a fixed rate of 47—slow, but securely strong. Today, 23 years later, it continues to beat steadily at that low rate.

Figure 1-5.   Poster by Bob Jones Announcing the 1975 Creativity Panel
Presentation

about three-quarters of which I sold.

Becoming a professional artist was much more for me
than just escalating a hobby. With the decision to relinquish
the safety of being an amateur and join the Stamford Art
Association's Professional Division, I committed to pursuing art as a full-blown second career, and to devoting to
it as much drive, concentration, and self-development as
I'd used in my career at GE. I opened a separate bank
account; designed and ordered cards, stationery, and logo
stickers; learned how to mat and frame professionally,
backing my paintings with paper instead of leaving them
open. I soaked up every bit of information I could, not
only about painting itself, but also about how to operate
successfully in the business of art. I studied distribution
channels for art and developed a marketing plan that included what shows to enter, what critics and collectors to
meet, what prices to charge, what wider potential-buyer
segments to address for my kind of paintings. I signed up
with regional galleries and committed myself to a series
of one-man shows. I sought out artists to befriend and
developed connections with prominent figures in the art
world. I achieved local prominence myself, as president
of the Stamford Art Association and later as Vice President
for Art Education and Music at the Silvermine Guild of
Artists. If I averaged a 40-hour week at GE, I must have
averaged close to that in my profession as a painter and
sculptor.

Grateful and awed by my own creative outburst, I
became entranced by the subject of artistic creativity and
in 1975 suggested that the Stamford Art Association convene a panel to address questions like: Where does creativity come from? What is it based on? How can we stimulate
it? The association directors agreed and asked me to serve

as panel moderator.

To prepare for the program panel, I began poking around the Stamford Public Library and, within an hour, experienced one of those wonderful moments each of us has during our lives when we feel suddenly illuminated by instant understanding.

THE FIRST AHA! OF ILLUMINATION

What I found in the library were contemporary reports describing historic breakthroughs in our understanding of the human brain. Laboratory experiments conducted by neurosurgeons and psychologists had given rise to a new theory of brain specialization. According to this theory, each of our two brain hemispheres is specialized for its own type of thinking. The left brain seems to control mental functions required for scientific thinking; the right brain controls functions used in artistic thinking.

Suddenly, here was a scientific explanation—soundly based on brain physiology—of my own duality, a key not only to the mystery of my own makeup and behavior, but to that of others as well. Up to that moment, it had never dawned on me that creativity might be related to specific, physiological aspects of the human brain. But at that instant, the obvious truth of this simple fact began a chain reaction that was to change my life in wonderful ways. I suddenly became okay to myself. In a flash I understood who I was and why I had done the things I had, things that at the time had been incomprehensible. I accepted and became confident in my own authenticity.

I couldn't wait to tell someone, so I cornered the librarian and blurted out my discovery. She looked at me

"Every human life involves an unfashionable mystery, for the riddle of man in his endowment with personal capacities. The stars are not so strange as the mind that studies them, analyzes their light, and measures their distance."
Harry Emerson Fosdick, D.D.

"Creativity may express itself in one's dealing with children, in making love, in carrying on a business, in formulating physical theory, in painting a picture."
Jerome Bruner

Figure 1-6.   Split-Brain Patient Experiment. Identification of Objects

Figure 1-7.   Split-Brain Patient Experiment. Image Identification using a tachistoscope

somewhat quizzically. So, in later exchanges, did many of my colleagues. Their responses hardly mattered—I was onto something! Where reading had once been a chore, it was now effortless. As if on roller skates, I glided through a dozen books—only the beginning of a joyous period of research.

Early Learning: The Two Brains in Our Head

The obsession with the idea of a dual brain turned out to be something I shared with a number of thinkers. Over 100 years ago, the French physician Paul Broca and the German neurophysiologist, Carl Wernicke, had deduced from their clinical observations of brain-damaged patients that "the left brain spoke." Both had noticed that damage to specific locations in man's left hemisphere caused *aphasia*, or speech deficiencies, while damage to other locations in the left hemisphere, or to the right, did not.

By the mid-nineteenth century, because it influenced and controlled language functions, the left brain was widely believed to be dominant over the right. Observers had not yet been able to identify the right brain with any specific mental functioning, so the verbal left came to be called the "major" hemisphere, while the non-verbal right was relegated to "minor" status.

Such conclusions were challenged, starting in the early 1960s, by the *split-brain* research studies conducted by Dr. Roger W. Sperry and his associates at the California Institute of Technology. Sperry, along with Joseph E. Bogen, Michael S. Gazzaniga, Jerre Levy, and other members of his group, worked with end-state epileptics in whom the corpus callosum, a thick band of nerve fibers connecting the two hemispheres, had been severed in an effort to relieve severe seizures. Remarkably, the split-brain patients showed virtually no obvious changes in personality, capacities, or behavior. But if severing this massive neural connection had no influence on temperament or behavior, why did it exist at all? And what was the function of the mute right brain? To find out, Sperry and his colleagues designed a set of subtle tests to isolate and reveal the functioning of each hemisphere. The findings of these tests revolutionized our understanding of the human brain—and earned Dr. Sperry a Nobel Prize in 1981.

The tests Sperry's team developed were based on thinking that differed significantly from earlier approaches. They already knew that in virtually all right-handed people, the left hemisphere controls both the right side of the subject's body and the speech center. So they posited that a split brain person could perform verbal functions in connection with physical control of the right side of the body. But what about the left side of the body—the side controlled by the right brain? How would it perform in connection with verbal functions? To find out, they had to be able to reach the separated hemispheres one at a time.

Sperry's Experiments with Split Brain Patients

In one experiment, the researchers concealed a split-brain patient's hands from his view, placed a familiar object in his right hand, and asked him to name it. As expected, he was able to do so. But when they put the same object in his left hand and asked him to name it, he could only guess at what he held. His right brain knew what the object was, but there was no crossover information available to his verbal left brain, so he couldn't accurately name it.

"Everyone has the potential for creativity. Some have more artistic outlets and special talents for expressing their creativity, but even the most 'unartistic' person can be creative. For creativity is defined as 'the process of bringing something new into being.' The 'something new' you create can be an idea, a plan, a rearranged living room, a new friendship, a work of art, and so on."
Unknown

"The main theme to emerge ... is that there appear to be two modes of thinking, verbal and nonverbal, represented rather separately in left and right hemispheres, respectively, and that our educational system, as well as science in general, tends to neglect the non-verbal form of intellect. What it comes down to is that modern society discriminates against the right hemisphere."
Roger W. Sperry

For another set of experiments, the team perfected a new visual input device called a tachistoscope, a specialized instrument with a screen on which a given image can be flashed to a single visual field—one controlled by *either* the right *or* the left side of the brain. The researchers seated a split-brain patient in front of the viewing screen and simultaneously flashed two different figures on the screen, one to each visual field. This meant a different image reached each side of the subject's brain. When asked to name what he had seen, the subject named the figure in his right visual field, the one he "saw" in his left brain. When asked to point to what he had seen, he pointed with his left hand to the figure he had seen in his right hemisphere.

With these and similar tests, Sperry and his colleagues demonstrated that: (1) sensing and motor control are distributed to one hemisphere or the other; (2) the hemispheres are specialized in function; and (3) the corpus callosum exists largely to unify attention and awareness and to allow the two hemispheres to share learning and memory. It links a divided brain.

But Sperry's work turned up even more information: Not only did each of the two hemispheres serve different functions, they also seemed to have emotional and value differences. In Sperry's words, "Each hemisphere of the divided brain seemed to have its own separate and private sensations; its own perceptions; its own impulses to act." (Excerpt from the film, *The Mind of Man*)

Case Histories of Our Rebellious Divided Selves

Anecdotal material confirming our duality is fascinating. In some tests, EEG activity showed that the left side of a patient's brain would suddenly jump into action when the right side had made a mistake in working on a task for which it was specialized. At the moment the left-brain activity spiked on the EEG, a frown or a scowl would appear on the subject's face. One side of the subject's brain was scolding the other for incorrect answers! Another example describes one patient's complaints that his "weird" left hand would keep doing things he didn't want to do—like untying his robe as his right hand struggled to pull it on!

In another case, a female split-brain patient kept complaining that her left hand became involved in activities she didn't want it involved in. It would just reach out and do things quite unexpectedly. She took to slapping it, but that didn't do much good. It only hurt! On one occasion, as the patient was selecting accessories with her right hand, her left hand reached out and selected a totally different outfit. Later that day, when she was having coffee with a neighbor, her friend asked why she seemed to be wearing two different outfits at the same time. The patient hadn't realized until that point that she had two outfits on!

Another story tells of a party at the hospital where the split-brain surgery was performed. Split-brain patients and their families were invited to join with doctors, nurses, and hospital staff to celebrate the success of this unusual surgical procedure. During the party, one male patient became abusive toward his wife and began to tongue-lash her in the middle of the party room. She gently led him off to a corner of the room, away from the center of attention, trying along the way to calm him down. Instead, he became even more abusive, now cursing her and becoming physically agitated. By the time they got to the corner of the room, he was shouting curses and began hitting her with one hand only. With the other hand, however, he was reaching out to protect her from the attack. His divided

brain had become the source of divided behaviors. Without the ability to integrate the differences mentally, all these individuals behaved simultaneously in strikingly opposed ways. Can you imagine how painful and disconcerting this must have been for them? While valuable for research, it is, from a personal standpoint, a scenario of nightmare quality, rather like having another being take over your body and being unable to make meaningful contact with it.

In terms of the implications for the rest of us, what impresses me most about these and many other anecdotes is how strikingly different the patients' two brain hemispheres are and, by extension, how double-minded we all must be.

So, not only does the right hemisphere have functions of its own, but each hemisphere has its own unique "mode of knowing." The left is verbal, involving logical, analytic, and sequential processing of information. The right is visuospatial and emotional; its functioning involves simultaneous processing, pattern recognition, and holistic thinking. Our mind is composed of wonderfully complementary parts, each enriching the other, and both crucially important to our successful functioning as human beings.

Lateralization: How Our Abilities Are Distributed in the Brain

The science of neuropsychology has confirmed and extended Sperry's work by establishing that many of our specific mental abilities are *lateralized*, that is, carried out, supported, and coordinated predominantly in one hemisphere of our dual brain or the other. Speaking, reading, writing, and thinking with numbers are now known to be carried out mostly in the left hemisphere for most people, while spatial perception, geometry, mental map-making,

*"..... poetry of many kin
great pleasure and ever
I took intense delight in
especially in the historic
also said that formerly pi
considerable, and music
delight. But now for man
endure to read a line of
tried lately to read Shak
found it so intolerably d
nauseated me. I have al
any taste for pictures or
mind seems to have be
machine for grinding gen
large collections of fact,
should have caused the
part of the brain alone, (
higher tastes depend, I
.... The loss of these tas
happiness, and may pos
to the intellect, and more
moral character, by enfe
emotional part of our na*
—from *Autobiograp*

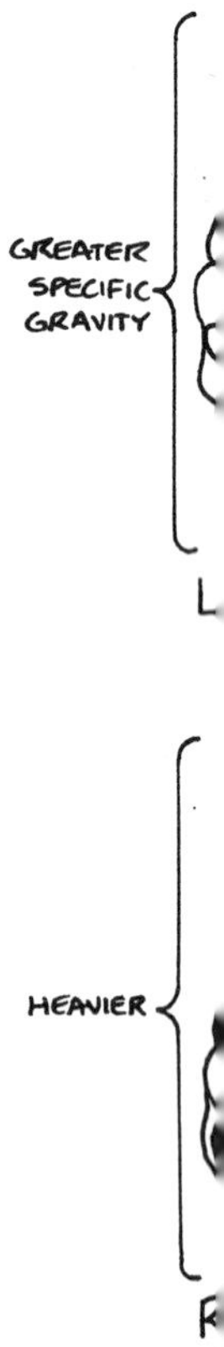

GREATER
SPECIFIC
GRAVITY

HEAVIER

Figure 1-8

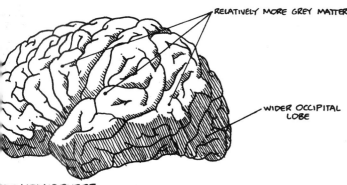

RELATIVELY MORE GREY MATTER

WIDER OCCIPITAL LOBE

...FT HEMISPHERE

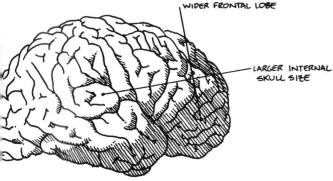

WIDER FRONTAL LOBE

LARGER INTERNAL SKULL SIZE

...GHT HEMISPHERE

Physical Asymmetry of the Brain

and our ability to rotate shapes in our mind are performed predominantly in the right hemisphere. However, it's not always that simple.

The major factor contributing to this left/right distribution of specialized modes of mental activity, I believe, is the location of the language center. The acquisition and use of language is one of the most compelling of human experiences. The most basic and influential reason for this is that the moment we begin to learn words, we open up otherwise unavailable ways to get our needs met. Neurologically, language can be overwhelming to other perceptual and processing activities. When activated in the brain, it's like a high intensity lamp, which, though small, dominates the eye so much that very little else can be seen except in reference to it. Even though words often fail to communicate what we want to convey, language touches almost everything we experience—work, play, sex, nature, God, family, and so on. In so doing, it fixes imposed concepts, a frame of reference. It also dictates a sequence of thinking that determines the way we take in, process, and give out information.

Since language is linear and sequential, the hemisphere in which it resides appears to take on all compatible modes of information processing, such as linear, sequential arithmetical thinking. When the language center resides in the right hemisphere, as is the case for a small percentage of left-handers, the associated modes of perception and thinking shift with it.

Can lateralization be changed? Yes, it can to some degree—especially in the young developing brain. If damage to the left brain occurs during childhood, the right brain can develop language ability to compensate for the loss. Even in adults, research has shown that, given certain

conditions, the right hemisphere is capable of simple language comprehension: There are cases, for example, of people with left-hemisphere damage who, while unable to speak, are able to sing simple songs. Stuttering also offers us windows into issues of lateralization. Some therapists theorize that people may stutter because a competing verbal capability from the right hemisphere comes and interferes with left-hemispheric expression. This could explain why some stutterers can sing without stuttering, and also why therapists have been able to reduce stuttering in some cases by tranquilizing patients' right hemispheres.

The Normalcy of Duality: Ornstein's EEG Studies

Most early investigators based their conclusions about localization of brain function and hemispheric specialization on studies of brain-damaged, clinically dysfunctional subjects. As a result, scientists questioned whether their findings could be safely generalized for the entire population.

In the early 1970s, psychologist Robert Ornstein, using electroencephalographic (EEG) techniques, was among the first to demonstrate scientifically that hemispheric specialization was not limited to abnormal people but could be identified and measured in all of us. The technique was simple, clear, and replicable. By attaching two EEG machines to each of his normal subjects, one to each brain hemisphere, Professor Ornstein and his associates were able to differentiate brain wave responses while subjects were engaged in simple tasks of replicating block patterns and writing letters. The data showed that while a subject performed the visuo-spatial block task, the left brain idled in a state of relaxed electrical activity. Conversely, when the subject engaged in writing a letter, the

"...dominance is part and parcel of the normal human condition....As a result of this dominance, we are handed, footed, eyed, and—in a general sense— 'brained'."

Ned Herrmann

*"But words are things, and a small drop of ink,
Falling like dew upon a thought, produces
That which makes thousands, perhaps millions, think."*

Byron

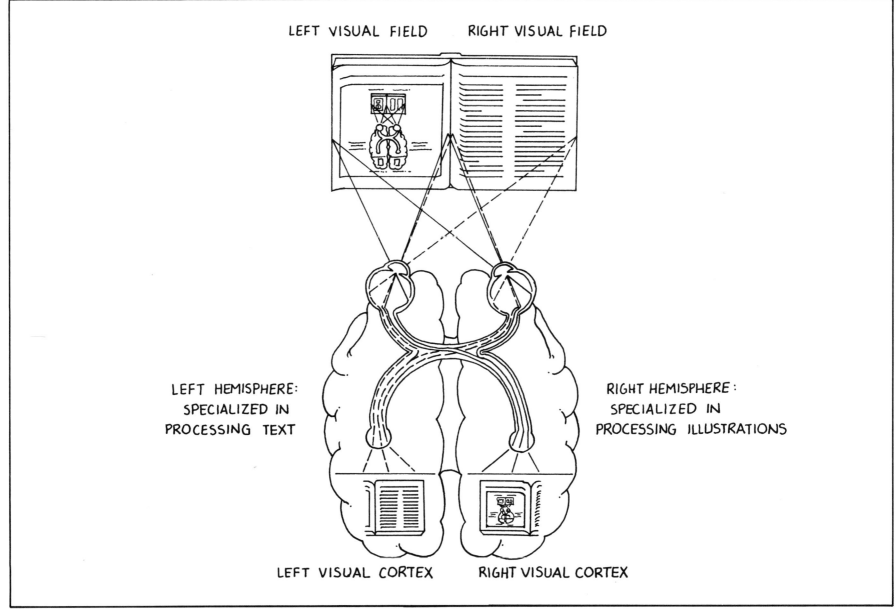

Figure 1-9.   Book Format

right brain idled while the left brain engaged.

Ornstein opened the way for a new wave of lateralization research into a whole array of specialized functions, thus extending the exciting new field of neuropsychological research. The new findings could now be directly related not only to the sick and infirm, but to healthy people engaged in everyday activities.

Since those first EEG studies, hundreds of dedicated researchers at universities and neurological institutes around the world have devised many other exciting experimental techniques to locate, identify, and measure the degree to which mental capabilities are controlled by one hemisphere or the other. Mental capabilities examined have included processing for audio, visual, and even tactile input. New medical technologies like PETT (Positron-Emission Transaxial Tomography), NMR (Nuclear Magnetic Resonance), and temperature mapping are also being used to track changes in electrical activity and blood flow in the brain as it applies itself to specific tasks. These research techniques are yielding an ever-growing mass of evidence in support of the concept of *brain asymmetry*—the idea that the two sides of the normal brain are different, naturally.

These discoveries are beginning to have a significant impact on our daily lives. A good example relates to the design format selected for this book. You may have already noticed that almost all of the illustrations and graphics are located on the left-hand pages, and that the right-hand pages are almost entirely text and quotes. The reason for this is the way in which the human visual system is arranged: The left visual field of each eye is combined in the optic chiasm and processed in the right visual cortex, and the right visual field of each eye is combined for processing in the left visual cortex. If this seems strange, remember that in terms of motor control, the left hemisphere controls the right side of the body, and the right hemisphere the left side of the body. Nature is consistent in this reversal pattern in terms of visual processing. When we look directly at the book, with the inside margins in the center of our view, the left hemisphere processes what we see in our right visual field and the right hemisphere processes what we see in our left visual field.

This being the case, I can improve my chances of communication if I format the book so that it delivers the different types of information to the part of your brain that can process them most effectively. Because the format was designed to favor the naturally most preferred modes of processing for your brain, you should find this book relatively easy and comfortable to read.

DOMINANCE: THE NATURAL HUMAN TILT

Not only do the two brains differ functionally, they're asymmetrical physiologically as well. The left hemisphere, for example, has a greater specific gravity, relatively more gray matter, and a wider occipital lobe. In contrast, the right hemisphere is heavier, with a larger internal skull size and a wider frontal lobe.

In its functional and structural asymmetries, the brain is consistent with the way things are in the rest of the body. Although they may look alike, our bilateral organs and appendages—such as eyes, hands, arms, and legs—are unequal in physical characteristics and different in what they do and in how we use them.

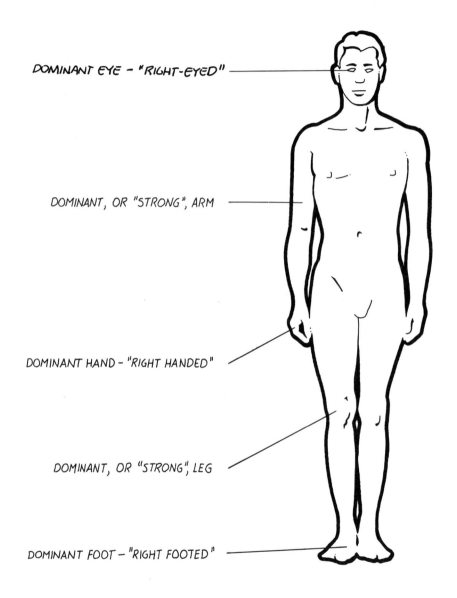

DOMINANT EYE - "RIGHT-EYED"

DOMINANT, OR "STRONG", ARM

DOMINANT HAND - "RIGHT HANDED"

DOMINANT, OR "STRONG", LEG

DOMINANT FOOT - "RIGHT FOOTED"

From infancy, we begin to develop preferences for one or another of these "twin" body parts. We begin, for example, to reach out with one hand as our preferred way of taking hold of objects. This preferred hand later develops into the one we use for writing. For 90 percent of us, it is the right hand—like the rest of the nerves and muscles of the right side of the body—that is controlled by the left brain. As it grows stronger, through repeated use, the right hand becomes increasingly preferred, ultimately becoming symbolic of strength itself. The left hand is controlled by the right brain. When less preferred and relatively unused, it takes a secondary, supportive role in working with the dominant right hand.

The same is true for our legs: We have two seemingly identical legs, but as we mature, one becomes dominant. We use the dominant leg to step forward, to kick a ball, or to center our balance. When we need to initiate a response, we go to it first, relying on the strength it has gained from repeated use.

We even have a dominant eye—one on which we rely to focus our visual field and through which we see more. Test for yourself. With both eyes open, extend your dominant arm in front of you and form a circle with your thumb and forefinger, placing a distant object in that circle. Alternately close one eye and then the other, and you will discover which one you use primarily to see with and which one supplies supplementary visual information. The eye with which you continue to see the object through the circle is the dominant one.

Figure 1-10.   Dominance in Bilateral Organs

Why Dominance? Why We Develop These Preferences

I believe the main reason we have evolved these preferences is that they provide us with two important benefits. First, dominance gives us an automatic lead response to any situation. If both hands and feet were to be preferred equally, wouldn't there be some confusion about how we should initiate action? Dominance enhances our ability to respond quickly and effectively by eliminating a decision-making step.

Second, dominance has given us higher skill levels than we could otherwise attain. A body part or organ that is favored is used almost twice as much as it would be if it weren't favored, and with such use, it continues to increase in strength and skill well beyond what it could if it were used only half the time. It isn't that we can't write with our non-dominant hand or kick a ball with our non-dominant foot. It's just that without such added use, parts of our body remain relatively unskilled in these tasks and are therefore clumsy.

In terms of dominance, or preferred usage, therefore, we are handed, footed, and eyed. And that is okay. Dominance is part of the normal human condition.

Dominance in Brain Function and How It Affects Behavior

Not surprisingly, this notion of dominance also applies to the brain. Brain dominance is expressed in terms of how we prefer to learn, understand, and express something. I call these cognitive preferences, or *preferred modes of knowing*.

Our preferred mode of knowing is the one we are most likely to use when faced with the need to solve a problem or select a learning experience. A *left-brain* approach to solving a problem would be fact-based, analytic, and step-by-step, favoring words, numbers, and facts presented in logical sequence. A *right-brain* strategy, by contrast, would seek out insight, images, concepts, patterns, sounds, and movement, all to be synthesized into an intuitive sense of the whole. So, our preferred mode of knowing correlates strongly with *what* we prefer to learn and *how* we prefer to go about learning it. A left-brainer may prefer to learn about engineering or law. A right-brainer might prefer studying psychology, art, or music. When approaching the subject of dance, for example, left-brainers may learn about dance by reading about it—the facts regarding names, productions, history, physiology, and positions—while right-brainers would likely learn about it by watching and doing it.

If we strongly prefer one mode, we may actually reject another. For some fact-based learners, even the idea of intuition is suspect, whereas for an intuitive person, factual data can seem distracting or boring. Thus, someone who strongly prefers to function in one mode usually finds it difficult or impossible to problem-solve in the other.

This has vital implications for human learning: You can see how failing to match a person's cognitive style with the delivery system of information to be learned can get in the way. The individual is likely to find the learning a great effort, frustrating, demanding, boring, non-productive, and un-fulfilling.

Differences in cognitive preferences have a downstream effect on other aspects of personality, especially work habits. "Phyllis" and "Sam" represent extremes of

Figure 1-11. Phyllis the Left-brainer

Figure 1-12. Sam the Right-brainer

what we describe as left-brain dominant and right-brain dominant types.

Phyllis, the left-brainer, acquires knowledge primarily by reading factual information. She tends to introversion and bookishness and has precise, elaborate concepts to order her thinking and data processing. In her work, she is meticulous and detailed, highly verbal, and as sharp as a razor in thinking and writing. Her office is organized for efficiency; she keeps it neat with everything in its proper place; on her desk is the current project and nothing else.

Sam, the right-brainer, by contrast, learns by "walking around" and tends to be more extroverted and experiential than Phyllis. People say he's "street smart." In his work life, he is at the other end of the spectrum from Phyllis. Although he learns the general concepts surrounding a problem, he avoids the minute details. He's intelligent—he grasps ideas quickly and is often able to tie very diverse concepts into a meaningful picture—but his insightful thinking often comes across as muddled because he has difficulty expressing ideas in words. His office is messy and his desk is covered with papers and books because he works on several projects simultaneously and doesn't want to spend the time being neat. Differences like those between Phyllis and Sam exist everywhere. Reflect for a minute on your family members and business associates, and you'll be reminded of many examples.

As I was learning about these differences, I wondered whether one brain surpasses the other. Today I can say, Yes, without a doubt—but *only for certain types of activities.* As you will see further along, we are marvelously made so that every part of the brain can play superbly the role it was designed to discharge.

Can Dominance Be Changed?

What if we want or need to do better at something that isn't one of our preferences? Can we influence our own dominance patterns? Can we change our children's patterns? Or are the differences genetically predetermined?

If all our mental preferences are predetermined genetically, then the answer would be, No! We can't change our preferences for certain thinking patterns. And one school of thought says we can't. Most brain researchers agree with the hypothesis that individual differences in behavior result at least in part from genetically determined differences in brain organization. They further agree that the hypothesis is worthy of continuing serious study. Of the numerous examples reinforcing this hypothesis, my favorite is Wolfgang Amadeus Mozart. His ability to compose and perform music was based more on what was born inside his own head than on what he, as a child prodigy, acquired through the teaching of his father and other court musicians. Mozart was musically superior to most of those around him by the age of six. His musical genius had to result more from his DNA than from the influence of his teachers. So the Mozart syndrome is more like 30 percent nurture and 70 percent nature—just the reverse of what I think is true for most of us. If the Mozart syndrome example were the rule, it would mean that virtually all our mental capability would have to be genetically predetermined, and change would be well-nigh impossible.

But I'm more hopeful than that. Despite Mozart, I would strongly argue, (and I expect future research to confirm), that the way a person uses the specialized brain results from socialization—parenting, teaching, life experi-

Figure 1-13.   As a Child, Mozart knew more than his Teachers

ences, and cultural influences—far more than from genetic inheritance. Although identical twins are a clear exception, I believe most of us are not as genetically programmed as we might think.

Here's my reasoning: We come into the world with a given genetic complement of cognitive capabilities, options, and mental strengths and weaknesses. As we respond to life's learning opportunities, it's natural that we learn to go to our strengths first, because they tend to win us praise and other rewards. As our behavior is positively reinforced by our mentors, we further entrench our favored pattern of mental response. Repeat usage leads to ever-improving performance, which, in turn, leads to ever-increasing praise, and, therefore, intensified preference! It is this performance-praise-preference feedback loop that can turn a small difference in hemispheric specialization into a powerful preference for one cognitive mode over another.

The performance-praise-preference loop works not only for individuals, but indeed for entire cultures.

THE COSTLY RISE OF THE LEFT

Of the many ways socialization influences our dominance patterns, I think the most compelling one is work. We reinforce those behaviors that are needed on the jobs society needs done, those tasks that have to be accomplished to keep the economy functioning smoothly at any given time. We can see this in the development of various nations and, more broadly, in the history of mankind itself.

In terms of our evolution as a species, right-brain

development preceded the left. Our Cro-Magnon ancestors apparently engaged in art long before they engaged in verbal communication. Then, as the need for higher levels of communication among humans grew, the feedback loop began to reinforce the development of the language center. The natural seat of that center on the left side was established: The need for fine hand control in the dominant right hand had already laid a foundation of fine motor control skills in the left hemisphere, just the kind needed for the complex act of vocalization.

Even after language became quite sophisticated, however, the right brain remained very important because right-brain skills were required for survival. Today pre- or non-industrial nations still reward skills that have to do with intuiting and sensing growth—the ability to nurse a sick animal, to understand the ecology of a forest, or to know where game can be found. Healing arts, nurturing land and beasts, sensing the currents and moods of the sea, finding the way across the trackless arctic ice—all these take on enormous importance in societies that live closer to nature than our own does. The Industrial Revolution and the accompanying scientific explosion changed all that for us.

In modern Western society—the "developed" world—the pendulum has swung to the other side as society has increasingly demanded and reinforced left hemispheric skills. As industrialization replaced agriculture, our civilization focused its attention on behaviors that served the interests of a production oriented, business-centered, financially driven style of social organization. It's the role of Alex Keaton that Michael J. Fox plays to the hilt in "Family Ties." It rewarded the left-brain cognitive mode—orderly, replicable, and verbal—which serves these in-

"As soon as you can say what you think and not what some other person has thought for you, you are on the way to being a remarkable man."
James M. Barne

*"What you must dare:
is to be yourself."*
Dag Hammarskjöld (1905-1961)

Figure 1-14.   Like Fingerprints, Each Human Brain is Different

terests better than the spontaneous, less structured right modes.

Although it emerged later, the left brain's cognitive focus on fact, rationality, and verbal communication eventually earned it a position of power over the quiescent modes of the right brain. It has done so within each of us, within most of our social institutions, and in all of our business organizations. The left-brain modes have become especially entrenched in our educational system, which typically emphasizes the "three R's" and neglects—or even attacks—the cognitive capabilities of the right brain, such as art, intuition, music, and dance. Countless references in Western languages insult the left hand and, by implication, the right brain.

There have been unfortunate—even devastating—consequences to this rigid emphasis on the left brain. Well-meaning parents unknowingly constrict their children by failing to recognize and honor right-brain as well as left-brain gifts with respect to education and career choices. Well-intentioned teachers take their students down the wrong learning path because they don't know how to discern and use the preferred learning style of each student. Dedicated spouses and managers reduce the performance of family members or associates because they are taught to discount rather than appreciate precious differences. As a result, our right-brain capabilities remain latent at best, and often atrophy, at great cost to our personal satisfaction as well as our effectiveness as problem-solvers.

RECLAIMING OUR RIGHTS

The easily dominated right brain needs all the help

it can get to reclaim improved status in the Western world. Until it does, we will experience a high degree of internal conflict and dissatisfaction in our society.

From a motor control standpoint, the brain's hemispheres are typically cooperative. The left and right hands work together. The left and right legs cooperate in walking and running. Each eye has both a left and a right visual field and the two eyes coordinate their movements in order to provide binocular vision. The auditory system functions non-competitively in the processing of auditory input.

However, in terms of thinking style preferences, research has shown that the right and left brains are in a constant state of competition. Our two minds tend to be divided against each other.

I believe it is human destiny to move beyond this mental conflict to a more integrated wholeness, reflecting a smoother collaboration among the specialized parts of the brain. However, we will need to become far more aware of how to handle thinking preferences than we are now. We need to emphasize all the mental skills people favor, so our repertoire of potential behavioral responses can develop fully. This will give us powerful advantages in dealing with life's problems—both personal and professional.

As you will see in the next chapter, the physiological precondition for wholeness already exists. The brain is already organized to allow for intercommunication among the specialized modes of knowing.

"... no animal species, no matter how humble, lacks cerebral dominance."
author unknown

"Our business in life is not to get ahead of others, but to get ahead of ourselves— to break our own records, to out-strip our yesterday by our today, to do our work with more force than ever before."
—Stewart B. Johnson

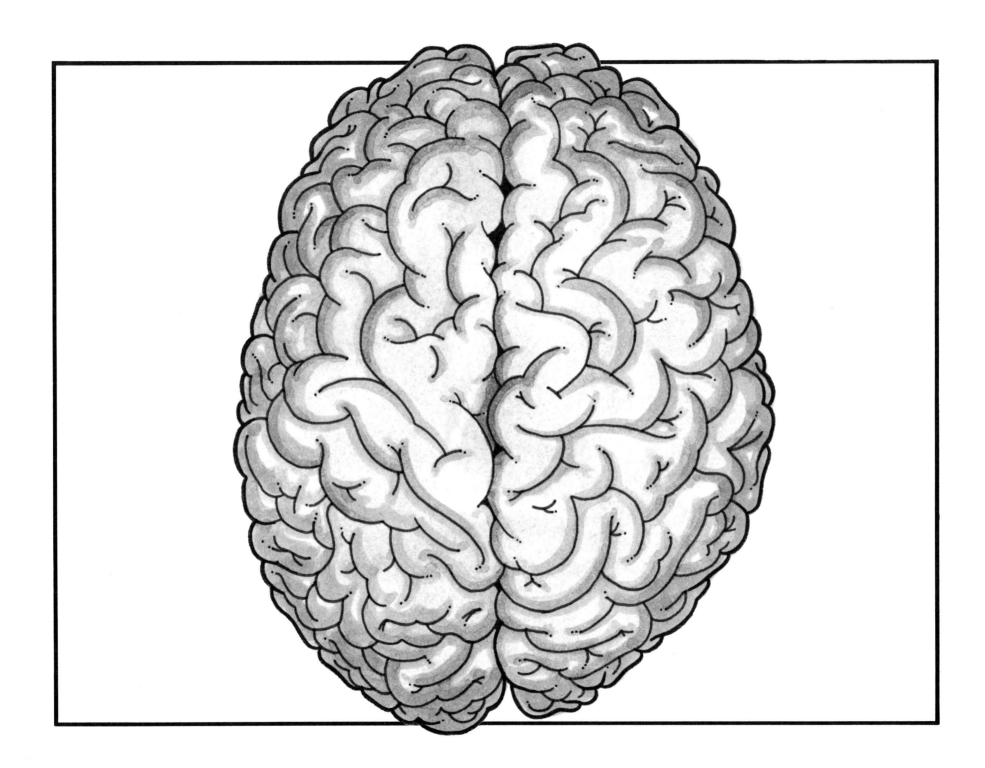

BRAIN 101:
A SHORT COURSE ON BRAIN BASICS

The insight I gained in the Stamford Public Library (that the brain is the source of creative process) led quickly to a new understanding of the learning process as well—my primary professional concern. If cognitive preferences varied from person to person, then doing a topflight training job meant discovering how to respond to individual learning styles—something management educators did only by luck and feel, if at all. Back in 1975, we didn't know how.

We needed to develop a new technology of learning. Fortunately, as manager of management education of one of the world's great corporations, I couldn't have been in a better position to figure out how to do it. You can imagine what an exciting prospect it was.

Even more exciting to me personally, it provided a way to integrate my creative and scientific selves. After three decades, my work finally began to provide a way for me to feel whole again.

I had some intuitive hunches about applying this new knowledge, but before experimenting in the classroom, I needed more information about the brain itself and about any applications of that information that had already proven successful. I began devouring books at a great rate and what they revealed was amazing. In this chapter, I will (1) summarize the history of those brain research breakthroughs that contributed most to my understanding

of duality; and (2) briefly describe the two major approaches to brain structure that led me to the integrated whole-brain model.

A CONCISE HISTORY OF BRAIN RESEARCH

What my research on creativity had uncovered was the growing literature on the subject of neuropsychology, a new science connecting behavior with the functioning of the brain.

Although the science of neuropsychology is new, two of its major ideas, the brain hypothesis and the neuron hypothesis, are old. Even the idea of duality is old—it's been linked with the brain hypothesis from the beginning. What's new about neuropsychology wasn't possible to know until we learned to measure electrical brain wave activity using the EEG (electroencephalographic device). Once we did that, the theories of duality in brain/mind functioning could be confirmed and expanded.

Milestones in Developing
the Brain Hypothesis

The brain hypothesis establishes the brain as the center of mankind's experience, control, emotions, and

Figure 2-1. The Human Brain (opposite)

Figure 2-2. Sperry, Ornstein and Mintzberg. Important brain researchers

desires. Today's acceptance of this hypothesis as the foundation of neuropsychology reflects centuries of theoretical investigations, experimental research, and debate.

The earliest milestone my study of the brain uncovered stands at a point almost 2,500 years ago, when the primacy of the brain was proclaimed by Hippocrates, the Greek physician considered to be the founder of modern medicine. He wrote:

> Some people say that the heart is the organ with which we think and that it feels pain and anxiety. But it is not so. Men ought to know that from the brain, and from the brain only, arise our pleasures, joys, laughter, and tears. Through it, in particular, we think, see, hear and distinguish the ugly from the beautiful, the bad from the good, the pleasant from the unpleasant. To consciousness the brain is messenger.

The observations of early Greek philosophers led Plato, too, to believe the brain was the central ruling organ in the body.

Aristotle, one of Plato's students, disagreed, siding instead with older Hebrew, Hindu, and Chinese traditions that the heart was the source of human intelligence and the center of the body's nervous system. Many of those favoring the heart theory thought the main purpose of the brain was to cool the body's blood supply. These two theories as to the true focus of thought, emotion, and behavior in human beings—the brain vs. the heart—were debated for hundreds of years.

Hippocrates not only asserted the brain was sovereign, he also introduced the notion of duality. In his personal notes on an epileptic patient, he wrote that the patient revealed a mental duality in his behavior, that there seemed to be two different minds in one brain.

TABLE 1-1   A PERSONAL LIST OF BRAIN DUALITY MILESTONES

DATE	RESEARCHERS	KEY LEARNINGS
450 BC	HIPPOCRATES	Within the brain of a patient, there can exist a *mental duality*.
1286	ROGER BACON	Humans exercise two modes of knowing: One through *verbal argument*, one through *non-verbal experience*.
1500	LEONARDO da VINCI	The human brain and mind are *different* things.
1684	THOMAS BROWNE	*Both* brain halves affect human behavior.
1844	ARTHUR WIGAN, M.D.	Man must have *two minds* with *two brains*.
1870	VICTOR HORSLEY, M.D.	We are not single animals: We are really *two* individuals.
1874	JOHN HUGHLINGS–JACKSON, M.D.	One of the two half-brains in humans takes the lead and is the *dominant* hemisphere.
1960	ROGER SPERRY, Ph.D.	The split brain experiments demonstrate that the left and right hemispheres are *specialized*.
1975	ROBERT ORNSTEIN, Ph.D.	The hemisphere of *normal* human beings are specialized in "predictable and measurable ways."
1976	HENRY MINTZBERG, Ph.D.	Humans can be "*smart and dull*" at the same time.

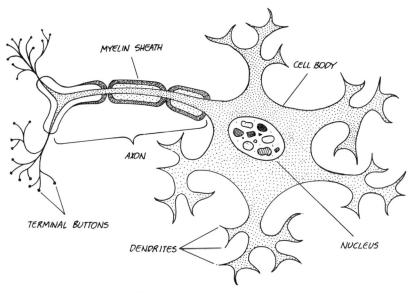

Figure 2-3. A Typical Neuron

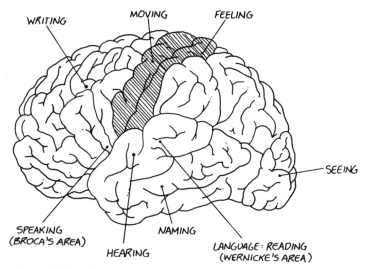

Figure 2-4. Major Specialized Functions of the Brain and their Locations

It was in A.D. 1268, well over a thousand years later, that the next milestone of the dual brain appeared. Sir Roger Bacon came up with the thought that humans exercise two modes of "knowing," one through "argument" and one through "experience." This translates into verbal and non-verbal modes.

The next breakthrough came in the 1500s, when Leonardo da Vinci differentiated between brain and mind and, in so doing, provided the basis for studying the physical organ separately from the results of its functioning, much as one would study the body separately from dancing.

Then, in 1684, came Sir Thomas Browne's posthumously published work, which proposed that both brain halves affect human behavior. In 1844, A. L. Wigan, M.D., reinforced the idea of two minds with his brilliant book, *The Duality of the Mind* (recently republished with an insightful foreword by Dr. Joseph Bogen, a neurosurgeon who worked with Dr. Roger Sperry). In 1870, Victor Horsley, M.D., observed that we are not single animals, but rather two individuals. In 1874, neurologist John Hughlings-Jackson introduced the idea of dominance with his hypothesis that one of the brain halves was the "leading hemisphere."

These early observations of duality were finally confirmed and expanded in this century in the 1950s and 1960s. Roger Sperry's work with split-brain patients, described in Chapter 1, helped us understand hemispheric specialization and modes of knowing. Psychologist Robert Ornstein then extended that understanding about specialization to include us all as a result of experiments in which he used EEG techniques with normal subjects.

Most of these men were scientists, doctors, and neuropsychologists of some note. But it was a medical layman who in 1976 made the most profound impact on my appreciation of the brain and its role in business creativity. Henry Mintzberg, professor of management at McGill University, asked the key question: "Why are some people so smart and dull at the same time?" This immediately brought into practical focus my thoughts about individual variations in brain dominance.

The brain hypothesis, then, has prevailed as the cornerstone of the evolving science of neuropsychology since the dawn of our modern age.

The Neuron Hypothesis

The second major idea of modern neuropsychology is found in the neuron hypothesis, which proposes that the nervous system is composed of discrete, autonomous, unique cells, called neurons, that can interact but are not physically connected. We now know that the brain is composed of 180 billion such cells, all of which are located in the cortex, or outer layer, of the brain's major structures. Each one can be considered a tiny information-processing system. Taken together, neurons comprise the working elements of the thinking regions of the brain. It is through their interaction that the physical organ of the brain gives rise to the living mind.

A typical neuron can receive synapses, or physical signals, from up to 15,000 other neurons immediately adjacent to it. Scientists have estimated that possible interconnections between neurons in a single human brain outnumber atoms in the known universe. Weighing only about 3 pounds and no bigger than a grapefruit, the brain in its organization is more complex than any other known struc-

"All seems then to prove that man is strictly made up of two complete and perfect halves, and that no more central and common machinery is given than is just sufficient to unite the two into one sentient being, and provide for the due synchronous action of the two animals.

To ask why this strange organization should have been established is futile. That it is for a wise and beneficient purpose the whole constitution of nature seems to prove; but when the philosopher attempts to search deeply into the cause, he is compelled to acquiesce at last in the reason that satisfies."

A. L. Wigan

"The longer you can look back, the further you can look forward".

Winston Churchill

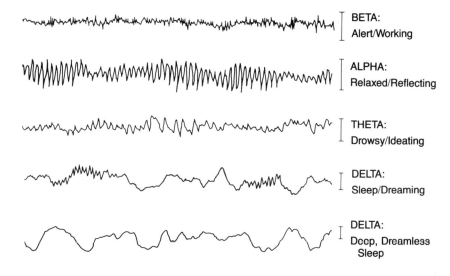

Figure 2-5.   Brain Waves

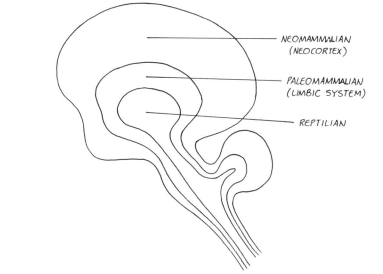

Figure 2-6.   The Triune Brain

ture. It is this extraordinary complexity that explains our amazing ability to imagine, think, deduce, and create.

Once having confirmed that the brain controls human behavior and that neurons are what conduct mental energy, researchers proceeded to explore which part of the brain controls specific functions and behaviors and how it does so. After some two centuries, by the 1860s, Paul Broca, Carl Wernicke, and others had confirmed only that language was localized in the left temporal lobe. Scientists have come a long way since then, thanks in no small part to the EEG.

The EEG—Listening in on Brain Activity

Like all cells in the human body, neurons generate electricity when they work. An active human brain can generate an easily measured 10 watts. This electrical neural activity is what creates the brain waves that EEG instruments measure. As the brain's pattern of electrical activity changes in response to changes in the situation, the wave forms also change—probably hundreds of times a day for the mentally active person. When the EEG measures these changes in a person who is carrying out specific activities, it's possible to localize brain functioning by revealing which parts of the brain are working hard and which are at rest.

CURRENT THEORIES OF HOW THE BRAIN IS ORGANIZED

There are several ways of looking at the brain physiologically. Traditionally, scientists have divided the brain's structures into three functional components: the hind-brain, the mid-brain, and the fore-brain. This description was taught in biology in the 1950s and 1960s. However, the division is mainly arbitrary, having relatively little to do with facilitating our understanding. Much more useful and increasingly popular today are the following two theories of organization:

1. The triune brain theory
2. The left brain/right brain theory

The Triune Brain Theory

Dr. Paul MacLean, head of the Laboratory for Brain Evolution and Behavior at the National Institute for Mental Health, has proposed the triune brain theory, according to which the human brain is, in reality, three brains, each superimposed over the earlier in a pattern of brains within brains.

The first is an ancient, primitive reptilian brain, so called because it strongly resembles the brain found in prehistoric reptiles, as well as in alligators and lizards today. This brain, comprising the brain stem, the mid-brain, the basal ganglia, and the reticular activating system, is a slave to precedent: Driven by instinct, it seems to contain the ancestral lore of the species.

The second and next oldest brain is the limbic, or mammalian brain, which encircles the more primitive brain, and which consists of the limbic system. It is thought to have developed between 200 and 300 million years ago. We share this brain with lower mammals such as rats, rabbits, and horses. The limbic brain registers rewards and punishments, is the seat of emotion, and controls the body's autonomic nervous system.

Finally, over the limbic brain lies the neocortex, or "thinking cap," the convoluted mass of gray matter that evolved with such rapidity in just the last million years to produce Homo sapiens. We share the neocortex with higher mammals such as chimpanzees, dolphins, and whales. What distinguishes the brains of Homo sapiens from those of these other animals is that the neocortex of man is so large in relation to both the brain and the body. It is the neocortex that seems to enable us to think, perceive, speak, and act as civilized beings.

When you see them in crosssection, the three brains look as if they were successively superimposed on one another. In the evolutionary process, each appears to have made some new starts and replicated older functions, so the functional divisions aren't easy to precisely define. While these three brains overlap in the functions they perform, they differ in style. The two older brains are thought to control genetic/instinctual behaviors: hierarchies of dominance-submission, sexual courtship, follow-the-leader rituals, mass migration, ganging-up on the weak and the new, defending territory, hunting, bonding, nesting, greeting, flocking, and playing. The older brains also mediate the autonomic nervous system, the body's involuntary internal responses. The newer neocortex, in contrast, seems more adept at learning new ways of coping and adapting. It deals more with voluntary movements and with external and environmental events.

The Left Brain/Right Brain Theory

To understand the left brain/right brain theory, you need to know about the following:

1. The left and right halves of the neocortex
2. The left and right halves of the limbic system

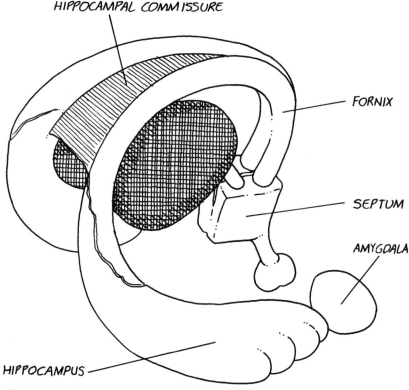

HIPPOCAMPAL COMMISSURE

FORNIX

SEPTUM

AMYGDALA

HIPPOCAMPUS

Figure 2-7. The Limbic System

3.   The connectors, which are structures that provide pathways along which the different parts of the brain send signals to one another

These specialized structures, plus two patterns of brain functioning—situational functioning and iterative functioning—comprise key aspects of left brain/right brain theory of organization as you need to know it to understand how I apply it to whole-brain creativity and learning.

The Neocortex—Left and Right

The neocortex accounts for about 80 percent of total brain matter, as well as for most of the brain's thinking cortex, or gray matter. It is divided anatomically into two halves, which are loosely referred to as the left and right hemispheres, but which should be called *cerebral* hemispheres. Taking place in these cerebral hemispheres are all the processes concerning vision, hearing, body sensation, intentional motor control, reasoning, cerebral thinking and decision making, purposeful behavior, language and non-verbal ideation.

The Limbic System—Left and Right

When Hippocrates concluded that the brain of man is "double," he was referring to the two large hemispheres of the neocortex. Had he gone a bit further in understanding the role of the two halves of the limbic system, he might have said the brain of man is twice double, for these two sets of bilateral structures, through their interconnections, comprise the four major parts of the brain controlling our primary mental functions.

Nestled into each of the two cerebral hemispheres are the two halves of the limbic system, which comprise much of the remaining portion of the brain's thinking cortex.

Although considerably smaller than the cerebral hemispheres in terms of cortex, the limbic system plays an enormous role in our functioning. If blood supply is a significant indication of importance, then it is worth noting that the limbic system has one of the richest blood supplies in the entire body. And no wonder! The limbic system regulates eating, drinking, sleeping, waking, body temperature, chemical balances such as blood sugar, heart rate, blood pressure, hormones, sex, and emotions. It's also the focus of pleasure, punishment, hunger, thirst, aggression, and rage.

We began to understand this system's role in our emotional lives when Dr. James Papez postulated in 1937 that emotion was produced specifically by the limbic system. His theory has been confirmed by subsequent research. The limbic system is physically located between the brain stem and the cerebral hemispheres and is connected to both areas through massive and highly developed interconnections. It is thus physiologically positioned to mediate brain activity that occurs both below and above it—and it does! It can, for example, overwhelm rational thought with emotional energy and thus completely neutralize logical modes of processing.

In addition to controlling our emotions, the limbic system also contributes to our cognitive processing. It is now known to be essential to the learning process because it plays a vital role in transferring incoming information into memory. We have three memory systems: very short-term, lasting a second or less; short-term, lasting about 15 seconds; and long-term, which has no time limit.

The limbic system is actively involved with all three of these memory systems:

"The more connections that can be made in the brain, the more integrated the experience is within memory."
Don Campbell,
Introduction to the Musical Brain. MMB, 1983

"If the brain is a computer, then it is the only one that runs on glucose, generates 10 watts of electricity, and is manufactured by unskilled labor."
David Lewis

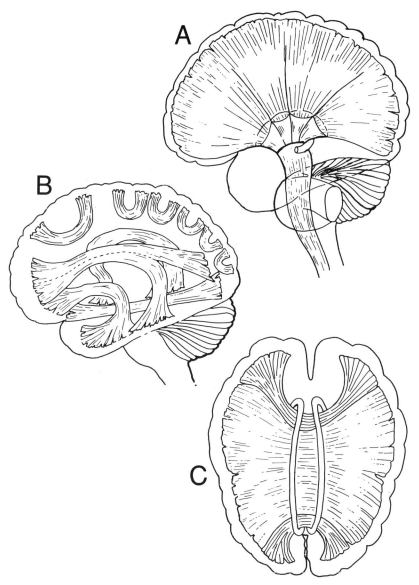

1. The limbic system converts information that the brain receives into appropriate modes for processing, constantly checking information relayed to the brain by the senses and comparing it to past experience.

2. The limbic system also directs information to the appropriate memory storage areas of the brain. This function is needed because memories are not stored in one specific place, but rather are distributed throughout the brain in the areas functionally associated with the nature of the memory to be stored. Words, numbers, and visual images, for example, are stored in areas associated with the language center, the calculation center, and the visual cortex, respectively.

3. The limbic system is also involved in the information transfer from short-term to long-term memory.

You may wonder, since you can remember longer than the medium-term memory of 15 seconds but forget things in a day or two, whether there is a medium long-term memory as well. Not as far as we know to date. The reason we "forget" isn't because we don't have adequate storage, but because our accessing systems are weak. None of that memory is lost. It's just that without constant use, it doesn't stay near the surface unless it has some emotional charge on it.

Interconnections in the Brain

The brain is full of *connectors*—fibers that carry the signals used by different parts of the brain for com-

Figure 2-8. Interconnections in the Brain—*(A) Projection Fibers; (B) Association Fibers (C) Commissural Fibers*

municating with each other. For our purposes, we can divide the connectors into two groups: those that provide links *within* each brain hemisphere and those that are links *between* the hemispheres and the two halves of the limbic system. Taken together, these connectors provide the physiological basis for wholeness in mental functioning.

Connectors *within* each half of the brain include two types, projection fibers and association fibers. *Projection fibers* radiate out from the brain stem to each lobe of each hemisphere, and this communication network relays impulses from the body and the brain stem to the cortex and back. *Association fibers* provide communication channels among the specialized regions located within each brain half, and thus form a complex communication network that allows each hemisphere to integrate its functioning.

Connections *between* the two half brains are provided by three bundles of axonic fibers called *commissures*.

1. The corpus callosum
2. The hippocampal commissure
3. The anterior commissure

These connections provide hundreds of millions of "hard wires" running from neurons in one half of the brain to mirror image neurons in the other. They thus enable the brain to coordinate the activities located in parallel regions of each cerebral hemisphere and also each limbic half.

The Corpus Callosum—A Feminine Advantage.

The *corpus callosum* connects the two cerebral hemispheres. The number of axonic fibers in the corpus callosum alone is variously quoted as being between 200 million and 300 million, making it the main channel for inter-hemispheric communication. The work of Roger Sperry

"The exponential growth of the human brain during the last two hundred and fifty thousand years is unique in the history of evolution. Even today we lack a satisfactory explanation of how it came about."
Richard Restak,
The Brain: The Last Frontier

"What we are learning about human intelligence may do more than double what we know. It may compel us to redefine it altogether."
Jack Fischer

"Let others praise ancient times; I am glad I was born in these."
Ovid (43 B.C. 17 A.D.)

and Michael Gazzaniga demonstrates conclusively that without such a connection, the brain has no way of integrating one specialized mode of knowing with its complement; it cannot, for example, develop a concept from a visual experience, then translate that concept into written or spoken words.

The corpus callosum is one area in which men and women differ significantly and women seem to have the edge in three distinct ways. First, studies based on autopsies have shown that the corpus callosum in females average about 10 percent larger than in males; there may be as many as 20 million more axonic nerve fibers present. Second, impulses from a neuron in one hemisphere to its mirror image neuron in the other travel 5 to 10 percent faster in females than in males. This more rapid, inter-hemispheric transit time means that many females can move ideas back and forth faster than the average male can.

Third, the corpus callosum in the female brain typically matures up to 3 years sooner than that of the male. By matures, I mean the myelin sheath surrounding and insulating each axonic nerve fiber forms more completely, and thus allows the fiber connections to function more fully. This earlier maturation occurs between the ages of 9 and 12, which gives the rapidly developing female brain extra time to learn to make better use of the specialized modes located in the two cerebral hemispheres. This may explain why young females feel so much more comfortable with their mental processes than do young males. It may also be what later manifests as a woman's higher comfort level regarding intuitive, non-linear functioning and the ability to verbalize those modes.

The Hippocampal and Anterior Commissures.

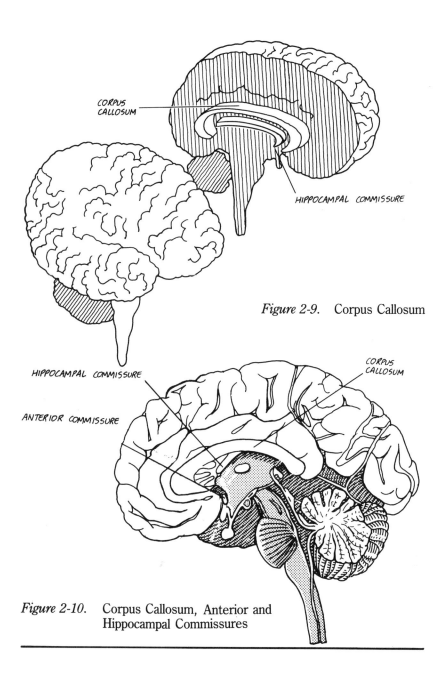

CORPUS CALLOSUM

HIPPOCAMPAL COMMISSURE

Figure 2-9.   Corpus Callosum

HIPPOCAMPAL COMMISSURE

ANTERIOR COMMISSURE

CORPUS CALLOSUM

Figure 2-10.   Corpus Callosum, Anterior and Hippocampal Commissures

Proportionately smaller than the corpus callosum are the hippocampal commissure and the small anterior commissure. The *hippocampal commissure* connects the separate halves of the limbic system, making it a complete bilateral structure. That commissure's millions of connecting "hard wires" facilitate inter-limbic communication in the same way the corpus callosum does between the two cerebral hemispheres.

The *anterior commissure* appears to perform an auxiliary function. Autopsies show that in human beings born with no corpus callosum, the anterior commissure is greatly enlarged to provide an alternate connection between the regions of the neocortex.

Like great telephone cables, these three commissures bridge the main structures of the two brain halves, providing the physiological means for information transfer, collaboration, and integration between them.

Situational Functioning

In addition to being interconnected in its structure, the human brain is also *situational* in its functioning. By situational, I mean that when presented with a situation, the local region of the brain specialized to perform the task called for in that particular situation is activated, and those regions not required for that task go into a resting state. We know that's what happens because the activated part of the brain gives electrical evidence that it is in a working mode by sending out beta waves. The parts of the brain that are relaxed exhibit alpha or theta patterns of brain waves. For example, when a person speaks, the language center is engaged; meanwhile, the calculation center, for example, is idling. When the person is not

The Two-Sided Man

Much I owe to the lands that grew-
More to the Lives that fed—
But most to the Allah Who gave me
Two Separate sides to my head.

Much I reflect on the Good and the True
In the faiths beneath the sun
But most upon Allah Who gave me
Two
Sides to my head, not one.

I would go without shirt or shoe,
Friend, tobacco, or bread,
Sooner than lose for a minute the two
Separate sides of my head.

Rudyard Kipling

CONCEPT IS FORMED AS SHE WATCHES FILM...

GOES TO THE LANGUAGE CENTER TO WRITE-DOWN INTERPRETATION...

AS OTHERS SPEAK, SHE COMPARES HER CONCEPT TO THEIRS...

GOES BACK TO THE LANGUAGE CENTER TO SPEAK...

Figure 2-11. Interation. An oversimplified example of the back-and-forth communication between hemispheres while a woman participates in a workshop exercise.

talking, but multiplying 9 times 12, the calculation center will switch into beta and the language center will rest in alpha. When a person is quietly painting, the language and calculation centers both idle in alpha and the visual and spatial processing centers switch into beta.

The ability to function situationally is crucial to a person's effectiveness. Just think a moment about what you would do if, while attempting to add a column of figures, you couldn't turn off awareness of movement and sound around you. As I mentioned earlier, right-hemispheric interferences with the left-hemispheric language center can cause stuttering. One needs to be able to turn off parts of the brain situationally so that those parts that are needed can function without competition or interference.

Iterative Functioning

Iteration is a back-and-forth movement of signals among the brain's specialized centers that takes place to advance work on a task. The iterative process can consist of a single back-and-forth transaction or many such iterative transactions, depending upon the complexity of the task. Iteration can occur either within or between hemispheres.

The following is a simplified example that involves moving back–and–forth between the brain structures specialized for spatial conceptual processing and those specialized for language processing. The iteration would take place through the corpus callosum, which connects the two key brain structures involved.

A group of people are shown a film that conveys a complex idea in visual metaphors. They are instructed that after the film is over, they'll be expected to write down their interpretation of its meaning.

Let's take one woman out of the group and follow

her mental processing. As she watches the film, the nonverbal/conceptual part of her brain processes the metaphorical information received visually and develops a spatial concept. To write down her interpretation of the film's meaning, she needs to wrap words around her conceptual understanding of the film. The first iterative motion occurs when the signals from the conceptual center are sent to her language center, enabling her to put the concept into words and physically write it down. As she writes, the iterative process repeats itself many times, translating pictures into words and words into pictures, until she feels comfortable with her interpretation. Then she is asked to share her thoughts with the group. Once again, the iterative process allows her to check what she has written against her conceptual memory of the film. As she listens to the interpretations given by others, she goes through the checking process again, comparing her thoughts to theirs, comparing what she has written to what she has heard, and so on. Even in a simple exercise, the iterative mental processing of information is extremely complex.

Specialization, interconnectedness, iteration, and situationality are four key characteristics that help explain the workings of the human brain. The description becomes more complete with the brain hypothesis and neuron hypothesis. When the triune brain and left brain/right brain theories are added, and we incorporate the reality of brain dominance, we have the essential elements of an organizing principle upon which a working model of brain function can be based.

Some of you will want to refer to the bibliography for supplemental reading; but for most of you, this summary is all that's needed to understand how the four-quadrant theory came together for me—a breakthrough you can read about in the next chapter.

"Strange that I was not told that the brain can hold in a tiny ivory cell God's heaven and hell."

Oscar Wilde

"If your head is wax, don't walk in the sun."

Ben Franklin

"To cease to think creatively is but little different from ceasing to live."

Ben Franklin

"By 1984, we should understand what the brain does when we think."

Lord Brain, 1964

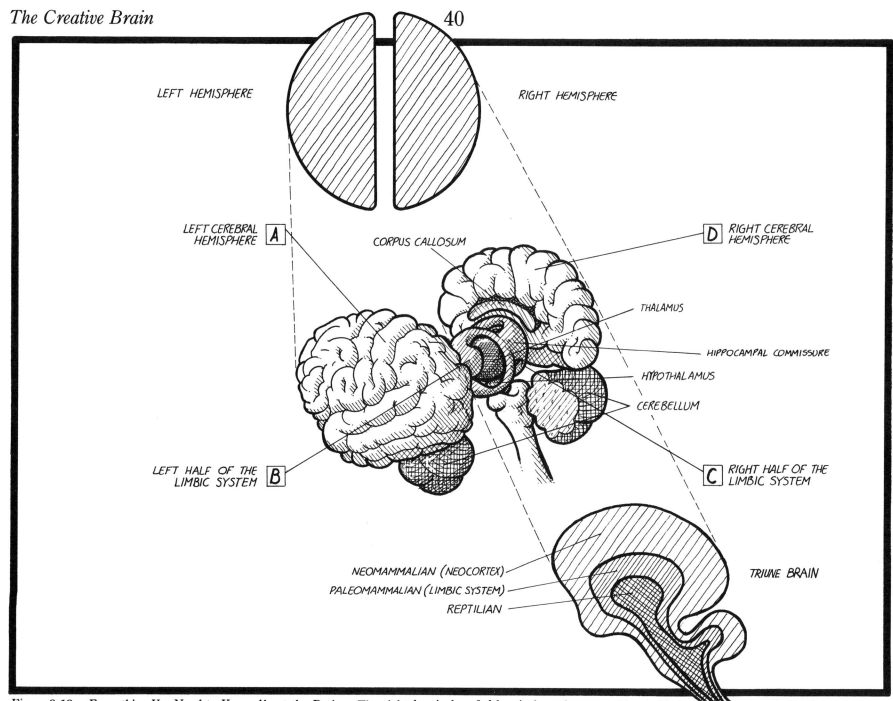

LEFT HEMISPHERE

RIGHT HEMISPHERE

LEFT CEREBRAL HEMISPHERE [A]

CORPUS CALLOSUM

[D] RIGHT CEREBRAL HEMISPHERE

THALAMUS

HIPPOCAMPAL COMMISSURE

HYPOTHALAMUS

CEREBELLUM

LEFT HALF OF THE LIMBIC SYSTEM [B]

[C] RIGHT HALF OF THE LIMBIC SYSTEM

NEOMAMMALIAN (NEOCORTEX)

PALEOMAMMALIAN (LIMBIC SYSTEM)

REPTILIAN

TRIUNE BRAIN

Figure 2-12.   Everything You Need to Know About the Brain.   The right hemisphere/left hemisphere theory combined with the triune brain theory

"There is no security on this earth; there is only opportunity."

Douglas MacArthur

"All glory comes from daring to begin."

Eugene F. Ware

"Some people say that the heart is the organ with which we think and that it feels pain and anxiety. But it is not so. Men ought to know that from the brain and from the brain only, arise our pleasures, joys, laughter and tears. Through it, in particular, we think, hear and distinguish the ugly from the beautiful, the bad from the good, the pleasant from the unpleasant....To consciousness the brain is messenger."

Excerpt from a lecture by Hippocrates, 5th century B.C. Reprinted in *The Mystery of the Mind* by Wilder Penfield

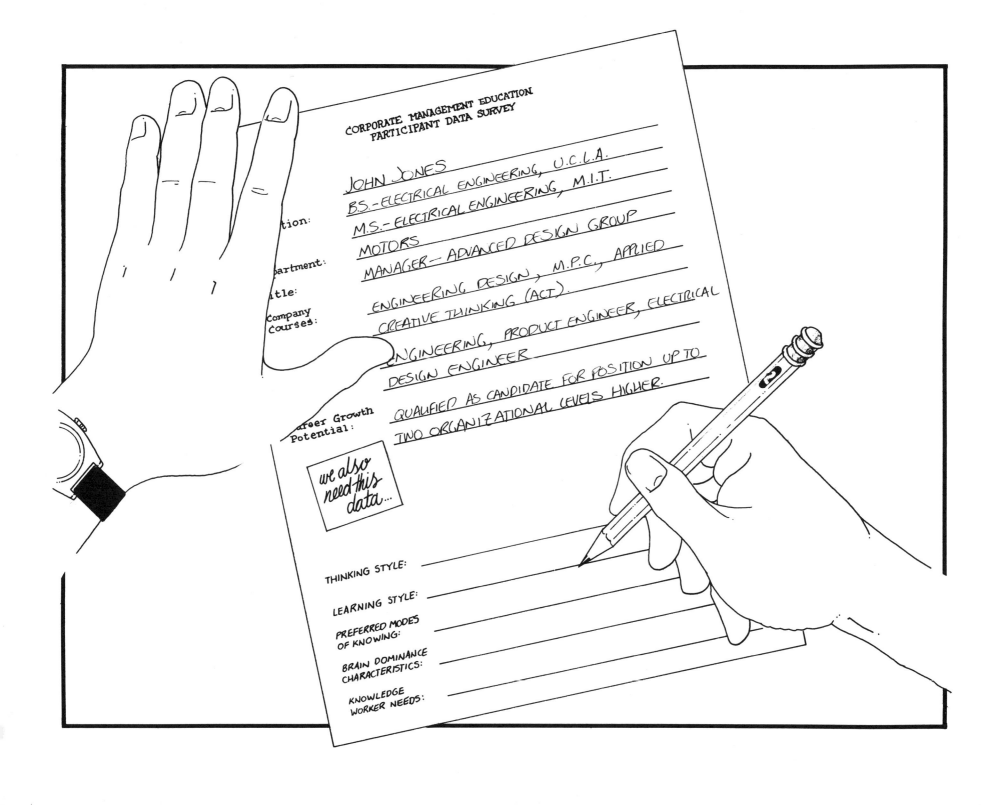

3

FROM DUALITY TO QUADRALITY: HOW THE HBDI WAS BORN

At GE my brain-related research began in earnest around May 1976, about 9 months after my first discoveries at the Stamford Library. As head of management education, I felt my job was to put GE ahead of its competitors through improved manager training. I believed we could move in that direction by revamping our management courses and seminars based on new learning about brain function, but we soon realized that we simply didn't know enough about our learners' thinking or learning styles. To do what we wanted, we first needed a way to identify what learning styles the individuals participating in the seminar preferred. We needed an accurate device for measuring brain dominance.

I'm taking the time and space to tell the story of the search for that device not only because it's of interest in itself to those involved in brain technology, but also because the way the Herrmann Brain Dominance Instrument (HBDI) was born and evolved illustrates a major message regarding creativity and the brain:

> If we want to expand creative functioning in our lives, in or out of the office, we need to learn to trust our non-verbal right brain, to follow our hunches, and to follow them up with careful, highly focused left-brain verification.

Read on and you'll see what I mean.

SEARCHING FOR A WAY TO MEASURE BRAIN DOMINANCE

In approaching the question of how to measure learning style preferences, my premise was—and is—that dominance is part and parcel of the normal human condition, not only physically (as in handedness), but mentally as well. In other words, it would be normal to find people who prefer using left modes of mental functioning rather than right modes and vice versa. As a result of this normal dominance, we are handed, footed, eyed, eared, and—in a general sense—"brained."

What I needed was a model, and it had to do two things. First, it would have to give us a scale for measuring preference in mental functioning, just as we measure handedness. Handedness among human beings exemplifies the distribution of dominance across a continuum from left to right. Handedness data collected on tens of thousands of subjects show that hand preferences range from 100 percent right/0 percent left, through 50 percent right/50 percent left (ambidextrous), to 0 percent right/100 percent left. Most people's hand preference is

Figure 3-1. Occupational Qualifications

around 75 percent right/25 percent left, which indicates that while both hands are useful, there's about a 3-to-1 preference for the use of the right hand over the left. A similar model for brain dominance would include preference for using each side of the brain, and thus for using the faculties characteristic of each, such as analyzing, sequencing, processing feelings, and conceptualizing. Preference for each of these would be measured on a continuum from left to right, through which a person would exhibit dominance in terms of preferred usage.

Second, the model would have to relate these measures of brain dominance to specific thinking and learning styles—what we call *preferred modes of knowing.* Preferred modes of knowing are crucial factors to take into account in management education or any teaching situation because they filter out certain data and allow other information through. For example, for people whose preferred mode of knowing is visual, what is presented in pictures will get through to them better than a lecture or book with text only. Thus, preferred modes of knowing shape our perceptions of the world around us and incline us to think about our experience in specific ways. It is these very perceptions and inclinations that we are trying to influence and shape when we design courses.

Let me give you an example of how knowing a person's preferred thinking and learning style might influence course design. Some people prefer logical, rational, quantitative, and fact-based thinking. This style underplays, misses, ignores, or avoids intuitive, ambiguous, feeling-oriented information. Let's say we have a manager—Manager A—whose perceptions are dominated by this mode of knowing. He might want to know about a car's engine in exquisite technical detail, but would be less concerned about its interior upholstery. He would likely read the *New York Times, Fortune,* or *Scientific American,* but probably not the *Daily News, People,* or the *National Enquirer.* He would be inclined to take courses in accounting and engineering, but avoid sociology and music appreciation. In his youth, he probably aspired to a career in finance, engineering, or law, but didn't even consider careers in recreation, nursing, and counseling. When asked the question, "What is wrong with education?" he says, "We have too many frills in our educational system. We need to return to the basics and teach the facts in an orderly way."

Say we're teaching a course on dealing with difficult subordinates, for example, and we want managers to learn to deliver and receive emotional communication so they can solve employee-related work problems. We cannot—we must not—assume that Manager A sees the value in expressing feelings and giving other people the opportunity to vent their emotions. Nor can we assume that watching someone else role play the process is going to convince Manager A of that value. It may go right past him. What he may need instead is an entire course of logic, explaining that: (1) feelings have a biochemical basis; (2) negative feelings denied or suppressed inevitably manifest in negative conscious or unconscious behavior; and (3) the successful manager is aware of any such behavior and provides the opportunity for clearing negative feelings. To reach Manager A, one will have to persuade him that dealing with feelings is a step in the process of meeting a set goal, an integral part of getting the job done, not a frill or a pandering to weakness.

By contrast, in the next chair, Manager C, who moves by intuition, may already know how to deal with feelings, but may discount the need to set firm limits and goals in definable, measurable ways. His staff may be happy, but his department performance is only average because they don't have a clear sense of what is expected of them and what the consequences are of failing to deliver. Reaching Manager C, however, means presenting the need to set goals and define numbers as part of the requirement for personal satisfaction. He needs to hear that: (1) people feel their best when they know specifically what they're shooting for, they know someone is holding them to a commitment, and they successfully discharge that commitment; and therefore, (2) people can't feel fully satisfied unless they have goals.

To experience the relevance and importance of dominance more fully, try the Dominance Sorting Exercise in table 3-1. It will help you become more aware of the behavior and communication patterns that differentiate some of the key people in your life. These often dramatic differences reflect underlying preferences in modes of knowing. Since this exercise will be referred to several times in later chapters, it will help your understanding of the book to complete it now. It should take you 10 to 15 minutes at most.

Dominance Sorting Exercise

The worksheet in table 3-1 is laid out in four columns: A, B, C, and D. Two (A and B) represent left-hemisphere-related modes of knowing and two (C and D) represent right hemisphere-related modes. The words in each column describe each of the four primary modes of thinking. Not all of the descriptors in a column will fit a given person equally, but taken together, the words in one column will fit a person better than the words in any other.

Here's how to do the exercise:

1. First, list the names of the important people in your life down the left-hand side of the page in this order: (a) *mother and father* (or significant caretakers when you were growing up); (b) your *present spouse*; (c) *past spouses* if you had them (you may even want to number them spouse 1, 2,); (d) if you are unmarried, but had or have a "significant other," enter that person in the Special Cases/Self category; (e) *brothers or sisters* and *children* (start with the oldest and move in order to the youngest); (f) *best friends*, the three or four truly best friends in your life; (g) *yourself*.

2. Now choose which set of column descriptors best fits each of these people and write his or her first name or initials in the appropriate column. Do that for each person on your list. Finally, being as objective as you can, enter yourself in one of the columns in the Special Cases/Self category.

3. Once you have the people on the personal side of your life classified, turn to the Business Associates category. This time, before you select which people to include, consider first their modes of thinking, and then choose just one associate for each category: A, B, C, and D. Sometimes people will seem to fit more than one category equally. If so, use someone else. Each person you choose for this part of the exercise should be most completely described by just one of the categories.

4. Finally, with all the columns now filled in, take a moment to think about the quality of the relation-

ships you have with each of these people. How well do you understand that person? How well do you think that person understands you? How well do they communicate with one another? What is the quality of the communication with you?

Think first about your mother. Note the column you placed your mother in and compare it with the column in which you placed yourself. Make the same comparison with your father. Disregard for the moment issues of affection, love, and family loyalty, and compare the quality of your relationship with each. Is it different? Now think about how your mother and father relate to each other. How well do your mother and father communicate with you? With your brothers and sisters?

Now shift your attention to your spouse and children. Again, disregard issues of affection, love, and family loyalty, and ask yourself about the *quality of understanding* between you and your spouse, between you and your children.

Are your children placed in different columns? Do you maintain different levels of communication with them? Do you treat all of them the same way, even though they may be very different from one another?

Are your best friends in the same column, adjoining columns, or widely dispersed across the spectrum? Think about a time when you were able to communicate with one of them soundlessly, with just a glance.

Finally, turn your attention to your business associates, starting first with the person who is in the same column as yourself. Then compare the quality of the relationship and ease of communication you have with one who is in the column the most distant from you. For example, if you are in column A, compare yourself with the person in column D. Next, compare yourself with the person in the same column as you. Since these are people you know, try to recall how these similarities and differences affect your ability to work effectively with each of them. Now, considering all four individuals, who would you seek out when in need of help or advice? Who would you avoid?

If a task force were formed of the four business associates in columns A, B, C, and D, how effective a team would they make? How well would they work together? How creative do you think they would be as a group? Visualize for a moment how you would function if you were a member of this group. If you were the manager, what would you have to do to make the group an effective community?

After completing the Dominance Sorting Exercise, take a moment to reflect on the similarities and differences that should have now become even more obvious with this group of special people. Focus especially on their differences as they might effect their modes of knowing and their ways of learning. The people you have in column A are likely to learn in ways similar to Manager A, and the people you have in column C will learn in ways similar to Manager C. Knowing these people as you do should help

DOMINANCE SORTING EXERCISE

LEFT-ORIENTED DESCRIPTORS		RIGHT-ORIENTED DESCRIPTORS	
A	**B**	**C**	**D**
FACTUAL	ORDERED	MUSICAL	ARTISTIC
LOGICAL	DETAILED	SPIRITUAL	HOLISTIC
RATIONAL	SEQUENTIAL	TALKATIVE	FLEXIBLE
THEORETICAL	CONTROLLED	EMOTIONAL	IMAGINATIVE
MATHEMATICAL	CONSERVATIVE	EMPATHETIC	SYNTHESIZING

PARENT

SPOUSE

BROTHERS AND SISTERS

CHILDREN

BEST FRIENDS

| BUSINESS ASSOCIATE A | BUSINESS ASSOCIATE B | BUSINESS ASSOCIATE C | BUSINESS ASSOCIATE D |

SPECIAL CASES/SELF

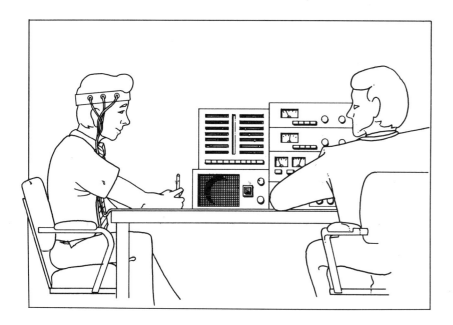

Figure 3-2. EEG Experiment

make it clearer that two sharply different learning styles are involved with A and C. When you add in B and D, there are at least four very different learning styles.

Back at the time of my search for a model, about all I realized was that differing brain preferences would have a major effect on teaching and learning so the potential for enhancing our programs became obvious. The next thing needed was some kind of measuring device to supply us with data about these individual preferences. It was with high hopes that I started a methodical search for an existing brain dominance measuring instrument. Over the next few months, I contacted all the known leaders in this emerging field, both nationally and internationally. I was surprised to come up totally dry. The need for such an instrument now seemed obvious, and it was amazing to me that none had been developed.

If I wanted a way to measure someone's brain dominance, it looked like I'd have to develop it myself. This was not a task I relished undertaking or even had a clear plan for accomplishing, but the sense of urgency to get it done was compelling. I was like a man possessed.

Initial Steps

No doubt because of my own technical background and interest in scientific measurement, I gravitated first toward biofeedback as a potential way to determine brain dominance. My search led me westward to Tod Mikuriya, M.D., Ph.D, a Berkeley psychiatrist who used biofeedback in his practice.

Biofeedback Experiments

The initial experiment we conducted involved my learning to influence my own brain waves as monitored by a bimodal EEG apparatus. This apparatus was an electroencephalographic instrument composed of two units, one connected to the brain's left hemisphere and the other connected to the right.

Using this biofeedback instrumentation, Dr. Mikuriya trained me to achieve an alpha state in each hemisphere individually, and then in both hemispheres simultaneously. While still wired up, we conducted additional experiments in which I drew graphic symbols, added up a column of numbers, sketched a landscape, worked an algebra problem, and read from a book that required both reading and interpretation of a visual diagram. The readings taken during these additional tests confirmed that brain wave responses shifted as the tasks changed. Specifically, the left hemisphere switched into a beta or active state when a task correlated with such specialized modes as number and language processing, but when it had to do with drawing and interpreting visual diagrams—right hemisphere modes—the left hemisphere shifted to an alpha frequency. In contrast, my brain waves showed that while my right hemisphere was stimulated for all of the tasks, it was far more active for the drawing and visualization ones.

This experiment directly reconfirmed for me the work of Roger Sperry, Robert Ornstein, and David Galin. It also gave me an explanation for my ability to carry on two divergent occupations: corporate manager and professional artist. My left brain responded situationally to numerous business-oriented tasks and my right brain stayed "turned on" generally, ready for artistic activity whenever the situation allowed. This probably isn't unusual. I believe all healthy human brains are waiting to respond situationally to the mental activities of the person involved.

"Recreation is nothing but a change of work, an occupation for those who live by their brains or the brains for those who live by their hands."

Dorothy Thompson

Figure 3-3. Berkeley Brain Tests (photo)

The Berkeley Brain Tests

My success with this initial experiment led to a comprehensive EEG research project performed in December 1977, referred to as the *Berkeley Brain Tests*.

These tests were designed in collaboration with Max Fogel, Ph.D., a Philadelphia-based psychologist, and Tod Mikuriya, M.D., Ph.D. They consisted of 55 different activities performed by a group of 14 volunteers who were hooked up to a bimodal, digitized Autogenic EEG apparatus and a Mind Mirror, which provided an analog (pictorial) display of the frequency states in both hemispheres at once. We captured the digital EEG data and the Mind Mirror data on a split-screen video, which also recorded the behavior of the subjects during the experiment.

The results reconfirmed the validity of hemispheric specialization, but did not produce a viable test for everyday application in the business world. Apart from the enormous expense and time required, it was simply impractical to wire up managers and executives and to put them through a testing procedure complex enough to demand that professionals monitor the testing protocol and interpret the biofeedback data.

There had to be another way.

Brain Update Workshop Data

While the search for a dominance-measuring technique was thus under way, I began, out of my enthusiasm for all this new learning, to share my new understanding with anyone who was interested. This was done in the form of one-day seminars called *Brain Update Workshops*.

With no more specific idea than the thought that it

might prove interesting to learn something about those attending, I put together a simple questionnaire called a *Participant Survey Form*. It requested data on educational background, job focus, preferred academic subjects, the work most enjoyed, hobbies, handedness, and also some open-ended questions that might elicit data I'd not thought to request specifically. It also included some adjectives describing different functions of the specialized brain, and asked people to select from among them those that pertained to themselves.

It was a full year before I knew why I was doing any of these things. Here's one of those points I told you about—evidence that the right brain has an uncanny instinct for doing the right thing, even when we don't consciously know how or why or when it's going to work out in the end. It's important to learn you can trust your right-brain ideas to take you where you want to go. I was trusting in this way when I decided to hold Brain Update Workshops and to survey the participants.

The purpose of the Brain Update Workshops was to give the pioneering participants an understanding of the specialized brain, and also to offer experiences that would provide clues to their own brain dominance. What I didn't know was that I was putting together the beginnings of an instrument to measure brain dominance. To find out which experiences changed participants' self-assessments, I captured their reactions to the experiences on a worksheet that had three scales of brain dominance ranging from left to right. About one-third of the way into the workshop, participants would mark the first scale, showing where on the left/right continuum they thought they fell, based on the information they had received thus far. They repeated this about two-thirds of the way through the

workshop and then again at the end.

The reaction to these early Brain Update Workshops was extremely positive. Before long there was a waiting list of interested people from all walks of life—teachers, artists, farmers, scientists, managers, housewives, executives, ministers, and associates from the GE Management Development Institute—and we were scheduling more than one a month.

After running 10 of these sessions over a period of 6 months, about 500 sets of participant data had been gathered. The two separate stacks of forms, paper-clipped and bundled together with rubber bands, sat on a corner of my desk for many months before it dawned on me that there might be a relationship between the personal demographic information contained in one stack and the participants' self-assessed brain dominance ratings in the other. The way that dawning occurred is another instance of how the mind "knows" even before one can articulate the knowledge. Here's how it happened.

I walked into my office after returning from a trip and found my desk neat and orderly. My secretary had cleaned up my normally messy desk. The two stacks of papers were gone. My secretary was out. Had they been thrown away? I panicked, dashed out of my office, and ran down to the basement area where trash was gathered for disposal. A frantic search turned up nothing. No, nobody in the maintenance area could recall any stacks of precious papers. When I got back to my office, my secretary had returned and I confronted her with the sad tale. She said, "Oh, I knew those were important to you. I stuck them in the cabinet with the rest of the stuff you get frantic about after its gone. Let me get them for you now."

Still not knowing what to do with those papers, but

BRAIN UPDATE WORKSHOP

PARTICIPANT SURVEY FORM

Please fill this out and then share it with some of the other participants. Feel free to add to or modify it during the course of the workshop. I would like you to turn this survey sheet in to me at the end of the day, so I can use it in my research.

Thank you,

Ned Herrmann

NAME: _____

COLLEGE MAJOR: _____

COLLEGE DEGREE(S): _____

OCCUPATION: _____

OTHER OCCUPATIONAL INTERESTS OR DESIRES: _____

_____

HOBBIES: _____

_____

ARE YOU RIGHT-HANDED OR LEFT-HANDED? _____

DO YOU WRITE WITH YOUR PENCIL ABOVE OR BELOW THE LINE? ____

ARE YOU DARK-EYED (e.g., Brown) _____

ARE YOU LIGHT-EYED (e.g., Blue) _____

IF YOU HAD YOUR CHOICE OF ACTIVITIES, WOULD YOU TEND TOWARDS THOSE REQUIRING

FAST RESPONSE TIME _____, OR THOSE THAT ARE MORE SELF-PACED _____

WHAT WERE YOUR BEST AND WORST SUBJECTS IN ELEMENTARY OR HIGH SCHOOL? _____

_____

WHAT KIND OF ACTIVITIES DO YOU SHY AWAY FROM? _____

_____

WHAT KIND OF ACTIVITIES DO YOU DO WELL? _____

_____

WHAT DO YOU DO WITH YOUR FREE TIME NOW? _____

_____

OTHER RELATED DESCRIPTORS: _____

_____

Figure 3-4. Original Version of the Participant Survey Form, 1976

convinced by my panic that there must be something important in the data and having taken the EEG testing into a blind alley, I decided to dig into those two stacks. To see what correlations might occur between the two sets of data, I retained Kendrik Few of Opinion Research Corporation to help me perform a factor analysis. The term *factor analysis*, for those of you who aren't familiar with statistical techniques, refers to an analysis focused on finding out what factors explain the correlations among the different items. There may be dozens of items, but only a few important factors. The analyst first sorts out what factors are common and then tries to make sense out of them.

Bingo! While the data base was relatively crude, consistent correlations emerged in just the right places. People who had taken engineering as a college major and who now worked in engineering occupations described themselves as logical, analytic, quantitative, and technical. They did well in math, but not as well in English. They said of themselves that they preferred rational, fact-based thinking; enjoyed golf and fishing as hobbies; and *saw themselves as left-brain dominant.* In contrast, people who were artists, salesmen, or owners of their own businesses did well in English and less well in math, tended to major in the humanities; described themselves as insightful, intuitive, and imaginative; enjoyed arts and crafts and photography as hobbies; and *placed themselves on the opposite end of the continuum!*

Kendrik Few's report arrived a scant 3 days before the first Whole Brain Symposium, an invitational group of 55 people I brought together at GE's Management Development Institute to share their research findings and enthusiasm for new emerging understanding of the brain. Because of the need to prepare for the symposium, I was unable to give the data more than a cursory examination—just enough to know that the results warranted mention.

When the time came to reveal that particular research to the audience, I laid the data out in front of me, correlating the Participant Survey Form questions and the left/right continuum data. While sharing these with the audience, it suddenly dawned on me that the striking correlations that had emerged might represent the basis for a measuring instrument. Right in the middle of my presentation I stopped and said to the audience, "My God! I think this might be the basis for a brain dominance instrument." Smiles, applause, and encouragement followed, including offers from these and many other interested people to share their own personal data.

Let me comment here on another lesson to be drawn from this story: In expanding your own creativity, it's very important to learn what it is that stimulates your creative process. It's different for different people. For me, it's frequently the pressure of an event. So it was in this case. Often I don't make certain kinds of innovative, imaginative connections unless I'm pushed, the way I was here.

Following this correlation study, I made some changes in the Participant Survey Form and administered the new version to about 300 people who'd attended the Brain Update Workshops during 1978. This first revision of the form has elements that have been retained to this day—through 19 additional revisions. We then repeated the correlation studies conducted with the original group of 500. On the strength of the very positive results, I went ahead with plans to develop a formal paper-and-pencil instrument, which eventually, at GE's insistence, was renamed the Herrmann Brain Dominance Instrument (HBDI).

"The Creative Dilemma: Every valuable, creative idea will always be logical in hindsight."
Willis Harmon

"Some extremely intense forms of creative learning lead to ecstasy. Ecstasy is the powerful process in which form (LH) and passion (RH) are united."
Source Unknown

Figure 3-5.   Left/Right Continuum. Two points

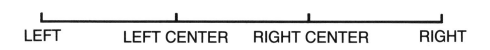

Figure 3-6.   Left/Right Continuum. Four points, two added for left center and right center

The First Formal Instrument

Formalizing the instrument meant simply that, having finally developed enough data and focus, I could get very deliberate and specific about what I was going after in designing it. Up until that point my conscious process was following my own interests, exploring, feeling my way. It was clear to me that something important would emerge, but, from a design standpoint, my process was very informal indeed! All that now changed. The first formal instrument was an expanded and honed version of the original Participant Survey Form, and it produced a linear scale showing a person having four ratings: two extremes, one for left and one for right; and two intermediate ratings, one for left center and one for right center.

Understand that at this point, physiological brain dominance was still the basis of my thinking. That is, I believed that if we monitored, on the EEG, a person who indicated strong left-brain thinking preferences, we would find that if given a situational choice, he would spend his major thinking time using the left brain, and we would know this because most of the time the left brain would emit beta waves and the inactive right brain would emit mainly alpha waves.

Later neuropsychological research called into question the appropriateness of this totally physiological basis as a foundation for my learning/teaching model. Accordingly, I soon shifted to a metaphorical model, which was derived less from a strict physiological interpretation than from the growing body of documented observations of behaviors. But this is jumping ahead of the story. I knew very little of this in 1979.

What I did know was that the instrument I'd developed was working. Even looking back from today's vantage point, this first version is amazingly on target. And it was doing what needed to be done. I was discovering enough about the learning process through the use of the instrument data in workshops that the goal of developing a whole-brain teaching and learning model felt only inches away. I could almost taste what it would be like to be able to design our courses at the Management Development Institute so they could reach everyone, not just those who shared the designer's assumptions and preferences.

Early Learnings About Learning

I experimented a lot with tailoring the way we presented key learning points in existing workshops. Some of the things I did were quite mundane and simple, but they clearly confirmed that participants had different needs based on their brain dominance. Some of the lessons learned were: (1) we had to cover all modes; (2) mental mavericks enriched the learning experience; and (3) many people fell into one or more of four distinct categories.

The Need to Cover All Modes

On one occasion, we had members of high-level GE corporate staff groups attending a five-day Motivation Workshop. At the time, from a design standpoint, this workshop was the most advanced course available at GE's Management Development Institute. As a matter of fact, it was so much more open and unstructured than the more traditional, functional courses that some people became uncomfortable with the lack of form and structure.

On this particular occasion, we started the workshop at 8:30. At the 10:00 A.M. coffee break, one of the key

"The miracle ingredient that would provide a respite from the strain of overchoice...not a single product or idea, but a way of organizing all products and ideas, not a single commodity but a whole lifestyle, a set of guidelines that help the individual reduce the increasing complexity of choice to manageable proportions."

Alvin Toffler

Figure 3-7.   Workshop Road Map

staff managers came up to me and said, "Ned, if I don't find out in the first five minutes after we reconvene what this workshop is all about, where it's going, and where it will end up, I will be leaving after lunch, and I will be taking with me all four of the people who work with me and anybody else who is as uncomfortable as I am at this minute!" I said, "I'm sorry you feel so uncomfortable. Let me see what I can do." I grabbed my colleague and co-leader, Bob Harper, and we went back into the workshop room and developed a detailed "road map" of where we had just come from, where we were going in the next two hours, where we would be before the end of the day, where we would be by the end of day 2, day 3, day 4, and where we would be at the end of the week.

When the group reconvened, I introduced the new road map as something that was built into the workshop design and walked the group through the details of "what had happened" that morning and "what will be happening" hour by hour later on. As I did so, I noticed at least five or six people looking visibly relieved. Expressions of hostility softened into expressions of understanding, acceptance, and comfort.

What had happened was this: The course had a deficit in the left hemisphere, and we had filled it with the structure and detail that those with strong preferences for that mode of knowing required in order to be comfortable with a new learning experience.

Another example of filling a deficit occurred during that same workshop. I noticed that while individuals were performing detailed verbally oriented work, the quiet became almost oppressive. People became uncomfortable. To ease the tension, I began to play a baroque music tape — a Bach flute sonata. Some eyebrows rose, but before long, people not only became comfortable with music, but actually complained when it wasn't played. The non-intervening, soothing melody and pulse-matched rhythms filled the deficit for an inspiring setting without intruding on the group's concentration in performing activities. Music is now an integral part of all of my workshops. (See Chapter 8 for more on music).

Why Mental Mavericks Help

Even at this early date, my explorations were confirming my belief that even though the brain is specialized, *no part works as fully or creatively on its own as it does when stimulated or supported by input from the other parts.* Of course, the other parts can also operate competitively, as Sperry's split-brain experiments showed. But *each part truly needs the others if it is to function at its best.*

At no time was that demonstrated more vividly to me in those early days than in what happened when the instrument was administered to a Motivation Workshop group that included some "course enrichers." *Course enricher* is a term I used to describe people I introduced into a class as a means of enriching the discussion.

The basic problem bedeviling this and most other in-house workshops was that the participants had such similar backgrounds (educational backgrounds, work assignments, experiences, and thinking patterns) that they agreed too quickly to have much of anything to talk about. Where no differences exist, there's basically nothing to discuss—and nothing much new is learned.

In an attempt to stimulate learning in these homogeneous groups, I began to include people who came from different occupations—art, social work, retailing—and from different companies, usually outside of big bus-

iness. A large proportion of these course enrichers were female. A group of 18 to 20 people normally would include about 4 of them. Their impact was immediate and positive. On any given subject, they could be counted on to come up with a very different perspective, a different point of view, a different set of experiences. By facilitating the discussion that developed around these differences, the leader was able to bring out learning points that were unavailable in more homogeneous settings.

The success rate was extremely high, but there were occasional failures—not because the course enrichers contributed negatively to the learning situation, but because they didn't contribute any fresh input at all. They weren't different enough. For instance, a female financial manager introduced into a group of male financial managers tended to be relatively indistinguishable from the men because she shared similar education, training, and brain dominance characteristics. She didn't enrich, she blended.

On numerous occasions, people who were to serve as course enrichers asked me what special role they should play. They were always surprised to hear, " I don't expect you to play any role at all. I just want you to be yourselves—to be completely authentic. Your uniqueness will automatically enrich the learning for everybody."

I was involved in the Motivation Workshop long before learning anything about the impact of brain dominance on thinking styles, so my influence on its design would have to be categorized as an intuitive solution to a problem that was felt rather than fully understood.

When several years later the instrument was available to administer to a workshop group, I could see immediately why the course enrichers had such an impact. They were usually right-brain dominant, which gave them an entirely

Figure 3-8.   Course Enricher

different perspective from the typical GE technical employee who tended to lean more left. This different perspective, in and of itself, provided the basis of their contribution to the learning process.

How Preferences Cluster

The linear profile produced by the early version of the instrument reflected the basic dichotomy between left-brain-related modes of mental processing and right-brain-related modes. It was like the distributed profile for handedness mentioned earlier. Using both analytic and intuitive techniques, I had classified all of the different specialized mental activities according to how much left or right was required to perform them. Then I had rank-ordered them, left to right, thus forming the basis of a continuum.

But as more people filled out the survey, the data base grew, and four distinct clusters emerged. Two clusters represented the end points of the continuum, the extremes of the dichotomy (logical, analytical, and quantitative on the left; intuitive, artistic, and imaginative on the right). The other two seemed to represent a pair of points centered between the extremes, which I called left center and right center. The left center descriptors had to do with planning, organizing, and administering; the right center cluster had to do with emotions, interpersonal aspects, expressiveness, and music.

Most early profiles showed distinct preferences for descriptors that fell within two of the four data clusters. Sometimes both preferences were at a primary level—very strong in both data clusters—and sometimes one preference would be secondary or less strong.

What's more, it was becoming evident that certain combinations of primary and secondary preferences tended to occur as characteristic of certain occupations, such as engineering, finance, social work, and entrepreneurship.

The Second Generation Instrument

I wanted more precision in measuring dominance. Although I could already predict behavior based on profiles, the instrument was still pretty rough and there were things I couldn't do. For example, one of the activities in the Brain Update Workshop involved having people seat themselves in the classroom along a left/right continuum. Because our participant groups were so homogeneous, however, five or ten people in each workshop would come out with the same general brain dominance profile, and I couldn't be sure of properly arranging them in relationship to each other.

To differentiate among people who had similar overall profiles, I expanded the instrument. Building on the work of Eugene Raudsepp, a writer well known in the area of creativity, I developed an array of 20 questions, including 10 questions that fell on the left side of the brain dominance continuum and 10 on the right. For each question, there was a five-point scale, which meant that the score from the 20 questions added a substantial quantitative measure to the metaphoric profile display. These numerical measures provided enough differentiation to break almost any tie between individuals who had identical nominal profiles based on the data supplied by the original instrument.

Now, even for a homogeneous group, the scores for individual profiles could be arrayed along a continuum from left to right, and the individuals could be seated left

"Questions are the creative acts of intelligence."

Frank King

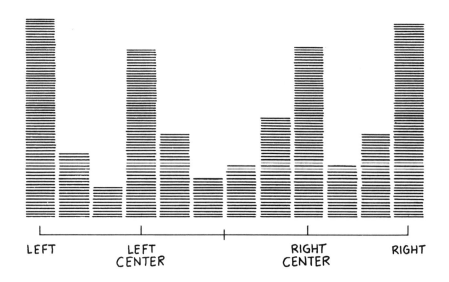

LEFT LEFT CENTER RIGHT CENTER RIGHT

Figure 3-9. Data Clusters. A Histogram representing the number of surveys that fell into each category

to right in a classroom accordingly. This made it easy to observe their reactions to the material being presented. For example, when I talked about the usefulness of guided fantasies in the workshop, those sitting on the right side of the room reacted with enthusiastic acceptance while those on the left were reacting in distaste and rejection. Similarly, when I introduced a subject involving the application of logic, the people receiving it enthusiastically were mostly on the left side of the room, while those acting puzzled and dismayed or bored sat to the right. Individuals on the far left exhibited discomfort with ambiguity and any activity that involved the expression of feelings, but responded favorably to facts that were backed up with documented references. They liked their instructions clear and explicit and their handout materials to be well organized and sequenced with all relevant detail. They performed repetitive tasks patiently and carefully. Such things were of little or no interest, by contrast, to those on the far right. These people were more interested in experimenting, taking risks, and moving physically. They greatly favored people-oriented activities with some emotional content. They preferred information displayed visually as well as in written form.

SETTING THE STAGE FOR A NEW VIEW OF DOMINANCE

The neuropsychological research of the 1970s on which the earliest versions of the instrument were based focused on the left/right dichotomies. Scientists believed then that the brain was specialized in an all-or-nothing way. They thought all language was in the left hemisphere together with all logic, while all spatial comprehension was in the right hemisphere together with all holistic thinking. So the design and interpretation of my early data gathering reflected this same left/right thinking.

However, some pieces of theory and data that were floating around didn't quite fit. For one thing, as the clustering in four separate regions spaced across the continuum became more distinct, I was impressed by the fact that *the overall data seemed equally distributed among the four regions*. This looked unusual, for the more typical pattern in any given continuum is to have a bell curve, with the fewest number of people falling at the extreme ends, and the largest number occurring somewhere around the middle. It was a while before my thinking evolved to accommodate this apparent oddity.

Another piece had to do with the limbic system. Early on, my research turned up general agreement within the scientific community that emotional processing, originating in the limbic system, was controlled by the right brain. Sperry's work on specialization had differentiated between the substructures of the brain, i.e., between the limbic and the cerebral hemispheres. But then he'd focused exclusively on the two halves of the cerebrum, leaving out the limbic. So we had a partial theory—the left and right combined with a bit of cerebral vs. limbic—but it didn't feel whole, so I kept searching.

Still a third important piece had to do with Paul MacLean's triune brain theory, which made a great deal of sense to me when I encountered it. It reminded me of the biological theory that "ontogeny recapitulates phylogeny," which means that each human being relives the evolution of the human species in his or her development. The neural tube,

"All appearances are verily one's concepts self-conceived in the reflections seen in a mirror."

Podma Sambhava

"It (the limbic system) is the central role in generating affective feelings, including those important for a sense of reality, ...and a conviction of what is true and important."

Paul MacLean

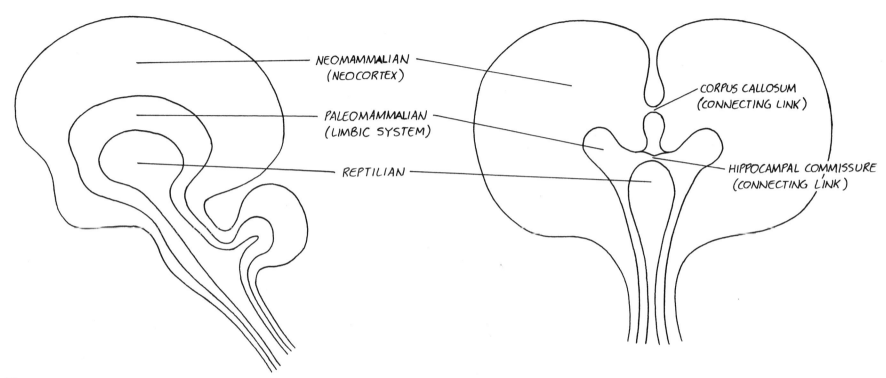

Figure 3-10.   The Triune Brain

Figure 3-11.   The Rotated Triune Brain

which is the beginning of the brain in a fetus, develops initially into the brain stem, which in turn develops a limbic system above it, which, in turn, is capped by the cerebral hemispheres.

I was sure the triune brain theory was valid, and even more sure of the duality of the left brain/right brain theory. But it took well over a year of incubation time before I was able to integrate the two. When I did, it took my thinking onto an entirely new plane, from which all the surrounding territory looked transformed.

The Quadrant Concept

Here's how it finally came together for me. One day, while driving the 35 miles between office and home, I was thinking about how to merge the triune and the left brain/right brain theories. Both theories initially appeared in my mind's eye the way they're always illustrated: The left brain/right brain concept I "saw" was a frontal cross section of the brain indicating two separated hemispheres. The triune brain appeared in a sideview crosssection cut between the hemispheres rather than through them. Then, in my visualization, the triune brain crosssection rotated through 90 degrees, so instead of looking at it from the side, I was seeing it from the back.

Eureka! There, suddenly, was the connecting link I had been searching for! When viewed from this unconventional perspective, it was obvious! The limbic system was also divided into two separated halves, and also endowed with a cortex capable of thinking, and also connected by a commissure—just like the cerebral hemispheres. Instead of there being *two* parts of the specialized brain, there were *four—the number of clusters the data had been showing*!

Instead of using a straight line with four clusters, I could simply bend the ends up and around to form a circular graph, which would also correspond to a cutaway of the brain from behind. So, what I had been calling left brain, would now become the *left cerebral hemisphere*. What was the right brain, now became the *right cerebral hemisphere*. What had been left center, would now be *left limbic*, and right center, now *right limbic*. The fact that each quadrant touched the next would reflect the connectors—the two commissures between the left and right sides of the brain, and the association and projection fibers that provide communication between cerebral and limbic on the same side.

The whole idea unfolded with such speed and intensity that it blotted out conscious awareness of everything else. I discovered after the image of this new model had taken form in my mind that my Stamford exit had gone by some time ago. The last ten miles had been a total blank!

Eventually, the insights from that day evolved into the four-quadrant model of preferred modes of knowing and brain dominance we still use in the twentieth revision of the instrument. Between that day and this one, however, lay major milestones.

One such milestone was the shift from the physiological model to the metaphoric. Another was confirming the validity of both the design of the instrument and the data it produced.

The Move to the Metaphoric Model

The whole-brain model, although originally thought of as a physiological map, is today entirely a metaphor.* The circular display represents the whole thinking brain, which then divides into four conscious modes of knowing, each with its own behaviors demonstrably associated with it.

---

* Since the initial publication of this book, I have developed a set of models describing the architecture of the brain model. These are displayed in Appendix E.

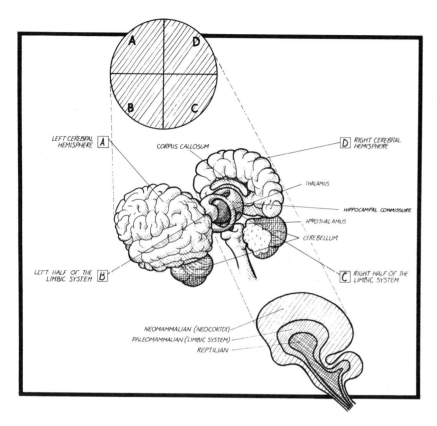

Figure 3-12. Everything You Need to Know About the Brain. Figure 2-12 with the addition of the four quadrant concept.

The move away from the physiological interpretation toward a more general, metaphoric one made sense for three reasons:

1. Determining precisely which part of the brain was doing what was looking more and more difficult, and less and less important. Researchers were discovering that brain lateralization wasn't as all-or-nothing as they'd originally thought: The operation of the brain was immeasurably more subtle, complex, and versatile than the dichotic model implied.

2. I believed strongly that the two center clusters of data I had gotten from the original instrument had something important to do with the limbic system, but even if they didn't correspond precisely, or they did and we couldn't prove it, the idea was useful because it provided a means of organizing and clarifying our thinking about modes of knowing.

   And that, after all, is what metaphors are: ideas that clarify understanding of something else, like—"Man's soul is the candle of the Lord" (Proverbs) or "The larger the island of knowledge, the longer the shoreline of wonder." (Ralph Sockman).

3. The data base was great! Daily occurrences confirmed that the four-quadrant modes-of-knowing model was producing data on human behavior that was consistent enough to have validity in its own right. Not only was the four-quadrant data consistent, it was richer than the simpler left/right data. Including visceral and emotional modes

along with the more abstract and conceptual ones produced information that permitted us to distinguish, for example, the left-brain preferences that make for good accountants from those that make for good bookkeepers; and those that make for good social workers from those that make for good facilitators. (Accountants and facilitators have cerebral preferences, whereas bookkeepers and social workers have more limbic tendencies).

Data from the four-fold metaphoric model also provided a way of describing dominance characteristics for those who are multidominant, that is, who have distinct preference for working in more than one mode. A study of 15,000 profiles indicates that 6 percent were single dominant, 60 percent double dominant, 30 percent triple dominant, and 3 percent quadruple dominant. In other words, 94 percent of the sample had primary preferences in more than one quadrant. The simpler dichotomized model cannot provide either this type or this level of discrimination.

To further soften the relationship between the physiology of the brain and the metaphoric model, I stopped using cerebral and limbic as discrete quadrant descriptors and, instead, labeled each quadrant with a letter—A, B, C, D, beginning with upper left and running counterclockwise to upper right. (These correspond, by the way, to the four columns, *A, B, C, D,* of the Dominance Sorting Exercise you did back at the beginning of the chapter.)

The reason for going counterclockwise in this way is that the circular profile display evolved out of the original linear continuum. I created the circular display by connecting upperleft A with upper-right D, and lower-left B with lower-right C, just as these physiologically specialized brain structures are connected by the corpus callosum and the hippocampal commissure.

VALIDATING THE INSTRUMENT'S DESIGN

In the process of carrying out the original project using the questionnaire from the Brain Update Workshops, I literally fell upon the design of the instrument. It was more intuitive than planned. There wasn't the kind of forethought that often precedes design. But as the instrument evolved, I went back to make sure that it did in fact measure what it was intended to measure, and did so in a way that eliminated as much as possible the chance of bias or omission. In so doing, I considered these questions:

1. What is the best way to administer the instrument and why?

2. How can we eliminate bias in answering the questions—trying to shape the answers to produce a certain profile, for example?

3. How can we prevent inaccuracies that might occur because of anxiety?

4. How can we make sure that people's scores aren't simply a result of misunderstanding?

5. How do we ensure that the survey questions are scored consistently?

6. What is the best way to present results so participants gain the most from the experience?

BIOGRAPHICAL INFORMATION

1. Name _____ 2. Sex: M ☐ F ☐
3. Educational Focus or Major _____
4. Occupation or Job Title _____
   Describe your work _____
   _____

HANDEDNESS

5. Which picture most closely resembles the way you hold a pencil? Mark box **A**, **B**, **C**, or **D**.

   A ☐   B ☐   C ☐   D ☐

6. What is the strength and direction of your handedness? Mark box **A**, **B**, **C**, **D**, or **E**.

   A ☐ primary left   B ☐ primary left, some right   C ☐ both hands equal   D ☐ primary right, some left   E ☐ primary right

BEST/WORST SUBJECTS

Think back to your best/worst elementary and/or secondary school subjects. **Rank all three subjects** identified below by entering a **1**, **2** or **3** on the basis of how well you did: **1** = best; **2** = second best; **3** = third best.

7. _____ math   8. _____ foreign language   9. _____ native language or mother tongue

Did you use each of the numbers **1, 2,** and **3** once and only once?

WORK ELEMENTS

Rate each of the work elements below according to your strength in that activity, using the following scale:
5 = work I do best; **4** = work I do well; **3** = neutral; **2** = work I do less well; **1** = work I do least well.
Enter the appropriate number next to each element. **Do not use any number more than four times.**

10. _____ analytical
11. _____ administrative
12. _____ conceptualizing
13. _____ expressing ideas
14. _____ integration
15. _____ writing
16. _____ technical aspects
17. _____ implementation
18. _____ planning
19. _____ interpersonal aspects
20. _____ problem solving
21. _____ innovating
22. _____ teaching/training
23. _____ organization
24. _____ creative aspects
25. _____ financial aspects

Please check: No more than four 5's, four 4's etc.? Correct if necessary.

KEY DESCRIPTORS

Select the **eight adjectives** which best describe the way you see yourself. Enter a **2** next to each of your eight selections. Then change one **2** to a **3** for the adjective which best describes you.

26. _____ logical
27. _____ creative
28. _____ musical
29. _____ sequential
30. _____ synthesizer
31. _____ verbal
32. _____ conservative
33. _____ analytical
34. _____ detailed
35. _____ emotional
36. _____ spatial
37. _____ critical
38. _____ artistic
39. _____ spiritual
40. _____ rational
41. _____ controlled
42. _____ mathematical
43. _____ symbolic
44. _____ dominant
45. _____ holistic
46. _____ intuitive
47. _____ quantitative
48. _____ reader
49. _____ simultaneous
50. _____ factual

Please count: only **seven** 2's and **one** 3? Correct if necessary.

HOBBIES

Indicate a **maximum of six** hobbies you are actively engaged in. Enter a **3** next to your major hobby, a **2** next to each primary hobby, and a **1** next to each secondary hobby.

51. _____ arts/crafts
52. _____ boating
53. _____ camping/hiking
54. _____ cards
55. _____ collecting
56. _____ cooking
57. _____ creative writing
58. _____ fishing
59. _____ gardening/plants
60. _____ golf
61. _____ home improvements
62. _____ music listening
63. _____ music playing
64. _____ photography
65. _____ reading
66. _____ sailing
67. _____ sewing
68. _____ spectator sports
69. _____ swimming/diving
70. _____ tennis
71. _____ travel
72. _____ woodworking
_____ other _____

Please check: only one **3** and a total of **six hobbies.** Correct if necessary.

ENERGY LEVEL

73. Thinking about your energy level or "drive," select the one that best represents you. Check box **A**, **B**, or **C**.

   A ☐ day person   B ☐ day/night person equally   C ☐ night person

MOTION SICKNESS

74. Have you ever experienced motion sickness (nausea, vomiting) in response to vehicular motion (while in a car, boat, plane, bus, train, amusement ride)? Check box **A**, **B**, **C**, or **D** to indicate the number of times.

   A ☐ none   B ☐ 1–2   C ☐ 3–10   D ☐ more than 10

75. Check box **A** or **B** to indicate whether you can read while traveling in a car without stomach awareness, nausea, or vomiting.

   A ☐ yes   B ☐ no

ADJECTIVE PAIRS

For **each paired item** below, check the word or phrase which is more descriptive of yourself. Check box **A** or **B** in each case, even if the choice is a difficult one. **Do not omit any pairs.**

	A / B		A / B
76. conservative	☐ / ☐ empathetic	88. imaginative	☐ / ☐ sequential
77. analyst	☐ / ☐ synthesizer	89. original	☐ / ☐ reliable
78. quantitative	☐ / ☐ musical	90. creative	☐ / ☐ logical
79. problem-solver	☐ / ☐ planner	91. controlled	☐ / ☐ emotional
80. controlled	☐ / ☐ creative	92. musical	☐ / ☐ detailed
81. original	☐ / ☐ emotional	93. simultaneous	☐ / ☐ empathetic
82. feeling	☐ / ☐ thinking	94. communicator	☐ / ☐ conceptualizer
83. interpersonal	☐ / ☐ organizer	95. technical things	☐ / ☐ people-oriented
84. spiritual	☐ / ☐ creative	96. well-organized	☐ / ☐ logical
85. detailed	☐ / ☐ holistic	97. rigorous thinking	☐ / ☐ metaphorical thinking
86. originate ideas	☐ / ☐ test and prove ideas	98. like things planned	☐ / ☐ like things mathematical
87. warm, friendly	☐ / ☐ analytical	99. technical	☐ / ☐ dominant

Please check the adjective pair items. Did you mark one and only one of **each** pair?

Figure 3-13.   The HBD Instrument *Panel 1*   *Panel 2*

■■■ **INTROVERSION/EXTROVERSION** ■■■■■■■■■■■■■■■■■■■

100. Check one box only to place yourself on this introvert–extrovert scale.

introvert | | | | extrovert

■■■ **TWENTY QUESTIONS** ■■■■■■■■■■■■■■■■■■■■■■■■■■

Respond to each statement by checking the box in the appropriate column.

	strongly agree ▼	agree ▼	in between ▼	disagree ▼	strongly disagree ▼
101. I feel that a step by step method is best for solving problems.	☐	☐	☐	☐	☐
102. Daydreaming has provided the impetus for the solution of many of my more important problems.	☐	☐	☐	☐	☐
103. I like people who are most sure of their conclusions.	☐	☐	☐	☐	☐
104. I would rather be known as a reliable than an imaginative person.	☐	☐	☐	☐	☐
105. I often get my best ideas when doing nothing in particular.	☐	☐	☐	☐	☐
106. I rely on hunches and the feeling of "rightness" or "wrongness" when moving toward the solution to a problem.	☐	☐	☐	☐	☐
107. I sometimes get a kick out of breaking the rules and doing things I'm not supposed to do.	☐	☐	☐	☐	☐
108. Much of what is most important in life cannot be expressed in words.	☐	☐	☐	☐	☐
109. I'm basically more competitive with others than self-competitive.	☐	☐	☐	☐	☐
110. I would enjoy spending an entire day "alone with my thoughts."	☐	☐	☐	☐	☐
111. I dislike things being uncertain and unpredictable.	☐	☐	☐	☐	☐
112. I prefer to work with others in a team effort rather than solo.	☐	☐	☐	☐	☐
113. It is important for me to have a place for everything and everything in its place.	☐	☐	☐	☐	☐
114. Unusual ideas and daring concepts interest and intrigue me.	☐	☐	☐	☐	☐
115. I prefer specific instructions to those which leave many details optional.	☐	☐	☐	☐	☐
116. Know-why is more important than know-how.	☐	☐	☐	☐	☐
117. Thorough planning and organization of time are mandatory for solving difficult problems.	☐	☐	☐	☐	☐
118. I can frequently anticipate the solutions to my problems.	☐	☐	☐	☐	☐
119. I tend to rely more on my first impressions and feelings when making judgements than on a careful analysis of the situation.	☐	☐	☐	☐	☐
120. I feel that laws should be strictly enforced.	☐	☐	☐	☐	☐

Panel 3

Administering the Instrument for Best Results

I designed the instrument to be self-administered. Why? Because I believe we know more about ourselves than anyone else does, even if we share openly with others. Of our total mental activity, I believe at least half is internally focused and, therefore, invisible to others. This being true, no one can complete an instrument for another person, even if that person is a very close family member, a best friend, a personal secretary, or a boss. In no way can someone understand enough of the invisible part of the other person to complete the questionnaire accurately. Numerous husband/wife, parent/child, and boss/secretary experiments have confirmed that information supplied by one person about the other is significantly inaccurate when compared to the data the same person supplies about himself or herself.

Eliminating Participant Bias

This decision to make the instrument self-administered introduced the question of how to keep participants from shaping the responses. The questionnaire would have to be devised so it would solicit natural responses rather than slanted ones. This meant meeting several requirements. First, the questions would have to range widely enough to cover the entire brain dominance spectrum and to fully characterize each quadrant. Second, a high proportion of them would have to be blind—phrased so the respondent couldn't figure out the conclusion that a given answer would lead to. Third, the instrument would need an internal validation section to evoke responses that would

Figure 3-14. No Test. The HBDI is not a test. There are no right or wrong answers.

provide a cross-check in each of the four quadrants. The HBDI meets all these requirements.

One of the strengths of the instrument is that its questions range over several key areas without giving any particular clue regarding what the answers are likely to suggest. The areas include:

1. Educational Focus
2. Work (career choice, occupation, and best/worst work elements)
3. The use of discretionary time (hobbies and athletics)
4. Inner Self Perception (key descriptors of self)
5. Values (20 Questions)
6. Inner/Outer Self (Introversion/Extroversion Scale)

These questions are referred to as *blind* because their implications are not generally known. Few people would guess, for example, that a relationship exists between what time of day the person experiences the most mental productivity and which brain quadrant he or she prefers. (And I would tell you what that relationship is, except that then the question would not be a blind one for you anymore.)

People usually guess that handedness might identify hemispheric dominance, which is only faintly so, but few know that writing posture can suggest much about the organization of an individual's brain dominance preference by indicating whether the language center resides in the left or right hemisphere. This is important because the language center strongly affects the other specialized modes in the hemisphere in which it resides.

Most people don't know the implications of the question regarding motion sickness either. Charles Mirabile, Jr., M.D., the expert in this field, developed a concept that differentiates individuals with a strong dominance in one quadrant from those with a strong dominance in the opposite quadrant on the basis of their susceptibility to motion sickness. I later found that this data also provided useful information about the readiness of some people to open themselves to greater use of less preferred modes.

Preventing Misinterpretation of the HBDI as a Test

The final way to eliminate bias also helps deal with inappropriate test anxiety, and that is to make absolutely sure the participants understand the HBDI isn't a "test," and scores don't refer to gradations in either performance quality or potential. Often people who believe they're being evaluated look for answers that are "right" instead of real. That creates not only bias, but for some people intensifies anxiety enormously. We work very diligently to get people to realize that *every quadrant brings critically important contributions to effective living and working*. What the HBDI is doing is measuring which type of mental activity a person is *more inclined* to engage in at a particular time. It's like we're looking to see if you like Chinese food, French food, vegetarian, or barbecue, so when you come for a meal we know what food to cook, and how to serve each course. Learning preferences aren't right or wrong, good or bad. They simply *are* and we should delight in their profusion. So instead of "test," we use the word *instrument* or *inventory* or *survey* or *profile*.

Unfortunately, we just haven't found an acceptable

"It seems that once you understand the organizing principle involved, you see many things in everyday life that fit the four-quadrant model."

Ned Herrmann

"Failure is the line of least persistence."

Alfred W. Brandt

word to substitute for the term *scores*. Too many people have attached the idea of right or wrong, good or bad to the word *scores*, just as they have to the word *test*. So we use *scores* for lack of a better word, but again, we emphasize—no one's grading anything.

We also make sure people understand that the HBDI scores have nothing to do with IQ scores. They're entirely different. The four-quadrant profile is a metaphor describing how a person prefers to acquire and process information, not how fast or accurately they do it. IQ tests purport to measure an individual's general level of intelligence. (In fact, they do not. IQ tests are oriented far too heavily toward the verbal A and B quadrants to test general intelligence accurately. The brain is much more versatile than mere IQ tests can possibly measure.)

Reducing Misunderstanding of Terms

To reduce the chance a person would characterize himself or herself inaccurately because of a misunderstanding of some questions, we provided a way to double-check the clarity of a person's preference for one mode of knowing. The adjective pairs force a choice between preferences representing a given quadrant and the remaining three.

To make sure participants clearly comprehend the choices before them, the adjectives used are very carefully defined on the survey form.

Making Sure Scoring Is Consistent

Today, each instrument completed is scored by a professional trained in brain dominance technology, certified in the use of the HBDI, and using a proprietary scoring protocol or set of procedures. This protocol emerged from the original validation studies and has been honed and refined by successive validations and by the experience of scoring tens of thousands of surveys.

Presenting the Results

The scoring protocol results in a quantified measure of an individual's preference for each mental quadrant, which is then charted on a circular grid to make a personalized visual metaphor. In addition to the graphic representations, a person's profile is also expressed in a four-digit numerical code that assigns a number to each quadrant, indicating the strength of preference for that quadrant.

- A *1* stands for a score of 67 or more points on any one preference and is considered a *primary*, or strong preference.

- A *2*, representing a score of 34 to 66, is considered a *secondary* and indicates neither preference nor avoidance.

- A score of 0 to 33, designated by the number *3*, is considered a *tertiary* and indicates an area of potential avoidance. This means even if the person has somehow developed good skills for operating in this quadrant, the mental activity is likely to be very demanding, even enervating.

While the demarcations between these three bands were initially just commonsense estimates, experience has shown in most cases they differentiate very appropriately.

The differentiation between a preference and an avoidance (a 1 and a 3), is important for three reasons. First, the behavioral effects of a preference combined with an avoidance tend to be cumulative—each reinforcing the other—particularly when they occur in different hemispheres, and even more so when in diagonally opposing modes: A and C or B and D. Second, an extremely strong preference for one end of a dichotomy combined with a rejection of the other end (e.g., when the primary score exceeds 100 and the tertiary score is under 30) can eliminate the potential for iteration between the two modes.

Third, when both the preference and the avoidance are extremes, the related behaviors become highly visible. For example, a person with a very strong preference for quadrant A—logical, rational, fact-based processing—and an avoidance of emotion and feeling in quadrant C can come across as cold and mechanical. Likewise, a person who strongly prefers imaginative, visionary, holistic modes (quadrant D) and avoids the planned, organized, detailed modes of quadrant B can come across as an unreliable, off-the-wall character who cannot be counted on to produce results in the real world.

So the scoring code uses ones, twos, and threes, and it assigns value to the quadrants, starting with upper-left A and proceeding counterclockwise around the continuum to upper-right D. The code 1-1-3-3, then, means the person has primary preferences in A and B and tertiary preference, or avoidances, toward C and D. The code 2-1-2-3 means the person's primary preference is for B, he uses A and C comfortably when needed, and avoids D.

Four quadrants with three strengths of preference each makes close to 100 possible profiles mathematically possible. But about 12 profiles account for over 80 percent

> *"What lies behind us and what lies before us are tiny matters compared to what lies within us."*
> William Morrow

> *"Genius, in truth, means little more than the faculty of perceiving in an unhabitual way."*
> William James

of the population surveyed to date.

VALIDATING THE RESULTING DATA

Scientific training as a physicist and work experience in GE's General Engineering Laboratory motivated me to seek the strongest possible validation of my instrument, both the design and the resulting data. In addition to my own instincts, winning continued endorsement and support in a company as scientific and technical as GE required anyone in my position to validate his or her work strongly, using accepted scientific methods.

If you're interested in reading about the validation study, concepts, and practices and results in detail, turn to Appendix A for a comprehensive write-up by C. Victor Bunderson, Ph.D. Dr. Bunderson was appointed Vice President of Research Management at Educational Testing Services while this book was in preparation.

For the non-technical reader, I will say only this much: Three major sets of studies confirmed the instrument's internal and external validity in 1980, 1981, and 1982, and since 1983, the validation process has continued: 28 doctoral dissertations have added to the supporting evidence and 20 additional doctoral studies are in progress as this book is being written. The most important studies were performed by the following:

1. C. Victor Bunderson, Ph.D, Chief Scientist of WICAT Systems, Inc., and President of its Educational Institute, and James Olsen, Ph.D, also of WICAT, performed a series of studies of internal and external validity. When combined, the results of those studies converted the scoring into a numerical system, validated the four-quadrant model, and factor-analyzed the results against established psychological indicators. Factor-analyzing, in this case, involved both internal comparisons among the views of the HBDI (to establish internal validity) and external comparisons with other established measurement devices to establish external validity. Bunderson and Olsen took other indicators and profiling instruments whose purpose was to measure some kind of preference or aptitude that the HBDI instrument also covered. For example, the *Myers-Briggs Type Indicator* measures (among other things) preferences for thinking versus feeling. For the HBDI, this should correspond with *quadrant A, upper left vs. quadrant C, lower right*. To validate the HBDI, those subjects showing a preference for A should also show a high comfort level for thinking over feeling. And they did.

2. Lawrence Schkade, Ph.D., Chairman of Systems Analysis Department, and Arthur Potvin, Ph.D., Chairman of Biological Engineering Department, both of the University of Texas at Arlington, used EEG techniques with a group of artists and accountants. Their work provides evidence for the external validity of the HBDI in two ways: First, the artists and accountants had the expected profiles; second, the two groups used their brains differently in responding to tasks.

3. In a Ph.D dissertation, Kevin Ho of HighT*ch Incorporated, has shown internal construct valid-

ity of the four-fold model through replicating Bunderson and Olsen's original internal validation study with a normative base of about 8,000 subjects. His research generated two familiar bipolar factors, clearly defining the same preference clusters as the original study, which used the earlier version of the instrument. The two bipolar factors have internal and external validity: A at the opposite pole from C, and B opposite D. This result further reinforces the four-quadrant model.

So where are we at this point? We have an instrument that produces consistent data regarding thinking patterns, and we've got a model that goes beyond the limitations of the left brain/right brain dichotic approach and include metaphoric expressions for the cerebral and limbic dimensions of mental functioning.

So what? The answer is, plenty, and it's in the next chapter, which describes ways to interpret profiles, and then describes how the profiles behave—at work, at play, and at home.

"It takes courage to be creative. Just as soon as you have a new idea, you are a minority of one."

E. Paul Torrance

II.
What the Brain Quadrants Mean to Us All

4

DISCOVERIES ABOUT BRAIN DOMINANCE PROFILES AND YOU

As we drew more and more people into our data base — we had about 10,000 surveys by 1979 — some clear patterns began to emerge, showing how preferences for different thinking modes affect our lives, especially our work lives. Today, now that our data base consists of hundreds of thousands of individual surveys, the major patterns we originally observed are strongly confirmed:

1. Although 81 possible combinations of preferences exist, about 12 main brain dominance profiles comprise over 80 percent of the population; with over a million surveys scored, generalizations regarding internal experience of individuals with different types of profiles are holding true.

2. Over 90% of our database is multi-dominant.

3. Individuals with different profiles tend to behave in specific, predictable ways with regard to such things as time, creativity, dress, money, problem-solving, and intuition.

4. Everyone has at least one primary preference.

5. Individuals with similar profiles tend to communicate more easily with each other even across cultural boundaries.

6. People of similar profiles tend to gather into tribes and may exhibit classic tribal behavior, both positive and negative, including shutting others out and making war.

7. Problems in groups can often be resolved when people understand their profiles, as well as the tribal tendencies and the opportunities that working with a variety of different profiles can open up.

This chapter elaborates on these fascinating findings. If you haven't done so already, let me urge you to complete your own Herrmann Brain Dominance Instrument (HBDI) now. As interesting as this book may be it can't possibly be as interesting to you as your own intriguing self. Having your own profile scores in front of you will bring this chapter alive for you.

INTERPRETING THE PROFILES

This section, which is designed to help you interpret dominance profiles (especially your own) covers the following:

Figure 4-1. Distribution of Occupations Based on Brain Dominance (opposite)

1. General comments about the brain dominance profiles
2. A description of each quadrant individually
3. Descriptions of profile categories — single dominant, double dominant, triple dominant, and quadruple dominant (if you want information on any one of the major types of profiles, turn to Appendix B, where each is described individually).

Overview—Some General Comments

As you learn about the major types of dominance profiles, it is very important to keep three ideas in clear focus.

First, a given profile is neither good nor bad, right nor wrong. Each person's profile represents nothing more than personal preferences at a given time. Any mode of knowing, if situationally applied, can be more useful than the others. Any mode of knowing, if adhered to without reference to the situation and its demands, can be inappropriate and cause problems. If your profile matches the content and expectations of your educational or occupational endeavors, you're likely to succeed. The closer the match, the better your chances.

Second, the HBDI measures preference for a mental activity, which is entirely different from competence in performing it. I can do bookkeeping very well, but I don't like it. Some people love to sing, but can't carry a tune. Preference for a given mode of knowing is a matter of attraction. Competence to perform a given task comes through training and experience and can be developed to reasonable, even superior, levels whether or not the person is attracted to

that task. Necessity can be the mother of competence. But true expertise and certainly world-class competence is achieved almost exclusively in our areas of preference.

However, preferences commonly do correlate with competence, because people tend to do best what they like best. For this reason, achieving world-class or superlative levels of performance in an area probably is not possible unless it is an area of primary preference. We willingly repeat, and thus reinforce, those tasks that we feel good about doing and that we can star in. It's more difficult and less fun to strive for competence in activities we'd rather avoid.

When the preference is there, but the competence isn't, remedies are readily available. Each quadrant contains several processing modes, and even though a person strongly prefers a given quadrant, he or she may have missed the chance to build a specific skill simply because the opportunity to develop that skill never arose. This can happen for any number of reasons: Someone with a strong overall preference for A quadrant may still be deficient in quantitative processing because his math training was poor, he fell ill during a critical learning period, he faced ridicule at home, or he simply had other interests that were stronger. The reasons don't matter. The point is, if this person's preferences for a particular quadrant are strong overall, he can correct specific deficits later in life if he so chooses.

Third, profiles tend to remain constant, but they can, and do, change. Hundreds of respondents involved in longitudinal studies (studies repeated over time with the same people) have demonstrated that over a period of time the profile's basic shape varies either not at all or only insignificantly. And this makes perfectly good sense since most of us tend to continue doing the same kinds of things in the same way. If a person's basic situation remains constant (he continues to perform the same kind of work in the same way, live in the same kind of environment, and does the same kinds of things), his profile holds steady, even if answers to specific questions change. (While profile shape remains consistent, profile size can change with mood: when people feel good, they tend to give themselves somewhat higher values in areas of preference.)

Having said that profiles tend to remain stable, let me hasten to add that changes do occur, for many people can and do change their preferences if they so choose or their life circumstances require. This is a very positive, hopeful fact. It means we can adapt, do what we need to in our lives (and even like it), despite our original or accumulated avoidances and preferences. The things that change the profile are significant life events and crises, major job shifts, or other significant learning experiences. For example, an individual who has just survived a near-fatal accident will usually correct imbalances in the values he or she assigns to the humble things of existence or to human feelings as a result of a heightened sense of being alive. That person might well begin to exercise previously avoided capabilities in B or C quadrant. Similarly, an artist who wants to enter the art market may learn to exercise A quadrant thinking modes in analyzing the market and D quadrant thinking modes to invent novel ways of reaching that market. He or she may find the new mastery rewarding and develop a liking for functioning iteratively in both cerebral modes. Another example is a young mother whose profile shifts to the lower-right C quadrant as she gives birth and nurtures her child. After six months or so, her preferences begin to return to her pre-pregnancy state,

"What we perceive comes as much from inside our heads as from the world outside."

William Jones

"Research is exemplified in the problem solving mind as contrasted with the let-well-enough-alone mind. It is the composer mind instead of the fiddler mind. It is the tomorrow mind instead of the yesterday mind."

Charles F. Kettering

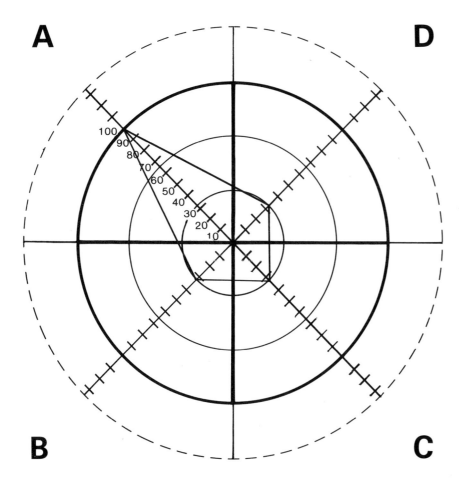

A

D

B

C

Figure 4-2. A-Only Profile

but now the profile shows an increase in the lower left, protective, safekeeping B quadrant to reflect her concerns about the welfare of her newborn. On a long-term basis, the overall profile of many mothers tilts toward the B and C limbic modes.

How do changes in a profile happen? HBDI scores reflect a person's experiences, but only up to the time the profile is drawn. After that time, since the brain functions situationally, it continues to respond to change, even (when necessity or motivation is strong enough) in areas of avoidance. As it does so, especially over a prolonged period, new *reinforcement loops* develop that reward new behavior, and eventually the dominance profile changes accordingly.

Understanding the Individual Quadrants

In the population overall, the data strongly imply that the preferences for each of the four quadrants are equal. What this means is if you add up all the primary choices —those with one, two, three, and four primary preferences —you'd come up with a roughly equal number of primary preferences for A, B, C, and D. You could say that the world taken as a whole represents a composite whole brain.

The following section describes each primary preference as if it were a person's only primary and only mode of operating. These aren't actual profiles: They rarely occur in nature, but they'll help you to get a sense of each quadrant's influence so that when you read about the multiple dominants, you'll have a better sense of the relative compatibilities and incompatibilities among preferences.

Please refer to Appendix B for generic descriptions

of the total array of profiles.

(In trying to give equal time to male and female pronouns, we assigned two quadrants to the men and two to the women. A-only and B-only are "he"; C-only and D-only for "she." Please understand that A and B are also for women and that C and D are also for men.)

A Quadrant Preference

Preference for A quadrant means the person favors activities that involve analyzing, dissecting, figuring out, solving problems logically, and getting facts. In making decisions, the person relies on logic based on certain assumptions, combined with an ability to perceive, verbalize, and express things precisely. The person favors reducing the complex to the simple, the unclear to the clear, the cumbersome to the efficient. Facts are crucial underpinnings for verbal statements. These statements can be abstracted to form even more succinct phrases such as, "Time is money." Moreover, the same method can be used to simplify statements used for decision making, such as, "Whatever the issue, saving time is the rule, so do it the faster way." The point is the whole logical structure must hang together in order to satisfy the A quadrant mentality.

Leonard Nimoy's portrayal of Mr. Spock is a wonderful example of the A quadrant personality at its highest functioning. But as he's only half human, we'll use another example to get a sense of what A is. Let's take a profile of 1-3-3-3, a primary preference for A and an avoidance for any of the other modes. (See Chapter 3 for a review of scoring). Let's call this person *A-only*.

A-only is a master of logic and reason: At his best he is constantly processing new information, even if it assails the validity of a treasured formula. The definition of real- ity is of prime importance, and no fact should long lack explanation for its existence. A-only's output takes the form of principles, mathematical formulas, and conclusions about where to go next. His abilities to generalize from the specific and verbalize those generalizations make him an ideal technical problem-solver.

When A-only does something—anything—he figures out the most efficient way of doing it so he can conserve effort, especially repetitive effort. He also calculates the odds, and if they're excessively high, he won't move. In business, as in other areas, he honors argument above personal experience, facts above intuition (which he may discount altogether as a fabrication). He tends to avoid emotion altogether: If there is trouble at home, for example, rather than asking how people feel and why, he'll look for needs he can fill without having to confront his emotions, e.g., by adding a new room or swimming pool or by simply discontinuing conversation on the subject. If he believes in God, it may be only because facts and logic have taken him to that conclusion, rather than because of any intuitive knowing or revelation.

With avoidances in B, C, and D, A-only would be severely handicapped in functioning. To survive in the world of business, for example, A-only would need to work in a quite isolated ivory tower of sorts, someplace where the fear of emotion, the distaste for detail, and the inability to visualize wouldn't matter. A-only would survive quite well on a diet of facts and questions about things. He would need computers and would prefer some obedient robots to run numbers and confirm calculations. He would dictate the results of his work into a machine and correct the type-written copy when it returned.

A-only's avoidance of other quadrants affects the way

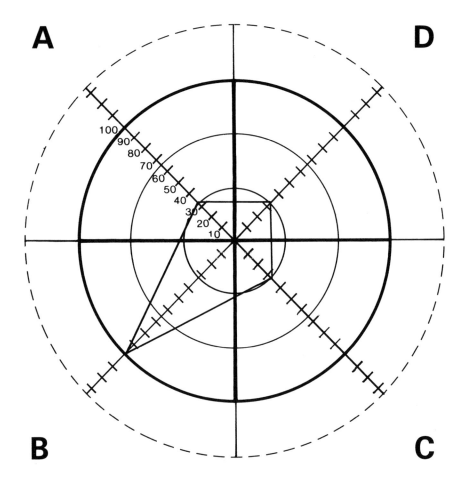

A

D

B

C

Figure 4-3. B-Only Profile

he strikes others. Because he is not an emotional person, he appears cold, aloof, and arrogant. Because he's not visual, he also may appear limited—which in B, C, and D quadrant modes he is. He tends to discount the importance of human feelings, boredom, fatigue, and need for beauty and refreshment. His solutions, while logical, are often impractical because he's ignored the very real barriers of, say, dealing with human inertia or fixed attitudes. And because his thinking is linear, he may embody the ultimate in logical brilliance, but his logic chains him to the ground: He can't make the creative leap required to set a new direction. His possibilities are limited by what is already known or deducible from what is already known.

But A-only is smart in his own way and if material can be presented to him logically, he is open to it. Spock, for example, in *Star Trek IV*, finds it illogical for an entire crew to put themselves in jeopardy to save one member. "But," he reasons at the ensuing trial, "that is how humans behave [fact]." And he may add, "I am, after all, half human."

B Quadrant Preference

B-only bears a number of similarities to his cousin, A-only. They are both verbal. They both take a linear approach to things and reject ambiguity—B-only even more so than A-only. Both distrust emotions and intuition. Both also tend toward controlling their environment and themselves, mainly by imposing thought over reality. They are also both efficient.

However, B-only differs from A-only in several significant ways. Where A-only focuses on facts, logic, and the here-and-now, B-only wants to know what has worked in the past ("If it worked before, it will work again"). A-only devises formulas, B-only tests them down to the last jot and tittle. B-only is basically action-oriented and may therefore have little patience or respect for the intellectual complexities that A-only finds so compelling. "Can we verify it? Is it an answer? Let others ask interesting questions." B-only wants answers-only.

B-only's heaven is a world where there's a rule and a place for everything; it's a neat, dependable world, where decisions are made according to long-established procedures. If something has worked before, let it keep working. "If it ain't broke, don't fix it." He thus preserves the tried and true, but often may defeat progress.

A-only and B-only each have their own kind of efficiency: B-only's efficiency has to do with making sure things are done on time and correctly to the last detail the first time around. No shortcuts for B-only. "Make the first time you do a thing the last time anyone has to."

One of the strengths of B quadrant is the ability to focus on one thing at a time. When you want to see things get done, watch B quadrant people work. They pick up one thing, finish it, put it down, pick up another, finish that, put it down. Sometimes B quadrant is like the tortoise in the race between the tortoise and the hare: Because of sheer dogged persistence, B quadrant people often win the race while others with equal or greater talent and vision, but no B power, fall away to the side.

If you want perfection in detail, B-only is the answer to your prayer. B-only is rigorous and demanding toward himself and his subordinates. Procedure and precision are sacred, and failure to conform to protocol is seen as threatening the entire operation—which sometimes it is, as NASA has learned to our sorrow.

B-only's preference is to keep things safe and predict-able — to such an extent that he typically lacks a sense of possibility. When his aversion to the unproven is extreme, he may even discount the evidence of his own eyes if the evidence fails to fit into established, verbally definable structures. He also rejects ambiguity of any kind, which immediately eliminates the sensual, feeling, and intuitive modes from consideration. As a result, others tend to see B-only as domineering and small-minded, boring, insensitive, and anti-social. Because he fears a loss of control, his efforts to control others often intrude and offend. For him, as for A-only, emotions constitute an unpredictable, and therefore unwelcome, variable. Those with preferences in other quadrants tend to write B-only off as dense. However, it's not true. B-only has an absolute genius for bringing order out of chaos. Starting with the smallest piece of an enormous pile he can eventually create neat categories of classifications, plus a procedure for keeping them precisely classified. Without the kind of efficiency and clarity that B-only makes possible, the world could not operate as it does.

Given the strain of keeping so much under tight control, it's not surprising that B-only has difficulty with change and emotions, because both have their own unique logic. The prospect of change means realigning every tiny detail so it is painstakingly ordered. It means the predictability B-only has labored so hard to establish is at risk. The consequences: loss of control and, therefore, loss of safety.

When faced with change, B-only may take one of two courses: (1) If he values procedure over practicality, he may narrow his perceptions to see only those portions of life that are still controllable, and ignore or deny those parts that are changing. (This syndrome was identified by Alvin Toffler as Future Shock: the phenomenon experi-

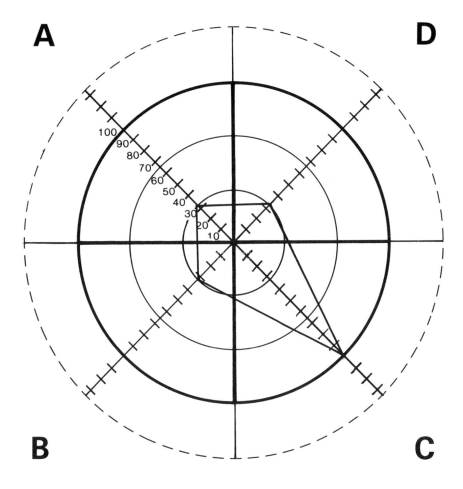

A

D

B

C

Figure 4-4. C-Only Profile

enced by people when the pace of change outraces their ability to adjust.) (2) B-only may work harder to establish an interim order of sorts until the new order has become apparent. In the first instance, B-only can endanger self and co-workers—the best thing to do is to accept his self-imposed constraints and place him in a limited role doing repetitive or procedural work that can't interfere with the conduct of other aspects of existence. Above all, his authority over others needs to be curtailed during this most stressful period. In the second instance, B-only helps in the transition period by: (1) carrying out those activities on which people are accustomed to relying; and (2) testing A-only formulas to see if they actually work, and providing feedback.

The modern world couldn't be what it is without B-only around to help stabilize it.

We turn now to the right-brain modes, which reject precision for a different kind of "knowing," and which in many ways are out of joint in this left-brained world of ours.

C Quadrant Preference

Of all the quadrants in the brain, C quadrant might be looked upon as the most sensitive and receptive. C-only sops up experience like a sponge—about mood, atmospheres, attitudes, and energy levels. She is a moment-by-moment barometer of what's going on with the people around her. She is as concerned with reality as A-only, but it's a very different reality, consisting not of words, but of emotional currents. When the mood of an individual or group changes, C-only is immediately aware of the change and is ready to respond to it, usually in a soothing or conciliatory way.

Although intensely aware of externals in terms of the world, and especially the people around her, C-only perceives them with her own body—through her own internal experience. She tends to be what is called *kinesthetic*, which means that perception and communication are experienced as a free-flowing sequence of body sensing and movement, more than of visual or verbal information. Not in the least linear in functioning, C-only has little time for logic or theory. For her, theory is something removed from reality, whereas experience *is* reality.

Her primary modes are emotional and spiritual. Her comfort with her body tends to give her an essential sense of belonging in this world. She seems to have an innate sense that a Creator exists who cares for all of us, that we belong to a spiritual family, and that we're here on earth to help each other be tender, grow, and change. Goals mean nothing if they violate human process. She has faith in groups and is open to the contribution of each person to a process or goal. Personal satisfaction is a prime measure of the success of anything. She is spiritual, empathetic, nurturing, and musical.

On the downside, because of her aversion to the A, B, and D quadrants, C-only can be flaky, undisciplined, sentimental to the point of being maudlin, and, when the time comes to get something done, impractical because of her refusal to deal with facts and goals, time and money.

Where B-only tends to constrict, C-only tends to expand. One of her modes of expansion may be conversation. Communicating is very important to her, and so it's rare to find a taciturn C. The problem is that most of what she's really talking about is very hard to verbalize, so the conversation flow—the connection—becomes more important than the content. Other C-onlys understand this

"I would rather have goodwill and cooperation than logic."
Jawaharlal Nehru

"We can have facts without thinking, but we cannot have thinking without facts."
John Dewey

"A word to the wise is not sufficient if it doesn't make sense."
James Thurber
-excerpt from *The Weaver and the Worm*

"I would rather be the man who bought the Brooklyn Bridge than the man who sold it."
Will Rogers

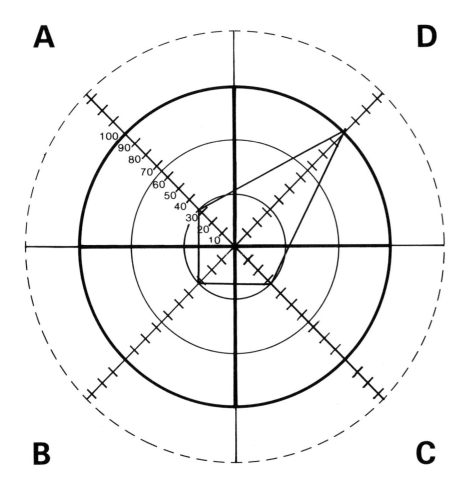

Figure 4-5. D-Only Profile

intuitively, but a verbal A or B can find the continual talk frustrating, unfocused, and demanding.

C-only and B-only share a preoccupation with the past, but in different ways. B-only wants to know what worked before so he can stay safe. C-only reveres traditions because of their emotional value: They comfort and inspire people.

Others tend to see C-only as agreeable, nice to have around, supportive of harmony and beauty, and quite often sentimentally so, and always people-oriented. C-only is also frequently thought to be somewhat of a non-conformist by A and B standards. Even more so is her cousin, D-only, to whom we now turn.

D Quadrant Preference

D-only is a 3-3-3-1; that is, a person with a very strong preference for D quadrant and avoidances in all other areas.

At first meeting, the most outstanding thing you would notice about D-only is that you probably couldn't understand much of what she was saying. Most of her conversation would be in metaphors, introduced by "It's like," but she would provide no translation of how the metaphor helps make "it" clear or even what the "it" is.

Once in a while, however, you'd catch a glimpse of what she is seeing, and you might be blown away by the sheer originality, beauty, or wildness of it. D-only thrives on the excitement of new ideas, possibilities, variety, oddities, incongruities, and questions that sound obvious but actually go to the heart of the matter. Surprises, non sequiturs, and uncertainties are all possibilities. With lots of that kind of grist for her mill, she tends to be a true visionary, in the best sense of the word. The visions may be just that: images of ideas in metaphoric terms.

The Beatles' movie, *Yellow Submarine*, is a D quadrant creation (made with a lot of A, B, and C quadrant support, of course). It is imaginative, colorful, artistic, fanciful, open-ended, and quite confusing from time to time. Even more suited to D-only taste is the movie, *2001*. Science fiction is the stuff of which D-only's daydreams are made.

Although D-onlys have their own language, they often don't understand each other or even themselves. But that's okay, because to them, as to C-onlys, understanding is less valuable than experience. That they understand!

D-only's downside, because she's unsupported by A, B, or C preference, is that under no circumstances can she be counted on to make a deadline or even complete a task at all. She also is not very good at working with others, not so much because of her unreliability, but for two other reasons. First, she's largely nonverbal. D-only has trouble explaining even something she's very clear about. She doesn't have many words—mostly she has pictures. It's hard for her contribution to be realized on a team, unless one of the other members has multiple preferences with a strong D so he or she can translate D-only for the rest of the team.

The second reason she's tough to have on most teams is that she's impersonal. Her own process comes first and she doesn't have C-only's need to connect. Moreover, she doesn't want to slow down to the speed she'd have to go at in order to let someone else catch up. Nor does she want to take the energy to develop a structure for presenting her material—that's A and B quadrant work for C quadrant reasons.

D-only actually fears structure because she feels it slows or stops the flow of ideas and energy. Words do the

same. (Imagine looking at a motion picture and trying to describe it to someone who can't see.) Logic also impedes free flow, because it's based on assumptions, which are based, in turn, on a fixed interpretation of what is already past. She doesn't even want to pay attention to the here-and-now: It also gets in her way, whether it's the material detail and procedures of the here-and-now B-only deals with, or the emotional here-and-now to which C-onlys are so attuned.

The challenge for D-only is to accommodate the realities of the other quadrants by considering them useful contributions to her own process, rather than as impediments only. She needs to learn that present reality can be a springboard, not just an anchor. She must also understand that she needs the rest of us poor mortals if her visions are ever to become a reality.

You now have an idea of the influence exerted on personality and perception by the individual quadrants. But in practice, no quadrant exerts exclusive influence over any person. Preferences occur in patterns or profiles, and those types of profiles are what we'll describe next.

Understanding the Profile Types

As of this writing, the total number of HBDI surveys scored exceeds 500,000. Several recent studies of large samples have indicated that approximately 7 percent of these are single dominant, 60 percent double dominant, 30 percent triple dominant, and about 3 percent quadruple dominant.

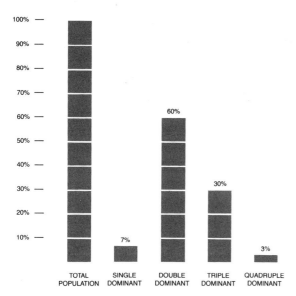

Figure 4-6.   Dominance Distribution.

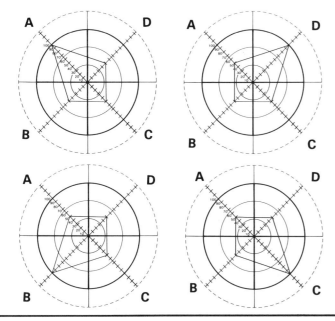

Figure 4-7.   Single Dominant Profiles

Single Dominant Profiles

Single dominant profiles are those that show only one primary, with secondary or tertiary preferences for the other three quadrants. Figure 4-7 shows the four basic single primary profiles.

Single dominant profiles make up only 7 percent of the population and are about equally distributed across the four quadrants. That distribution will probably reveal a cultural bias in the population, i.e., California has more C and D and Ohio shows more A and B; Germany more A and B and India more C and D.

The advantage of having a single dominant profile is that the person goes through life with relatively little internal conflict. Perceptions and decision-making processes tend to be harmonious and predictable. The single-dominant person tends to see the world through a consistent set of lenses, and not to see the world through the lenses others use.

The other side of the coin is that while the 7 percent who have single dominant profiles have the benefit of living a harmonious life internally, externally it can be quite different. The remainder of the population (a good 93 percent) has other profiles and sees the world differently from them. Getting along smoothly in life requires some ability to see things the way the other guy does. This can be quite difficult for the single dominant unless he or she lives or works in an environment where either (1) people of like profiles predominate; or (2) the differences are acknowledged, honored, and appreciated.

A positive environment would help handle another single dominant handicap: Single-dominants often have reduced capability to iterate internally between quadrants, which reduces their abilities for independent creative processing. An environment that celebrates differences would promote external iteration between people of different preferences.

Double Dominant Profiles

In the Same Hemisphere

Like people with single dominant profiles, people with double dominant profiles in either the left or right hemisphere tend to feel internally integrated. Both left quadrants, A and B, are verbal and structured in their thinking, efficient, time-oriented, linear, and precise. Having both of these primaries actually strengthens the quality of both A and B thinking. The same internal harmony tends to prevail for C and D double-dominants. These two quadrants are intuitive, nonlinear, experientially oriented, and sensitive to beauty. In addition, the gifts of the D quadrant are deepened and made more available to others because of the service concerns of C. The sensitivities of C take on a broader character because of the visionary inclinations of D quadrant.

However, like those with single dominant profiles, people with two primaries in the same hemisphere tend more strongly to avoid the modes of the other hemisphere —the double dominance has a cumulative effect. The double dominant right can look flakier and less reliable to others; the double dominant left, more controlling, pedestrian, and less agreeable to be around. This can present a problem when dealing with those with preferences in the other hemisphere.

It's particularly important for double-dominants, right or left, to develop an appreciation for the other modes, not only because it will help them get along better

"Learn to discern the real from the false, the ever fleeing from the everlasting. Learn above all to separate head learning from soul wisdom, the Eye from the Heart doctrine."

H. P. Blavatsky

"Order is the sanity of the mind, the health of the body, the peace of the city, the security of the state. As the beams to a house, as the bones to the body, so is in order to all things."

Southey

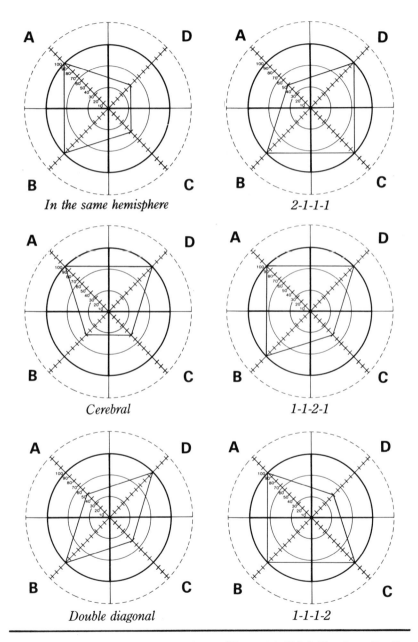

In the same hemisphere

2-1-1-1

Cerebral

1-1-2-1

Double diagonal

1-1-1-2

Figure 4-8. Double Dominant Profiles   *Figure 4-9.* Triple Dominant Profiles

with others, but because the ability to iterate, required for truly creative functioning, is limited without it.

Double Dominant—Cerebral or Limbic

When the two primaries occur in opposing hemispheres directly across from one another, in A and D or B and C, a new set of advantages and difficulties arises.

The advantages are that the person has an expanded ability to iterate—to access major aspects of functioning that relate to left and right hemispheres generally. For example, the person who is double dominant cerebrally can understand nonlinear thinking and verbalize it (to the extent it can be verbalized). He can switch from fact-based, rational functioning to experiential modes. He can move from the focus on external to the focus on internal. This enhances his iterative abilities, improves the quality of his thinking, and helps him make his thinking more accessible to others.

The disadvantages are that the person now has two quite different options for going about things, and it may take some years to figure out which modes are appropriate for which types of situations. Working that out takes time, although the similarities between laterally opposed quadrants help. The cerebral quadrants are both interested in action, while the limbic quadrants both value tradition. The abilities of each often support the other's concerns.

Double Dominant Diagonal Opposites

Double dominant diagonal opposites are profiles that have primaries in either A and C or in B and D. To the extent that physiology affects the model, it's worth noting that no direct connection exists in the brain to link the cerebral left with the limbic right or the cerebral right with the limbic left. In both the model and the actual brain, all iteration between these two modes must go through another quadrant or brain structure first.

Of all the types of profiles, these are potentially the most problematic — not only internally, for the individuals themselves, but externally as well. The major modes are in quadrants that oppose one another in almost every way. They pit: (1) ideas against action; (2) feelings against thinking; (3) people against things; (4) the future against the past; (5) risk-taking against staying safe. As a result, people with double dominant preferences in diagonal opposites frequently find themselves caught between decisions based on two entirely different sets of values. When things are working well, they can integrate the two in decision-making. But in pressured situations, they often find themselves erratically switching from one mode to another or, even worse, paralyzed between the two.

On the plus side, the person who learns to integrate his functioning has an enormously powerful combination of abilities. An entrepreneur for example, with a 2-1-2-1 profile, can envision the business as it can be and do the down-and-dirty detail work required to get it there. A financial person with a 1-2-1-2 profile has not only the A quadrant necessary for determining the best financial arrangements, but also the C quadrant, which gives him the interpersonal ability to package and present his services effectively on a face-to-face basis.

A good way to integrate diagonally opposed preferences is to enhance abilities in one of the other two quadrants, either of which has direct physiological connections and clear commonalities in functioning with both of the opposing primaries.

Triple Dominant Profiles

Triple dominant profiles have only one quadrant that isn't primary. These profiles account for 30 percent of the profiled population. Of the total surveyed population, the profiles 2-1-1-1, 1-1-2-1, and 1-1-1-2 represent a full 25 percent. (See Figure 4-9.) The others account for the remaining 5 percent of triple dominant profiles.

The linguistic ability of triple dominant profiles is even more expanded than that of double-dominants, for they can speak to fully three-quarters of the population without strain. They can iterate freely among quadrants, and, while they may spend less time in the less-favored quadrant, for most of the triple-dominants that fourth quadrant is a good strong secondary. It is entirely available to them in terms of competence and the ability to iterate.

The drawbacks to triple dominant profiles are simply that they may take longer than the others to mature, because they incorporate the same decision-making oppositions as the diagonally opposed double dominant profiles. On the other hand, there is a third primary preference already available to ease the impasse.

Quadruple Dominant Profile

The quadruple dominant profile (1-1-1-1), which occurs in less than 3 percent of the population, expresses primary level preferences for every one of the four modes. This gives the person a unique advantage: It makes iteration between any and all quadrants entirely available. With no aversion to any operating mode, and the ability to experience the legitimate value favored by every type of mental mode and viewpoint, quadruple-dominants are capable of developing an extraordinarily balanced view of

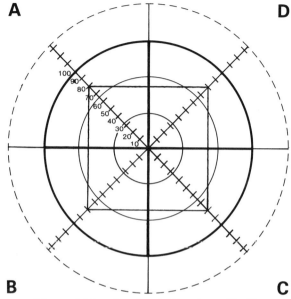

A　　　**D**

B　　　**C**

Figure 4-10. Quadruple Dominant Profile

Figure 4-11. Time Sensitivity

any given situation. They can also communicate easily with people who favor one of the other quadrants, and act as translators among people of different mental preferences.

Though their potential is great, people with such profiles experience many of the difficulties other types of profiles have. Like the single-dominants, they see the world in a way that seems quite out of step with the rest of the population. Like the opposing double-dominants, they experience considerable internal conflict during their early years and must learn to integrate very divergent sets of values. Like the triple-dominants, they may have to spend considerable time learning to reconcile their many different impulses and interests, particularly if they were raised to take a more singular approach to life.

CONTRASTS IN HOW THE PROFILES BEHAVE

The preceding section examined preferences for each quadrant mainly in terms of internal experience. As we've seen and will continue to see more and more clearly in the coming chapters, a person's brain dominance characteristics and associated preferences for modes of knowing powerfully affect everyday observable behavior. In this section, we take just a few examples that highlight contrasts in this behavior. These examples concern time, views of the creative personality, dress, money, preferences for different kinds of activity at work, and occupational patterns.

Time

Individuals relate to time very differently, depending on their mental preferences. People who are dominant and developed in the left hemisphere (A and B) typically stay very conscious of time, and they place a great value on it. They frequently wear a watch, often take note of the time, and may even know what time it is, day or night, without even consulting a timepiece. In contrast, C and, particularly, D dominant individuals tend to relate to time only irregularly. They value it less, wear a watch only infrequently, and ignore it when they do. They assign highest priority to non-time-related issues. The watches selected by left mode dominant individuals tend to be the digital, multi-function types that display numbers; watches selected by right mode dominant people are usually the simple analog types with hands.

Views of What A Creative Person Is

In the ACT Workshop, which is discussed in Chapter 8, we ask participants to bring a written description of "The Most Creative Person" they know. Here are four responses to that exercise that vividly display the differing perceptions of creativity and descriptive styles of each of the four quadrants. Note the differences not only in the words used, but also in the styles and formats.

Other contrasts in quadrant-specific behaviors occur in the areas of dress and handling money.

"There are some enterprises in which a careful disorderliness is the true method."

Herman Melville

"Many of the things you can count, don't count. Many of the things you can't count, really count."

Einstein

"I must have a prodigious quantity of mind; it takes me as much as a week sometimes to make it up."

Mark Twain

I cannot say that I have met what I consider to be a
a creative person in my working career. My perception of
a creative person is best depicted by some college professors
I have met.

Figure 4-12. A Quadrant View

MOST CREATIVE PERSON:

1.0 Who

The person I am describing is Sally Blank. I know her only as a casual friend; hence, I cannot relate to regarding all of the points outlined in exercise 1-B.

2.0 Points FROM EXERCISE 1-A

2.1 IMAGINATION

Sally's imagination is best exemplified by her quick and cunning wit. Likewise, it is apparent in her original recipe cooking and home decorations.

2.2 DRIVE AND LOGICAL THINKING

Sally was secretary to the owner and manager of a Lynchville cleaning franchise named "ServiceMaster." The franchise having never been successful, was offered for sale. She borrowed the money and bought the franchise. Under her management, the business has been successful for ten years.

3.0 PRODUCTIVITY

I believe that Sally's productivity is also explained in paragraph 2.2 above.

4.0 CREATIVENESS

Over the past ten years, she has hosted many parties. These parties are usually organized around a central theme or idea. At these parties, Sally always managed to "create" lots of interesting activities or games.

5.0 INTERACTIVE ATMOSPHERE

When having a general conversation with Sally, it becomes apparent that she is a very intelligent woman. She tries to involve each person in the discussion. In a typical conversation, her position is usually the most different from everyone else's.

Figure 4-13. B Quadrant View

This exercise required little time, only a quick hand to capture all the thoughts that flowed. A close friend, Susan Dubois, surely is my most creative individual. This unique lady has eyes that can see art in a seed pod and draw it, can capture love from the sky through her camera and frame it, can find a subject for her canvas in the exposed ceiling of a room and paint it, see a man in a block of clay, glass, oils, watercolor, ink, paper, cloth, wood — even useless junk and I am sure that with a little time, the results will be either useful, artistic, clever, silly, odd, innovative, etc. But most important, it will happen and will be created at that moment and it will never happen again with the same impact. She can listen to Bach, Beethoven, Black Sabbath, Styx, a preschooler sing and find some value and beauty in each. Being at the right place at the right time is not enough, but being at the right place, at the right time, and hearing the music is what Susan is all about.

Figure 4-14.   C Quadrant View

Precocious musings register
Sensory inputs high noon,
Expanding wealth of experience,
With mind and body in tune.

Heart and mind working together,
In the midst of the marketplace roar;
Seeing and feeling relations,
Where none existed before.

Visualizing what she is thinking,
Believing in what she feels,
Happy examing pieces,
Before the bell finally peals.

Dresses as comfort demands,
With fixins that take little time,
Smiling, straight-talk and humor,
Articulating ideas in rhyme.

Behaves as if hard work is fun,
Listens to what people say,
Knows that success is subjective,
But people are vital today.

Produces by standards she sets,
Keeping her eyes on the dress.
Remembers that life is for living,
And doing, not having's the cream.

Confident walking in darkness,
Before the sun's brilliant roar,
Playfully understanding
That life is a green metaphor.

Figure 4-15.   D Quadrant View

Figure 4-16. A Quadrant Dress

Figure 4-17. B Quadrant Dress

Dress

An A quadrant person aims to strike a balance between wearing the right thing and spending the least possible amount of time on the matter. Whether or not the person is sensitive to color, he or she will tend to confine choices to a few colors and a few styles, which relieves the decision-making burden. In a situation where "correct" dress is unimportant, expect the A quad to wear the same thing every day.

The B quadrant individual, on the other hand, while equally or even more concerned with being appropriate for a given occasion, will spare no effort to be sure every detail is correct. Normally, the dress is on the conservative side, with subdued colors and classic cut; perfectly centered knot in the tie; starched collars; precise, straight hems; and polished, spotless everything.

The C quadrant individual's clothing is, first of all, comfortable to move in. Being kinesthetic, the C quad

Figure 4-18. C Quadrant Dress

Figure 4-19. D Quadrant Dress

wants nothing that would cause physical stress and thus distract from sensing the signals of his or her own body. Color is equally important to the C quad, carrying with it a distinct emotional impact that affects both self and others. Sensitivity to others' feelings may incline the C quad to assume whatever local style prevails—especially if there are many influential B quads around. If the personality is also artistic, the clothing style and color tend toward the dramatic and unusual, especially if the person also has a strong D preference.

The D quadrant person, like the C quad, insists on being comfortable, but is highly individualistic about clothes—preferring very unusual cut and cloth with unique accessories, interesting color combinations, and styles that are experimental. If occupied with other things, of course, D quads will pick up whatever thing is closest, but when they are dressing, they can be flamboyant and outrageous.

Money

The A quadrant person tends to handle money well, guided by a sense of overall purpose and direction: Often impatient with the details, an A quad nevertheless understands their importance. He or she tends to delegate well what can be delegated and systemizes the rest—e.g., pays bills once a month (or whatever works most efficiently) and reviews accounts periodically for any departure from expected patterns.

The B quad values money, knows where every penny is, was, and will be—to the extent that it's possible to know. He or she pays bills on or ahead of time and records transactions accurately and in meticulous detail in checkbooks and with running totals up to date. Often blessed—or cursed—with a prodigious memory, the B quad remembers prices, comparison shops, and exacts value from every purchase. Frequently B quads maintain an inventory of property with original values noted.

The C quadrant person, without A or B competence, handles money erratically and with difficulty. Often impulsive, frequently undisciplined, and even more frequently untrained, C quads consider money important mostly as a support to people's sense of well-being; in and of itself, it has no great value. C quads often pay bills all at once only after some of them are overdue. Their records are poor, and they tend to have trouble billing, especially when clients show any reluctance to pay. When C quads team up with A and B quads, they usually end up fighting over how to handle money.

The D quad considers money simply as a means to an end and, apart from employing it whenever a great idea demands it, is much happier leaving financial details to others. D quads tend to pay bills whenever not paying them gets in the way of something else, keeps records erratically, if at all, and is inclined to gamble on ideas with very little calculation to support the risk-taking. Extreme examples include entrepreneurs who make money and lose it several times before somebody rescues them from themselves.

Work Preferences

Work preferences comprise another set of behavioral patterns that are consistently predictable according to the HBDI profile. This predictability has been tested many, many times in both individual and group settings: We've observed well over a thousand people in groups of 16 to 20, over periods as long as a week. In addition, I've led several hundred public demonstrations where, after being exposed to basic brain theory, audiences have accurately predicted how homogeneous groups of people with specific single dominant profiles would respond to a certain kind of work assignment.

In my early demonstrations, I would select one group from the logical, analytic, rational, verbal end of the brain dominance spectrum, and the second group from the intuitive, holistic, insightful, imaginative opposite end of the spectrum. I would then give both groups the same task to perform. The following is an actual example of such a demonstration conducted as part of a conference called Brainstorming: The Art of Whole Brain Education, sponsored by the Syracuse University School of Education in May, 1981.*

The demonstration was carried out as follows. I displayed the names of five people in group 1 and group 2

---

* This demonstration was conducted in advance of developing the four quadrant model.

on an overhead projector, and called them up to the front of the auditorium. I did not identify which group was of which dominance. I gave both groups the same assignment: "What work turns you on? What are the common characteristics of the work? Reach a group consensus, make a brief report, be back in 15 minutes." The groups were sent to identical break-out rooms, each containing a table and chairs, a flip chart, and felt tip markers. During the 15-minute interval before their return, I teased out of the remaining 150 people in the audience their prediction as to what each group would report and how each group would behave. Precisely at the end of 15 minutes, group 1, the left-brain dominant group, burst into the room, marching in a line with the lead person carrying a flip chart sheet aloft. They looked triumphant, were smiling, and were obviously pleased with themselves. I asked them if they had a spokesperson and would that person make a report. The individual with the flip chart pages then made the following report:

Group 1 (Left-Brain Dominant Presentation)

- We read the directions and we got to the task immediately.
- We didn't fiddle around, we didn't have any conversation.
- After we made our lists, we had to list them according to what was important.
- We need to know if we did what we were supposed to do.
- The most important thing which we asterisked and "arrowed," is that our work must be multifaceted.
- We like to be in control.
- We have a high need for success and recognition.
- We like a structured place.
- We have to have closure.
- We are task-oriented.
- We like to see results.

"Practice and persistence are the necessary ingredients of creativity."
Source Unknown

"To find out what one is fitted to do and to secure an opportunity to do it is the key to happiness."
John Dewey

Chart A

4 GROUPS (A, B, C, D) - 4 PEOPLE IN EACH GROUP

A UPPER LEFT	D UPPER RIGHT
We were all analytical and logical and very meticulous in our approach. We like to work on tough problems. We agreed that we are task-oriented. We like to get things done and we feel good about our accomplishments. We considered ourselves "number" people. None of us checked emotional.	7 out of 8 work elements matched. We had many similarities and agreed that integration and conceptualizing were our favorites. Common characteristics of our work were strategic development, design consideration, and conceptualizing tough problems. We like to have other people implement our plans. We love new stuff and get bored easily, particularly with financial details and administrative chores.
Planning and organizing were key elements. We all wanted to be very organized. Our common characteristic was a results orientation--implementing plans, carrying out projects was a "turn on." We all felt we were good administrators and liked that kind of work. Three of us had quality responsibilities, but all of us get a kick out of getting the job done right, on time, and meeting cost targets.	We agreed on most everything, particularly if it had to do with people--that was the common denominator. Expressing ideas, teaching/training, and persuading were "turn ons." None of us checked implementation or logical. We agreed that other people thought of us as pretty emotional, and three of us would include spiritual in that description.
B LOWER LEFT	C LOWER RIGHT

Chart B

4 GROUPS (A, B, C, D) 4 PEOPLE IN EACH GROUP

A UPPER LEFT	D UPPER RIGHT
We consider ourselves left-brained. We found lots of commonality. We like to make order out of chaos. We are analytical, logical. We like to solve problems. We like to use our expertise to solve problems-- analytically and logically. We like to analyze by ourselves first and then get our point across based on that analysis. We don't think of ourselves as creative.	We think we are right-brained. We felt we were remarkably similar. Even though we all come from different backgrounds, we agreed on these work elements: conceptualizing, expressing ideas, innovating, and creative aspects. We like new things and ideas. We are bored with repetitive tasks. One of us is in finance work, but he says--"It's creative finance!"
We felt similar. We like administrative, planning, and organizational work leading to a successful outcome. We like to implement for tangible results. We are interested in the organization of people. We are not interested in technical aspects or innovation. Implementation is the key word.	There was a lot of similarity in our group. Work elements that we all agreed on were: expressing ideas, teaching/training, and interpersonal aspects. We like to facilitate interaction--doing things with others--one on one. We are open to different opinions and we like to get a group to function well together. There is a lot of people involvement in our "turn on" work. We like to express ourselves and sell our ideas.
B LOWER LEFT	C LOWER RIGHT

Figure 4-20.   The Four Quadrant Results of Two Public Demonstrations

- We are always busy doing something constructive.
- We like to make lists.
- We love to cross things off our lists.
- We love an ordered environment.

Following this report, a comment was made by one of the group that they had actually finished in 13 minutes, but were reluctant to come back early so they took the additional 2 minutes to prioritize the listing of key characteristics contained on their flip chart.

At this point the right-brain group 2 had not returned and so an emissary was dispatched to get them. When they did return, it was approximately 20 minutes after they had been sent to the break-out room. They drifted in one at a time and proceeded to meld into the audience; and it was only after a lot of encouragement that I got them to assemble at the front of the room. There were no flip charts, and there was no obvious spokesperson. After some pleading from me, one of them volunteered the following report:

Group 2 (Right-Brain Dominant Presentation)

- First of all, we were confused by the word "work."
- We couldn't make a decision.
- Some people mentioned painting, drawing, gardening, and athletics.
- Liking a lot of space.
- Viewing the task from a whole point of view.
- Seeing the end at the beginning.

Following this report, I asked group 1 (left-brain dominant) to comment on how they characterized the work that "turned on" group 2 (right-brain dominant). Their response was, "It seems puzzling." The left-brained group then offered, gratuitously, the comment, "We want you to know that we are glad we are who we are." Then, since the right-brain group had not heard the other group's report since they had not returned early enough, I asked the left-brain group to recapitulate, and they did so with these key words:

- Task-oriented
- Need for Closure
- In Control
- Structured
- Successful
- Organized

I then asked the right-brain group to characterize the work that "turned on" the left-brain group. Their response was a simultaneous, unanimous "BORING."

Now the point of all of this is that people, by reason of their dominance, have different mental processes and different mental preferences, and this affects their choice of work and activities. In a summary of over 50 similar studies, 75 percent of the group 1 (A quadrant) participants felt uncomfortable or somewhat confused about group 2 work, while 90 percent of the group 2 (D quadrant) participants were bored by A quadrant work and used that exact word to describe their feelings.

My 100 most recent demonstrations have all been based on the four-quadrant model. Instead of just two groups, I select four groups of three or four people, with each group representing an exclusive preference in one of the four quadrants: A, B, C, or D. The exercise is similar to the two group version, but for reasons of logistics, the groups work in place rather than being sent to remote break-out rooms. Figure 4-20 shows the results of two four-quadrant demonstrations conducted in 1986.

I believe these results have important implications for the way we structure work to be done in our businesses. We managers tend to ignore the mental aspects of work in most work settings and, as a result, pay an enormous price in both productivity and human pain (this is discussed in more detail in Chapters 5 and 11).

"It's what you learn after you know it all that counts."

Ethel Barrymore

"Life is like music—it must be composed by ear, feeling, and instinct, not by rule. Nevertheless, one had better know the rules for they sometimes guide in doubtful cases, though not often."

Samuel Butler

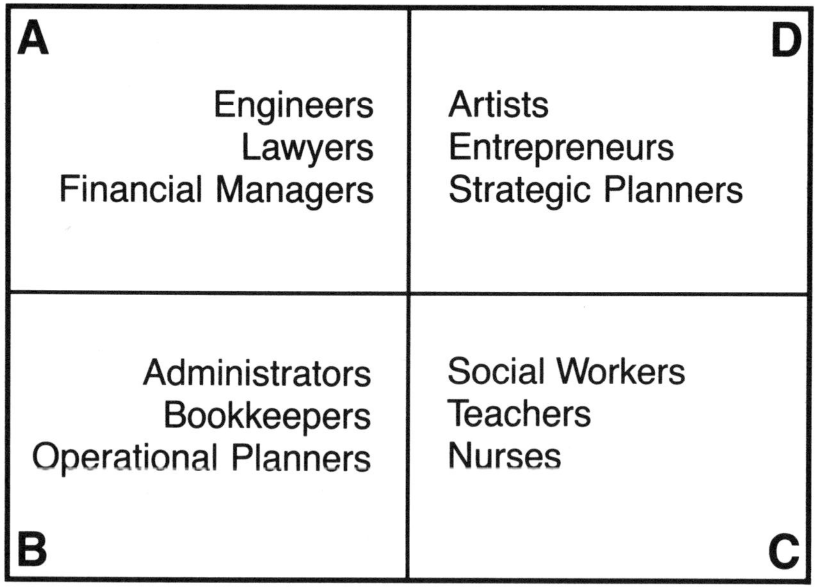

A		D
Engineers Lawyers Financial Managers		Artists Entrepreneurs Strategic Planners
Administrators Bookkeepers Operational Planners		Social Workers Teachers Nurses
B		C

Figure 4-21. Occupational Patterns

Occupational Patterns

Given the consistent way people of different dominances respond to questions about work preferences, it's not surprising to find that certain profiles show up more in some occupations than in others. In fact, the patterns are quite dramatic.

Figure 4-21 shows some examples of the most pronounced patterns: As you see, engineers, financial managers, systems analysts, and lawyers tend to favor upper left A. B is favored by administrators, bookkeepers, and operational planners. The empathetic lower right shows up in profiles of social workers, teachers, and nurses. And, finally, upper right is a consistent feature of artists and entrepreneurs. Multiple dominance shows up in occupations that require the ability to call on more than one mode either for activity or translation. For example, double dominants are found in financing, radiology, and manufacturing. Triple dominants occur in social work, nursing, training, and about half of all CEOs. And finally, quadruple dominants include CEOs, personnel executives, politicians, and executive secretaries.

Profile Norms for Selected Occupations

Certain occupations attract people of particular brain dominance profiles. We refer to the most common or average profile for a certain occupation as occupational norms. Here are just a few samples of typical occupational profiles selected from the many occupations in our growing data base. Other examples are shown in Appendix C.

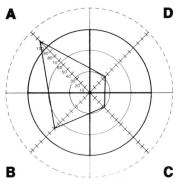

Figure 4-22.   Radiologist

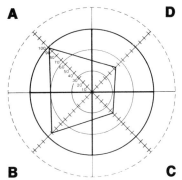

Figure 4-23.   Engineering Manager

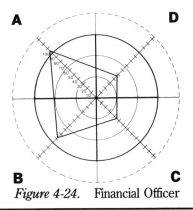

Figure 4-24.   Financial Officer

Radiologist

The normative profile of a radiologist features a strong preference in the A quadrant and also a prominent primary in the B quadrant. This profile is also characterized by tertiaries in both C and D, with the C quadrant typically being the less preferred of the two.

Engineering Manager

A good example of an occupation that has a strong preference in the A quadrant is an engineering manager in a medium-to-large, technically oriented business. Here, the strong A preference not only characterizes the educational preparation for the work, but also the principle orientation of the work elements in the occupation. Typical descriptors would include: logical, analytical, technical, and quantitative. The occupational norm, especially with regard to the B and D quadrants, can vary significantly, depending upon the orientation of the work. If the work involves manufacturing and production, the B quadrant is usually stronger. If the work tilts toward design and development, the D quadrant is more preferred. However, all these show the C quadrant as the least preferred.

Financial Officer

This profile represents individuals who are responsible for financial matters in businesses, institutions, agencies, or organizations. Their most preferred quadrant is A, with a very strong second primary in B. The degree of preference for the D quadrant is influenced by the degree to which the more global aspects of finance are involved in the work. Typically the higher the person's organizational level, the stronger the D quadrant preference will be. In almost all cases, the C quadrant is the least preferred.

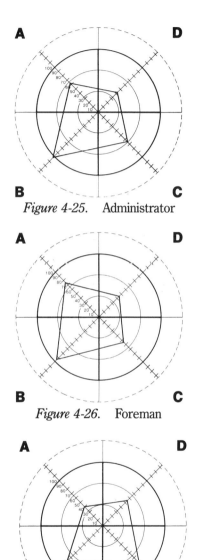

Figure 4-25.   Administrator

Figure 4-26.   Foreman

Figure 4-27.   Secretary

Administrator

Occupations labeled "administrator" occur in many organizations—hospitals, business offices, municipal agencies, educational institutions. In this occupation, the B quadrant stands out clearly as the most preferred. Since most administrative occupations also involve personnel, there's also usually a strong preference in the C quadrant, but this is typically a low primary or a high secondary. The least preferred quadrant for this occupation is D since imaginative, innovative approaches are usually outside the role of the administrator.

Foreman

The typical profile for foremen is quite similar to that of administrators. The most preferred quadrant is B, with an emphasis on the planned, organized, and procedural aspects of the tasks to be performed and the rules, procedures, and disciplines associated with production work. The second most preferred is the A quadrant with an emphasis on logical, analytic, and quantitative modes of processing. The next most preferred quadrant is C, which reflects the interpersonal aspects associated with the foreman role in dealing with people. The least preferred quadrant is D. In most foreman situations, a strong preference in the D quadrant would be counter productive to carrying on the work in accordance with established procedures.

Secretary

The typical secretarial profile is double dominant in the limbic mode with relatively equal preferences in the B and C quadrants. These preferences correlate with the nature of the work, which requires planned,

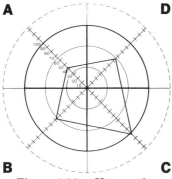

Figure 4-28. Homemaker

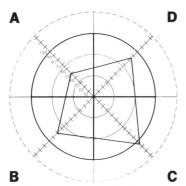

Figure 4-29. Social Worker

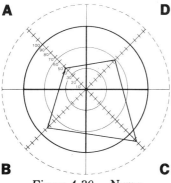

Figure 4-30. Nurse

organized, administrative activities, and interpersonal, human relations-oriented activities. The least preferred quadrant for this occupation is almost always A.

Homemaker

The occupational norm for the homemaker is double or triple dominant with emphasis on the B, C, and D modes. Typically, the least preferred quadrant for the homemaker is A, the most preferred, C. The next most preferred is B and the third quadrant of preference is D.

Social Worker

Generally, social worker profiles are triple dominant, with the most preferred quadrant being C, the next most D, and the third, still a primary, B. The least preferred quadrant for social workers is almost always A. The social worker, having an occupation that epitomizes the helping professions, would typically have a primary score greater than 100 in the C quadrant. The surprisingly high value for the B quadrant in the social workers' occupation reflects the large caseloads and the administrative aspects of the social worker role.

Nurse

The typical nursing profile shows the most preferred quadrant to be C, with relatively equal lesser primaries in both B and D. The least preferred quadrant is A. The strong C quadrant preference of the nursing occupation is characteristic of the "helping" professions. Supervisory nurses would tend to have the B quadrant as their most preferred, followed by C, D, and A.

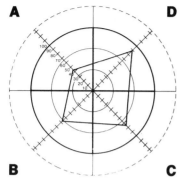

Figure 4-31. Sales Manager

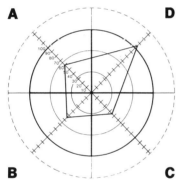

Figure 4-32. Strategic Planner

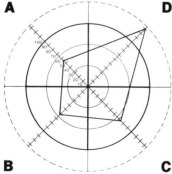

Figure 4-33. Entrepreneur

Sales Manager

The sales manager's profile features three primaries of which two are opposing primaries. The most preferred quadrant is D, with a lesser primary in B. D represents the outer-directed strategic interests in making the sale, while the B quadrant preference reflects the structure and discipline required to deal with the operational planning and follow-up to the selling activity. The strong C quadrant primary reflects the interpersonal, expressive aspects of the sales occupation.

Strategic Planner

This profile features a strong D quadrant preference, a considerably lower primary in A, and a high secondary in B. The C quadrant is frequently the least preferred for this occupation. This profile is characterized by a very strong preference for the D quadrant, since strategic thinking is based upon global understanding and intuitive and insightful processing of relevant facts; and often a primary or high secondary in A, where the processing of facts, analytically and logically, takes place. The strategic planning profile contrasts sharply with the more operational planning profile that typifies administrators and middle managers.

Entrepreneurs

The entrepreneurial profile features a very strong D quadrant preference, with moderate to strong secondaries in the other three quadrants. The entrepreneur's profile

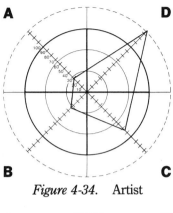

Figure 4-34.   Artist

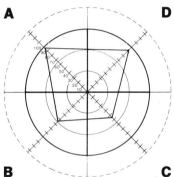

Figure 4-35.   Physicist

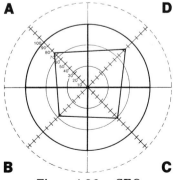

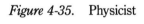

Figure 4-36.   CEO

is oriented to risk and opportunity. Key descriptors include holistic, intuitive, simultaneous processing preferences. The strong secondaries (or low primaries) in A, B, and C quadrants indicate situationally applied competencies to specific areas of work such as finance, planning, and interpersonal relationships when necessary.

Artist

The artist's profile shows an extremely strong preference for the D quadrant, a low primary in C, a low secondary in B, and a tertiary in A. The extreme preference for D represents the locus of the artist's mental orientation. Key descriptors include artistic, holistic, intuitive, conceptual, imaginative, and spatial.

Physicist

The physicist's profile is double dominant cerebral, two equally strong primaries in A and D. The next preferred quadrant is B, with a moderate secondary. The least preferred quadrant is C, with a low secondary. The physicist contrasts sharply with the chemist, who has perhaps the most upper-left-oriented occupational profile of all of the technically oriented occupations.

CEO

The CEO profile is characterized by a balance of at least three of the four modes. The normative profile shows slightly higher scores in the A and D quadrants. This multi-dominance tends to characterize people who are leaders of diverse, multifunctional organizations, made up, for example, of the occupations whose profiles are listed in this section.

NATIONS, TRIBES, AND TERRITORIES

Another key finding is that people with similar mental profiles tend to form into communities or tribes, both professionally and socially.

The word tribe fits because it implies that members share not only mental preferences, but also experiences and perceptions of the surrounding world, a common language to describe them, and, frequently, a great deal of time together. When people of similar profiles work in the same company, they tend to lunch together; engage in sports or recreation together; and generally find support and comfort in their tribal relationships. Some occupational tribes (such as accountants, lawyers, psychologists, and medical doctors) have the added glue of professional jargon and educational similarities to strengthen the tribal bond.

Sometimes it takes only minutes for people of like profiles to find one another, as the following example illustrates. When I am going to give a seminar, I routinely draw profiles in advance and then array the participant seating plan accordingly. One such seminar (for a group of public relations executives) included a preliminary social hour, at which I was able to watch these 30 people break spontaneously into smaller conversational tribes. Sure enough, those who had gravitated naturally to one another during the social hour were largely the same individuals who found themselves together in the formal seating array during the seminar.

You can see this same clustering pattern on a much larger scale at conventions of professionals. Members of the same tribe tend to dress in similar ways, wear their hair in similar ways, and select similar concurrent sessions.

If, for example, you attended the separate conventions of the American Psychological Association and the Association for Humanistic Psychology, respectively, you would see two distinctly separate tribes. Since they both deal with the human psyche, they are actually two tribes within a community that are separate because of the difference in their specializations and mental preferences. The two tribes differ significantly in terms of program content, meeting schedule, dress codes, and the like. The American Psychological Association, for example, emphasizes technical papers delivered in lecture format, and the audience usually wears suits, ties, and dresses. In contrast, the Association of Humanistic Psychology features a looser agenda, with many informal and experiential sessions. Some of these are delivered out on the lawn, with people dressed in blue jeans and tee shirts. Some even sport loose, flowing hairstyles and wear sandals. Neither way is better; it's just different to suit different mental preferences.

Throughout history, tribes, once established, have carved out their territory and invented weapons to keep others from invading it. Tribes based on brain dominance do likewise, protecting themselves from outsiders in several ways: by requiring certification to become a member, by communicating through newsletters and conventions (which are available only to a limited audience), by lobbying politically for special treatment under the law, or by accumulating a body of humor to put down the outsiders. Thus doctors are known to resist the idea of nurses entering their domains of medical care, lawyers erect fences to keep paralegal assistants at a distance, accountants who are CPAs market that tribal certification.

The process of erecting walls against outsiders strengthens tribal bonds in both insider and outsider groups. It's a classic phenomenon understood and used by political regimes: Create an outside enemy and the people will pull together to both attack and defend.

When tribes form for reasons that don't relate to mental similarities, *sub-tribes* often form within them to fill the void. This is true within the medical profession, which exemplifies how widely people can vary within a single occupational continuum. These variations range from pathologists and radiologists, who both tend to have 1-1-2-2 profiles, to pediatricians and psychiatrists, who tend to have 2-2-1-1 profiles. Between these extremes, and largely favoring logical, analytic, quantitative, factual, and rational modes of knowing, are the disciplines of surgery, internal medicine, gynecology, and general practice. Physicians' profiles of preferred ways of knowing translate into visible behaviors. Pathologists tend to be introspective, often work alone in basement laboratories, remain aloof from patient contact, perform their tasks with excruciating attention to detail and technique, and form their evaluations with scientific detachment. Pediatricians, on the other hand, are generally flexible, extroverted, loving, and willing to play with children. They decorate their offices brightly and have a special place for children and mothers that includes toys and other distractions. They relate strongly to their patients and the parents of their patients. They tend to communicate openly.

The July 10, 1987 issue (Volume 258) of the *Journal of the American Medical Association* lists 280 organizations of medical interest. As examples of these many sub-disciplines or sub-tribes I have randomly selected 30 separate medical groups that feel different enough to have established their own separate organizations:

American Academy of Psychosomatic Medicine
American Ambulatory Pediatric Association
American Academy of Allergy and Immunology
American Academy of Child Psychology
American Academy of Cosmetic Surgery
American Academy of Dermatology
American Academy of Family Physicians
American Academy of Neurology
American Academy of Opthamology
American Academy of Orthopaedic Surgeons
American Academy of Otolaryngic Allergy
American Academy of Pediatrics
American Academy of Psychiatry & the Law
American Academy of Psychoanalysis
American Academy of Thermology
American Association of Anatomists
Association of Pathologists
American Broncho-Esophagological Association
American College of Allergists
American College of Cardiologists
American College of Cryosurgery
American College of Gastroenterology
American College of Obstetricians & Gynecologists
American College of Radiology
American Dermatological Association
American Geriatrics Society
American Lung Association
American Otological Society
American Opthamological Association
American Pediatrics Society
American Psychiatric Association

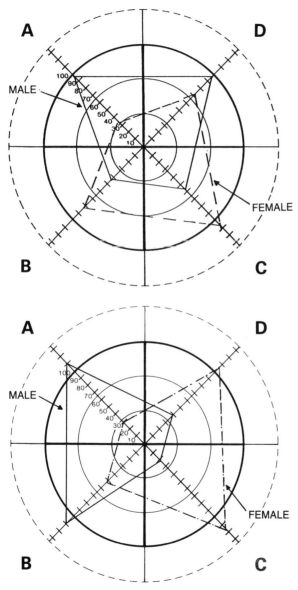

Figure 4-37. Married Couples Profile

American Psycho-Analytic Association
American Psychosomatic Association
American Society of Anesthesiologists
American Society of Hematology
American Society of Internal Medicine
American Thoracic Society
American Thyroid Association
American Urological Association
American Society of Toxicology

Keep in mind that these sub-tribes are just a few selected organizations and represent only a fraction of the total in the medical profession. There appear to be strong professional and social needs for these groups to form and meet regularly.

Sub-tribes have also formed within the teaching profession, labor unions, and other aggregations of people whose coming together was based on social or economic issues rather than on similarities in mental preferences.

When the sub-tribes within a tribe become large enough, they may find their needs sufficiently different from those of the other sub-tribes to warrant forming a separate organization—amicably or otherwise. Amicable separations aren't unheard of. When the Reparenting School of Transactional Analysis was born from the membership of the International Transactional Analysis Association, for example, most of the new association's members even retained their membership in the larger body. However, other examples of splitting off are nowhere near as friendly.

Most of us though witness disputes between tribes, let alone between sub-tribes. This scenario most commonly occurs at the workplace where there are literally hundreds of examples of chronic hot or cold wars year after year. Finance, sales, engineering, manufacturing, personnel, and legal departments are obvious examples of functional tribes that engage in such activity. In addition, there are "headquarters" tribes, the "operating" tribes, the "region," the "staff," the "bean-counters," and the strange people in the "skunkworks." In school systems, it is the teachers vs. administrators. In the advertising field, it is the "creatives" versus the "administrative" tribes.

Not all of the dramatic examples of disputes occur in business. In fact, the most painful ones often strike us when we walk in through our own front door.

MARRIAGE AND FAMILY PATTERNS

The data suggest two major findings, the first having to do with mating patterns, the second with family tribalism.

Mating Patterns

Given what we know about profiles and tribalism, you would think we'd gravitate toward those of similar mental preference when seeking a mate. Not at all.

Studies of over 500 married couples show clearly that opposites attract. (Your grandmother could have told you that, right?) In over 75 percent of the cases, the profiles of husband and wife differ significantly. In the majority of cases, the husband had a left-oriented profile, the wife, a right-oriented one. However, in those cases where the husband had the right-oriented profile, the wife invariably

"Grown-ups love figures. When you tell them that you have made a new friend, they never ask you any questions about essential matters. They never say to you, 'What does his voice sound like? What game does he love best? Does he collect butterflies?'"

St. Exupery
The Little Prince

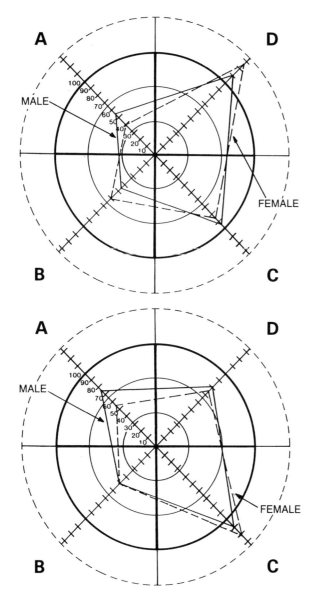

Figure 4-38. Living Together Couples Profile

leaned left. Also, in the majority of cases, the husband was cerebrally oriented and the wife limbic, the males more conceptual, and the females more visceral in their thinking processes. *In less than 20 percent of the marriages I reviewed were the profiles similar enough to be called homogeneous.*

In contrast to the normal pattern of heterogeneity in married couples, emerging data suggest that unmarried couples living together have *similar* profiles, which makes them highly compatible. What does this mean? We don't know yet, so it's dangerous to generalize, but we can probably safely say it relates to commitment and the search for wholeness. Male and female "opposites" unconsciously seek personal wholeness through marriage, which gives them tremendous motivation and strength to make it work long-term. Are members of living-together couples more aware that wholeness is an internal matter? Does the ability to be best friends easily obviate the need for a marriage contract commitment to keep the relationship viable? Or are they settling for less? We really don't know, but I'm eagerly awaiting the results of additional research on the subject.

Quite often when married couples are having difficulties, tensions ease when they see their respective HBDI profiles and understand their differences in terms of preferred modes of knowing. Each suddenly discovers that the other person is truly different, that his or her behavior isn't a deliberate ploy, but is a genuine consequence of a differing mental preference. A typical response when they see their profiles are strikingly different is: "Oh! You *are* different, but I had no idea *how* different! I thought you were doing those things on purpose just to get my goat, but now I see it's because you really are different."

The potential power and creativity in a marriage between extreme opposites is immense when each spouse accepts the other's differences as being legitimate, stimulating, and enhancing. The process of learning to accept those differences can be very difficult, but the rewards of success are well worth the effort. (My wife, Margy and I speak from hard-won experience, as Chapter 9 describes in more detail). A 1-2-2-2 male married to the 2-2-2-1 female, for example, makes up a composite brain that is cerebrally double dominant; this enables them to iterate back and forth between themselves as well as internally. This iteration is an essential ingredient for synergistic creative functioning and relates directly to my earlier statement that all quadrants of the brain are crucially important to full mental functioning.

When children join the equation, even greater creative potential develops—along with greater potential difficulties: When the number of people is increased, tribal patterns can come into play. Then what frequently develops is what I term the "Weird John" syndrome.

The Weird John Syndrome

Weird John is an actual person. Here's the story. As often happens, I was asked to use the HBDI to diagnose a family problem. A father concerned about his son, John, asked for a profile of him. The conversation went as follows: "I am really interested in finding out more about my son," he began. "He is really a different kid. Weird. My wife and I sometimes joke that maybe the hospital made a mistake and we took the wrong baby home. He's so different from us and the rest of the family that we really wonder about him. We don't understand him and have trouble communicating with him. I am really con-

"Measure a thousand times and cut once."

Turkish Proverb

"I used to think that anyone doing anything weird was weird. I suddenly realized that anyone weird wasn't weird at all and that it was the people saying they were weird that were weird."

Paul McCartney

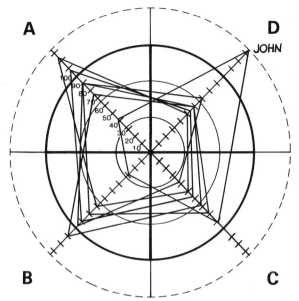

Figure 4-39. Weird John and His Family with Profile

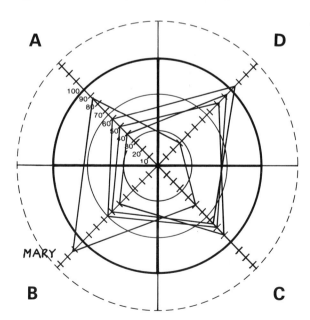

Figure 4-40. Desperate Mary and Family with Profile

cerned about his future. I don't like his friends and I can't stand his hobbies. He doesn't seem to be able to develop a career path that fits in with our family background. As a father, I really don't feel I can help him very much. Would you please do his profile and those of the rest of our family?"

Figure 4-39 is a composite profile of Weird John and his family. As you can see, his 3-2-1-1 is a mirror image opposite of the profiles of his parents and siblings. The four of them make up a tribe, and as is typical of tribes, they managed over the course of years to dig a moat, build a wall, and invent an "anti-John" weapon—the word, *weird*—which successfully kept John at a distance for most of his young adult years. The father looked at the composite family profile and said, "My God, what have I done?" I asked him if John ever went out with his friends. He said, "Oh yes, often." I said, "In that case, fantasize John's talking to his friends about his 'weird' family." For the father, that was a new idea.

On his return home, the father proceeded to call a family meeting around the dining room table. Each member had a copy of the family's composite profile. At first, no one said anything. Then one brother ventured an exploratory, "Hi, John." The rest of the family, each in their own way, then joined in welcoming John back to the family group from which they had previously excluded him.

There was nothing wrong with John. He was—and is—simply different from the rest of his family. His preferred mode of knowing is nonverbal, nonlinear, and "soft," which renders him vulnerable to verbal rejection and criticism from those of opposing preferences. John's visible behaviors accentuated the differences. His hair, his dress, his hobbies, his music, his school program, his leisure activities all differed from the tribal culture of his family. Viewed from the tribal perspective, John was a misfit. Viewed from John's perspective, he was an outcast.

When families understand the value of welcoming differences, they enhance the synergistic possibilities inherent in their relationships. In this case—which is not rare, by the way—simply seeing the composite profiles was enough to initiate a flow of understanding that brought John back into his family and helped the family to understand him. John was married a short time later to a young woman whose profile matches that of the rest of his family. Together, with understanding, he and his bride can make a mental whole brain.

A family's Weird John isn't always a child. A woman approached me in some distress and, indicating that she felt estranged from her family, asked me for a composite survey of her family. The composite (see figure 4-40) revealed that "Desperate Mary" married her opposite, created with him a family whose culture reflected his dominant modes rather than hers, and then was ostracized by the tribal group she had helped to create. She felt cast out by and estranged from her own children and husband simply because her preferences differed from theirs. Once again, a family council enhanced understanding. Instead of being "weird," Mary is now accepted as unique, but normal.

Whether applied to relationships at home or at work, knowledge of our brain dominance empowers us as individuals and groups to achieve more of our full potential. As we become aware of our own preferred modes of knowing and sensitive to the preferences of others, we greatly enhance our ability to communicate with the people around us.

In this chapter, I've concentrated mainly on patterns as they manifest in our individual lives. These same patterns also operate powerfully in much larger groups—churches, communities, businesses, states, and nations—where the original family patterns may be echoed over and over.

The major opportunity and challenge is to learn to capitalize on and celebrate our differences rather than use them as reasons for rejection. Nowhere is this more dramatically demonstrated than in the world of business to which we now turn.

"We can't cross a bridge until we come to it; but I always like to lay down a pontoon ahead of time."
Bernard M. Baruch

"The brightest flashes in the world of thought are incomplete until they have been proven to have their counterparts in the world of fact."
John Tyndall

5

WHAT DOES THE BRAIN HAVE TO DO WITH MANAGEMENT, ANYWAY?

My first full-scale research activities on brain function caused quite a stir at the GE Management Development Institute. Most people couldn't see how it connected with my professional work in management education, although it seemed to me at the time that I had specified its relation to creativity and learning very clearly. My experiences had already affirmed my ability to communicate effectively, but I still had a lot to learn about the enormous communication chasms created by the divergent ways in which people of different brain dominance preferences think.

A vivid illustration of this is a dining room incident that occurred in 1977 at the Institute. It had been my practice to visit with groups with whom I had no direct classroom contact by joining them at lunch to discuss their experiences at the Institute and to answer any questions they might have. I approached one small table of three high-potential middle managers and introduced myself as a member of the staff. One of the people said, "Oh, you're the guy doing brain research. That sounds really interesting; I'd like to hear about it."

In response, I began giving a brief overview of my activities, focusing on some of the exciting new insights into brain functions that were emerging. As I spoke about the fact that the hemispheres were specialized, and that brain dominance caused most of us to have distinct mental preferences for using one part of the specialized brain or another, the young man seated on my right became visibly uncomfortable with the topic. As I continued describing how some people can be quite logical and analytic in their thinking, while others can be very intuitive and insightful, he became more fidgety, and, finally, after several more minutes, he reached out to touch me on the shoulder and interrupted me by saying, "Ned, this is very interesting, very interesting indeed. But I really have a need to know —and mind you—I'm interested in these new developments but I really need to know—what does the brain have to do with managing?"

A dead silence followed his question. I looked at him for a moment and then looked at each person seated at the table; after waiting about 20 seconds to see if anybody would say anything, I responded, "Well, in your case..."

Now, ten years later, it is far less likely that I would answer such a question with so little understanding, for I've learned a great deal since then about the communication chasms that exist between people of different brain dominance profiles and about bridging those gaps.

In fact, the question "What does the brain have to do with managing?" was perfectly appropriate from his point of view and verbalizing the answers clearly is important for us all. The brain and our new learning about brain

Figure 5-1. The GE Dining Room Incident (opposite)

dominance have everything to do with managing, because they both answer and pose some fundamental questions in critical areas.

1. *Planning*. What differentiates strategic planning from operational planning?

2. *Job Design*. How should work and jobs be designed to win 20 to 40 percent in additional productivity?

3. *Supervising*. How can supervisors reach subordinates regarding behavior that needs to be changed? What can supervisors do to motivate subordinates?

4. *Teamwork*. How should teams be staffed? How should a CEO and his staff relate in terms of brain dominance?

5. *Top Management Training*. What can a CEO who is already installed do to enhance his leadership capabilities? How should we be training the CEOs of 2010?

6. *Corporate Culture*. How can a CEO keep his corporate culture flexible, especially for dealing with change and preserving innovative vitality?

7. *Communication*. How can communication bridges be established between valued executives of divergent mental preferences to make the most of all available talent?

8. *Creativity*. How can an organization establish a climate for creativity, build a creative team, and manage it?

9. *Career Aspirations*. What brain dominance patterns would make a person ideally suited for functional positions, such as engineering and finance? Managerial positions? Entrepreneurs? Top line and staff positions? Chief Executive Officers?

My exchange with the young man was a classic example of communication mismatch, sharpened by differing frames of reference. A *frame of reference* is a system of concepts and assumptions about a subject—how it relates to other subjects, how it is structured internally, and how the person who holds the frame of reference interacts with the subject.* Here was a multidominant person (myself) functioning for the moment in the D mode, talking with a strongly B dominant person who had a different frame of reference regarding the brain and the relationship of quadrant C and D activities to management. His thinking about the brain most likely began and ended the last time he saw a picture of one in a high school biology lab. In his thinking, C and D activities were defined as strictly vacation behavior (such as daydreaming while waiting for an unwary trout to strike).

Anyone can shift a frame of reference, but to do so, a B dominant person, being very literal, first needs proof that the new frame of reference is valid—this proof being hard evidence supporting clearly articulated ideas, facts, and interrelationships. People functioning in D mode, however, change frames of reference quite easily and often. Moreover, when they do so, they feel little or no need to define or verbalize the logic of the shift, or to justify the new connections.

Nowadays, our frames of reference about the brain and management are changing very rapidly as more and more alert managers soak up this new knowledge about the brain. They're learning that this new brain dominance

---

*I discuss frames of reference at greater length in Chapter 9.

technology is both valid and relevant, not only for management, but also for everyday life on all fronts. But this wasn't so at all at the beginning of my investigation—not even for me. My main focus was that of an artist seeking to understand the nature and source of creativity. The lights didn't go on regarding the brain's connection with management until I read an article in the *Harvard Business Review*.

SMARTNESS AND DULLNESS

Why are some business people so smart and dull at the same time? The question, that summer day, was like all the stadium lights turning on suddenly at midnight. Not only did the brain relate to our artistic creativity, it was fundamental to business structure, management process, and my own job!

The moment is still vivid. It was in late June 1976. I arrived one morning at the Management Development Institute to find the latest issue of the *Harvard Business Review* in my mail tray. I picked it up and was casually scanning its table of contents, when my eye lit on the title, "Planning on the Left, and Managing on the Right" by Professor Henry Mintzberg. Could he be talking about the brain? He was! A short way into the article, he raised the key question:

> Why are some people so smart and so dull at the same time, so capable of mastering certain mental activities and so incapable of mastering others? Why is it that some of the most creative thinkers cannot comprehend a balance sheet, and that some accountants have no sense of product design? Why do some brilliant management scientists have no ability

"People are always neglecting something they can do in trying to do something they can't do."

Ed Howe

"To get creative behavior, we must reward it."

Paul Torrance

"I am more stupid about some things than about others; not equally stupid in all directions; I am not a well-rounded person."

Saul Bellow

Figure 5-2. Two managers with Different Profiles React to the Same Data.

to handle organizational politics, while some of the most politically adept individuals cannot seem to understand the simplest elements of management science?

I remember saying to myself, "My God, I think he's talking about me...but he's also talking about my staff, my boss, my family, and all my friends." Although all were successful in what they did, not one was equally "smart" across the entire brain spectrum. We were all smart and dull at the same time. He was talking about everyone!

Mintzberg went on to connect the new knowledge about brain specialization with different styles of managerial thinking. Essentially, he proposed that different aspects of the work of managing required different parts of the brain. For example, operational planning makes use of left-brain modes, particularly the B quadrant. Other aspects—such as dealing with people, having a vision of the business, and using intuition—employ the C and D modes of the right. Translated into the everyday world of business, Mintzberg was saying that some managers are very smart at detailed planning and less smart at envisioning the whole business while for other managers, it's vice versa. If you consider the entire spectrum of thinking required in managerial work, Mintzberg's concepts make it easy to explain the vast differences between one manager's perceptions of the work to be done and the way in which other managers carry out that work.

As if I needed any further encouragement, Professor Mintzberg concluded by explicitly raising the issue of management education. He called on management educators, first, to rethink the work of managing in light of the new learning about the specialized brain and, second, to change the management education process accordingly. Professor Mintzberg had proclaimed the need to rediscover the brain not only for artists, but for managers as well.

OPERATIONAL VS. STRATEGIC PLANNING: THE REAL DIFFERENCE

One of the first realizations to which Mintzberg's article led me concerned the nature of the difference between operational and strategic planning and how to teach it.

Several years earlier, GE's corporate executive office had commissioned me to develop a strategic planning seminar as part of the effort to move GE's culture to approach business more strategically. In response, my Executive Education colleagues at the Institute had developed a week-long workshop directed at the company's top 200 general managers and planning executives. A brief time later, the CEO, Fred Borch, requested a shorter seminar for the 10,000 key downline managers in the company whose understanding of strategic planning was needed to further this planned cultural change. While the seminar I developed was judged very successful, the sense of somehow having missed the boat persisted. I didn't feel the seminar fully conveyed what strategic thinking really means, but I couldn't figure out what I should have done instead. It took Mintzberg's article to provide the first clue.

Strategic planning differs from operational planning mentally. Operational planning, which requires more structure deals with facts, logic, analysis, sequence, detail, time, history, process, and procedure. In strategic planning, which is more experimental, we work with vision, insight, inference, intuition, trends, patterns, integration, synthesis, projections, risk, and global thinking.

"The fixed person for the fixed duties who in older societies was such a godsend, in the future will be a public danger."

Alfred North Whitehead

"A man to carry on a successful business must have imagination. He must see things in a vision, a dream of the whole thing."

Charles M. Schwab

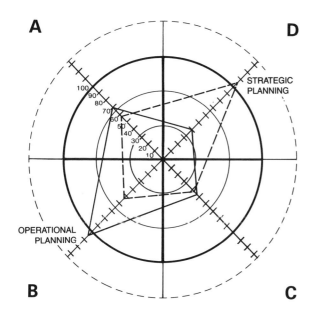

A

D

STRATEGIC
PLANNING

100
90
80
70
60
50
40
30
20
10

OPERATIONAL
PLANNING

B

C

Figure 5-3. Operational vs. Strategic Planning Profile

Since none of us had thought about the mental differences between operational and strategic planning, neither the content nor the delivery of the workshop took into account the critical shift required from the *safekeeping*,* lower-left B quadrant modes called for in operational planning to the experimental upper-right D quadrant modes crucial to strategic planning. Unwittingly, we had largely ignored the right-mode quadrants. From beginning to end, the strategic planning workshops and seminars emphasized A and B quadrant processes and techniques while overlooking the major aspects of C and D thinking modalities required to make full use of those techniques.

Even more crucial, we had greatly underestimated the learning challenge inherent not only in this short seminar, but also in the entire cultural shift. Any move from a preferred or primary mode to an area of secondary or even tertiary preference sharply heightens the demand on a person's mental energies, especially if that person's normal operating mode happens to be diagonally opposed to the mode of the material being taught. Since the vast majority of people participating in those programs had strong preferences for the logical, analytical, rational, and operational planning modes, it was an enormous leap for them to comprehend strategic thinking and planning, let alone learn how to implement it.

The teaching challenge was finding new ways to help B quadrant people access the D quadrant, affirm their ability to make use of those modes, and then develop skills for them to apply to strategic tasks.

With that exciting understanding clear, I began to

---

*Safekeeping is a term used loosely to describe the protecting and safeguarding aspects of individuals and companies who guard against risks, change or variance in procedure, or anything that may upset a set plan which would generate set results.

re-examine our workshop subjects and delivery processes in terms of which quadrants they called on or needed to access. It was too late at that point to revamp the strategic planning workshops—they'd already been delivered. But since then, I've developed dozens of techniques for helping people make just that kind of shift. To give you an idea of the options in designing workshops, here are just a few I used recently when working with a high-powered oil industry group.

In addition to the standard planning approaches, I used a series of guided fantasies* that staged the thinking from the present to 5 years out and finally 15 years out to the year 2000. In between these meditative excursions, the participants built a model of their perceptions of the problems they were trying to solve, using a wide variety of creative materials, including clay, wood, wire, paint, construction paper, colored yarn, feathers, and the like.

Before and after the model building, I took the group out on Lake Lure to search for parallels in nature—metaphors around which to develop potential strategic solutions. Then, to develop a last metaphor for modeling the final 15-year stretch, I took the group up to Chimney Rock for a spectacular aerial view of Lake Lure so they could gain a more holistic perspective of what they had seen the day before. The group then consolidated their thinking by returning to the creative materials and producing a new set of models that now revealed key elements of a solution.

The final-stretch fantasy provided the basis for combining all these elements into: (1) an array of strategic alternatives, and (2) a strategy for presenting them to top

*Guided fantasies: an exercise where the instructor has you close your eyes and focus on taking a mental trip which he or she guides you with narrative and music.

"An idea that appears radical, bizarre, or way-out one day, may be readily accepted the next day."
Source Unknown

"Almost all men are intelligent. It is method that they lack."
F. W. Nichol

management—a critical step usually left out.

The combined effect of using conventional and new techniques gave the individuals and the total group permission to think in D quadrant ways and, in the process, to discover strategic solutions that more traditional approaches alone would not have revealed.

Understanding operational and strategic planning in these terms opened up the whole question of what *other* business activities were being viewed from the wrong quadrant. That thinking led even further to the subject of brain-related management in general.

THE IMPORTANT MOVE TO WHOLE-BRAIN MANAGEMENT

From a business training standpoint, and in terms of brain understanding, one could say that the mid-1970s were the Dark Ages. Most businesses were so left-mode dominant that their cultures were impervious to any attempt to introduce whole-brain techniques. For many companies, this continues to be true. Even executives who have strong preferences for right-mode functioning lack the understanding needed to honor and utilize those intuitive strengths fully.

As I'll explain later in more detail, this is a very hazardous situation, for, without deliberate cultivation of the right modes, the left will tend to take over a company and render it increasingly incapable of innovative operation. Both for my own small company and for businesses in general, a more conscious whole-brain approach to management is becoming less of an option and more a necessity for three

© 1981 AMERICAN MANAGEMENT ASSOCIATION AND JOSEPH FARRIS

"*I appreciate your fresh, innovative, and perceptive thinking. Unfortunately, here we prefer stale, tried-and-true thinking.*"

Figure 5-4.   A Whole-brain Organization is Better

compelling reasons.

The right brain (especially D quadrant) is the only part of our brains that deals effectively with change. As essential as left-brain modes are to business success, they spell slow death for a company when used without the right-brain modes. Left modes (particularly the B quadrant) resist change, but the right modes (especially D) frequently stimulate it, welcome it, produce appropriate responses to it, and are able to make critical decisions after the facts have run out.

If change is a constant, in order to compete effectively in a world characterized by change, business managers *must* function in all four of the brain's different modes, right as well as left, cerebral as well as limbic. This needs to happen at all levels of management, not just at the top. In today's world, the CEOs can no longer spread themselves far enough to supply all the right-brain leadership capabilities needed in their companies. As true as this is today, it will be even more true tomorrow as the pace of change continues to accelerate.

Heterogeneous groups produce more creative, effective solutions than do homogeneous groups. This isn't an altogether new thought. The saying, "Two heads are better than one," has been around for a while. As Chapters 7 and 8 explain in more detail, creative or innovative functioning can be effective only if all four quadrants collaborate to contribute their specialized modes.

But the heterogeneous group is much harder to manage because traditional, authoritarian forms of managing don't work. Why not? Because authoritarian management is essentially left-brained. Imposing A and B quadrant values on a whole-brain team is constricting and, therefore, usually counterproductive. If we're going to tap the power of the whole-brain team, we'll need to learn whole-brain ways of managing. However, in a large organization, the odds against whole-brain functioning are high.

The left-brain modes increasingly dominate an organization as it ages unless leadership consciously cultivates and encourages the right. The basic factor powering this phenomenon is fear: We are all insecure. None of us likes to be wrong. This fear gives special power to four factors leading to the leftward lean.

First, "tried and true" methods tend to entrench themselves because it's hard to argue with success. If something worked before, we think, maybe we can squeeze another year out of it—even if we feel uneasy about it. The cry goes up, "If it ain't *broke*, don't *fix* it." But this attitude, according to Edward de Bono, internationally known author of *Lateral Thinking* and many other books, may well be the single most powerful contributor to the decline in American industry.

Second, people with A and B preferences tend to perform in a way that inspires confidence and invites more responsibility (and authority). They take action, finish what they start, meet deadlines consistently, and document occurrences so they have proof, records, and numbers.

Third, it's hard to argue with numbers. Their clarity alone makes them powerfully persuasive, as I mentioned in Chapter 1. That clarity—the clarity of A and B modes— has been a major reason many elements of our society, particularly business and education, have become so left brain oriented.

Fourth, when we experience fear, we protect ourselves by doing the *B quadrant downshift*, reverting to the B quadrant, which is a safekeeping mode. You can watch it happen when a company is in crisis: Management takes action—

any action—as long as it is in the "right direction." They slash budgets, close sales offices, chop research efforts, eliminate promotion and advertising — anything as long as it provides a visible signal of the downshift. While some of these actions may be appropriate, these edicts frequently add up to overkill and can be severely counterproductive. Whether they work or not, these behaviors tend to place great power in the hands of people who perform the safekeeping functions (e.g., financial, operational, administrative management), and once given, that power is difficult to reclaim.

What Whole-Brain Management Is and Isn't

I'll explain in a moment what I do mean by recommending a whole-brain approach to management, but first let me say what I don't mean.

I'm not proposing that business deemphasize the A and B modes. The very nature of most business enterprises dictates a left-mode tilt toward the everyday conduct of its activities. We *need* our B dominant people to keep records, follow uniform procedures, monitor cash flow, plan and control inventory, keep files in order, figure out how to keep track of salesmen's expenses, and a hundred other important functions. We *need* technical people, financial analysts, accountants, engineers, and lawyers using their A quadrant to engineer products, measure performance, report facts, solve problems logically, and act rationally.

I'm not proposing we put the C and D right-brain modes into exclusive ascendance. This is not a campaign for D quadrant thinking throughout the accounting function, for example, or the legal department. D quads don't suffi-

ciently appreciate the need for consistency, rules, tradition, facts, schedules, or reliability. I'm not suggesting we hire the majority of engineers with C quadrant preferences. Engineers need, above all, to devise ways for things to work; although human emotions and feelings need to be factored into solutions, they mustn't dominate the activity of achieving them.

I'm not proposing we mentally restructure the corporation. The way American businesses are structured mentally is essentially sound: (1) At lower levels most managers show strong left-brain preferences; (2) at higher levels the *proportion* of people with multiple preferences increases; (3) at the very top level, the CEO is almost invariably triple or quadruple dominant with strong D quadrant leanings. This structure is appropriate because the nature of the work to be done at different levels demands it. Middle management work is 60 to 80 percent left-mode oriented; this includes technical, financial, analytic, administrative, and planning work, together with functional activities such as engineering, manufacturing, marketing, finance, and personnel administration. By contrast, to manage these major subordinate functions well, the CEO must be strong in each of the four quadrants of mental preference—particularly in the ability to speak all four "languages" in order to function effectively as a multidominant translator.

Those three points represent what I *don't* mean when I say businesses need to become more whole-brain oriented.

What I *do* mean is this: When designing and implementing responses to business issues and challenges, *the human brain functions at its most innovative, productive best only when all four quadrants engage situationally and iteratively in the process.* The A and B quadrants define the problem or issue. The B and C quadrants provide the visceral and emotional ingredients. The C and D quadrants incubate and permit solutions to rise to awareness. The A and D quadrants then process those solutions iteratively to check the logic of the imaginative solution. Finally, the A and B quadrants, along with C and D quadrants, verify and refine the solution during the planning, implementation, and control processes.

This need for all four quadrants applies to individuals, groups, teams, divisions, and even whole companies.

Whole-brain management may have the competitive edge. The First Law of Cybernetics says it another way:

> The unit within any system that has the most behavioral responses available to it controls the system.

In mental terms, this means no organization that restricts its mental options to A and B quadrants alone can hope to prevail over the organization that uses A, B, C, and D and maximizes the number of potential responses these can make. To compete effectively, companies within markets as well as individuals and groups within a company need to employ all four quadrants. That doesn't mean we need to spend equal time in each mental quadrant. It *does* mean that we function situationally—that we have *equal access* to all four quadrants so that when the situation calls for a given type of mental function, we can give our best response. After all, taken as a whole, the world out there is a composite whole brain!

Barriers to Whole-Brain Functioning

If you accept my analysis, you agree that situational whole-brain functioning is unquestionably crucial to corporate health. However, change may be slow in coming.

"It is easier to seek forgiveness than permission."
Female Admiral in the U.S. Navy

"A good creative idea always collides with an established idea, and some individuals find this very frightening."
Source Unknown

Figure 5-5. Shoe Store Comparison: The More Styles You Have the More Customers You Attract

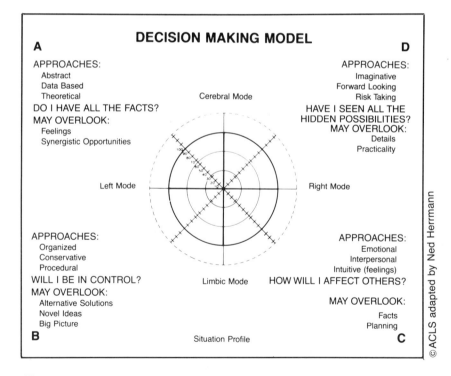

Figure 5-6. Whole-brain Decision Making Model

In addition to the normal inertia that impedes all change, our excessive reliance on the left modes presents a number of barriers to implementation: ignorance, excessive conservatism, and tribalism.

Ignorance

The first barrier is *ignorance*. Although writers have popularized the right brain/left brain dichotomized model of the brain in relation mainly to the difference between artistic activity and the analytic aspects of accounting, many very savvy people still understand little or nothing of the brain's significance for management decision-making. They are simply not informed.

Safekeeping Frame of Reference

Closely related to ignorance of new thinking, the second barrier consists of a *safekeeping frame of reference* about business that arises mainly from the B quadrant. From the B quadrant perspective, firmly grounded in what has worked in the past, new, improved ideas often look too risky to tolerate. Lacking widespread historical data and measurements to prove the validity of whole-brain functioning, individuals with this safekeeping frame of reference may well consider any new idea unfounded/ungrounded ivory tower stuff that is draining energy which would be put to better use elsewhere.

Tribalism

The last barrier is *widespread tribalism*, to which I've referred in Chapters 1 and 4. As I mentioned earlier, despite the cooperation left hemispheres exhibit in mentally managing the physical operation of the body's right side and vice versa, our various modes are frequently at odds. This mental conflict between left and right modes both contributes to and is exacerbated by tribal patterns.

The mutual lack of understanding and appreciation between tribes for their differing modes of knowing, and for the work styles that emanate from them, costs American companies a bundle. This is true both directly—in terms of immediate dollars—and indirectly, in the longer-term productivity costs of dissatisfaction and lack of fulfillment. An obvious and classic instance of direct dollar costs occurs in the eternal war between sales and manufacturing. How many sales have been forfeited because of excessively rigid production schedules? How many unnecessary hours of costly overtime have wiped out profit margins because some salesperson didn't plan ahead, communicate a customer's need in time, or check to see if the factory could build what he was trying to sell. American corporations have been paying through the nose for these wars.

Even so, high as they are, these costs have simply not constituted enough incentive to resolve the impasses among tribes. It's a sad commentary, but achieving better working relationships between traditional adversaries within companies is more likely to be a bonus at the end of the move toward whole-brain management than an impetus to begin it. The motivation to manage in a whole-brain way will instead come from more compelling sources.

Why the Barriers Can't Stop the Trend toward Whole-Brain Management

One or more of four compelling factors will ultimately draw corporations into consciously utilizing whole-brain

"To give a fair chance to potential creativity is a matter of life and death for society."

Arnold Toynbee

"How good bad music and bad reasons sound when we march against an enemy."

Freidrich Nietzsche

"No matter how far you have gone on a wrong road, turn back."

Turkish Proverb

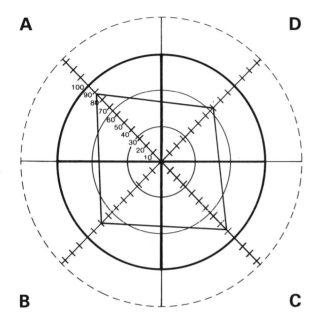

Figure 5-7. CEO Profile

technology in the next few years.

1. **The Wave.** Once understood, the power of the four-quadrant model of the brain is like the tide— almost irresistible. People get hooked when exposed to it and to even just a small sample of the creative empowerment it facilitates. Again and again, the impact of the idea on individual lives keeps the knowledge and enthusiasm spreading. In addition, general knowledge of brain functioning is increasing at an explosive rate, as are favorable reports of the results of applying this new knowledge.

2. **The Boss.** The person in a corporation most likely both to appreciate the advantages of whole-brain functioning *and* to see that it gets implemented in a balanced way is the chief executive officer. Of all the occupational categories, the CEO shows quadruple dominance profiles (1-1-1-1) most consistently and, in my experience, grasps the implications of the four-quadrant brain model most readily.

3. **The Carrot.** Surveys have shown that after receiving their personal profile results from the HBDI, many knowledge workers estimate their productivity will increase 30 percent now that they know what their preferred modes of knowing are and can match those with the work that "turns them on."

4. **The Stick.** The competitive disadvantage of not utilizing the new brain technology when other companies do can be prohibitive.

The benefits from applying whole-brain management are in accordance with the Law of Cybernetics mentioned earlier. In layman's terms, the company that controls the market is: (1) the most versatile, innovative, and creative; (2) consistently more forward-thinking than its competitors in marketing, engineering, product line, and manufacturing versatility; (3) consistently one jump ahead of the pack; (4) more efficient, reliable, and orderly; and (5) legally and financially impeccable.

Would you rather be with the controlling company—or with the company that competes against it? Silly question—except that some people will choose to remain with the company that believes what worked in the past works best, rather than changing and reaching for what this new knowledge can win for them.

In the remainder of this chapter, I'm going to address the subjects of creativity and productivity. However, they are presented under different headings in the order in which you might proceed toward whole-brain management if you were a CEO or a manager exploring its possibilities.

THE MULTIDOMINANT CEO

CEOs are an unusual breed, for more than any other occupational grouping, they tend to have strong preferences in at least three, and sometimes four, quadrants. While the composite profile of all CEOs averages out to be a 1-1-1-1, there is a whole array of multidominant profiles in that average. Nine percent of all CEOs have the 1-1-1-1 profile. The 1-1-1-1 profile occurs three times more often in this occupational group than in the population as a whole.

The chance of finding a 1-1-1-1 CEO is ten to twenty times greater than finding a 1-1-1-1 engineer, financial director, lawyer, or medical director. Quadruple dominant profiles are rare overall, but they appear more often in the CEO occupational group than any other. The task of the CEO demands a multifaceted, multitalented, and very often, a multidominant person. Thirty-three percent of the CEOs surveyed are triple dominant. Forty-one percent are double dominant, and seventeen percent are single dominant. Figure 5-8 shows a sampling of the more common profiles for CEOs.

You may notice from the CEO statistical analysis of profile frequencies that many have a 1 for the fourth digit of the profile, which indicates a strong preference for the D quadrant functions (risk taking, experimenting, future-oriented, holistic). As a matter of fact, 83 percent of the CEOs profiled have a primary preference for the D quadrant. In many cases, the CEO has a greater preference for D than any of his staff members.

The multidominance of the CEO may explain the puzzlement that people often feel when trying to "psych out" the CEO. Unless they themselves are multidominant, and have a significant preference for the D quadrant, the CEO will often seem to be able to speak their language, be a regular fellow, but then switch to some strange or difficult personality that unpredictably interrupts the first, more familiar functioning. The CEO also seems to "know" things that no logical process would give him a handle on. "How does he *do* it?" people ask. "She picks this stuff out of the air," another might comment.

As often as not, the other party's puzzlement is

MULTIDOMINANT

2111 ....11%

1112 ....7%

1111 ....9%

DOUBLE DOMINANT

1121 ....15%

1122 ....11%

1221 ....11%

2211 ....22%

2121 ....8%

SINGLE DOMINANT 17%

Figure 5-8. Distribution of CEO Profiles Chart

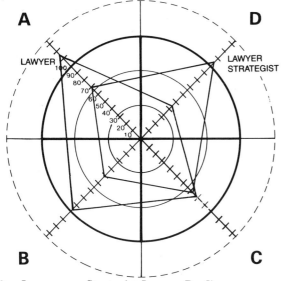

Figure 5-9. Lawyer vs. Strategist Lawyer Profile

matched by the CEO's own. I often encounter CEOs who don't recognize the mental processes they are using. Usually they believe what they do is simply using logic and common sense.

Believing in this logic does no harm except that, being unaware of their options, CEOs often fail to capitalize on their own versatility in certain situations. And those situations arise frequently: Interviews with CEOs, personal observations, and an analysis of random weeks of their calendars show that as much as half of the work they do can benefit from the application of the right-brain modes of knowing. It's very useful for a CEO to know that. In our left-brain dominant corporate world, even CEOs need all the encouragement they can get to utilize their full capabilities.

My experience with hundreds of managers, including many CEOs, reveals that the more they appreciate their own mental preferences, the better they understand and work with their staffs, other key managers in their organizations, and the outside groups with whom they interact.

One CEO talent that tends to manifest automatically, however, whether the person is aware of having it or not, is the ability to translate ideas from the language of one quadrant to that of the next. This translation role comes naturally to the multidominant CEO. CEO candidates exhibit this talent for translation early in their careers. It's a crucial ability when the time comes to translate ideas into action, advance facts toward conclusions, articulate concepts, incorporate human factors into those concepts, *and* synthesize many ideas into a few. The power to communicate clearly for a variety of internal "tribes" so they can work together is absolutely essential.

There's no law saying that an A-B dominant person

(1-1-2-2) can't also rise to the top. But it takes extra energy to operate in an area of secondary preference, so the A-B dominant CEO will need to work harder and be lucky in the C and D areas. He will also need to have on his staff a person who can serve in the multidominant translator role. I've seen this quite often. For example, one lawyer functioned far beyond law per se to include advising the CEO on a wide range of internal and external strategic and political issues. Not until he saw his own profile could he articulate the source of the differences he experienced between himself and the majority of his legal colleagues. His new understanding of himself was instantaneous. As you can see in Figure 5-9, given his stronger preferences for upper-right D, he is an unusual lawyer.

The CEO's Left-Mode Support Staff

While CEO profiles tend to be multidominant, their supporting staff departments lean left. The composite average for the profiles of typical CEO staff groups showed distinct preferences for A and B thinking. In studies of dozens of staff groups, the majority of their members strongly preferred A, had a nearly comparable preference for B, exhibited a clear secondary in D, and were uniform in their lack of preference for C. Figure 5-10 is a typical corporate staff showing the relationship of the staff to the CEO.

When you look at the profiles of senior staff members who manage the primary functions of a business, they usually epitomize their occupation. Therefore, the head of an engineering division is usually an engineer himself, a successful one who develops managerial skills to organize his staff. Even though he is now a manager, his profile

"The reasonable man adapts himself to the world; the unreasonable man persists in trying to adapt the world to himself. Therefore, all progress depends on the unreasonable man."
George Bernard Shaw

"The greatest enemies of creativity are crusty rigidity and stubborn complacency."
Source Unknown

"We believe that knowledge feeds creative fire. There must be a stronger new bond, a closer relationship than ever before between the analytical and creative sides of our business."
Source Unknown

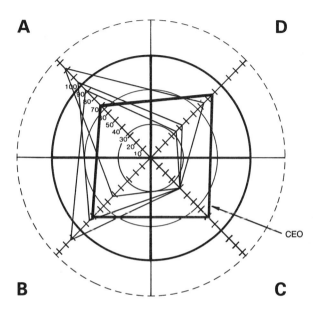

A

D

B

C

CEO

Figure 5-10. Staff vs. CEO Composite Profile

still matches the norm for engineers in the given organization. The same is true for senior executives in the other major staff functions of business, such as finance, manufacturing, legal, human resources, research and development, and marketing.

The CEO, by contrast, not only shows preferences that are quite evenly distributed through all four quadrants; he also has, in many instances, stronger right-mode preferences than any other single member of the staff, regardless of function. It is these preferences, particularly for upper-right D, that provide vision, global thinking, a bridge to the future, and the ability to conceive a business strategy in holistic terms. I think it's safe to say, based on the data, that the mental quality distinguishing the policy maker from the implementor is the ability to access and use the D quadrant.

Once alerted to these distinctions in modes of knowing, most CEOs recognize their validity immediately. During a Brain Update Workshop I gave for the CEO and staff of a $20 billion company, the CEO turned to his staff and said, "With a few exceptions, you're all left-brain dominant and that is what *you should* be. That's the work I need to have done. You are, individually, and as a group, the best in the world. I brought you into these positions deliberately because of your functional capabilities. You are the experts. It's my job to integrate and synthesize the functions you represent and add any missing dimensions that are required to meet our corporate needs." What this CEO was saying was that he needed to understand each one of his staff members when they were representing their functional responsibilities, and that he had to be able to translate that understanding into the languages of other functions in order to integrate them all.

How does a whole-brain person float up out of the depths of a basically left-oriented organization? In my observation, CEO candidates have all their preferences in place early on, including right-mode preferences, but they *begin* their journey upward by developing and excelling at left-mode A and B skills. Thus, while winning their spurs, and for some time afterward, they restrict their right-mode behaviors on the job: They stay within organizational norms, keep a low profile, and step out on a right-mode limb only when the left-mode preparation and documentation has been done so superbly that they can't be faulted. That is what the system requires, and that is what they deliver. They gradually begin operating in a more overtly intuitive, experimental way only when they command enough authority to reveal themselves as different without the risk of being penalized for it.

Women as CEOs

The profile data on CEOs are especially interesting in relationship to the trends concerning women in business. Today, while women are joining the corporate management ranks more than ever before, many are also leaving large corporations to become business owners or CEOs of smaller companies. There are several reasons for this. The *first reason* women are striking out on their own, of course, is that American big business isn't keeping pace with their managerial aspirations. Not enough women are making it in traditional organizations to satisfy their urge for leadership.

Second, in terms of mental preference, many of the women are well equipped to make it on their own. They bring to their leadership positions an enhanced capability

"A dreamer is one who can only find his way by moonlight and his punishment is that he sees the dawn before the rest of the world."

Oscar Wilde

"Forget 'what's available' out there. Figure out instead what kind of job would make you happiest because the kind that would make you happiest is also the one where you will do your best and most effective work. As David Maister says, 'If the thing turns you on, you'll be good at it; if it doesn't, you won't.'"

Richard Bolles
Hints

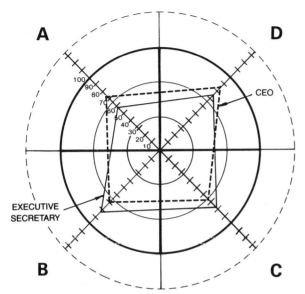

Figure 5-11. Executive Secretary vs. CEO Profile

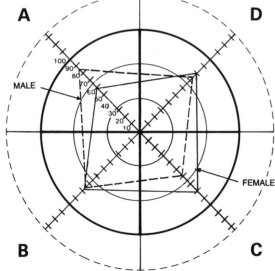

Figure 5-12. Male vs. Female Profile

that results from their larger, faster, and earlier maturing corpus callosums, brain chemistry and enculturation differences. All these differences help women to be potentially more inter-hemispheric in their processing than are men. Thus, women are, on average, more whole-brain oriented, more intuitive, and less fact-based, more open to new ideas than to status quo, more people-oriented than thing-oriented. Therefore, they perceive their surroundings more sensitively, manage the innovative process more comfortably, and respond more rapidly to changing environmental circumstances.

Think about this: Other than the CEO, the person who most frequently has a 1-1-1-1 or whole-brain profile is the executive secretary. How many of the women who, in times past, would have worked supporting the CEO are today occupying that desk themselves?

Third, women want a more whole-brain environment and have mental preferences that give them advantages in creating it. Let me explain what I mean in terms of profile data. Comparative data on male and female CEOs and business owners show they differ significantly in two of the four quadrants. Both men and women tend to have strong preferences for the lower-left B and upper-right D quadrants, with only minimal differences between them. However, in quadrant A and quadrant C, male and female CEOs differ markedly. On the average, upper-left A is the most preferred quadrant for males and the least preferred for females. Lower-right C is the most preferred for females and the least preferred for males.

In sum, the profile data indicate that female CEOs, with strong C quadrant preferences in whole-brain profiles are capable of building unique and effective organizational cultures. What's more, they're actually out there doing it.

I'm going to speak more about this later, but let me just note that men would do well to learn how their own profiles relate with those of their women colleagues. On an average, (please note these are *averages*), men have clear advantages in rational, fact-based functioning and women have clear advantages in intuitive, emotionally oriented functioning. Put the two together in a cooperative way, rather than in competition or conflict, and you have the potential for tremendous iteration and, therefore, genuine synergy. Even more to the point—*without both* A and C capabilities in abundance, you leave out important parts of the creative equation. Men and women in business need each other, and my feeling is that American business will be a whole lot better off as we learn how to work that out.

There is now a great need for companies to be open to change and to manage the innovative process comfortably. This is one reason women will tend to make successful CEOs and why corporations must become internally more whole-brained, despite the barriers that exist against such cultural change.

WHY RESPONSES TO THE CREATIVE IMPERATIVE FALL SHORT

CEOs have been making speeches proclaiming a "fresh commitment to creativity," urging an entrepreneurial approach to the business, and actually committing huge dollar sums to research—but the results have been disappointing. Why? Because the CEO is calling for a D

"When opposites supplement each other, everything is harmonious."
Lao Tsu

"In a rapidly changing world, the ability to create and adapt is a priceless asset."
Source Unknown

"No idea is so outlandish that it should not be considered with a searching but at the same time with a steady eye."
Winston Churchill

quadrant response while the management organization is thinking in rational, safekeeping, and stewardship terms, primarily B quadrant preferences. As a result, companies usually apply those dollars to shoring up the existing product line rather than exploring the truly new. The frustrated CEO asks: "What must I do to get action from my people? I tell them what I want, but nothing happens!" The managers appear to understand, applaud sincerely, but are mentally unable to implement. They have been hired, trained, and rewarded for operating well in a left mode and now, when they're being exhorted to move to the right, they can't respond effectively. They feel uncomfortable and insecure when operating in a mode that they neither trust nor understand.

Businesses have tried various strategies (in addition to speeches) to encourage creativity, but without a proper understanding of the mental aspects of the issue, they usually don't work. Let's take a look at some of those strategies and see why not.

Intrapreneurship

Intrapreneurship, introduced several years ago, is simply entrepreneurship within the organization. The idea, though popular, promises more than it delivers because, like the CEO'S speeches, it's an attempt to carry out a D quadrant function in a B quadrant frame of reference. The solution in a large organization: Because creativity is a mental process, management must organize *mentally* to stimulate creativity. That means, management must create a mental climate to stimulate creativity, and then nurture and manage it. All this takes understanding, time, and investment, but it can be done.

Skunkworks

When traditional business approaches to encouraging innovation don't work, some managements have taken a chance on non-traditional ones. Generally speaking, these approaches involve going outside the established corporate structure, system, or mainstream. A good example is the *skunkworks* approach.

Skunkworks refers to a small, high-powered organization working on a special project in a secluded facility that brings together in one place everything needed for the project to succeed. The approach is based on the idea that certain special work requires unique people working in ways that are legitimate, but that differ so much from the ongoing culture of the business that they cannot be contained within it. So a special place must be set aside for them, not only separate from the rest of the organization culturally, but also separate physically—in a facility that allows project people to work most efficiently. This invariably means flexible work hours, relaxed dress codes, and a specialized physical environment, all of which differ visibly from the parent organization.

The original and most successful skunkworks was created by the legendary Kelly Johnson of Lockheed Aircraft. An extraordinary engineer devoted exclusively to the design and development of secret military aircraft, Kelly Johnson has been responsible for some of the most important technological design breakthroughs in American aviation history. Working with the team in his Lockheed skunkworks (officially named Advanced Development Projects), Johnson designed the world's highest performance aircraft—including the U-2, the SR-71, and the YF-12.

In his autobiographical book, *Kelly*, written with Maggie Smith, he describes how he pestered top management to let him set up an experimental department where the design engineers, mechanics, and shop artisans could work closely together to develop airplanes without the delays and complications of intermediate departments to handle administration, purchasing, and all the other support functions. He wanted a direct relationship between design and manufacturing, which meant that all the functions required for the project would have to be able to operate independently of the main plant. He finally won the chance to try it out, and what he created as a result became the first skunkworks.

Johnson doesn't know exactly where the name skunkworks came from, but one story has it that a Lockheed engineer asked, "What the heck is Kelly doing in there?" "Oh, he's stirring some kind of brew," came the answer. This brought to mind Al Capp's popular comic strip of that day, "Li'l Abner" and the hairy Indian who regularly stirred up the brew, throwing in skunks, old shoes, and other likely material to make his "Kickapoo Joy Juice."

Kelly Johnson's success can teach us important lessons on how to do things quickly, inexpensively, collaboratively, and creatively, and to tailor the approach to the degree of risk involved in each project. What he did and how he did it was generally outside—and in many cases, in spite of—the so-called regular system. He created a unique new form of leadership, in which he felt he owed the members of his skunkworks team these things: challenging, worthwhile jobs, stable employment, fair pay, a chance to advance, opportunity to contribute, good management, sound projects, good equipment, and good work areas.

"Entrepreneur: A high rolling risk taker who would rather be a spectacular failure than a dismal success."

Jim Fisk

"A flash of inspiration can burst out anywhere. For Archimedes, it came in the bathtub and for Isaac Newton beneath an apple tree. But for Alastair Pilkington, it came one misty October evening while he was washing the dinner dishes. Staring at the soap and grease floating in the dishwater, he suddenly conceived of float glass—a way of making glass more cheaply by floating it in an oven on a bath of molten tin."

1964 Newsweek Magazine Article

What makes this different from other forms of leadership? It took place within an enormous, highly structured, and slow-moving corporate behemoth—a place where his kind of creative efficiency is all too rare.

He proved that a skunkworks approach works well, even spectacularly, when top management and project champions understand what they are doing, when the right people work in the right setting under the right leader, under the right top management, providing the right support.

Johnson's basic operating rules for the skunkworks are enumerated in his book. Since I believe his approach applies to projects far beyond the strictly secret military hi-tech kind, I've adapted Johnson's rules to suit a more broadly based and creatively oriented project. Here they are:

1. The skunkworks head should:

    (a) Be a competent and directive "champion" with a "hot line" to top command to be used at his discretion, plus enough authority and autonomy to implement decisions immediately and put him, for all practical purposes, in complete control of all aspects of his program.

    (b) Report to the highest level possible—division vice president at least.

    (c) Be mentally multidominant; capable of accepting and integrating people of divergent mental preferences; and able to operate in a way that balances authoritative and participative styles.

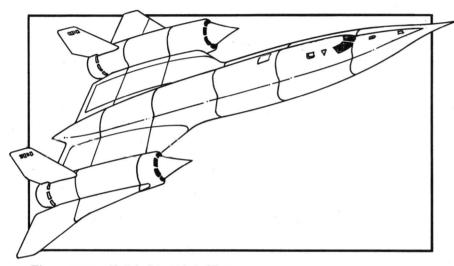

Figure 5-13.   Kelly's Blackbird: SR71

2. The skunkworks staff should be composed of especially capable and responsible people, numbering less than 25 percent of the normal organization. This staff should:

    (a) Include all required functions (engineering, advanced design, manufacturing, finance, personnel, strategic planning, etc.)

    (b) Explain any and all changes in the work situation to everyone as they occur.

    (c) Be able to obtain special competence by bringing in experts as needed.

3. The work should be structured and assigned so that:

    (a) All members either are doing work that directly advances the project toward completion or are closely involved with that work.

    (b) Jobs call for mental capabilities in a combination that makes for enhancement of functioning—e.g., a job requiring highly creative thinking ideally calls for 60 to 70 percent D and C quadrant work rather than 80 percent B quadrant work.

    (c) People's mental preferences match the mental requirements of the work they do.

    (d) Individuals can take advantage of their best work times, consistent with the needs of the project.

4. Communication with all staffers should be ongoing, skillful, intense, and comprehensive so that the entire staff is fully cognizant of the project. That way, decisions in one aspect of the project

"Far and away the best prize that life offers is the chance to work hard at work worth doing."

Theodore Roosevelt
Labor Day address, 1903

"A man becomes creative, whether he is an artist or a scientist, when he finds a new unity in the variety of nature. He does so by finding a likeness. This is not a mechanical procedure, and I believe that it engages the whole personality in science as in the arts."

Jacob Bronowski

Figure 5-14. Juryrigging

can account for events and objectives in other parts of the project. For example:

(a) Work should be designed to keep reports and paperwork to a minimum, but all important work must be recorded thoroughly.

(b) Any and all changes in the work situation should be explained to everyone as they occur.

(c) All families should be kept aware of the project status and should be familiar with the work activities.

5. The work facility should provide the team with:

(a) Whatever privacy they need to carry out their work free of invasion or undue influence by surrounding organizations.

(b) Free access by all team members to all essential equipment and creative materials.

So a skunkworks is far more than a place. It is an enterprise that arises spontaneously out of an organization, usually powered by the vision and drive of one or two champions who take advantage of the loopholes in an organization or culture that allow for such endeavors to grow. Champions reach for and claim creative space. The top management wise enough to identify and acknowledge the champion and allow the endeavor to take place can do no more than create the right environment.

The skunkworks concept seems so simple, but most of them bomb out. Why? Primarily because creativity can't be legislated. Too often a company desperate for innovation simply "plugs in" a skunkworks or matrix concept and it crashes because management didn't really understand the mental requirements for making creative endeavors work. One typical bombing-out pattern: Top management creates a special task force to deal with a major corporate issue, charges them with developing an innovative solution, and then poisons the work climate by punishing the task force for not being able to prove in advance to what degree the solution will work. Another pattern: Management builds specialized research and development facilities designated as creative space, but neither the design nor the goals arise from within the organization, so the project lacks both vision and a champion to lead the way toward it, and the facilities don't fit the creative task to be done.

Juryrigging and Bootlegging

For top management to impose a creative strategy on a company is just as silly as it would have been to try to legislate juryrigging and bootlegging on the U.S. Navy's Seabees during World War II. The Seabees were responsible for establishing bases for various navy units, mainly in the Pacific. Since no one could ever think of everything in advance, and no local hardware store was available to supply what was forgotten, the Seabees became absolute masters at scrounging, begging, borrowing, and bootlegging (polite word for stealing, forging, and related activities). What they couldn't bootleg, they juryrigged. Juryrigging is invention using only what's immediately available. In fact, it became a Seabee signature. The outfit took enormous pride in their creativity, especially when they said it"couldn't be done."

Can you imagine the impact on the Seabees if an admiral from the Regular Navy ordered them to bootleg and juryrig as a military strategy? It would have spoiled everything.

By the way, the term *juryrigging* originated in the days of the tall ships. When an emergency breakdown occurred, no matter what kind it was, the captain would call all the functional heads together to devise a solution. If the mast broke, for example, the bosun, the blacksmith, the chandler, the sail master, the bosun's mate all would come together (like a jury) to figure out and rig up some way to get the ship afloat and head for land. The jury was, in effect, a corporate whole-brain matrix team, with instant innovation as the single, unifying purpose. Once again, we have here an idea that has far more validity when presented in mental terms than it does when described in organizational terms alone.

Remember, I'm not advocating that anyone do away with B quadrant thinking. Not at all. What innovation requires more than anything is *all* the preferences, functioning together situationally to serve an innovative purpose. The B quadrant planning, preparation, verification, and implementation modes are crucial, not only in ongoing operations, but in setting up innovative projects of any kind.

Matrix Management

Matrix management is a term given to a multidisciplinary organization (usually temporary) or team of people brought together to achieve a common goal. Team members are specialists from all the functional areas or disciplines required to achieve the goal. Unlike the makeup of most project teams, which remains constant for the life of a project, matrix team membership can change frequently to accommodate work requirements. When a person's specialty is no longer required, that person drops out. Specialists are added as needed. Companies assign various labels to the matrix team's brand team, project team, task force, etc. The name doesn't matter—the idea is still the same: to assemble a group of people from different parts of the business or organization to accomplish a specific task, and then when the task has been completed, to disband the group. The team leader is a functional rather than administrative head who supplies work direction for the task at hand, but has no authority to change salaries or attend to such supervisory activities as development and vacation policies.

Like many organizational concepts, matrix management makes a lot of sense as far as it goes: Unfortunately, it hasn't gone far enough: (1) The matrix concept hasn't been understood and appreciated in terms of brain dominance; and (2) because of this ignorance, groups have dissipated their energies in internal strife rather than multiply it through synergistic iteration.

Figure 5-15 is an actual-and-typical example. This composite profile represents the members of a matrix-type task force assembled to accomplish a specific short-range task. The people assigned to the group brought all the skills and business experience thought to be essential to the task, but when the team was analyzed using the four-quadrant model, two difficulties showed up. First, the team clearly lacked strong A quadrant preferences for logical, analytical thinking. It therefore faltered in analyzing and interpreting the data on which the project relied, and undoubtedly failed to iterate well enough to function synergistically. Second, the leader, although equipped with the

business information needed to play the leader's role, didn't have the profile needed to function effectively as a multidominant translator. In addition, he was representative of the largest functional tribe, which exacerbated the group's tendency to polarize internally into "us" against "them."

Sure enough, within a few days the group bogged down with an impasse between the more conservative, controlled, safekeeping members and the more adventuresome, experimental, and risk-taking members. In essence they neutralized one another.

It wasn't until this brain dominance diagnosis brought to light the lack of A quadrant strength and the absence of a multidominant translator that the job could get done. To resolve the impasse, the original leadership roles were largely preserved, but the CEO joined the task force to take the translation role, and two consultants with very strong A quadrant preferences were also added.

Thus, making matrix management requires three factors:

1. Leadership that understands all the dialects and how to manage differences rather than simply impose line authority

2. A pool of potential team members that is large and varied enough to contain people of all the preferences need to assemble a composite whole-brain team and a multidominant leader

3. An organizational climate that encourages understanding and expression of differences

In light of these requirements, it's safe to say that the

main reason matrix management fails is probably because it places a demand for heterogeneous management skills on managers who have learned management almost exclusively with mentally homogeneous groups. This background ill-prepares them to deal with the polyglot of differing functional languages and widely diverse values and styles required for highest-level creative functioning. In a homogeneous group, it's possible to manage based on lines of authority, whereas in a heterogeneous group, authority needs to derive from the ability to communicate across mental boundaries, to bridge vast differences in values, beliefs, assumptions, biases, prejudices, and brain dominance characteristics.

The reason one must be able to lead without authority is that the team itself becomes part of the managing resource. The unique backgrounds and different competencies of the individual members are the key resources. Traditional line authority tends to stifle differences, but these resources can be made available for use through leadership that encourages differences and is able to synthesize them into a whole. Even in homogeneous environments, high-calibre traditional management requires multifaceted communication. Less-than-high-calibre management has either to abdicate or to fall back on lines of authority in the hierarchical sense. Any manager who has to choose either one of the above options will be pushed well beyond his level of competence when put into a matrix leadership situation.

Given that most managers tilt to the left and aren't used to leading such diverse groups, it is very important that they develop skills in how to manage differences. The more they know about how important diversity is to creativity, the more obvious this need will become to them.

"The minute you say that a thing cannot be done, you are through with that thing. And no matter how much you know— even if you are an expert—if you say it can't be done, you are all through. And someone knowing nothing about it, but thinking it can be done, now is a better man for the job than you."
Harry Myers

"Logical consequences are the scarecrows of fools and the beacons of wise men."
Thomas H. Huxley

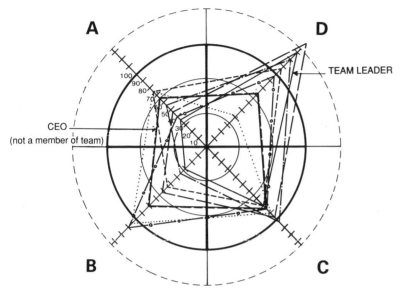

Figure 5-15.   Matrix Type Product Design Task Force

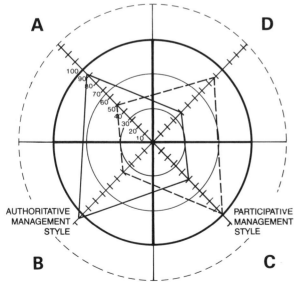

Figure 5-16.   Authoritative vs. Participative Management Profile

THE FOUR-QUADRANT TEAM: KEY INGREDIENT IN THE CREATIVE EQUATION

To open up the highest potential for innovation and synergy, it's important to assemble an innovative project team that comprises a composite whole brain. Ideally, the group includes at least one person with a preference in each quadrant, and one or more members who have triple or quadruple dominance so they can function as translators. Larger groups should also include all four double dominant profiles: left (A and B), right (C and D), upper half (A and D), and lower half (B and C).

The only problem with this kind of group staffing is that it is much more difficult to manage than the homogeneous one. Take a moment to go back to the Dominance Sorting Exercise in Chapter 3 and review the four business associates you chose. The four people in columns A, B, C, and D are all extremely different. Putting aside their different disciplines for a moment, imagine now what it would be like to have them all functioning together on one team. Members of heterogeneous teams differ so much in the preferred modes of knowing that they often find working together an effort—even a trial. Many misunderstandings and other kinds of interpersonal bumps can occur if the working climate doesn't recognize and honor differences.

By contrast, members of homogeneous groups tend to think alike and reach consensus easily. This makes them feel good about their task performance, and, although potentially misleading, this group pride appeals to any manager. In fact, though theoretically able to access all quadrants and iterate among them, the homogeneous group members, in their single-mindedness, often choose to reach a consensus quickly, not considering the full range of alternative possibilities before making a decision. Consequently, they deliver results that may be adequate but that are seldom superior.

It follows from this that for any organization striving to make its workplace creative and innovative, the central need is learning how to manage differences—something that is much more difficult for some managers than for others. A manager whose own mental preference is limited to just one quadrant often finds it hard to accept and honor the mental uniqueness of employees whose preferences are radically different. These managers are much more competent and comfortable with homogeneity and typically lack the level of sophistication required to lead a heterogeneous team without organizational authority.

Learning to manage differences isn't easy. It takes study, experimentation, and a period of stumbling over personal blindnesses and intolerance. It takes time and a commitment to develop sensitivity to others.

Is it worth the trouble? My experience with hundreds of groups says, Yes, unquestionably, the heterogeneous approach is the way to go. When it works, it works superbly. In the right setting, with appropriately knowledgeable, competent team members, it will work almost every time. When it doesn't work, the failure is almost always a result of inappropriate leadership or an improper work climate.

"The power of intuitive understanding will protect you from harm until the end of your days."

Lao Tsu

"A man of genius makes no mistakes. His errors are volitional and are the portals of discovery."

James Joyce

STEPS TOWARD ESTABLISHING THE RIGHT CLIMATE

If you are head of a company, division, or another organizational unit and you are now committed to introducing situational whole-brain project teams into your company to enhance innovative productivity, here are the steps you will want to take.

1. *Become very well-acquainted personally with the mental preferences of the entire top management group (your own included), and hone/expand your own leadership skills.* This understanding, while only the beginning of the task, is crucial to acquire not only intellectually, but also *experientially*. This book—and especially the next three chapters—is devoted to enlarging your understanding of creative functioning, and included are many exercises to make the learning as experiential as possible. But ultimately, no book can substitute for the kind of personal experience from which true commitment develops. You will need to have such experience, for without the commitment that comes from it, you are likely, when push comes to shove, to withdraw your support for less structured styles. In such cases, management tends to become even more one-sided than before.

2. *Demonstrate personal commitment to whole-brain functioning.* Once your personal belief and commitment are solid, it is crucial to demonstrate it to the organization *in a consistent manner.* That means accepting others' personal uniqueness and celebrating—noticing, enjoying, and praising—human differences. This is not an issue of policy so much as of role-modeling: "Do as I say, not as I do" never worked, never will!

3. *Identify those characteristics of the corporate culture that work against heterogeneity and change them.* This step is crucial, but easier said than done. In fact, management scientists have been pushing in this direction in vain for almost 25 years. They've been advocating a more horizontal, participatory approach to management, one that softens the organizational distinctions between layers and allows for communication not only down the line, but upward as well.

Introducing Participatory Management

In contrast to authoritarian forms, participatory forms of management are more whole-brained and assume that the preferences of the right mode, both cerebral and limbic, are valid and needed situationally as much as those of the left are. Whole-brain management means *whole* brain, not just right mode or left mode. While this form of management is more holistic, strategic, communicative, able to deal with ambiguities, and far more humanistic in its approach, it is, in its best form, carried out with the understanding that not all employees share any given preference in terms of their own preferred modes of knowing. Whole-brain participatory management affirms all operating modes.

One of the contributions that brain research has made to the participatory management issue is to explain, in understandable terms, why managers at all levels of an organization consistently fail to take advantage of new approaches to management. Managers aren't simply perverse: It's just that their preferred modes of knowing clash with the mental orientation of the management system they are trying to apply.

Participatory management is generally accepted in organizations where C and D modalities and values prevail; but where A and B dominate, the participatory approach seldom if ever takes hold without a very conscious effort to expand or shift the organization's thinking preferences. In a management group whose culture is profiled as strongly preferring highly structured, tightly planned, organized, disciplined, and administratively focused modes of operation, you can expect outright rejection of a management approach that also tolerates ambiguity, considers intuitive thinking valid, respects emotional expression, considers its employees unique and intrinsically valuable, is flexible in its administration, and trusts employees to do what they think is best.

Even with a conscious effort to expand preferences, the change in essential frames of reference is enormous. For this reason, what virtually any large company will probably need to do is to search out and develop employees whose preferences include the C and D right-mode quadrants. They are probably already on the payroll doing work mismatched with their preferences. If they're not, they should be hired. When I push clients to come up with a composite whole-brain group—and this means female participation as high as 50 percent—most say it isn't possible within their culture. When I cite the advantages and

"Argue for your limitations and sure enough they're yours."
Richard Bach

"Most advocates of realism in this world are hopelessly realistic."
Jawaharlal Nehru

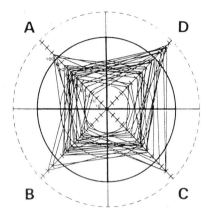

Figure 5-17. A Typical Profile of an Organization

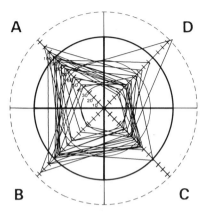

Figure 5-18. A Typical Profile of an A/B Dominant Organization

Figure 5-19. "We Hire in Our Own Image"

continue to insist, more and more appropriate candidates are "found," and the desired balance is more nearly achieved.

Although what I'm talking about here is really only a moderate *behavioral* shift in situational functioning—toward the increased use of C and D quadrants as warranted by the situation—the *cultural* shift is nevertheless profound. Some of our, and society's "anti-right" attitudes, are deeply rooted. There are equally strong anti-left attitudes, especially among the disenfranchised right. All these will take a generation to loosen.

The task of introducing such changes would seem to be overwhelming except that: (1) the technology available is so powerful today; (2) the competitive demands and pace of change in the economy require it; (3) the time is ripe for this kind of change.

Effecting the Cultural Change

We can define an organization's *culture* as the aggregate of the thinking preferences and resulting behaviors of the people in that culture, particularly of those who manage and lead it. A culture can be profiled in much the same manner as an individual. Figure 5-17 shows a typical one. Once established in a company, such cultural profiles tend to persist, because when managers recruit, they usually look for high-potential candidates with similar profiles—we hire in our own image.

Swimming against the cultural tide can be costly. The profile of today's organization in Figure 5-18 shows us its culture is dominated by the faculties of the A and B quadrants. Succeeding in such a culture requires left-mode responses, which can and do elicit substantial rewards. Divergent responses, however, resulting in behavior that departs from organizational norms, can evoke equally substantial penalties. Individuals who behave in ways that match a strong C and D quadrant preference are usually considered mavericks and are ejected or ostracized. If not, it's only because they exhibit an exceptional A and B performance, but even then, suspicion persists and the person may get put down (or be pushed out) for taking risks in unconventional ways. Ironically, such a person is often the budding intrapreneur responding directly to top management's call for innovation.

In some organizational units, such as strategic planning, where right-brain modes of thinking are required for the success of the enterprise, a savvy CEO or senior manager may provide a protective haven or sheltering wing for a D quadrant individual. But woe betide that sheltered person if the sponsoring officer's departure or promotion leaves him or her exposed and unprotected. Unless these individuals have a strong sense of self-protection, left-dominant tribal groups usually force them out. (Even if the tribes try but don't succeed, intrapreneurs often decide the struggle is too much. They then go out, start their own operation, and compete against the very outfit they were trying to serve). Those remaining are extraordinarily sensitive to this kind of expulsion. They see very clearly that the price of non-conformity may very well be their livelihood—with this employer at least—and they keep their heads even lower.

Some business watchers assert large corporations are incapable of providing the kind of environment that can accommodate entrepreneurial or "maverick" behavior. Are they correct? The jury hasn't really heard the evidence because we haven't understood the mental aspects of the

"Education, learning, and changing are so closely related to problem solving that they may all be names for the same thing."

George Prince

"There are two ways of spreading light: to be the candle or the mirror that reflects it."

Edith Wharton
"Vesalius in Zante," *Artemis to Acteon*

question well enough to offer alternative solutions that can work. (Read Chapter 10 for a fuller discussion of how to establish a creative environment.)

I myself am still hopeful about what can be done if management chooses to commit to this kind of environment. What would be required to accommodate the entrepreneur is actually an ideal economic unit. It's a whole-brain workplace with a slight right tilt: more experimental than safekeeping, more open than closed, more participative than authoritarian, more led than supervised, more mentored than disciplined, more humanistic than procedural, more entrepreneurial than administrative, more flexible than constrained, more visionary than reactionary, more future-oriented than precedent-based. At the same time, the ideal workplace environment would support—and be supported by—timely implementation; careful verification of important decisions; impeccable financial management; attention to legal issues; detailed operational plans for translating strategic plans into action; and sound procedures, practices, and administrative controls to support dynamic leadership.

How does one create and sustain such an environment? I think it takes a *champion*—an influential leader who intuitively understands the mental aspects of management and has the courage and skill to bring about needed change. The ideal champion would be able to sense any imbalance in management priorities and direction and take the necessary action to set the organization on course while keeping it open and flexible. My observation of many top-management staffs indicates that candidates for this leadership role are frequently already in place, but don't yet know how to function effectively as change agents. I believe creativity is the most promising path to dealing

positively with change and offer specific suggestions on how to "go creative" in Chapter 11.

Corporations will be able to make a lasting cultural shift when: (1) brain dominance technology is common knowledge and practiced in the business classroom; and (2) our frame of reference for teaching business subjects honors right-brain modes. We're getting there. As of August 1987, over 45 Ph.D dissertations based on the concepts and instrumentation described in this book have been written. But until these concepts are taught and practiced in the classroom by our business colleges and universities, we will not have truly conducted the experiment. Applying these concepts in the teaching/training environment is vitally important to their success on the job.

Opening Up Management Education

As I see it, management education should aim to balance the development capabilities in all four quadrants, but is highly skewed instead toward developing the left-oriented A and B quadrants. One of the management education acronyms from the 1950s and 1960s is POIM, which stands for "planning, organizing, integrating, and measuring." Of these, only integration reflects a right-mode preference; the other three are strongly left-mode oriented. This three-to-one ratio favoring the left is not an unfair assessment of management education as it operates in the 1980s.

In the relationship between businesses and business schools, we see elements of a closed system that feeds on itself. Not only is management education tilted left, but by reason of its content and orientation, it attracts people who prefer to think in those modes. It preaches to believers. The result is an army of business school graduates whose training makes them all potential victims of restricted vision. Many don't shed their blinders for years—if ever. The irony is that these institutions, whose charter is to train business captains, are targeting their programs instead toward the operational end of the organizational hierarchy. Graduates come into companies at high salaries, yet many find it difficult to progress to positions of command requiring competencies outside their specialized left-mode training, such as strategic and intuitive capabilities.

This view is confirmed by the data contained in the *Forbes Magazine* June 1987 cover story, "The Boss," which analyzes the 800 most powerful people (797 men, 3 women) in corporate America.

Examining the educational degrees of the top 100 of this group is revealing:*

Bachelors degree	50
No college degree	18
MBA	17
PhD	5
JD	3
MS	3
MA	2
Other	2

The message seems clear—specialization is not the best route to the top. Our concentration on narrow functional work can be limiting when the primary work requirement is multifunctional and, therefore, situationally whole-brained.

*Sixty-eight percent of the top 100 have no advanced degree or no degree at all.

Now I'm going to shift gears somewhat. Up to this point, I've been discussing a global approach to utilizing brain technology to increase innovation and productivity, the corporate-wide way. What I want to do next is to take a brief look at individuals in jobs, and how to get greater productivity from the people who hold those jobs.

BRAIN-RELATED JOB DESIGN: KEY TO PRODUCTIVITY

On the whole, jobs are structured around specific tasks, and pains are taken to make it possible to assign accountability to the individual so his or her performance can be measured for the purposes of evaluation. This makes good sense as far as it goes, especially in jobs where collaborative, creative effort isn't a priority.

Several difficulties, however, keep us from achieving the optimum design from a productivity standpoint.

1. To begin with, in designing the jobs, the responsible manager seldom takes preferred modes of knowing into account. As a result, the mix of tasks may or may not support carrying out the most important of those responsibilities.

2. As needs change over time, managers add new responsibilities to these jobs without reassessing the entire spectrum of activity required. The new responsibilities may or may not suit the incumbent. Furthermore, when the next incumbent takes over, the manager never goes back to

re-examine the suitability of the assignment.

3. As new people occupy a given position, little attempt is made to match the specific job to the incumbent's mental preferences.

In some areas, this doesn't present much of a problem. Most accounting activities match the preferences of the people who carry them out. Most lawyer profiles correlate with the types of legal activities they perform.

Beyond the functional departments and professional categories, however, it's a different story. Most people have jobs in which they do a great deal of work for which their mental preferences are ill-suited.

Now I want you to be clear about what I'm saying. There are two things about work:

1. People gravitate toward occupations where they can exercise their preferred modes of knowing. That's why we can develop HBDI occupational categories that contain "typical" profiles for certain kinds of jobs.

2. However, once workers occupy jobs—specific positions in specific organizations—they often find themselves laden with work that demands they spend large blocks of time operating in areas of lesser preference or even avoidance.

The *Peter principle* expresses one manifestation of this. People rise in an organization until they reach their "level of incompetence." A classic example is the salesman who is promoted to manager, not because he has managerial tendencies (preferences in A, B, and C quadrants), but

Figure 5-20.   Square and Round Pegs. Matching the individual to a job.

because he's a brilliant D quadrant salesman. He may or may not get training for his new job—often he doesn't—so it's a matter of sink or swim. As manager, he gets to do little or none of what satisfies him, and he wreaks havoc in the department because he hates the detail and can't supervise his subordinates. He's unhappy and bored and finally gets fired for not measuring up.

Another manifestation of the position/person profile mismatch is the high turnover among very promising young employees. Companies hire professionals today much as they did 35 or 40 years ago. They spend great sums recruiting on college campuses and advertising for talent. An army of well-intentioned and highly motivated managers using the latest recruiting techniques descend on college campuses each year to bring in the next crop. As a matter of policy, they deliberately overshoot in terms of candidate quality. Often they make offers only to the top 10 percent of the graduating class.

Then what happens? Instead of finding out what this promising, highly salaried young employee is likely to excel at, they hand him or her an entry-level position that amounts to a grab bag of jobs no one else cares enough about to fight for. There is no correlation between outstanding academic performance, mental preferences, potential, and job assignment. The employee starts out mentally over-qualified and mismatched. A few years later, motivation, productivity, and commitment to company goals are all lukewarm at best. These people start looking around and, when the right chance comes, leave. And the company—many thousands of dollars poorer—goes out to find a replacement.

Employees who don't leave, endure a "management development career path" that may or may not have any-

"People do not get tired out from working where work is intelligently handled. Work, if it is interesting is a stimulant. It's worry and a lack of interest in what one does that tire and discourage. Every one of us should have our pet interests—as many as we can handle efficiently and happily. Our interests should never be allowed to lag or get cold so that all enthusiasm is spent. Each day can be one of triumph if you keep up to your interests—feeding them as they feed you."

George Matthew Adams

thing to do with what they do best. Many companies use as the main vehicle for long-term professional development an arbitrary job rotation program that moves people from one job to another with no regard to their mental preferences. Some people are lucky in these programs, but even for them, mismatches inevitably occur that greatly reduce their performance, productivity, satisfaction, and morale. Procrastination clearly results from such mismatches.

Such mental mismatches, persisting over the years, sharply increase stress and anxiety, which can and does raise not only the incidence of flu and colds, but also heart attacks, nervous breakdowns, alcoholism, and drug abuse. Even when motivation to do a job well is high, people who are mentally mismatched find it difficult to keep up with the job's demands, and they must often work extra hours in order to accomplish what others could do in less time. This takes away from their personal time and can erode family relationships.

Does this sound overdramatic? If so, consider this: One out of every five American workers walks off the job each year. Talk to the middle managers of American business and industry today and discover for yourself how turned off many really are. Their problem is that they are survivors of a crude system that all too often works against productivity instead of for it. In studies I myself have conducted over the years, I have found only a handful of instances where the incumbent has felt his or her job is a perfect match. More typically, incumbents feel they know a much better way and would use it if given half the chance. I frequently urge them to do so.

In working with business people at all levels of an organization, I recommend that when they have the freedom to act independently, they adjust their work to fit their mental preferences and competencies. Most have far more freedom of action than they realize or admit. Where they don't have such freedom, I urge them to take the initiative with their managers to make changes in work priorities and job content. Doing so can produce win-win-win outcomes: win for themselves, win for their manager, and win for the company. I recommend to managers that they provide a climate encouraging their employees to take such initiative.

The productivity and work satisfaction gains can be enormous, and this is no small thing in the productivity equation. Satisfaction is in many ways both a measure and a source of self-esteem, which is a vital ingredient contributing to excellence and high productivity on the job. People with high self-esteem don't do sloppy work. I think it's safe to say that operating in preferred modes of knowing is a major source of self-esteem and thus of productivity.

When working with business audiences, I sometimes ask them to pick a percentage figure describing their own productivity, to write down this private piece of information on a piece of paper, and then to stick it in a pocket. Later on, after talking about the business applications of my work and the opportunity to design jobs and reassign people to those jobs, I ask them to write on another piece of paper what their productivity could be if their work offered them the opportunity to be "turned on," and to put this piece of paper in another pocket. At the end of the day, just before the session ends, I would say, "Oh, incidentally, what are you going to do about those two pieces of paper in your pockets?" People volunteer that the difference between the two numbers ranges from 10 to 50 percent—with the higher number always in favor of the "turn on" work.

Based on this and other observations, I believe the potential productivity gain in the average business group is 30 percent. To check this out, just look inward. What would a perfect job match do to your productivity? What would "turn on" work do to your job satisfaction?

So what is common sense here? To keep the highest quality candidate, provide the highest-quality work. Spend as much time and money on designing the right work as we spend on recruiting the people to do it. Make sure the candidates' preferred modes of knowing and competencies match the mental requirements of the job to be performed.

I speak more of this issue in Chapter 11, because its application and solutions are relevant for settings beyond corporations. Productivity is not just a business issue, but also a work issue; not just a knowledge-worker issue, but also an any-worker issue; not just an American issue, but also a world issue.

We've covered a great deal: from the need for corporations to adopt whole-brain functioning; to the role of the CEO, and particularly women, in effecting that change; to what makes for innovation in a company and how to get it going by using whole-brain teams, establishing an environment, and redirecting business and management education; and, finally, how enormously mental matching can improve the productivity of people in individual jobs.

In the next chapter, I'm going to look more closely at the issue of communication across mental boundaries between people of different preferences. It's both a profound and a hilarious subject, and no one escapes the consequences.

"If you aren't fired with enthusiasm, you will be fired with enthusiasm."
Vince Lombardi

"To love is to be engaged is to work is to be interested is to create."
Lina Wertmuller

"Every job is a self-portrait of the person who did it."
Source Unknown

6

WAR OR PEACE? COMMUNICATION ACROSS MENTAL BOUNDARIES

Nowhere do our differing mental preferences show themselves more dramatically than in the way we do and don't communicate with one another. This chapter begins by introducing brain dialects, both verbal and non-verbal, then proceeds to the subject of humor, and finally ties back to Chapter 5 by offering some business-related example of brain impasses.

Our communication with each other is one of the most visible manifestations of brain dominance similarities and differences. One of my favorite examples consists of a series of interchanges that took place a few years ago. After a five-year search for a building site, my wife, Margy, and I finally found what we considered to be the ideal place to build a "whole brain" home to serve as our residence and headquarters. It was in Lake Lure, North Carolina, at a resort complex now called Fairfield Mountains. After much research and contemplation, we finally settled on an architect, Lou Bruinier, from Portland, Oregon, to help us design the house, and we set up a date to have him fly out and view the site.

The appointed morning was a perfect September day in the mountains. I led Lou along the pathway skirting the ridge to a clearing on the mountainside that provided

a breathtaking view of the lake, the valley below, and the surrounding mountains. The architect was visibly moved by what he saw. He just stood, drinking it in. After a bit I asked, "Well, Lou, what do you think?" And without turning to me he answered, "What a place to build a home. What a place to live forever. I feel as if I'm doing God's work. Thank you for the privilege!" He then took out his sketchbook and entered the first lines of his design.

The plans were ready about a year later. After interviewing a number of builders who were candidates to construct the house, we selected Grover Wilson, the local "Sultan of Homes." I took Grover up to the building site and he naturally moved close to the same position that Lou had occupied. It was another perfect September day. After he looked out at the view and around the building site for a minute or two I asked, "Well, Grover, what do you think?" After a minute, he turned, peered at me, and said, "Oh, I've seen a lot worse than this."

Another year went by and while in the process of arranging for a construction loan and mortgage, I invited the banker to come up to the mountainside and inspect the building site. It was another beautiful September day. He made his way along the path to the clearing, carefully

Figure 6-1. View of Lake Lure (opposite)

Figure 6-2. View of Lake Lure with Builder

Figure 6-3. View of Lake Lure with Banker

A		D
FACTS		**FUTURES**
logical analytical technical financial		integrative imaginative insightful visionary
WHAT	**WHY**	
HOW	**WHO**	
organized detailed business-like sequential		interpersonal emotional people-oriented helpful
FORM		**FEELINGS**
B		C

A	D
WAYS TO COUNT	**WAYS TO SPEND.**
"money"	
WAYS TO SAVE	**WAYS TO HELP**
B	C

Figure 6-4. Four Dialects of the Brain

skirting the brambles to avoid snaring his three-piece suit or scratching his attaché case. When we got to the clearing, he seemed naturally to gravitate to the spot previously occupied by Lou and Grover. He turned to me but didn't say anything. I couldn't resist asking him, "Well, Jack, what do you think?" Jack looked me straight in the eye and said, "Ned, you'll never grow corn on this land." I had tried to anticipate his response, but this was beyond my imagining.

How different is the view from each of our brain dominance perspectives, and how different are the meanings we attribute to the words we use to describe those perspectives.

SEPARATED BY A COMMON LANGUAGE: INTRODUCTION TO THE DIALECTS OF THE BRAIN

The old saw about the Americans and the English being "two peoples divided by a common language" applies to those of us with dissimilar brain dominance profiles. Since English is the *lingua franca* for most of us, we assume that we share its meanings in common. But people have vastly different perspectives and attach different meanings to the words that they use to describe those perspectives. In fact, differences in brain dominance preferences can be so great that they create separate and distinct "languages" or *dialects*. While superficially employing the same vocabulary, these dialects assign different meanings to the same words and use them to describe worlds seen from vastly different perspectives.

"If there is any secret of success, it lies in the ability to get the other person's point of view and see things from his angle as well as from your own."
Henry Ford

"Harmonia is an atunement of opposites, a unification of the many, a reconciliation of dissentients."
Theon of Smyrna

"Hundreds of people can talk for one who can think, but thousands can think for one who can see."
John Ruskin

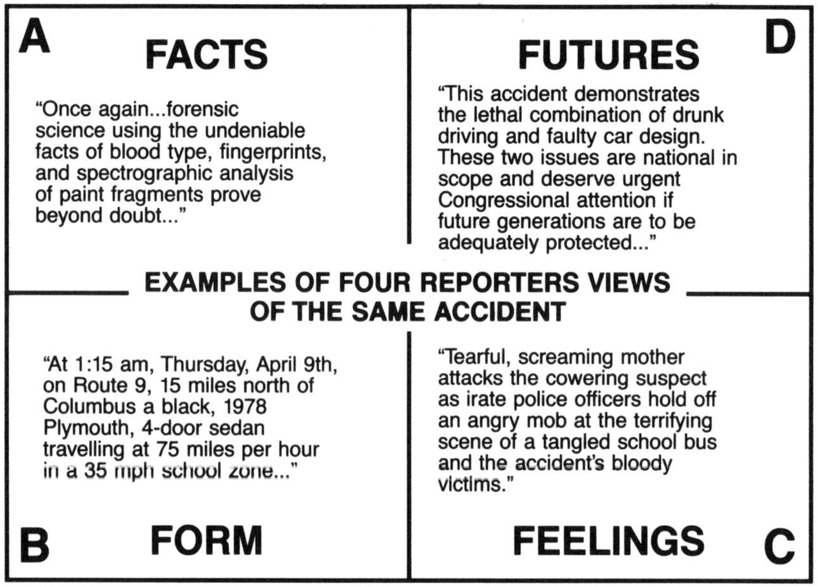

A FACTS	FUTURES D
"Once again...forensic science using the undeniable facts of blood type, fingerprints, and spectrographic analysis of paint fragments prove beyond doubt..."	"This accident demonstrates the lethal combination of drunk driving and faulty car design. These two issues are national in scope and deserve urgent Congressional attention if future generations are to be adequately protected..."

EXAMPLES OF FOUR REPORTERS VIEWS OF THE SAME ACCIDENT

"At 1:15 am, Thursday, April 9th, on Route 9, 15 miles north of Columbus a black, 1978 Plymouth, 4-door sedan travelling at 75 miles per hour in a 35 mph school zone..."	"Tearful, screaming mother attacks the cowering suspect as irate police officers hold off an angry mob at the terrifying scene of a tangled school bus and the accident's bloody victims."
B FORM	FEELINGS C

Figure 6-5. Four Views of the Same Accident

UPPER LEFT **FACTS** (Rational)	UPPER RIGHT **FUTURES** (Visionary)
Looks O.K. The facts seem to check out-the numbers add up. It could be a "go".	What a terrific idea! I can see it ten years out! I can really see the future in my mind's eye.

FOUR REACTIONS TO A "HOT" IDEA

It's possible, but I see some potential risks here. I'd wait until all the questions are fully answered.	Oh, Wow It's a winner! I've got tingles all over my body!
FORM (Safekeeping) LOWER LEFT	(Gut) **FEELING** LOWER RIGHT

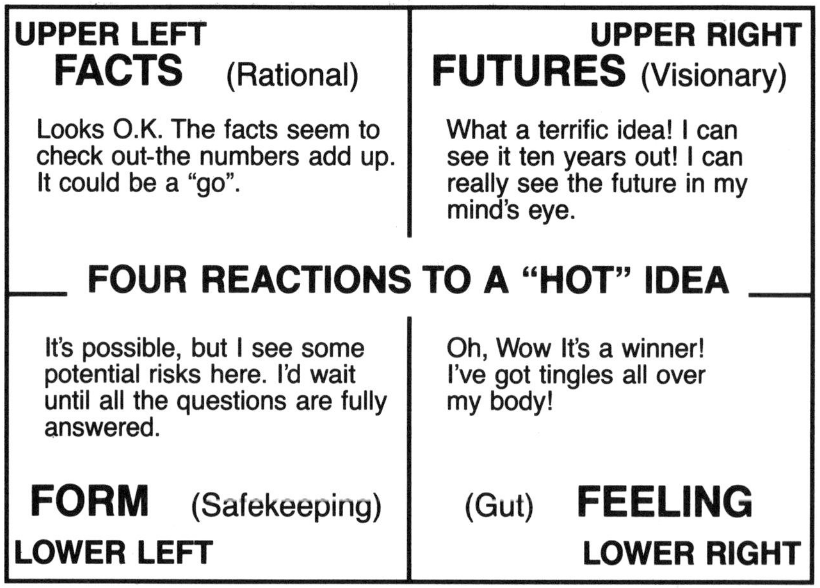

Figure 6-6. Four Reactions to a "Hot Idea"

Although we all speak these dialects every day, most of us do so with no awareness of the possible miscommunications, and so we all miscommunicate everyday in large or small ways.

We've discovered that these dialects can be classified according to brain quadrants, as the following model shows. Thus, there is the language of logic and reason (A), the language of structure and control (B), the language of feelings and emotions (C), and the language of intuition and imagination (D).

These dialects manifest in both verbal and non-verbal communication.

Examples of Verbal Dialects

For examples of how these dialects can communicate very different meanings, look at Figure 6-4. Four different views of the same imaginary auto accident, shown in Figure 6-5, have been written by four reporters, each of whom has a preference for a particular mode of knowing.

As you can see, each reporter's brain dominance preference influences not only the language used but also perception and response, and, hence, the direction a story takes.

In the next example (figure 6-6) of how the dialects differ from quadrant to quadrant we see how people of four different preferences react to a "hot idea."

We can also classify periodicals in terms of the mental preferences addressed. Two popular magazines that speak to the cerebral left A mode are *Scientific American* and *High Technology. Popular Mechanics* fits here too because it focuses on mechanical and engineering matters and overflows with data and gadget specs. *Omni* and *Venture*, which appeal to the upper-right D, sport dramatic and unusual

layouts, pictures, and words. The *Harvard Business Review* and *The Bureaucrat* (a U.S. government publication), reflect the lower-left B primarily. And serving the lower-right C, we have *People, Life*, and *Guidepost*.

Using brain quadrant dialects, we can likewise classify movies, books, works of art, and almost every other expressive aspect of our existence. All of them reflect their readers', viewers', and creators' preferred modes of knowing.

Of course, not all interpersonal communication is verbal. It's quite the contrary, in fact.

Examples of Non-Verbal Dialects

Definitive studies by Albert Mehrabian prove, much to most people's amazement, that 55 percent—well over half—of our face-to-face communication is achieved not with words, but with facial gestures, body language, dress, and other non-verbal cues. Vocals (pitch, volume, rate of speech, and inflection) account for another 38 percent, leaving words to carry only 7 percent of the message!

The year 1979 brought me an opportunity to learn not only about non-verbal patterns, but about how profoundly our brain dominance preferences affect them. Naomi Frankel and Indie Luria, then candidates for master's degrees in art therapy at Brooklyn's Pratt Institute, introduced me to a fascinating technique called *interactive drawing*, which they had adapted for use in business communication. The purpose of interactive drawing is to provide a powerful experience of nonverbal communication. This is especially useful for people accustomed to thinking of communication as primarily verbal.

Here's how it works. Two people are given a theme and asked to respond alternately on a single sheet of paper, without talking or writing words. One of the two people

Figure 6-7. Steps of Interactive Drawing

begins to interpret the theme by drawing lines, shapes, forms, or squiggles; then the other follows, adding more lines, shapes, and forms. The entire communication takes place on the paper. As they work, they can change tools — from pencils to crayons to felt tip markers, for example. As they go back and forth in this way, communication between them evolves.

After playing with the idea for a day or two, it dawned on me that if people with similar and dissimilar brain dominance profiles were paired, interactive drawing could demonstrate the impact of mental preferences on non-verbal communication. The first experiment, which took place in the very next Brain Update Workshop, produced dramatic results as you'll see — enough to make these exercises a permanent part of many of my workshops.

Working with 18 people who represented a good distribution across the brain dominance spectrum, I divided the group first into homogeneous pairs (both dominant in the same quadrant) and assigned them the theme of "flower." The drawings evidenced their ability to communicate without much coaxing or instruction: The flowers looked like flowers. Flowers drawn by pairs from one end of the brain dominance spectrum differed markedly from flowers drawn by pairs at the other end. And they all looked coherent, as if each pair agreed easily on a single concept of flower and a single way to express that concept smoothly. In the next exercise, the pairs were heterogeneous, made up of people from opposite ends of the dominance spectrum. The theme was "tree" and, as expected, these drawings indicated that participants had more difficulty communicating. They shared neither the concept of the tree nor the approach to drawing it. Here are some examples.

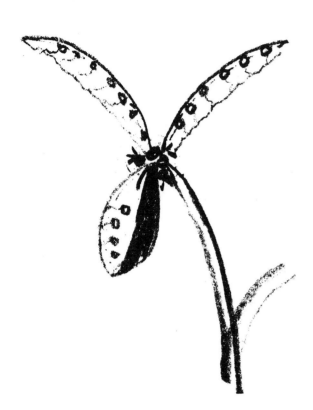

Figure 6-8.   Right-brain Pair Flower

Figure 6-9.   D Quadrant Pair Flower

In Figure 6-8, we see how effectively a homogeneous right-brain pair can create an attractive flower. Both individuals felt good about the outcome and enjoyed the experience.

Figure 6-9 illustrates how the aesthetic qualities of extreme quadrant D preference influence the shape and form of the drawing. It looks as if it were done by one person rather than two. Both participants thoroughly enjoyed the experience.

The most problematic combinations, as usual, involve those quadrants that oppose each other diagonally across the model: A with C and B with D. They seem unable to establish common ground and typically end up in a mild (or pronounced) power struggle. In figure 6-10, person

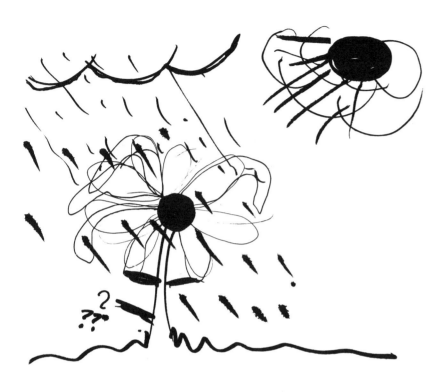

Figure 6.10. Troubled Flower

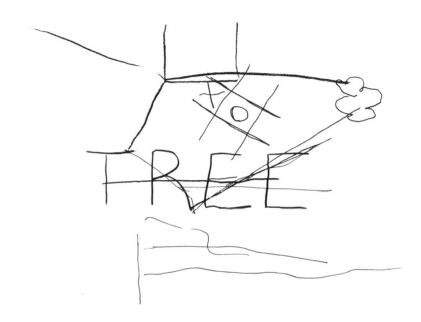

Figure 6-11. Tree Turns to Tic Tac Toe

#1 and person #2 combine to draw the simple flower. They had trouble enough with the flower. The weather only compounded their communication difficulties: Person #1 created the sun and person #2 contributed rain. When person #1 returned to draw the sun's rays, person #2 intensified the rain, building toward a communication impasse.

Figure 6-11 shows a drawing with even greater difficulties. The members of this heterogeneous pair, reflecting preferences for B quadrant and D quadrant respectively, seemed totally unable to communicate with one another. You can see several attempts to start a collaborative trend around the theme, "tree," but nothing developed. In frustration, the pair began to play tic-tac-toe, and, fi-

Figure 6-12.   Homogeneous Pair Emphasizes Structure

Figure 6-13.   Homogeneous Pair Emphasizes Innovation

nally, in order to complete the assignment, one took the initiative to write out the word "tree." These two people were both vice presidents of the same large American company and had sat at the same conference table for years, entirely confident that they understood each other's meanings!

In figure 6-12, the interactive drawing theme is "house." This house, very linear and structured, plain and simple, reflects the quadrant A preferences the two people shared.

In contrast, the house in figure 6-13 is imaginative and more welcoming. It features an extraordinary spiral staircase, a colorful round window, and a most unusual entrance. This drawing was done by an enthusiastic D quadrant pair.

Figure 6-14. A/B Dominant vs. C/D Dominant Design

Figure 6-15. Confusing House Design by Heterogeneous Pair

Figure 6-14 is a drawing produced by a double dominant heterogeneous pair. These individuals started out interactively, but soon began working in parallel, with the A/B dominant individual undertaking the floor plan and the C/D person furnishing it with a conversation pit, sauna, and pool. The two worked independently of each other, totally engaged in their personal part of the drawing and paying little attention to the other's.

In Figure 6-15, the heterogeneous pair dealing with the theme "house" were totally baffled by each other's initial forms. One drew Grecian-like columns, the other a pygmy hut that was in complete contrast to the first person's direction. When they discussed the exercise afterwards, they simply looked at each other and asked quizzi-

Figure 6-16.   An A and B Dominant Pair having it out on Paper

Figure 6-17.   Executive Mismatch

cally, "What in the world were you trying to do?" Here is another mismatch of two senior executives who probably assumed they could communicate effectively.

Of course, competition isn't the exclusive privilege of opposites. Figure 6-16 shows a case in point. In the beginning the individuals in this A and B dominant homogeneous pair proceeded in a way consistent with left mode

thinking. But then person #1 saw person #2 misinterpret one of #1's lines and he proceeded to shoot down #2's bird. Whereupon, #2 chopped down #1's tree. They were about to run over the bicycle when I ended the exercise.

In figure 6-17, we see a classic mismatch between a D quadrant CEO paired with his B quadrant vice president of security. In response to "house," the CEO developed

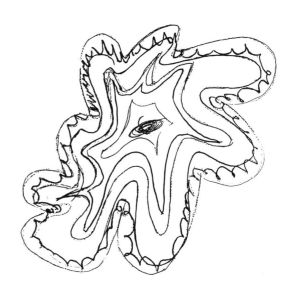

Figure 6-18. Sound Communication at work

Figure 6-19. "Themeless" by a D Quadrant Pair

the theme of the bird's nest, but the security officer could not make sense of it until, at the very end, the figure of the bird was added. At this point, the security officer made a tentative identification of the theme by writing the word house on the side of the drawing. The CEO was totally baffled by his VP's inability to grasp his meaning.

In contrast, Figure 6-18 shows a very appealing draw-

ing done by two similar, multidominant people able to sense a common design direction. You get the feeling that this house could almost be built.

Amazingly, these communication patterns hold even when there's no theme at all. Figure 6-19 is the product of two people with similar D quadrant preferences who, responding to the assignment "themeless" have drawn an

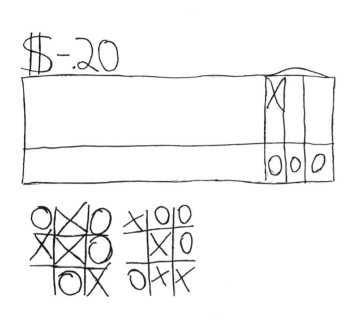

Figure 6-20.   An A Quadrant Approach to "Themeless"

Figure 6-21.   An Artistic Approach to "Themeless"

abstract theme that reflects a common interest in curved shapes and color combinations.

In sharp contrast, figure 6-20 shows an A dominant pair that has responded to themeless by drawing a series of line, letters, and numbers.

The drawing in figure 6-21, done by a homogeneous pair, shows a very abstract scene, revealing strong cerebral

right preferences, and an aesthetic, artistic quality.

I will conclude with one of my favorites, another response to the "themeless" exercise. In figure 6-22, person #1 intended to project the theme of "ship." Unfortunately, person #2 was unable to grasp that direction and saw, instead, "bird." Person #1 persisted, and continued with the ship until the two ended up with a "chicken ship."

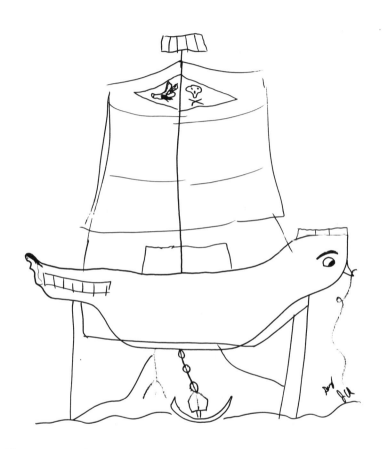

Figure 6-22.   Chicken Ship

Figure 6-23.   Reuben Nakian

Given the power that non-verbal communication carries, it's not surprising to find that sometimes some of us would do better to skip talking altogether. Consider my friend, the late Reuben Nakian. A sculptor of international reputation, with works of art exhibited in museums throughout the world, Reuben died only recently, well into his 80s. A tiny gnome of a man with a shock of white hair, he had an elf-like appearance, and a somewhat wobbly gait that belied his truly prodigious talent. When Reuben was selected by a distinguished panel to receive the 1977 Brandeis medal for lifetime achievement in art, he invited me, along with many other friends from Stamford, to attend the presentation ceremony at the Guggenheim Museum. On our arrival, we found a large stage on which were five seats of honor, plus the podium and seating for the committee members. The ceremony consisted of a brief citation for each recipient, delivered by the chairman, followed by up to five minutes of response by each honoree.

The first person honored was the poet Robert Lowell. After being cited for his distinguished record of achievement, he rose, fished a piece of paper from his inner coat pocket, and recited about 30 seconds of flowing poetry written for the occasion.

The second person cited was a young film director, who, following his introduction, gave a very articulate four-minute overview of a director's wide-ranging work.

The third recipient, an elderly publisher, began to detail the story of his career from the very beginning through letters he had received from the many authors with whom he had been associated. In his need to verbalize his response sequentially and in detail, he lost all track of time and went well beyond the allotted five minutes.

The sculptress Anne Frank was another recipient. She walked halfway to the podium, looked out at the audience, and said in a very emotional voice, "Thank you all so very much for this wonderful day."

And, finally, came the turn of my friend, Reuben. Following his introduction, the old man walked slowly toward the podium, but somehow never got there. Instead, he stopped, peered at the committee, looked out over the audience, then glanced at his honorers. Holding out his hands, he suddenly convulsed his body and face in an expression of wordless acceptance, pleasure, and frustrated helplessness at being unable to find adequate words. He then turned and walked the short distance to his seat amidst thunderous applause.

Think about these responses. Can you assign them to a particular brain quadrant? The more familiar you become with the model, the more visible these verbal and non-verbal behaviors become.

WHAT TICKLES YOUR FUNNY BONE?

For meaningful communication to occur between two people, either both must speak the same mental dialect or one or both must know such dialects exist and be sensitive to them. Not surprisingly, this principle also extends to humor. Generally, what we think is funny correlates with preferences for pairs of quadrants—either left or right or limbic or cerebral. And much of our humor pokes fun at modes that we ourselves don't prefer.

Over the past few years, I have collected cartoons that appeal mainly to one or more quadrants of mental preference. Experiments with several hundred groups have con-

Figure 6-24. Upper Left Cartoon

Figure 6-26. Upper Right Cartoon

Figure 6-25. Lower Left Cartoon

Figure 6-27. Lower Right Cartoon

firmed that people's taste for humor correlates strongly with their brain dominance profile. One person may laugh out loud at one or two cartoons, be mildly amused by a third, and show no response at all to a fourth, while the person next to him may react in exactly the opposite way.

Figure 6-24 shows four classic examples of quadrant-oriented cartoon humor.

EXAMPLES OF COMMUNICATION MISMATCH IN BUSINESS

Communication mismatch can be very costly to a business enterprise, and the cost is usually directly proportional to the executive level at which it occurs. Here are two examples of what I mean.

The Executive and the Speech Writer

When managers are still rising through a company's organizational hierarchy, they tend to write their own speeches. As a result, what they say and how they say it tends to reflect accurately their values, beliefs, assumptions, expectations, biases, prejudices, experiences, and brain dominance preferences. In short, what they communicate is consistent with their personal style and with the way in which they shape their corporate culture.

As they advance to higher echelons, however, time pressures make writing their own speeches increasingly impractical. Enter the executive speech writer—and up go

"Humor provides the therapeutic jolt that shifts things into their proper perspective. You have to be relaxed and have fun to be creative. You can't do it when you're too serious."

Source Unknown

"I quote others only the better to express myself."

Michel de Montaigne

"Men are most active when evading real issues, most powerful when rejecting real values."

Jean Toomer

Figure 6-28. Personal Package

the odds for miscommunication. It's sure, given the nature of their occupations, that a CEO and a speech writer will prefer different brain quadrants and, therefore, think differently. What's wrong with that? Just this: Both people, without fully knowing what's happening, allow the speech writer's thinking to shift the CEO's communication beyond the CEO's thinking and, thus, create inconsistencies between what the CEO communicates and what he's actually willing to introduce into the personal culture he has built up over the years.

This happens most commonly when a CEO becomes enamored of a neat phrase or idea that sounds great, but that is either impractical to implement or simply inappropriate as corporate policy. One of my favorite examples is the phrase "parallel paths of progress," composed by a speech writer for a vice president of engineering of a large American company. The writer believed that the managers and the individual engineers in this vast engineering operation, although they have separate career paths, should have equal career potential—hence, "parallel paths of progress." On seeing the phrase in his speech, the vice president said, "This will really knock 'em dead! I like it!" What he liked was the nice turn of phrase, but the truth was that he never genuinely committed himself to the concept. Thirty years later, the myth persists and thousands of people at that company still complain that there are not now, nor have there ever been, "parallel paths of progress."

The Innovator and the Administrator

Let's listen in on the dialogue between a vice president of advertising and administration of a large corporation and his number one creative person in the advertising department. In terms of dominance profiles, these two men represent a classic mismatch. They have no mental preferences in common, and their primary preferences occur across diagonal opposites. Walter, the VP, strongly prefers the logical, analytical, factual, rational modes, and he wants them exercised in a structured way—planned ahead, organized beautifully, and highly detailed. He plays it safe whenever possible, preferring proven strategies over riskier experimental or less established ideas. He favors fact and form over feeling, and avoids unstructured interpersonal situations. His preferred modes are A and B, and his least preferred are C and D.

By contrast, John, the creative director, shows an extreme preference for risky, innovative, experimental modes. He lives by intuition and also values art and beauty for their own sake. He sees the big picture and tends to let others deal with detail. He strongly favors emotional, interpersonal, musical activities. He avoids structure where possible, preferring to let others supply logical, analytical, quantitative components. His preferred modes are C and particularly D. His least preferred modes are A and B.

The dialogue begins as John walks into the VP's office with a portfolio under his arm and a smile on his face. The VP is sitting behind a large desk, surrounded by imposing office furniture and decorations. John walks about eight feet into the office and stops. Walter, the VP, looks up, sees John, and without changing his expression says, "I wasn't aware that we had an appointment, John—but you look as if you have something you want to say."

John: "Yes, I do. I need to tell you about some new developments on our campaign for this year's new product line. As you know we've made

"You have a shilling. I have a shilling. We swap. You have my shilling and I have yours. We are no better off. But suppose you have an idea and I have an idea. We swap. We have increased our stock of ideas 100 percent."
A. S. Gregg

"Unless you know what it is, I ain't never going to be able to explain it to you."
Louis Armstrong

"In human relations a little language goes further than a little of almost anything else. Whereas one language now often makes a wall, two can make a gate."
Walter V. Kaulfers

Figure 6-29. John and Walter

such a departure in the new designs that we've been struggling with ways of presenting these ideas in this year's Fall Campaign.

Walter: "OK, John, but keep it short. I've got to prepare for an important meeting upstairs."

John: "Well, Walter, I think I had a breakthrough this morning, just after waking up. As I was lying there slowly coming awake, it suddenly dawned on me that our previous approaches to this campaign missed the main concept of the new line. As I lay there mulling over that thought, I began to see..."

Walter: "What is the point, John? I'm on a schedule here. Don't take me through your whole 'Good Morning America' sequence."

John: "Well, Walter, it was important to me to tell you where the idea came from and how it evolved."

Walter: "John, you know me well enough to know that all I'm interested in is the end result—the bottom line—not all the hokey stuff that leads up to it."

John: "Yes, I do know that and I don't want to take time away from your important work, but it just seemed to me that this was a crucial campaign, and it needs not only your approval but also your support in making it happen."

Walter: "John, get on with it."

John: "Well, the central concept is that instead of featuring individual elements of the product line, what I think we ought to do, and what came to me in my visualization, is a large format piece showing the whole product line, with visuals showing how each separate product is related to each of the products in the line."

Walter: "OK, that seems obvious, so what's the big deal?"

John: "Well, the vision I had of our marketing strategy is oriented to the whole system rather than the product pieces and that's why the campaign needs to be expanded to a global approach rather than focused on the parts."

Walter: "Well, John, we've done pretty damn well around here talking about the parts! I don't see why we should risk a new approach when we've done so well with the kind of campaign we've had for the past few years. And anyway, are our competitors talking about the whole system? Hell, no! Before we go sailing off into the blue, I'm going to need some hard facts that support such a costly shift in our normal approach."

John: "Well, Walt, I really haven't gotten to the issue of cost yet, but it seems to me we have a good chance of bringing this thing in at the same cost and with a greater impact."

Walter: "John, I've told you time and again in previous discussions that there are certain ground rules in bringing things to my attention. The first of these is that you have a complete presentation, starting with the cost of the project and the breakdown of the critical elements of it. Second, that you have a schedule showing the beginning, the middle, and the end of the project. Third, that you have sufficient copies of these support materials available so that I can send them to other members of the staff to check out, and fourth, that you make an appointment in advance."

John: "Walt, I'm aware of these ground rules, but I felt that since my idea was so hot I would make some quick sketches and some preliminary layouts to show you while the idea was still fresh, so that we could take advantage of the possible time saved by making a quick decision to go in this direction. Take a look at these layout sketches..."

Walter: "Dammit, John, you know I can't do that. We've got to take these things up in an orderly way and deal with them in a way that factors in the costs and the time to accomplish the task. Now when you're ready to present your advertising campaign proposals to me on those terms, I'll gladly give you more time. Until then, I'm not available on this subject. So get cracking!"

See if you can experience what it's like to be each of these two men. Reread the dialogue twice, asking yourself these questions: What is valid here? How do I trip myself up in the same ways? When is this kind of behavior appropriate? The answers may be extremely important to you and to those with whom you live and/or work.

What these and hundreds of other examples prove is that mental differences not only exist, they stand between us in powerful, sometimes funny and sometimes heartbreaking ways as the story of Weird John, in chapter 4, illustrated. Our ignorance brings us up short again and again. We're sure we've been clear—so sure that when others don't get it, we even suspect they're being deliberately obtuse.

What's the answer? First, we need to learn more about our own mental preferences and the dialects that we use because of those preferences. Second, we need to learn more about how others' preferences and dialects differ from our own so that when we need to communicate across the boundaries between brain dominance quadrants, we have a better chance at both sending and receiving the message correctly. This applies to all our interactions in all our relationships: in business, between co-workers, managers, subordinates; and at home, between spouses, parents, children, and friends.

Finally, we need to develop greater respect for one another's differences and appreciate the powerful contributions that we can offer one another because of those very differences.

Developing that respect becomes a lot easier as we move fully into creative functioning, which is what our final chapters are about.

"Jazz piano lessons: Step-by-step approach to improvisation."
Alex Damien

"There are those who take their body for granted. I do not; mind and body are like Serbs and Croatians, unhappy members of a single state."
Pat Goodheart

"We must learn to live together as brothers or perish together as fools."
Martin Luther King, Jr.

III.
The Creative Life
and How to Enhance It

7

ZIGZAG LIGHTNING: CREATIVITY AND THE WHOLE BRAIN

Prevailing mythology has it that creativity is the exclusive domain of artists, scientists, and inventors—a giftedness not available to ordinary people going about the business of daily life. Partly as a result, *ordinary* people often hold the *creative* person in awe, finding little gradation in genius. It's either the Sistine Chapel ceiling or nothing.

CREATIVE? WHO, ME?

Our awe of creativity is like a dragon that blocks the gate to our personal creativity, and that we must slay before we can enter our own creative realm. For many of us, the dragon is a balloon, one of our own making, like a fugitive from the Macy's Thanksgiving Day parade. It is a fear inflated by our minds into a monster before which we shrink, trembling. We've created this dragon to protect ourselves from something worse: the possibility that we might really go for it, do the very utmost we can do—and find people out there who still don't think it's good enough and reject not only what we've done, but *us* as individuals.

What we need to understand is that by refusing to risk being creative at less than genius levels, we are already rejecting ourselves, passing judgment without evidence. While that judgment mechanism may have served to protect us from censure as children, we as adults no longer need to feel as vulnerable as we did when we were young. What we need to do instead is assume full responsibility ourselves: for encouraging our own inner child, for applauding our courage to try something, for praising our own spontaneity, for admiring our own willingness to start again when something comes out differently from the way we expect, and for delighting in our small and humble expressions of creativity, of which there are many every day.

In fact, most individual creativity is pretty humble—no Sistine Chapel ceiling, no Beethoven's Ninth Symphony, no Thomas Edison invention, just a solution to such a mundane problem as getting the microwave merry-go-round to work by turning it over and using it upside down, or finding a new way home, or writing a silly verse to a friend, or arranging and decorating a living room. One man got a faulty thermometer to shake down by attaching it to the blades of a fan and running it for a minute; he thinks that's "just technical," but it's fully creative. It's creative to design a house, develop a new business, paint a picture, lay out a garden, solve a new problem, fix a way to feed the cat when you're away for three days. All of these are valid examples of creative behaviors, because the doing of them includes an element of newness, novelty, and difference.

Figure 7-1. **Having Our Creativity Blocked by Our Self-Inflated Dragon**

Figure 7-2. Applied Creative Idea

Exposing Myths about Creativity

If we understand creativity in this sense, three things are clear:

1. All human beings are capable of being creative—it is part of our birthright.

2. It is not necessary to be a genius to be creative.

3. No matter how severely our creativity may have been repressed in the past, it can be reaccessed, stimulated, and developed through life experiences and specialized programs.

I would expect that less than 1 percent of the total population could rank in the genius category, yet of the thousands of people I've worked with (who by and large didn't consider themselves creative), a good 70 to 80 percent have been able to demonstrate to their own satisfaction that: (1) they do have creative abilities, and (2) exercising those abilities can bring them a great deal of joy and profit.

This good news isn't only for the creatively uninformed or uninitiated. The same techniques that can open the creative world to a novice can set off a creative explosion in the adept. One GE inventor—with 34 patents to his credit—took our ACT I Workshop and said, "If I had known all this 25 years ago, I would now have a hundred patents!"

Obtaining Keys to Your Creativity

What made the difference for this inventor and for thousands of others who've moved into creative functioning? The keys are these:

1.   An understanding of the creative process and its component stages, and how the four modes of knowing come into play at each stage

2.   An understanding of what hinders each mode at each stage

3.   A commitment to heightening one's own creative awareness and functioning

This chapter, the first of four devoted to helping people who want to heighten their creativity, elaborates on each of these areas of understanding.

WHAT IS CREATIVITY, ANYWAY?

I resist defining creativity: Each person's experience of it is so unique and individual that no one can formulate a definition that fits everyone else. However, you need to know what I'm talking about, so in this section I will be defining the word. Add to this extended definition in any way that works for you.

Many people think of creativity purely in terms of inventiveness, and that is surely part of it. "Hot" ideas are great and we revel in them when they hit. But if the process stops there, the "flash" evaporates. The world goes on, unchanged. The idea is usually lost. What's more—and this is the point—ideas in and of themselves, if they begin and end in our heads, produce neither growth nor full satisfaction because there's no basis for feedback to encourage more ideas. The reinforcement loop doesn't close.

"Also, creativity can be learned. Once you have become convinced and aware that you can bring new things into being, then it is simply a matter of choosing a particular way to create."
                                         unknown

"Creativity is so delicate a flower that praise tends to make it bloom, while discouragement often nips it in the bud. Any of us will put out more and better ideas if our efforts are appreciated."
                                         unknown

"Discipline and focused awareness contribute to the act of creation."
                                         John Poppy

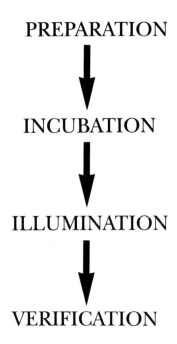

PREPARATION

INCUBATION

ILLUMINATION

VERIFICATION

Figure 7-3. Wallas's Four Stage Creative Process

My own thinking, is that *creativity in its fullest sense involves both generating an idea and manifesting it—making something happen as a result.* To strengthen creative ability, you need to apply the idea in some form that enables both the experience itself and your own reaction and others' to reinforce your performance. As you and others applaud your creative endeavors, you are likely to become more creative.

Defining creativity to include application throws the whole subject into a different light, because:

1. While *ideas* can come in seconds, *application* can take days, years, or even a lifetime to realize.

2. While *ideas* can come out of only one quadrant, *application* ultimately calls on specialized mental capabilities in all four quadrants of the brain.

3. While *ideas* can arrive in a single flash, *application* necessarily involves a process consisting of several distinct phases.

Defining creativity to include application also makes creativity totally applicable in the world of business, where it tends to go under the label of *problem-solving.*

THE SOURCE AND PROCESS OF CREATIVITY

Creativity's source is the brain—not just one part of the brain, but all of it.* Today, this theme song is well established and accepted, but when I first proclaimed it in 1975, it was a new idea and some of my associates in the training

*I'm speaking physiologically here, *not* philosophically or spiritually.

field thought I was nuts. Why? Because none of the well-known literature on creativity mentioned the brain once! It simply wasn't part of the prevailing frame of reference regarding creativity. I made the connection when others hadn't simply because: (1) I had specifically been asking about where creativity comes from at the moment of stumbling across the split-brain research, and (2) my awareness of duality had been strong since childhood. Others, whose frame of reference and background differed from mine, simply couldn't relate to what I was saying.

Knowing that creativity arises in the brain makes an enormous contribution to our ability to access, stimulate, develop, and apply the process, because it tells us: (1) what process we need to follow, and (2) how that process calls on the brain's specialized capabilities at each stage.

Researcher Graham Wallas, many years ago, set down a description of what happens as people approach problems with the objective of coming up with creative solutions. He described his four-stage process as follows:

1. In the *preparation* stage, we define the problem, need, or desire, gather any information the solution or response needs to account for, and set up criteria for verifying the solution's acceptability.

2. In the *incubation* stage, we step back from the problem and let our minds contemplate and work it through. Like preparation, incubation can last minutes, weeks, even years.

3. In the *illumination* stage, ideas arise from the mind to provide the basis of a creative response. These ideas can be pieces of the whole or the whole

"Our creativity is limited only by our beliefs."

Willis Harmon

"Once we are destined to live out our lives in the prison of our mind, our one duty is to furnish it well."

Peter Ustinov

"The weakest among us has a gift; however seemingly trivial, which is peculiar to him and which worthily used will be a gift also to his race."

Ruskin

Figure 7-4. The Making of the Pat Sculpture at Various Stages

itself, i.e., seeing the entire concept or entity all at once. Unlike the other stages, illumination is often very brief, involving a tremendous rush of insights within a few minutes or hours.

4. In *verification*, the final stage, one carries out activities to demonstrate whether or not what emerged in illumination satisfies the need and the criteria defined in the preparation stage.

This four-stage description has helped me define what happens in my own creative endeavors. Consider, for example, my approach to creating a sculpture of my daughter, Pat.

Pat: A Whole-Brain Sculpture

One of my goals was to complete sculptural portraits of my wife and daughters. The sculptures of Ann and Laura were complete and the one of my wife, Margy, nearly so when I decided to do one of my oldest daughter, Pat, next. In both painting and sculpting, it is my general practice to commit to the next project just before or immediately upon completing the current project. This allows me to incubate on a new project while going about other business.

In contemplating how to approach *Pat*, I visualized the completed head. As I did so, images came to me of the process of working the clay, creating the mold, casting the piece, and finally finishing it for display. I used the 45-minute commute from Stamford to New York City to incubate the idea.

Illumination came after several weeks of periodic contemplation, when an exciting new concept of the sculpture of Pat exploded in my mind. *Pat* would be more than a sculpture, per se, it would be a *sculptural event*. It would include a multimedia presentation showing photographs

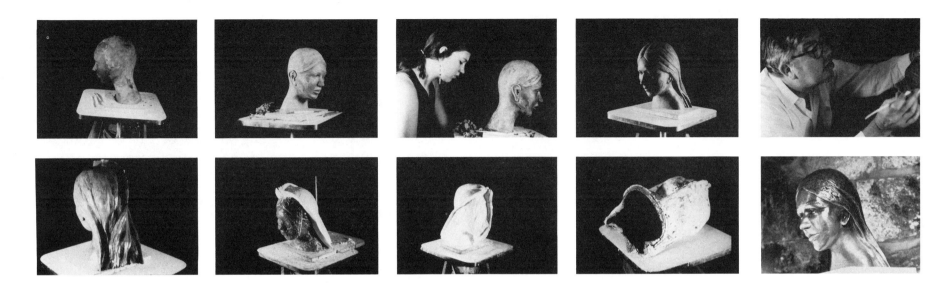

of the evolution of the sculpture from the bare armature, through the clay original, on to the creation of the mold, and then through the casting process, to the finished cold cast bronze. These photographs would be shown on a screen accompanied by music Pat and I would choose for each stage in the sculpting process and they would reflect Pat's frame of mind and view of life at that particular time. The show would conclude with an unveiling of the finished sculpture.

I will never forget my ecstasy when that whole idea presented itself. *I had to tell somebody about it to help fix it in my mind.* I happened to be sitting next to a casual acquaintance as the commuter train approached New York, and I interrupted his reading of the paper to tell him about my wonderful idea. Although somewhat puzzled, he reacted favorably. Some months later, the project was successfully completed and has since been presented dozens of times as a multimedia art exhibit.

Because of its complexity, the sculpture of Pat exemplifies well both the four-stage creative process and the functioning of the various quadrants throughout that process. Let me walk you through it.

To begin with, the integrated concept of the sculptured event itself was a clear D quadrant holistic idea. Then handling the multimedia aspects of the project required the specialized capabilities of both A and B quadrants. Before the clay was even touched, there had to be a very detailed, sequential plan for staging and capturing the evolving sculpture on film. Soon, my small and already cluttered studio had crowded into it a complex array of photographic equipment and stereophonic tape decks and speakers. One camera was mounted on a tripod so that, with a remote trigger system, it could capture the emerging portrait as it evolved. On either side of the camera were the stereo speakers for the music that Pat and I had selected in advance and that would be played during the sculpting

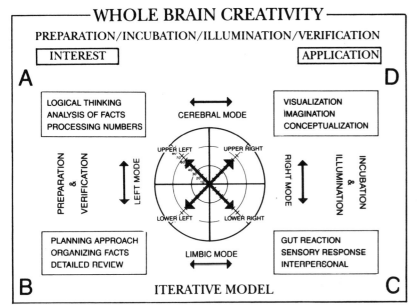

Figure 7-5. Whole-Brain Creativity Model

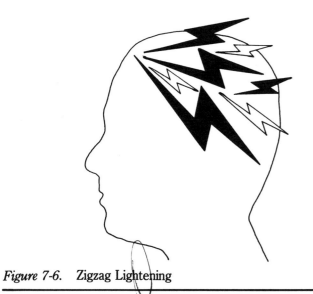

Figure 7-6. Zigzag Lightening

process. This music would be matched later with the photographs taken at the time. Getting all this to work on cue presented a number of technical problems, all of which had to be solved in advance of starting work with the clay. While working out these details, I had to go back and forth between the purely artistic aspects of the sculpture, and the technical and planning aspects of carrying out the photographic recording of the artistic process.

The C quadrant was also vital to this project. The sculpture of Pat offered an opportunity for me to become closer to my daughter. This was both a requirement and an opportunity. Capturing my daughter in a three-dimensional portrait required more than simply seeing her, it also required my sensing her inner, less visible self. If I lost touch with who she was, the project would fail, and a precious opportunity for intimacy would pass me by. We initiated the deeper converting process through our doing a photographic study of her; this also gave us time to discuss what music to use in the final presentation as well as in the sculpture process itself. All of these things required my accessing and using the C quadrant of my brain throughout the entire project.

Once modeling began, the D quadrant was required for sculpting, and A and B were required to deal with the enormous problems that arose, especially with the molding and casting process. These involved technical solutions that drew on my knowledge of chemistry and physics.

Putting the final multimedia presentation together involved selecting and sequencing about 100 slides from the many hundreds of photographs taken during the process and synchronizing them with the music Pat and I had pre-selected. This was an interactive, whole-brain process calling for emotional sensitivity, attention to sequence, conceptual consistency, appreciation for the flow of ideas, and awareness of the coloration provided by the music.

The final result created a wonderfully encouraging feedback/reinforcement loop. Professionally, *Pat* was very well received, winning three Blue Ribbons and one Best in Show in juried exhibitions as a straight sculpture. Even more important to me, audiences have been genuinely moved when viewing *Pat* as a multimedia event, which tells me that the presentation truly captured the experience my daughter and I shared.

To sum up, I made use of all four quadrants of the metaphoric brain model in the process of carrying out this complex creative act, not all simultaneously or in fixed sequence, but iteratively and repeatedly as the situation demanded. Artistry, vision, spatial capability, and holistic conceptualizing were contributed by the D quadrant. Sensitivity to my daughter, the incorporation of the music, and the moment-to-moment interpersonal exchange required to pose Pat successfully during the extended sitting process made full use of the C quadrant. The planning, sequencing, organizing, and structuring of materials and processes required to document and capture the sculpting process took advantage of all the B quadrant thinking modes. And finally, my A quadrant qualities provided the logic and analysis required to convert the holistic idea into a practical, doable project as well as the knowledge of chemistry and physics needed to solve the technical problems that arose throughout the project.

One could accurately describe this project as both left-brain (A and B) and right-brain (C and D), and also as both cerebral (upper quadrants A and D), and limbic (lower quadrants B and C). It is a good example of a whole-brain creative activity.

The Quadrants and Zigzag Lightning

This project clearly illustrates the basic relationships between the four phases of Graham Wallas's creative process and the use of the four brain quadrants. In addition, I've found it necessary to enclose Wallas's process between two other key brain-related stages—interest and application. The resulting dynamics are as follows:

1. *Interest* is general, probably distributed across all four quadrants.

2. *Preparation*, on the other hand, calls primarily on the A and B quadrants because it consists of gathering facts, organizing, and developing a plan of action.

3. *Incubation* occurs in the right modes C and D, and involves contemplation, subconscious processing, reflection, mulling, visualization, and sensory perception.

4. *Illumination* is also a right-mode activity, particularly associated with the D quadrant. It is in this stage that the idea is formulated non-verbally, and sometimes comes in the form of an Aha! moment.

5. *Verification* begins with the left-mode activity of recording or capturing the idea, and then checking it out to see if it resolves the original problem. This calls for engagement of the left-mode quadrants, A and B.

6. *Application*, the final stage, is usually distributed among all four quadrants, but typically starts in B and then subsequently involves A, C, and D.

Inclusion of *interest* and *application* to begin and end the creative process recognizes the need for mental motivation to start the preparation phase, and the need for mental satisfaction to complete the process with an action-oriented ending.

While this six-stage process sounds very orderly—and even is, occasionally—in practice, a person moves back and forth between the steps, sometimes recycles the whole process at various points, and may do some parts very quickly and others over a period of years. The person may even, in the process of responding to one creative challenge, include other tasks whose accomplishment then contributes new perspectives, awareness, and approaches to meeting the original challenge. This expanded version of what has been referred to as iteration has been called "zigzag lightning in the brain," a phrase first used to describe the highly versatile mentality of Winston Churchill. On any given weekend, Churchill might: work on a speech for Parliament, paint a picture, walk in the garden with his grandchild, plan a military campaign, write on the history of Western Civilization, engage in spirited conversation, contemplate a major political strategy, or carefully plan a detailed sequential operational plan. So zigzagging can be understood as representing rapid movement back and forth between highly diverse activities, each one of which requires a particular mix of specialized mental processes, and all of which, when put together, feed the creative mechanism.

As uneven as the process may be in real life, most people, nevertheless, relate easily to the six-stage overall process because it describes creative events they have experienced in their own lives.

Even more exciting, they can use the description to help diagnose the causes of creative difficulties when they encounter them.

WHAT HINDERS THE CREATIVE PROCESS

The creative process is a very delicate one, especially in its early phases, and it's important that the correct quadrant be activated during each phase. That doesn't always happen.

Excessive dominance in any one of the four quadrants can upset the inherent balance that makes whole-brain applied creativity so powerful. For example, we've seen that in the preparation and verification phases, the A and B quadrants should be accessed—gathering information, defining objectives, measuring results, etc. But strong dominance in either C or D can complicate the creative process by increasing the likelihood the person will: (1) get bored with detailed research and leap to a solution without doing the necessary preparation; (2) stick exclusively to intuition rather than check facts and follow them to logical conclusions; (3) fail to capture a good idea and follow it up; and/or (4) proceed to costly commitment to application without first verifying that the idea addresses the problem at hand.

An even more common impediment is the inhibiting effect of one of the left quadrants (A or B) on the development of ideas. The influence of A, when excessive, may lead one to discount the power of appeal to human values, or the realities of implementing something in a world where one must use mere mortals to get anything done. People whose B quadrant dominates strongly experience the most difficulty, for it is in B quadrant that we judge and criticize ourselves most severely. Preferences in the B modes are so powerful that they can shut down the open, free-flowing processes of the D quadrant entirely.

As disruptive as single quadrant dominance can be on creativity, it isn't nearly as unbalancing as the influence of double dominance in pairs of adjacent quadrants—double dominant left (A-B), double dominant right (C-D), double dominant cerebral (A-D), or double dominant limbic (B-C). The pairing of strongly related modes can completely cut off avenues to the essential contributions needed from the other two contrasting modes and severely reduce the level of iteration needed for synergistic functioning.

In Business and Government Organizations

Nowhere, in my opinion, do the inhibiting effects of A and B modes manifest themselves more clearly than in business settings. Not only the solutions that creative work produces, but also the very process itself is suffocated by exaggerated A and B attitudes. Two examples: First, in most business contexts, the creative process is labeled problem-solving. This, in and of itself, means something has to be judged as a problem—something negative—in order to evoke a creative response. People forget that defining and meeting a need may have more to do with seeing an

"Fear of failure is the most devastating block to creativity."
Unknown

"As is true of any other area, idea production can be implemented by certain techniques—especially by deferment of judgment during ideative effort."
Alex Osborn

"It hinders the creative work of the mind if the intellect examines too closely the ideas as they pour in."
Friedrich von Schiller

"Creativity involves breaking out of established patterns in order to look at things in a different way."
Edward de Bono

opportunity—a plus—than with defining a problem, a negative.

I have taken a positive step towards bridging this gap by developing a business-oriented workshop called "Creative Problem Solving." More information about that can be found in Chapter 9.

Second, most people think of problem-solving as strictly a left-brain process—orderly and straightforward, a step-by-step analysis and application of logic. That view of the process eliminates a wide array of enormously effective C and D mode techniques and activities, such as modeling, simulating, doodling, intuiting, thinking metaphorically, and synthesizing (combining things to create something new whose worth far surpasses the total of what each idea could be worth separately). These C and D techniques produce the visions that power truly innovative contributions.

You'd think that given the enormous power of these C and D mode activities we'd assign them greater value. Why don't we? Why not? In large part, we're just doing what we've been taught to do in school.

In Schools

Part of the reason is that so much of our educational system is directed toward teaching A and B mode activities — the preferred mode of most school superintendents, principals, and administrators. But there's a more fundamental cause for our lopsided education, and that has to do with the brain itself. In her book, *Drawing on the Right Side of the Brain*, Betty Edwards cites the crisis in art education that seems to occur in most of us around the age of ten. Most of us draw before beginning school, but by

age ten, we no longer can. Our native talents have been overpowered by language-based logic. The language center, situated in the left hemisphere, tends to involve and then overwhelm the other talents. The earlier we teach what language gives rise to (grammar, vocabulary, spelling, and composition), the earlier and more completely the left hemisphere begins to dominate the right.

Isn't the honoring of all of our non-verbal, intuitive modes as important in human development as our concentration on the verbal and rational? Life in reality is a balance between these differing, but potentially synergistic modes.

Isn't the attainment of visual literacy of equal value in our education? Visual literacy enables us to understand what we see, as contrasted with the words we read or the numbers we manipulate.

Even if we were to turn our educational system around today, there would still be millions of adults for whom other solutions would be necessary. School's already out. Fortunately, remedies exist to correct an excessive left-mode bias, and that's what we turn to next.

In this chapter, thus far we've seen that: (1) the creative process includes application; (2) all four quadrants need to be used in a certain way for that process to work; and (3) if the quadrants are activated in the wrong phase, creativity can come to a screeching halt.

We turn now to examine ways to reclaim and enhance our creative gifts—to correct some of the biases acquired in our educational and work lives.

To introduce this topic, I want to lead you on what may seem a roundabout path, but is actually a direct route. We're going to look at what people who are already creative are doing right.

WHAT CREATIVE PEOPLE DO RIGHT: CREATIVITY IN THE ARTS AND SCIENCES

People often ask if the creativity inherent in art differs from the creativity inherent in science. My response is that the essential processes are almost identical, but they differ in how people see them and what they emphasize.

What links the two types of creativity? (1) They both use the same mental processes; (2) they are both iterative; (3) they are both situational; and (4) the results of both can be enhanced by a better understanding of those processes and by finding ways of achieving greater access to them.

The two processes differ in that each emphasizes a different end of the creative continuum. The artistic creative process is relatively more right-mode oriented, that is, non-verbal, visual, imaginative, conceptual, and aesthetic. Scientific creativity, on the other hand, focuses relatively more on logic, factual knowledge, and technology — left-mode concerns. These emphases are natural reflections of artists' preferences for right modes, C and D, and scientists' preferences for the left, A and B. Not surprisingly, people perceive them accordingly: Artistic creativity is perceived as aesthetic and amorphous, while scientific creativity is perceived as more defined, focused, and deliberate.

But here's the gold: What becomes clear when one studies the lives and writings of scientific and artistic geniuses is that what made many of them extraordinary

"The arrogance of logic obstructs the use of new ideas."
Unknown

"Imagination must submit its work to the scrutiny of the critical faculties."
Morris I. Stein

"Stand firm in your refusal to remain conscious during algebra. In real life, I assure you, there is no such thing as algebra."
Fran Lebowitz

"I shut my eyes in order to see."
Paul Gamarin

Figure 7-7.   Einstein Rides A Rainbow

was their use and trust of modes that are non-dominant in their particular fields.

The most vivid example of this is the multiple dominant scientific and artistic giant, Leonardo da Vinci. Set his dozen major art works side by side with his dozen major scientific designs and you would be hard pressed to decide which were the greater. Leonardo's artistic genius was matched and enhanced by his genius for scientific understanding and invention. Each was the beneficiary of mental processes emphasized in the other. His artistic vision posed challenges of how to depict a person. His eye for structure and mechanics led him to study anatomy through dissecting corpses and building skeletons; then he expressed his new understanding through drawing body parts and painting wonderful pictures.

It is well documented that Albert Einstein dreamed of himself riding on a beam of light as a prelude to conceiving the theory of relativity. Einstein considered his gift for fantasy much more important to his thinking repertoire than the more rational and organized modes of thought. He felt that he really had only two "big" ideas in his entire life, and that he had spent many years either preparing for them or confirming their validity. For him, the acquisition of knowledge, facts, data, and statistics were simply preparation for the intuitive process from which his epochal ideas emerged.

August Kekulé is widely described as having conceived of the benzene ring through a dream about a snake grabbing its own tail in its mouth. This powerful metaphor provided him with the basis for solving the riddle that he had been struggling with—the molecular structure of benzene. Of all subjects, chemistry is among the most strongly dominated by A quadrant mental modes and activities.

Yet here was an individual who, while he nurtured and exercised his A quadrant mental process, also took advantage of and trusted his D quadrant visual, intuitive, and dream-processing modes.

Both Kekulé and Einstein had enormous iterative capabilities. Being double dominant (at least in A and D), they could go back and forth between these two specialized modes through the corpus callosum and thus bring together two different mental processes into a synergistic whole.

The synergistic breakthrough—the dream or fantasy that illumination usually consists of—is rarely planned or scheduled. Neither Einstein nor Kekulé set up their fantasies; they simply experienced them and took action as a result. The connection occurred in the subconscious and manifested itself through a mental process that "speaks" metaphorically in fantasy or dreams. That dreaming or fantasizing occurs naturally and spontaneously in ways we don't understand. This isn't to say that individuals can't fantasize or dream deliberately, because they can. Many of us routinely focus on a problem or issue before going to sleep, with the objective of dreaming a solution to it and then capturing it upon awakening. But for most of us, most of the time, illumination isn't a planned event—it just happens. We can help it happen more often by learning to tap our dreams and fantasies, and by having a capture system ready to record the resulting ideas.

In terms of creative expression, the world, in my opinion, consists of: (1) the *already creatives*—people who actively exercise their creative gifts for pleasure and profit; (2) the *sometimes creatives*—people who experience moments of creative brilliance, but only occasionally; and (3) those who can be creative, but who have yet to tap into

that potential.

In the first group are thousands of creative people who have never considered the importance of the brain and their own creative process and who are functioning successfully in very high-powered, highly productive ways: art directors, designers, advertising executives, producers, editors, writers, musicians, artists, inventors—the list goes on and on. In every case their profiles correlate strongly with the norm for creative occupations. These profiles are frequently skewed toward the D quadrant, which is not surprising, since most already creatives are idea persons. In my experience, professional creative people are largely unaware of what goes on inside them during the creative process. Nor do they know why they are better at one aspect of the creative process than at another. When these people see their profiles, however, they instantly understand such things. They see, for example, that to successfully bring a creative project to completion, they may have to seek outside help because certain aspects of the creative process fall outside of their areas of preference.

Those already creatives who are most successful within organizations are the ones who make effective use of other resources therein: sales support, marketing, business administration, finance, personnel, and technical resources. By contrast, creative people who have to function independently need to provide those services for themselves. Not surprisingly, such people tend to show quite a balanced profile: Their primary preference for D quadrant is supported by strong secondary preferences in other quadrants, enabling them to function situationally to complete the creative task. Moreover, strengthening these supporting capabilities often enhances their original preference.

The already creatives who have attended workshops

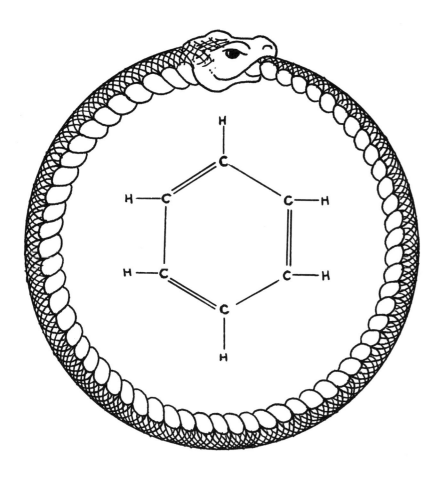

Figure 7-8.   Kekule's Snake Dream Led to His Development of the Benzene Ring Formula

like ACT I and CPS universally report that their creative potential has been significantly enlarged, and that they feel capable of performing even more challenging, creative work.

In the second category, *sometimes creatives*, we find individuals who report moments of creative expression, including inventing something, painting a picture, or writing a piece of poetry, but for whom such moments are rare. This demonstrates again the situational capabilities of the specialized brain. While these individuals don't have their primary preferences for such imaginative functioning, their strong secondaries allow them to access and use such capabilities when stimulated to do so: when a project urgently requires an original solution to a technical problem; when they yearn to capture a beautiful scene while on vacation, or translate feelings of love into poetic form.

The third category of people includes those who may or may not function creatively, but in any case, just don't know it. These are people who have mis-defined creativity, or who, for one reason or another, have yet to explore their latent potential.

It's clear, then, that in both artistic and scientific fields, creativity makes use of all types of thinking. In fact, *creativity is activated more by multiple intelligences than by high IQ*, and many of these intelligences are non-intellectual— hunches, intuition, feelings, and kinesthetic, sensory, visceral modes of mental activity. Creativity benefits from the involvement of all of our mental quadrants: left and right brain, cerebral and limbic, taken singly or in combination.

We all have multiple intelligences, even if we aren't geniuses, so can't we all be more creative (even if we are already creative)? And if we can, how do we begin manifesting and enjoying additional creativity today?

KEY TO CREATIVE LIVING: RECLAIMING OUR PASSION

A major key—perhaps the key—to living creatively is passion. By passion I mean a highly compelling, energetic attention to something. Turned-on people of all kinds are passionate. So are people who've just fallen in love. So are collectors, sports nuts, horse-crazy kids, boys who've just discovered baseball cards or video games, computer hackers.

Little children are passionate about almost everything they see. In fact, they are passionate about seeing itself, and feeling, and smelling, and hearing, and tasting, too. Their passion embraces life itself with all its experiences. Even timid children, once they've been reassured, have enormous enthusiasm. They reach out for everything they can—spiders, flowers, butterflies, blocks, hands, eyes, cats, food, wind, water, worms, you, music—everything. They are natural experimenters, dedicated explorers, fascinated examiners of you-name-it. As time goes on, they begin to make connections between things: One child, seeing oil in a puddle of water, exclaimed, "Oh look! A dead rainbow!" So extraordinary and novel are their perceptions that Art Linkletter made his reputation by interviewing children. Apart from committing the indiscretions that horrified their parents and delighted the audience, they resensitized us repeatedly to the wonder of the world around us.

The natural passion for life in all its unexpectedness

"Play teaches children to master the world."
Jean Piaget

"When the artist is alive in any person, whatever his kind of work may be, he becomes an inventive, searching, daring, self-expressive creature. He becomes interesting to other people. He disturbs, upsets, enlightens, and opens ways for a better understanding. Where those who are not artists are trying to close the book, he opens it and shows there are still more pages possible."
Robert Henri

"The idea is there, locked inside. All you have to do is remove the excess stone."
Michelangelo

Figure 7-9.

that characterizes children also features strongly in the personalities of people who have chosen to retain or reclaim their own creativity. They are constantly exercising their curiosity, trying new things, and delighting in the experiment for its own sake — even if the results themselves don't please. They are open to the moment for whatever it may bring. They approach life with expectancy, enthusiasm, and energy.

How do we reclaim our passion if it has been allowed to dim in our lives? What if we are one of those many people whose zest for life has grown faint or even faded. If we despair of having an original thought all our own? One way—an important way—is to increase the amount of genuine pleasure we allow into our lives. There are many things that make life more pleasurable—listening to good music, exercising, eating what nourishes your body— but I want to concentrate in this section on four things:

1. We can learn—or re-learn—from children.

2. We can affirm ourselves and others, and accept affirmation.

3. We can take stock of our lives—ask if the way we are living truly satisfies us, and if not, what must be changed so it does.

4. We can provide ourselves with proof that reclaiming our passion is worthwhile and possible.

Children Are Our Best Teachers

Children have a lot of special talents to offer. Their pursuit of novelty and wonder is both a cause and an effect

— a gift of the life fully lived and one of the things that makes life worth living. Anyone who knows children can tell you that they do the following:

Children follow their interests. If a kid is bored, you know it. None of this polite interest stuff the rest of us get stuck in. What they like, they do, and this teaches them that following what they like makes them happy—so they do it some more.

Children seek out and risk experimenting with new things. If kids are confronted with something unfamiliar, they will take a chance and try it out. They prod and poke it, smell it, look at it from all angles, try using it in different ways, look to see what you think about it — maybe even give it to you to see what you do with it. We adults, by contrast, slap a label on it, say, "I know what that is," and dismiss it. What we're really saying is, "I know what I already know about that, and there's nothing more worth knowing," which is almost never true of anything or anyone.

Children pay attention to their own rhythms. We grownups tend to drive ourselves until something's done, or until a certain hour strikes, but children do things when they feel like it. Naturally, since someone else tends to their necessities, they may have more time and freedom to do that, but we would do well to follow their lead where we have the choice. When we work during our most productive times and rest during our other times, we make the most of our energies. That means if we do our best work between 4 P.M. 2 A.M., then we should strive to arrange our day to make use of those hours. We become more trustworthy to ourselves and others.

Children honor dreams and daydreams. Children pay attention to, talk about, and follow up on their dreams and

"If children developed as they were intended from birth, they would all be pure geniuses."
Johann Wolfgang Goethe

"It takes a long time to grow young."
Picasso

"Creative thinkers make many false starts, and continually waver between unmanageable fantasies and systematic attack."
Harry Hepner

"By the time the child can draw more than a scribble, by age three or four years, an already well-formed body of conceptual knowledge formulated language dominates his memory and controls his graphic work. Drawings are graphic accounts of essentially verbal processes. As an essentially verbal education gains control, the child abandons his graphic efforts and relies almost entirely on words. Language has first spoiled drawing and then swallowed it up completely."
Psychologist, Karl Buhler

Figure 7-10.   Removing the Barriers to Creativity by Slaying Our Mental Dragon

fantasies. They may draw pictures they saw in their dreams, conduct conversations with dream characters, and try to recreate something experienced in dreams and day dreams. These are all creative acts. Moreover, they are important: Mankind has learned that dreams are a language the subconscious uses to communicate to the conscious. Many people say they don't remember their dreams, but I know of no serious effort to connect with one's dream life that hasn't succeeded. Those who succeed often report an experience of waking and sleeping that is like living two lives, each one feeding and nourishing the other.

Children consider mistakes as information, rather than as something unsuccessful. "That's a way it doesn't work. I wonder how else it doesn't work?" For children, the process of figuring something out is in itself a win. We, however, are hung up on outcomes, so we lay judgments on our mistakes—"We did it wrong" and what is worse, we take it further—therefore "People won't love us," "We're never good enough," and "We'll be all alone." No wonder mistakes frighten some of us so deeply. Patterns like that aren't learned overnight, and changing them may take more than a few tries, but they can be changed.

Children play. Kids make a game out of everything. Their essential business is play, so to speak. They delight in spoofing each other, parents, and personalities. They love to mimic, pretend, wrestle, hide and seek, surprise, play practical jokes. They love to laugh, tell secrets, devise stories of goblins and fairies and giants and monsters and heroes. They're not hung up on accuracy. When in doubt, they know they can always make it up. Many adults, however, have withdrawn permission from themselves to be silly, to expose the part of themselves that feels young.

We've become overly concerned with violating cultural or institutional norms — of appearing "unmanly" or "unfeminine." Even today, women march to echoes of, "Don't be unladylike" and "Nice girls don't wrestle, yell, get angry, or compete." We accept other people's judgments of what's okay behavior and disregard our own, all in the name of security.

Not that security isn't important; it is. Without security, both children and adults experience their energies diminished and fragmented by anxiety. We need to fit in, to feel that, to some degree at least, we belong. We need some predictability to keep the magnitude of decision-making within manageable limits. We need to know our survival isn't threatened before we are free to play. However, security without the fresh stimulation and joyfulness that comes through an open, experimental, playful mind will ultimately drive all but the most fearful to venture out of safe cubbyholes in search of that undefinable "more."

The fact that doing those things children do nurtures creativity is obvious. To confirm this, all you have to do is compare a group of people who are actively creative with a parallel group of people whose creativity is latent or inactive: You will find the creative group more concerned with what sparks their interest, more willing to take risks, more in tune with and responsive to their own personal rhythms and needs, more fanciful and inclined to honor and follow their dreams and fantasies, less concerned with being "right," more rebellious and non-conforming, and considerably more playful.

What determines whether a person retains these characteristics and talents or not? How can we who are parents at the moment help our children preserve and enhance this aliveness?

Affirmation Deflates Our Dragon

One major factor that I believe contributed to retaining my own creative abilities was my parents' unfailing support of any creative act that took my fancy. My father, while much the silent type, modeled creativity for me. He painted — one of his paintings hangs in my office today. He also built radios and hi-fi systems, striving always to make something that performed better than what you could buy. Often he succeeded. Even if the radio wasn't better, building it was good because it enabled him to experiment, an inherently good thing to do.

My mother provided the even more powerful verbal praise, encouragement, and support that most reinforced my creative behavior. She arranged for me to take singing lessons long before I was even aware that I had a voice worth training. When I came home with a good grade on a mechanical drawing exercise, she immediately bought me a drafting table. When I had the urge to build a reflecting telescope, she took me wherever I needed to go to get the pieces and parts. It didn't matter whether she understood the current project or not. She said sincerely that she thought I was wonderful to be doing something so clever and creative, and she supported me with concrete action.

You parents whose children are still young can do for them what my mother did for me, and what in turn I'm doing for my children, even though they are now grown. Tell them they are wonderful. Give help, but only when asked. Pay attention to the process, and let the end result be wonderful—just because your children did it. Ask them what they have learned, and applaud the learning. Tell them that finding out what doesn't work is just as important as finding out what does.

Equally crucial, *tell yourself these same things*. Let your results be wonderful just because you produced them and like doing it. Do it yourself if you can, and if you need help, request it from people who want you to learn as much as they want to show off. Find out what you have learned and applaud yourself for it. Tell yourself that learning what doesn't work is just as important as finding out what does. And don't be afraid to tell yourself that you are truly proud of your willingness to "try it out," no matter what "it" is, no matter if it's humble or grand, just because it was something you liked.

As an adult, by far the most meaningful and continuing source of affirmations for me have come from my wife, Margy. Her enthusiastic support of my acting, singing, painting, sculpting, house building, and a flock of other high-risk adventures — including starting several businesses—has never wavered over a span of 40 years. Fully equipped with her own islands of brilliance, Margy has always encouraged me to go beyond where I have been seemingly plateaued. It was she who encouraged me to paint in the first place and then gently prodded me to try other media than oils—a search ultimately leading me to gouache—the most glorious and versatile painting medium for me. It was Margy who kept telling me that I had sensitive, creative hands and should try sculpting. Two years of gentle, but persistent affirmations finally motivated me to slay the fierce dragon guarding that door to my creative castle. In many ways, sculpture has proven to be the source of my most creative expressions. Without Margy's positive influence, I would have never even attempted it.

There are consequences, of course. My success as an artist led me to the brain which has in turn overwhelmed art as the priority focus of my creative energy. But Margy is my partner in this new brain life as she has always been in my past lives. The power of unlimited affirmation and support is life-giving. I feel highly motivated and truly blessed by Margy's support.

Counting Our Days Cures Indifferent Living

While I have had more than my share of affirmations, I have also had more than my share of near-death experiences. As a result, I have taken stock of my life ten times and I can tell you that it also provides a wonderful impetus to live life fully. In one experience during the war, I survived a flaming plane crash that was fatal to many others. In another, an onrushing car swerved just enough at the last moment to avert certain death, while totally destroying both cars. In yet another, my life flashed in front of my eyes as I was blacking out — on my way into a concrete wall at 40 miles per hour. There were seven others — the most recent only six months ago.

Without getting mystical about it, I must tell you that this kind of experience virtually forces you to ask questions: "What is my life for, anyway?" "Why am I alive?" Furthermore, it forces you to come up with a satisfactory answer, even if it's only, "Well I don't really know, but I'm not about to just drift my way through the rest of it."

Please don't take this as an invitation to take up skydiving, motorcycle racing, or some such thing: You can heighten your appreciation for life in simpler ways. Here are some exercises:

1. Imagine that you've just been handed 10 million dollars a year income, tax-free, that no one else knows about it, and that you are free to do whatever you like with it for the rest of your life. How would you live your life?

2. Imagine that you have a year to live, in good health, with no money problems, and with absolutely no longer than 12 months no matter what. List the things you would do with that time. How does that list compare with how you're spending it now?

3. Write your epitaph. What does it say? What would you like it to say? What would you have to change in your life in order to make that epitaph true? What would that take? Are you willing to do it?

What people find, when they do these exercises, is that many of the things they would do if they had a million, if they knew they would die in a year, if they were to look back, are already possible. You don't need to have a million a year to make an impact on hunger, for example—you can join any of 20 different organizations dedicated to solving that problem and make a significant contribution. You don't have to have a million to start your own company — you need an idea, friends, and determination. You don't need to be looking death in the eye to write letters of love and gratitude to people who've been important to you— you can do it today. It doesn't take anticipating the end of your life, or going through a life-threatening crisis to try something you've always wanted to do—like pick up a paint brush, visit Alaska, or write.

In fact, the possibility that you might have only a year

He sought to sign In the integration of frivolities

"Everything is relevant; making things relevant is the creative process."
William J. Gordon

"The mere foundation of a problem is often far more essential than its solution, which may be merely a matter of mathematical or experimental skill.
Unknown

"To raise new questions, new possibilities, to regard old problems from a new angle requires creative imagination and marks real advances in science."
Albert Einstein

is real. None of us knows when we'll be called. Creative people live as if there were no tomorrow, which is part of what enables them to be passionate about today.

Proving the Opportunity Exists: One Breakthrough is All You Need

Another way to renew your passion for life is to see the chance to do so, to realize that living more fully is a real possibility, not so far out of reach after all. Here are some ways to prove to yourself that it's possible.

First-timers who are seeking to discover more about themselves and wish to explore mind-expanding opportunities can attend programs at Esalen Institute, Big Sur, California; the Monroe Institute of Applied Sciences, Faber, Virginia, near Charlottesville; the Omega Institute in Rhinebeck, New York; the New York Open Center, Inc., New York City; Wainwright House, Rye, New York, and many other similar educational institutions that cater to human development. Almost all these institutes have an array of programs to suit you, whether you're a beginner or advanced. Some courses will be very appealing, others, not at all. Follow your interests and sample their offerings, like a smorgasbord. For the physically adventurous, who want to jump in on the deep end, there's Outward Bound and a whole array of similar programs, including Larry Wilson's wonderful LEAP program, which combines both physical risk-taking and educational stimulation. I have experienced many of these programs personally — most recently the LEAP Program at Pecos River Ranch near Sante Fe, New Mexico.

High-growth programs related to brain dominance technology include the HBDI Certification Workshop and the ACTAL (Applied Creative Teaching and Learning) Workshop conducted by my organization in Lake Lure, North Carolina. Both of these not only provide certification in the use of my instrument, but also represent important personal development programs in their own right.

Idea-generating workshops are also available, most particularly those offered by the Synectics Corporation in Cambridge, Massachusetts, directed by George Prince. George is responsible for the notions of Experimental and Safekeeping that I refer to throughout this book. An annual event for both beginners and advanced students is the CIPSI Program run by the Creative Education Foundation of the University of Buffalo, under the leadership of Sidney Parnes, one of the best known and respected educators in the field of creativity. Also, there are the outstanding Solstice Workshops, conducted annually by Bob Samples, author of *The Metaphoric Mind*, and numerous other books. The workshops are held at Windstar (the John Denver Center) in Colorado. Workshop listings of the type just described regularly appear in the *Brain/Mind Bulletin*, published by Marilyn Ferguson, author of the *Aquarian Conspiracy*, and also in the *New Age Journal*.

In my none-too-modest opinion, the world's most cutting-edge workshop in the area of creativity and personal growth is the Applied Creative Thinking Workshop (ACT I), which Chapter 8 describes in detail.

Metaphors are *"word pictures that give language power and richness by involving our senses in the experience."*

Gabriele Lusser Rico

"Every child is an artist. The problem is how to remain an artist after he grows up."

Picasso

"Man's most serious activity is play."

George Santayana

8

ACT I: BREAKTHROUGH TO CREATIVITY

In the last chapter, one of the ways we recommended for reclaiming creative passion was to seek out experiences that confirmed to you that the opportunity to be creative is actually available to you. In line with that idea, we now describe our flagship workshop, Applied Creative Thinking Workshop or ACT I, which is designed to provide as many of those creative experiences as it is humanly possible to fit into the space of five days.

No book can substitute for the actual experience, of course, but we try in this chapter to provide you with some vicarious experience of ACT by describing it in a whole-brain way. We hope you will come to realize that if the people in these pages can reclaim their creative passion, so can you. Creative functioning—full creative functioning—is a basic human capability.

A TYPICAL ACT BREAKTHROUGH

See two people, one, a high-ranking military officer, strongly prefers analytical, quantitative, factual modes of thinking and dismisses the emotional, interpersonal, intuitive approaches (loves A, avoids C). The other, a music therapist, strongly prefers insightful, intuitive, feeling, and

Figure 8-1. Music Therapist and Military Officer Problem Solving

sensing modes and avoids, even cringes away from, rational processing (loves C, avoids A).

Their assignment is to solve a problem together. The statement of the problem includes a lot of facts, many quantifiable, but not enough to lead one to a logical conclusion. Missing elements and gaps in the data call for more than strictly linear problem solving.

The ways in which these two approach the problem reflect their extreme preferences. The army officer, with intense A quadrant preferences, quantifies the elements of the problem and pushes for a mathematical solution. The music therapist, on the other hand, feels frightened by all the facts and data and can't understand what the officer is doing. As he works, she moves away to a place near the window, where she ponders the problem while looking out into the garden. After the preliminary discussion, no one speaks for 10 or 15 minutes. Then, when the colonel is on the third page of his mathematical treatment, the young woman turns to him and said, "I've got it."

He responds, "What do you mean, you've got it?"

She says, "I don't know how to describe the answer, but I know it's right."

"What do you mean, you know it's right? And how can I tell what it is if you can't even describe it?"

"I can draw it for you," she replies. Taking some

crayons, she draws some symbols representing the elements of the problem and the relationship between them.

"Okay, I see that," he admits, "but I don't see the solution." She then says, "Well, let me show you," and proceeds to move her body in one way to express one aspect of the problem and then in another way to express another aspect. And then, again, through movement, she shows how these two elements come together to form a solution. The colonel is dumfounded, because she has indeed grasped the answer.

The assignment calls for a report to the group, and the colonel says, "Since you got the answer, you give the report."

The woman replies, "There's no way I can explain what I just demonstrated." Whereupon, the colonel answers, "Well, I still don't know how in the world you did it, but I'm satisfied that you did do it and I can explain not only what you did, but why it's the right answer."

Returning to the group, he articulates both the problem-solving process and the answer.

Awed, the music therapist exclaims, "My God, that's wonderful! Teach me how to do that."

Smiling, the army colonel responds, "I will, but only if you teach me how to do what you did."

In under an hour, these two individuals learned that *one's best mode can be enhanced by adding a mode one discounts or even fears.* Both people reordered their value systems and priorities accordingly to accommodate and develop modes of thinking that they had deprecated and avoided for most of their adult lives.

This incident was only the beginning. Talking with me more than a year later, the colonel said, "That moment was one of the most important in my life. Intuition always seemed like an absurd idea to me, not based in fact, and

certainly not something serious that professional people would employ in their business lives. I've now changed my mind. For the past year, because of that personal experience and this new knowledge of the brain, I've been using and developing my own right-brain modes. Observing my wife and playing with my grandchildren has taught me a lot. It turns out many of my colleagues use intuition when no facts or data exist to support a logical conclusion. They all seemed reluctant to acknowledge it's their intuition they're using, but with this new understanding, I now know what it is."

The music therapist, who had been experiencing severe career difficulties because she couldn't plan or organize well enough to express her ideas out in the commercial world, began to succeed in these areas. Her initial experience with the colonel, plus later conversations with him and others, provided initial access to her own left-brain capabilities. Within the year, she had greatly improved her professional relationships, had reclaimed her work from exploitative colleagues, and had marketed commercial products, which launched her on a career previously unavailable. Today, instead of running from those modes, she honors and uses them in achieving concrete goals.*

Wouldn't it be wonderful, you might say, if such learning could be an everyday occurrence?

In fact, it can be and is. It's been repeated literally thousands of times in hundreds of our courses. We've proven that the deadening (albeit well-meaning) mistakes made by parents, teachers, spouses, bosses, colleagues, and friends *can* be rectified. We *can* reclaim our rights to function in all ways, and we *can* validate ourselves and others in the process. What's required is a teaching and learning

---

* I would give more details, but it is inappropriate to reveal the answer to the famous "Doodlebug" exercise.

climate that *celebrates differences*. The colonel and the therapist learned *because of their differences, not in spite of them.*

Even more good news: Once experienced, a learning climate that celebrates differences is usually internalized. This is why learners retain the benefits of their new understanding and can continue their growth and development independently. It is for the privilege of participating in such experiences that many teachers enter the profession in the first place, only to find themselves constrained by concepts and practices so rigid and linear that breakthroughs begin to sound like fairy tales. Today, learning about the brain gives us the chance to renew our original calling as developers of the human mind—the whole human mind.

The word is spreading fast. Just since our first ACT I in 1979, many new creativity training programs have been initiated throughout the country, some very compelling and others less so, but the tide has turned. ACT I, now in its eighth year, continues to be the cutting-edge workshop in this growing field. When the larger corporations had a chance to experience ACT I, they immediately expressed a desire for a shorter version available to the many employees they wanted exposed to the ACT concept, but couldn't free up for a full week.

The answer was to develop a new two-and-one-half-day version—the Creative Problem Solving (CPS) Workshop—and train a faculty to deliver it at corporate plant sites anywhere and everywhere. CPS was an instant hit when introduced in 1984 and is now the core development program for a number of major corporations.

If you're a teacher or student and want to turn with the tide toward creativity training, both personally and

"He who has imagination without learning has wings and no feet."
Joseph Joubert

"With their heavy emphasis on communication and early training in the 3 R's, our educational system and modern society generally discriminate against one entire half of the brain. In our present school system the attention given to the minor (right) hemisphere of the brain is minimal compared with the training lavished on the (left) or major hemisphere."
Roger Sperry

Figure 8-2. "How Many of You Would Like to Draw?"

professionally, and want to introduce whole-brain methods into your environment, this chapter was written with you particularly in mind. Specifically:

1. The story of introducing ACT I into GE can be mined for lessons on introducing innovation into institutionalized environments.

2. Three new models: teaching and learning, and composite whole-brain learning group reveal the conceptual basis of the workshop design.

3. The several metaphoric and four-quadrant descriptions of how the course works today can provide useful ideas and understanding of whole-brain instructional design.

4. The postlude (AFTER ACT) suggestions can enrich your personal experience of whole-brain creativity.

HOW WE GOT ACT TOGETHER

Mintzberg's premise, you will remember, is that people are smart and dull in their work. My corollary to that premise is that we must also be smart and dull in our *learning*. And so we are, as you've seen. When we began to redesign GE courses, *everyone*, regardless of their mental preference, began to get smarter.

While learning about how to cover the entire brain

dominance spectrum in making key points in a course, more and more often I delivered each point not in just one way, but in three or four ways, and sometimes even five or six. I might use facts and data first, then show a graphic model, develop a case study, interpret it using a metaphor or a film, and follow up with an experiential simulation, with a written statement requested at the end.

Wasn't all that repetition tedious and time-consuming? you might ask. Not at all. Participants loved it, not only because of the variety, but also because each type of delivery expanded their grasp of the subject. You can learn about a car in a limited way from a written description, more fully from a snapshot, more fully still by touching it and getting inside, and even more so by driving it, looking under the hood, or going to an automobile factory.

Thus, the multidominant teaching ensured that students mastered the material as it was designed to be understood. And as for time-consuming, if a person's educational goals are meaningful in the first place, how can a course where people really learn cost any more in time and money than a course where people don't learn?

Greatly encouraged by these early course modifications, I resolved to find a way to design a whole-brain learning experience from scratch. It wasn't long before I received an invitation to do so that was all but engraved. Sitting in an audience, I heard a vice president say something like, "GE urgently needs a training program that will release the creative potential of employees so they can apply it on the job." I made a mental note to myself that said, "You know how to do this. Take the new things you have just learned about the brain and apply them to the design of a creativity workshop. Send this guy a proposal within 24 hours. This is the opportunity you've been wait-

ing for to put it all together." Returning to my office, I immediately developed and sent the VP a written proposal for a creativity workshop.

Nothing happened. I sent another copy of my original proposal with a covering note. Another month passed with still no response. Not to be denied, I telephoned the VP and said, "I'm going to be in corporate headquarters next Tuesday, and I would like to stop in and talk about my creativity workshop proposal." He said, "Okay, but you better have something better than your written proposal to convince me."

Now what to do? the V.P. was not only exceedingly sharp, he was also unusually gifted as a strategist on human resource issues. I was going to have to get smart in a hurry!

What If You Could Draw?

An experience just a few hours after my phone conversation and before my visit provided me with a much better but highly risky strategy. While speaking to a workshop group of about 100 managers on the subject of leadership, I got the beginnings of an Aha! that prompted me to take an unusual poll. "How many of you can draw?" Five or six immediately raised their hands, followed more slowly by two or three others. "How many of you would *like* to be able to draw?" Now every hand was in air, even those who had said they could draw already. Surprised and delighted, I then asked, "How many of you think you're creative?" Three or four raised their hands. "If you could draw, how many of you would then believe you were creative?" About 75 hands went up. Aha! People equate creativity with artistic capability! I then asked this question: "If I could teach you all how to draw, how many of you

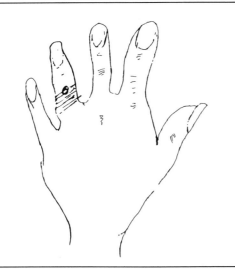

Figure 8-3. First Drawing of Hand

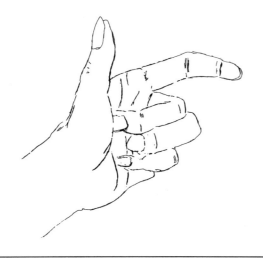

Figure 8-4. Drawing after Exercises Given By Betty Edwards

would be interested in learning?" Almost every hand shot up immediately. I was elated by the possibility of a new strategy for dealing with my vice president.

Musing over the coming meeting while driving over to corporate headquarters that Tuesday, one point kept coming back to me. My success as an artist carried over into my business career: Because I had achieved recognition as an artist, people thought of me as being creative, and they called on me when creative input and approaches were needed. Now if they accepted my creativity because I could draw and paint, and if I could provide them with drawing skills or some other capability they thought of as "creative," then might they not accept and access their *own* creativity, and even convince others they are creative?

Meeting with the vice president, I first reviewed my proposal in straightforward terms. When I finished, the VP said, "That's all well and good, Ned, but I'm not convinced you can do what you say you can do."

"What would convince you?"

He answered, "Some visible means that demonstrates people are able to do something creative they couldn't do before they came."

"If I can give you the demonstration you just asked for, will you approve my going forward with the workshop design?"

He quickly answered, "Yes."

"Okay," I said. "Let me ask you this question. Can you draw?"

He replied, "Not very well."

"Would you like to learn how to draw?"

"I'd love it," he said with a broad smile.

"If I could teach you how to draw, would you consider yourself more creative?"

"Absolutely."
Bingo!! Bull's-eye!! Eureka!! Touchdown!!

The First Drawing Class

I immediately contacted Carl Coleman in the Nuclear
Energy Division in San Jose, a friendly advocate of my
work, and he arranged to convene a group of nuclear
engineers for my purpose. They were obvious candidates
for the experiment—all A and B quadrant people, and
not one of them could draw.

I next invited my friend and colleague, Betty Edwards,
to collaborate with me in putting the session together. She
agreed to the challenge. Betty Edwards, you'll remember,
is the author of the best-selling book, *Drawing on the Right
Side of the Brain*, which was just being published at this
time. In it, she teaches people how to draw on the basis
of the mental aspects of "seeing" as opposed to the traditional approaches to art instruction. Her work represents
a phenomenal leap in art education.

We scheduled a session for that September weekend,
beginning with a two-hour Brain Update session Friday
night, in which I presented the premise of the specialized
brain, introduced Betty, and paved the way for the drawing
activity to follow the next day. On Saturday, Betty took
the group of volunteers through her process, emphasizing
repeatedly how it relates to the brain. She started by asking
each individual to draw his or her hand, label it "Unin-
structed Drawing," and sign it. Later on, after giving a
number of exercises (which you can read about in her
book), she asked each person to draw his or her hand
again, using the new ability to "see" that had been developed during the workshop. Then at the end of the day,

"Almost all creativity involves purposeful play."

"The ultimate creative capacity of the brain may be, for all practical purposes, infinite."

George Leonard

in a concluding mini-art show, we all compared these two drawings, the befores and the afters. The differences were quite spectacular, as you can see for yourself in the examples provided.

When he saw the actual evidence of the changes the session had produced, my vice president was greatly impressed, so much so that from that point onward, he functioned not only as my high-level boss, but also as an enthusiastic sponsor. We proceeded immediately to firm up our strategy for introducing the workshop.

Strategy of the Introduction

Keeping a low profile was essential to the success of the workshop project, because we needed the freedom to do whatever worked best, even if it was countercultural. Anyone who also wants to introduce new ideas into an old structure might consider three things I did to secure this freedom:

1. *I focused the initial proposal on the outcomes rather than on processes*, which ensured that any approval would authorize us to head for the goals, but which headed off potential interference in deciding how to reach them.

2. *I chose an offsite location* because such things as biofeedback, playing with creative materials, and visualization experiences would be inappropriate to conduct at the corporate Management Development Institute. We needed privacy to allow for the development of a creative learning climate. For that first workshop and for every one

since, ACT's home has been the International Training and Communications Center (ITCC) at the Monroe Institute near Charlottesville, Virginia.

3. *I avoided giving the impression that the workshop would be "too far out."* With my manager's endorsement, we entitled the workshop Productive Problem Solving—PPS for short— because we didn't want to risk something called "creative" to bomb out. We also thought the word *creative* might put GE operating people off; like *motivation*, it was not a word used frequently in the culture at that time. We needn't have worried. Unlike most pilot workshops, which take 6 to 12 months to work out, success was so incredibly dramatic that we changed the name for the very next one to what it is today, Applied Creative Thinking (ACT I).

ACT's Design

With these decisions made, we turned next to detailing objectives and approach, developing models, and creating tests for comprehension. The wording of these course components has evolved over the years, but the essence has remained unchanged, so the remainder of the chapter presents them in the form they are used for ACT today.

Two major players who had a part in creating ACT must be mentioned. Naomi Frankel and Indie Luria, the consultants who introduced me to interactive drawing, not only contributed many original ideas, but also were enormously influential and helpful in stimulating my thinking about every aspect of the workshop. More recently, Alison

Strickland and Ted Coulson have contributed many original ideas and have added significantly to the reinforcement and enhancement of the design. Ted and Alison have become extremely effective leaders of the ACT experience and are now the principal workshop faculty.

Course Objectives and Approach

The purpose of the workshop had already been defined: *to unlock the individual's creative potential on the job.* What I knew then was that the key to achieving that purpose was, is, and always will be personal affirmation, affirmation, and more affirmation.

Let me explain why affirmation is so critical to unlocking potential. As I've stated, many people believe they haven't ever been or could never be "creative." When focused on, that belief often functions as a self-fulfilling prophecy. The root of that belief is very often a fear of expanded mental activity. One of the first tasks in developing a person's creativity, therefore, is to alleviate that fear. Psychotherapists say two antidotes for fear and anxiety are: (1) information to reduce uncertainty, and (2) reassurance to provide a feeling of nurture and well-being. ACT provides information in abundance. Reassurance comes most powerfully in the form of encouragement and acceptance of individual differences, and ACT provides for this both externally and, even more important, internally. People develop the internal information and reassurance for themselves through personal experience by working on (1) assignments presented during the workshop, and (2) personal and business problems they face in their own lives and bring to ACT as grist for the process.

As people complete activities that prove they can indeed both visualize and think logically at the same time,

"To live is not to learn, but to apply."
Legouve

"To recapture childhood's wonder is to secure a driving force for grown-up thoughts."
Charles Sherrington

"Just as we can throttle our imagination, we can likewise accelerate it. As in any other art, individual creativity can be implemented by certain techniques."
Alex Osborn

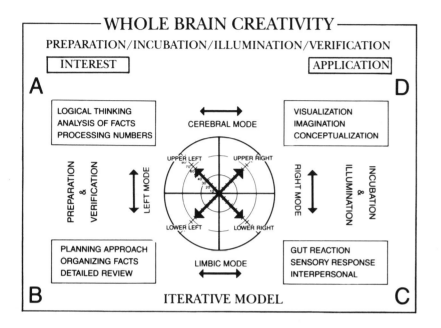

WHOLE BRAIN CREATIVITY

PREPARATION/INCUBATION/ILLUMINATION/VERIFICATION

INTEREST

APPLICATION

A

D

LOGICAL THINKING
ANALYSIS OF FACTS
PROCESSING NUMBERS

CEREBRAL MODE

VISUALIZATION
IMAGINATION
CONCEPTUALIZATION

PREPARATION & VERIFICATION

LEFT MODE

UPPER LEFT UPPER RIGHT

LOWER LEFT LOWER RIGHT

RIGHT MODE

INCUBATION & ILLUMINATION

PLANNING APPROACH
ORGANIZING FACTS
DETAILED REVIEW

LIMBIC MODE

GUT REACTION
SENSORY RESPONSE
INTERPERSONAL

B

ITERATIVE MODEL

C

Figure 8-5. Whole-Brain Creativity Model

they quiet their inner critic—that ever-watchful part of the left brain that leaps to protect us from the risk of rejection. Once the inner critic is quieted, people are free to open up new possibilities for themselves: For the A or B dominant person, the new possibility is a chance to experience an Aha! moment, to validate an intuitive perception, to "see" something in a new way. For the C or D dominant person, the new possibility may be an enhanced experience of control, of the power to actually manifest an idea, of an improved ability to appreciate the finiteness of a subject or problem.

What affirmation does ACT convey?

1. Your own style of functioning in a creative environment is okay and important.

2. Other, different styles of functioning in that same environment are also okay and important.

3. You can access and use mental modes not thought to be available to you.

4. You can further expand your creative options if you chose to do so.

The Whole-Brain Models for Achieving These Objectives

For me, a whole-brain workshop meant whole-brain everything:

1. Whole-brain content

2.   Whole-brain delivery

3.   Whole-brain learning group

4.   Whole-brain environment*

For each of these aspects of the workshop, I used a model. Let me just say a word here about models for those of you who aren't familiar with them and how they are used. A model is a standard—something against which to compare or measure something else. In a sense, a description of any concept, structure, or process is a model. It describes in generic terms a standardized version of something—a widget, for example, that you've decided every other widget must match in certain ways, in order to qualify as a widget.

Models take many different forms. Here, for example, is one of an ideal executive learning center that I use when examining conference centers for holding courses.

The learning center buildings should be attractive and situated on a secluded site of great natural beauty. The center should be located on 10 to 20 acres, preferably on a hill overlooking a lake and adjoining a full-scale resort facility. The learning center site would be a private world, separate from the resort, but close enough to take advantage of its resources and amenities without having them invade the learning space. It should be less than one hour from a jetport and should be available by limo service and private car. The facility should consist of two or three buildings especially designed and dedicated to their independent conference functions.

The first building, the learning center, should provide a minimum of 150 square feet of learning space per person. This includes general conference space as well as break-out rooms for small group work. The ideal conference room size for a group of 20-24 people is 40 by 55 feet. Break-out rooms should be about 10 by 12 feet. All should be fully air-conditioned and equipped with a complete inventory of high quality audiovisual equipment and professionally designed and installed lighting systems appropriate to the learning situation.

The second building, the residential hall, should provide accommodations for at least 30 people: up to 24 participants, 3 faculty, and 3 on-site staff. Bedrooms should be moderate in size and single, with a small television set and high-fidelity music system with provision for control through a master sound system. The residential hall should have a recreation room, a physical fitness room, and an inviting, private social lounge.

The third building could be either part of or separate from the residential hall. It would contain the private dining facilities and food preparation area. Food would be of the highest quality, with balanced menus oriented to seminar activities, rather than heavy, high calorie foods. Located near these buildings should be a private, well tended open field suitable for outdoor recreation, e.g., kite flying, boomerang throwing, volleyball, and the like. The roads that lead to and encircle the learning center site should be suitable for walking and recreational running without concern for traffic or questioning residents or tourists.

When choosing a place to hold specialized courses, such as ACT, I compare existing facilities against this ideal model and attempt to come as close as possible to it. If I were constructing new facilities based on the model, I would do the same. If the facility includes all the features of the model, it is in full compliance. To the extent that it does not have comparable facilities and surrounding environment, it is out of compliance.

Whole-Brain Creativity Model. To express my premise that creativity is whole-brained, I wanted a model to

---

*Refer to Chapter 10 for an in-depth discussion on this topic.

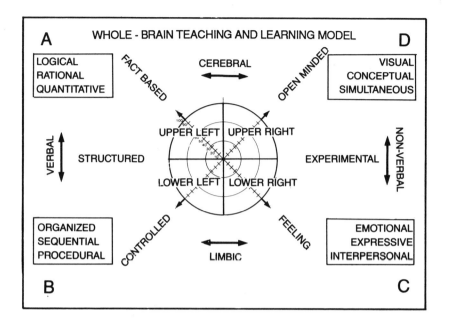

Figure 8-6.   Whole-Brain Teaching and Learning Model

show how the brain works while engaged in the creative process. To serve as that model, I took Wallas's four stages of the creative process (preparation, incubation, illumination, and verification) and related them to the four brain quadrants. After working with the model, it became clear that interest and application were significant steps in the process and needed to be added. Figure 8-5 shows the complete creativity model. Along with the six phases, the model has arrows to show how mental activity iterates back and forth among the four principal modes, drawing on the special skills resident in each quadrant.

The whole-brain model is dependent on all four quadrants, being situationally available during all four phases of the creative process. Close one down and the creative potential is diminished. Close down two or more quadrants or phases and applied creativity as a desired outcome ceases. The process stops. Block the iterative path between the quadrants and the creative potential is again diminished because the basis of synergy has been denied. The creativity model helped me develop ACT I because it synthesizes the twin metaphors of the creative process and brain specialization into a unified whole upon which the design of learning content can be based.

Whole Brain Teaching and Learning Model. In addition to the model of whole brain creativity, which set a standard for the content, I needed a second model to set a standard for the delivery. This model, the whole-brain teaching and learning model shown in Figure 8-6 first divides the learning process into the four brain quadrants, then summarizes these into two categories: *structured* (left) and *unstructured* (right). In the structured modes (A and B), we have some *hard processing* dealing with logical, rational, critical, quantitative issues and activities, and we have some procedural activities involving planned, organized, and sequential elements of the learning process. These more structured modalities contrast sharply with the non-linear, non-verbal, unstructured modes (C and D) of the right brain: visual, conceptual, and simultaneous processing; and the *soft processing* involving emotional, expressive, and interpersonal activities. Together, these comprise the full range of preferences for teaching and learning.

In designing the workshop, I checked every key learning point against the model to make sure the material was delivered through media that respond to preferences for each of the four mental modalities. At the least, that meant every learning point would be expressed through some kind of experiential or unstructured medium in addition to verbal, didactic information.

The Whole-Brain Learning Group Model. The ideal or model whole-brain learning group consists of 18 people, preferably 9 women and 9 men, arrayed across the total brain dominance spectrum so that as a group they constitute a composite whole brain. Before participants are admitted to our workshops, they complete the Participant Survey Form and we do their profiles so we can see where they fall in the total brain dominance spectrum. That enables us to make sure that, as a group, the 18 participants make up the best whole-brain composite we can assemble.

In such a whole-brain group, failing to reach people with preferences in any one of the quadrants would lower the potential for their understanding and, thus, for synergy in the group. It is imperative, therefore, to have a good test of understanding.

"Where there is an open mind, there will always be a frontier."
Charles Kettering

"Everything is relevant; making things relevant is the creative process."
William Gordon

"We succeed in enterprises which demand the positive qualities we possess, but we excel in those which can also make use of our defects."
Alexis de Tocqueville

Figure 8-7. Ship/Plow Metaphor

The Test of Metaphor

Instructors often can't tell whether students understand classroom material or not. All too often, student non-verbal behavior, such as head-nodding or smiling, tells an instructor they do understand when, in fact, they don't at all. Students aren't untruthful, they just see through the filters of their own brain dominance preferences, and, where those filters differ from those of the course designer, they redefine what was intended so it means something different. And then they think they get it, but actually they frequently don't.

Since a very high level of understanding is crucial to the iteration and synergy whole-brain design intends, we absolutely have to have a measure that tells us from moment to moment during the workshop whether or not understanding has occurred. Without such a measure, we'd end up with the dilemma this whole effort was designed to resolve to begin with: finding out—or worse, *not* finding out—we'd given a course and the participants had missed the point.

We'd already raised our chances of getting through to participants simply by using whole-brain teaching techniques. Moving back and forth between different modalities when teaching a learning point helps an instructor detect when someone has yet to grasp a point, because somehow the process seems to encourage participant questions and this helps the instructor get a sense of the people's comprehension levels. (If you're a teacher, you know how precious are the chances to clarify misunderstandings or misinterpretations before they become embedded in the mind.) That method helped, but we needed more.

The "more" that we needed was supplied by

metaphor. A *metaphor* is the use of one subject to clarify understanding of another. Dictionary examples include: "The spirit of man is the candle of the Lord" (Proverbs 20:27), and "A book should serve as an axe for the frozen sea within us" (Franz Kafka). The candle is a metaphor for the spirit, the axe for a book, and the frozen sea for our minds and hearts. Metaphors can be verbal and non-verbal, written or visual, mute or audible. They can bridge cultures, languages, and brain dominance preferences. A product of the right brain, a metaphor can be thought of as a translation from one mental language to another, from the literal to the analogic. Its power is the instant understanding it brings by reason of the translation. To be fully validated, a metaphor must be translated, and that can be done accurately only with full understanding. With understanding, there will be a direct hit.

Here's an example of how one might use a metaphor to test understanding: A farm boy who has never seen the sea and is unfamiliar with ships might develop an understanding of a ship's motion with the metaphor, "The ship plows the sea." As he grasps the visual image, he might say, "Oh, I get it. The ship moves through the water like the plow moves through the land. The bow of the ship cuts through the water like the plow cuts through the earth. Yes, I can see it in my mind's eye." When asked to demonstrate his understanding, he might say, "A ship slices through the water like a knife cuts through the icing of a cake," whereupon the teacher would say, "Yes, that's the idea."

Metaphors are an excellent test of comprehension because they magnify the degree of understanding—or lack thereof—so it becomes visible.

In ACT, metaphors are far more than measuring

"Reason can answer questions, but imagination has to ask them!"
Ralph W. Gerard

"It is not easy to describe the sea with the mouth."
Kokyu

"Take a music bath once or twice a week for a few seasons, and you will find that it is to the soul what the water bath is to the body."
Oliver Wendell Holmes

The Creative Brain

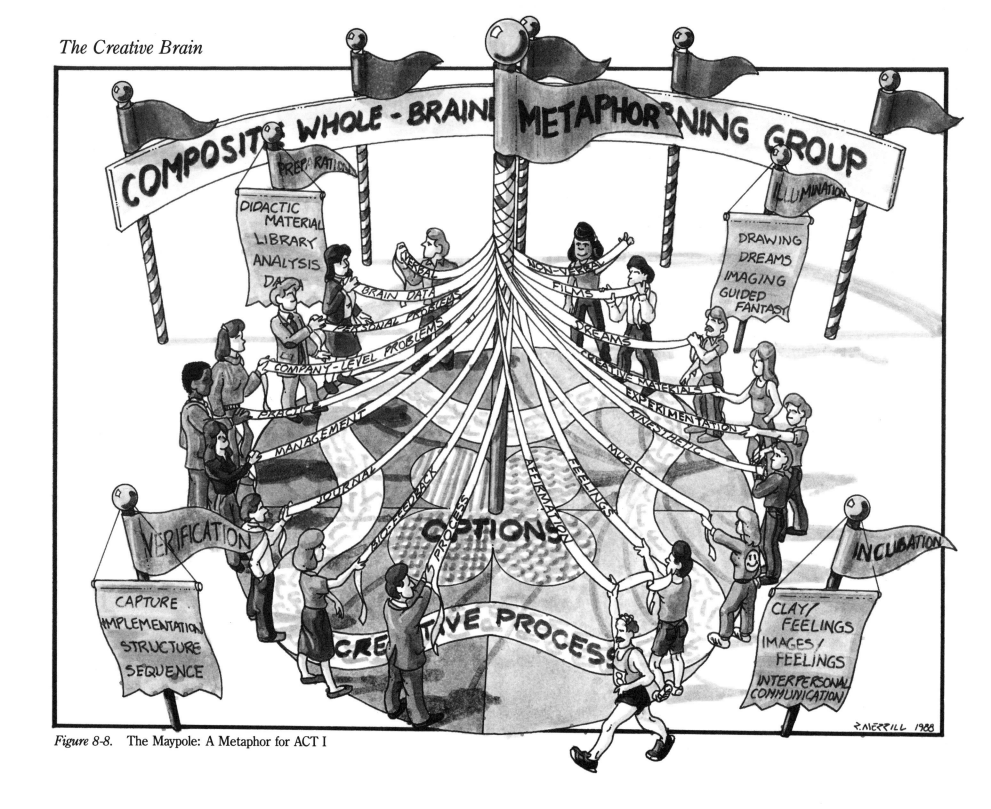

Figure 8-8.   The Maypole: A Metaphor for ACT I

tools, more than a way of thinking, and more than a useful technique for processing a problem solution. They are also fresh and rich and fun. In a larger context, the metaphor has been the principal means of communicating the concept of the four-quadrant specialized, dominant, situational whole brain. Metaphors have enabled us to develop useful understanding even though we still lack details of how the brain works physiologically. The metaphoric models allow us to accept areas of ignorance and still explain why the concepts work.

I am forever indebted to Bob Samples, author of *The Metaphoric Mind*, not only for writing that landmark book, but also for his gentle, patient, extraordinarily effective way of teaching me the power of the metaphor.

WHAT HAPPENS IN THE ACT WORKSHOP

Describing the Indescribable

There are at least two things about the ACT I Workshop on which there is universal agreement. The first is that it is an extraordinary learning experience—for many, the most significant in their lives. The second point of consensus is that the experience is indescribable. In writing a chapter for his new book on creativity, Morris Stein, professor of psychology at New York University, and an internationally recognized creativity expert, said that although he was highly impressed, it was impossible for him to describe fully his experience as an ACT I participant. The co-mingling of content, environment, and experience is too rich, complex, and multidimensional. Knowing that

ACT defies description, I'm going to do my best anyway and hope you come away with a taste of it, at least. I'll start, fittingly, with a metaphor.

The Maypole Metaphor

The illustration accompanying this section shows ACT I as a "maypole" type of experience being carried out on a four-quadrant field that has pathways indicating the creative process, which represents the core of ACT I. Ringed around the maypole are the 18 participants, who, taken together, represent a composite whole brain. They each hold a learning content streamer. If this metaphor were a movie, you would see that as they experience the creative process, they move in and out and around the four quadrants, taking their content streamers along these varying paths. In addition to participating, each of the 18 people is also a major element in the design and provides a critical ingredient in the total mix of resources. Their very uniqueness is crucial to the dynamics of the interactive learning that takes place. As a result, every ACT I Workshop, though it follows the same schedule, is unique.

Each quadrant of the maypole playing field is represented as containing those activities, exercises, and events of the workshop experience that fall mainly in that quadrant. For example, the data associated with the HBDI and the didactic materials describing the whole-brain model are located in the A quadrant, which also directs the *preparation step* in the four-stage creative process. The B quadrant, which can be thought of as the *verification* portion of the process, is where structure and sequence of the workshop activities becomes critical and where the capture and implementation of workshop learning resides. The C quadrant, which represents the *incubation* part of the creative process, is where feelings-oriented interpersonal and communication exercises and events take place. Finally, the D quadrant is the home of *illumination*, and in it are located activities and exercises dealing with idea-generation, such as drawing, imaging, modeling, guided fantasies, and dreams.

Central to the workshop experience is the concept and application of metaphor. So this is shown as a royal standard flag flying from the top of the maypole.

Equally important is the idea of play, which the metaphor of the maypole suggests, and which characterizes the ACT I experience. As intensely as people work and as much as they learn, participants play, and their sheer enjoyment contributes enormously to the learning. ACT is a special environment in which the playful idea of a maypole is legitimate, valid, and instructive, in addition to being a delight to the eye.

In the center of the playing field, covering all four quadrants, is a region labeled *options*. This represents the time and opportunity for participants to try things out, experiment, test themselves, or simply internalize the experience.

Also occupying space in the center are the two additional phases in which I've enclosed Wallis's original four-stage definition of the creative process: the initial stage of *interest* and the final stage of *application*. Both of these are multidominant in nature and tend to take on an aspect unique to each participant.

From day one through day five, each unique individual moves through the process combining, disengaging, and recombining with other unique individuals, first in homogeneous then in heterogeneous groups. This means that as they experience the creative path, they do so both with people who share their mental preferences and with other people whose view of the world is very different. It is the richness of this interaction, which takes place as the workshop rhythms and experiences roll on day to day, that makes the experience so meaningful and successful. Close your eyes for a moment and visualize this maypole coming to life. As you visualize that motion, color, and aliveness, you will have some grasp of the essence of the ACT experience.

This next section offers another way to discover ACT. It is composed of "Introductions to ACT" that might have been written by single dominance people from each of the four quadrants. Each one describes various aspects of the workshop content and experience differently. This first example is the A quadrant entry. B, C, and D quadrant entries follow.

ACT From Quadrant to Quadrant

A Quadrant

ACT I was designed in 1979 by Ned Herrmann (with the assistance of two creativity consultants, Naomi Frankel and Indie Luria) for the General Electric Company. Over 55 sessions have taken place as of January 1988, with an average of 18 participants per session. The workshop is held at the International Training and Communications Center (ITCC) on the grounds of the Monroe Institute in Faber, Virginia. The Monroe site is approximately 880 acres in size. Ned Herrmann personally lead the first 25 workshops. Since 1985, he has turned over leadership to Alison Strickland and Ted Coulson, who have both contributed to the current design. Participants are profiled using the Herrmann Brain Dominance Instrument and represent a composite whole-brain learning group.

The workshop premise is based upon Graham Wallis's four-stage model of the creative process (preparation, incubation, illumination, and verification), supplemented by the additional stages of interest and application. The workshop is a five-day program running from Monday morning to Friday noon. Well over 100 companies and organizations have sponsored participants. The workshop is under continuous redesign and is currently in its twentieth revision.

The workshop is intended to have a participant group balanced not only in terms of brain dominance characteristics, but according to gender. However, the norm during the last eight-years has been 60 percent male/40 percent female participation.

B Quadrant

The ITCC facility at Monroe Institute is located approximately 1.2 miles off Route #6, which is in turn 2.0 miles from Route #29 and a total of 27.2 miles south of Charlottesville, Virginia. Participants who drive are provided with maps. Those who fly use the Charlottesville Airport, which is approximately 45 minutes from the Monroe Center by the ITCC van.

The Center consists of three main buildings—the residential hall, the conference hall, and the Monroe Institute of Applied Sciences Research Laboratory. The residence hall will accommodate a total of 24 people in various combinations of single, double, and triple occupancy with each person having his or her own private controlled, holistic, environmental chamber (CHEC unit). The CHEC unit is equipped with audio, video, and fresh-air vents. Well-prepared meals are served on a timely basis that matches the workshop schedule.

The conference center is named the David Frances Hall in honor of one of Bob Monroe's principal supporters. It was built with special considerations given to the needs of ACT

workshops. It consists of a 40' X 55' main meeting room, along with four break-out rooms, a supply room, and storage rooms.

Participants arrive Sunday afternoon or evening in time for an 8 A.M. start on Monday morning. The daily schedule includes breaks, meals, and a social hour with optional health and fitness activities. Evening sessions end about 10:30 P.M.

Music is used throughout the workshop, including morning wake-up. Approximately 25 films are screened during the daytime workshop sessions and in the evening. Participant guidebooks, class workbooks, and capture notebooks are supplied, along with all necessary creative materials. Individuals are given a cassette tape of a guided fantasy through the brain and a special narrated journey through the creative process.

Workshops are scheduled to avoid extreme weather conditions both in the winter and in the summer. Approximately eight workshops are scheduled each year, with this schedule supplemented on the basis of demand.

The workshop is sequenced on the basis of the 4-stage creative process, with each day representing one stage as its focus. Within each day the structure and sequencing of content is arranged in accordance with the whole-brain model.

C Quadrant

I'm so glad you're going to attend ACT. What a fabulous experience! You'll never forget it. I remember on the last day writing about what I'd learned. I couldn't believe it was only three days ago that three rooms full of creative materials were opened up. It was like walking into a huge playpen! The first learning I remembered was that incredible moment when I discovered I could see my hand well enough to be able to draw it—I can really draw! On a break later, I saw a wonderful old barn and did a sketch of it. It was good! I'm going to hang it in my kitchen to remind me of how wonderful it felt. I also learned about how to solve that miserable personal problem I told you about. After all this time, it wasn't what I thought at all, but now I know I'm seeing it for what it is and I know my partner and I can work it through. Part of what helped was the creative process tape. It showed me I really did see the problem now and could deal with it. Writing that final letter was hard. I knew I was supposed to say what I learned, but there was just too much to get down on paper. The films alone are worth the trip. People told me ACT was great and that the films were especially 'good.' But, I had no idea! 'Superb,' 'incredible,' 'marvelous,' would have been more accurate. If all I got out of it was what they taught, it would take me a lifetime to integrate it all.

Now I'm remembering how fluttery my stomach felt when the leaders brought out the clay and told us to use it in expressing our feelings. I never thought I could do something like that, but it turns out I'm not *nearly* as bad as I thought and that an awful lot of other people have even more difficulty. Together, our group made a lot of progress that I'm going to take away with me. I especially loved working in the heterogeneous group of six. I will never forget the first time the six of us got together and tried to come up with a theme. Although we probably all tried, none of us really knew how to deal with the differences in that group and what we finally did come up with was in the last three minutes of the hour! It was ridiculous! Boy, did we ever get the point! The next time we were put into that same group we worked together wonderfully. Before the end of the workshop, we had solved a really major problem. The process was like magic, and if we hadn't been so different—backgrounds, experiences, the way we see things—it never could have worked so well. It's too bad we don't have a videotape of our community at work. It could

have been a model back home!

They don't tell you your brain dominance profile till almost the end. Yesterday afternoon when I first saw mine, I absolutely knew it was me. We all did. The workshop really helped us discover who we were, each of us, so the profile just confirmed it. I'm sold—if the profiles can accurately peg 18 people in a five-day period, this thing is valuable. I'm going to arrange to have profiles for my family and my staff at work.

During option time I tried something I'd never done before. My hand and the barn drawing were so exciting that I asked for some clay from the 'feeling' exercise and I modeled my hand. Now, *that* I am going to take home with me, because it's the best thing I have ever done in my entire life!

Does it sound like I've been working or playing? We've accomplished so much that you'd have to say we've worked, but we've had such a good time that you'd also have to say we've played. Wait till you try the interactive drawing exercise. It is hilarious! And of course, the last night... well now, that's really indescribable, but memorable to the outer limits.

It was hard to leave the place, even those crazy CHEC units, which I grew to love sleeping in. And those wonderful people—the participants and the staff. I've taken a lot of courses, but I've never experienced such a terrific group. I hear all the ACT groups say that. If it's true, it's still hard to believe, but then so are a lot of other things I didn't believe before either.

I'm very eager to begin applying some of the things I've learned about what it takes to stimulate creativity. Because I'm a manager, there are some things I can do immediately, both to claim my own creative space, and to help others in my group claim theirs. But the first thing I'm going to do is thank my boss for making ACT available to me! I didn't fully understand what she was asking of me before, and I want to thank her for showing me.

D Quadrant

Figure 8-9. The D Quadrant Introduction to ACT: The Personal Dragon is Slain by the Experience

KEY COMPONENTS OF THE ACT WORKSHOP

Thus far, the workshop image I've created may sound like a loose assemblage of independent modules. In actuality, ACT I is an incredibly complex, tightly coordinated program with split-second timing and careful sequencing. The ACT tapestry interweaves left and right, cerebral and limbic material, alternating didactic and experiential units. Up to now, I've concentrated on the conceptual and metaphoric material. Now we turn to the left for a little organization and linear/sequential reinforcement.

Some of the components of ACT I fall into these classifications:

1.   Didactic lecture material

2.   Films

3.   Music

4.   Individual and group exercises

Didactic Material

After an informal warm-up on Sunday evening, we devote Monday (the first full day) to an information blitz. This is specifically designed to prove to the A and B quadrants, our inner critics and protectors, that what we're doing makes sense, and that we don't need to defend against making fools of ourselves.

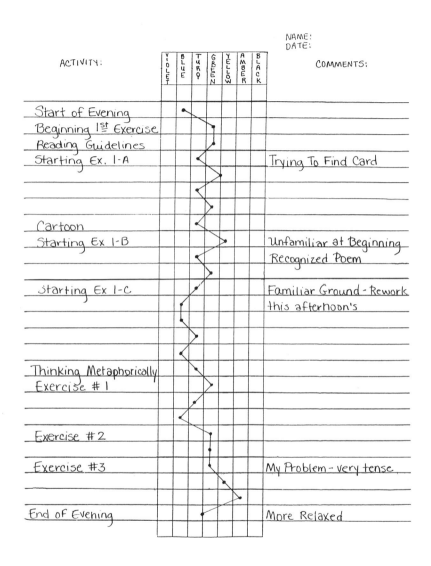

ACTIVITY:

NAME:
DATE:

COMMENTS:

VIOLET | BLUE | TURQ | GREEN | YELLOW | AMBER | BLACK

Start of Evening
Beginning 1st Exercise
Reading Guidelines
Starting Ex. 1-A — Trying To Find Card

Cartoon
Starting Ex 1-B — Unfamiliar at Beginning
Recognized Poem

Starting Ex 1-C — Familiar Ground - Rework
this afternoon's

Thinking Metaphorically
Exercise #1

Exercise #2

Exercise #3 — My Problem - very tense

End of Evening — More Relaxed

Figure 8-10. Typical Biofeedback Record Sheet from the ACT Workshop

To keep C and D dominant types stimulated and connected, we carefully spice the talks with visuals, films, cartoons, jokes, movement exercises, peeks into the future, and breaks. After Monday, we return periodically to the didactic material to let people know where we are and where we're going. However, once A and B are reassured, ACT moves far more strongly into C and D modes with quick returns to A and B to provide whole-brain balance.

Films

Because films communicate meaning marvelously, we screen as many as 25 during the week-long program. Many are animated and non-verbal, and at least 70 percent are metaphoric. All promote effective communication between different brain dialects and different cultures. These visual metaphors reinforce and expand the didactic learning points and provide a rich basis for group interaction and discussion. The films used in ACT are consistently rated as about the best array of visual inputs the typical participant has ever seen.

Music

I instinctively used music, especially Baroque music, in workshops for years before it was proven to be conducive to learning. My experience during those years demonstrated that music not only assists the learning process generally, but also has more specific uses. I sort music into two categories: intervening and non-intervening. *Intervening* music stimulates physical activity. It also shifts attention to itself and away from the learning activity, so we use it to disrupt the continuity of whatever is happening and to redirect a group's attention. In contrast, *non-intervening* music sustains and supports learning activities, and ACT incorporates at least four hours of such musical reinforcement in each day. Music is piped into the individual private CHEC units from 6:00 to 7:30 A.M., and is specially programmed from Monday to Friday in keeping with the evolving nature of the workshop. In a similar sense, music is used at meals and breaks to help create an appropriate atmosphere for the time of day and workshop activity. By Thursday night, the music has moved from Classical and Baroque to guitar and foot-stomping country and rock 'n' roll.

Individual Exercises

The exercises constitute the meat of ACT because they are the mechanisms through which people begin to construct their own inner affirmation. ACT intersperses individual exercises with exercises done in dyads, triads, and groups of six. The main individual exercises include: drawing, biofeedback, visualization through dreams and theta states, creative problem-solving, and creative materials work, which includes designing a personal logo and modeling a problem three-dimensionally. The group exercises begin with communication in dyads and end with a heterogeneous six-person team problem-solving assignment.

In all these exercises, the individual ones especially, we go beyond simply demonstrating that everyone can draw, for example. We ask, what *else* can you do? If you can draw, when three hours ago you thought you couldn't, then *what else* can you do to exercise your creative potential and your own mental processes?

Drawing

I described the drawing exercises Betty Edwards de-

veloped earlier in this chapter. The ACT I version is substantially the same, only compressed into less time. The results are equally impressive, however.

After teaching people to draw in ACT I, by the way, I like to teach them to sculpt in ACT II. People who have learned to sculpt have been stunned by their sudden ability to do something really "artistic" they'd always thought beyond them.

Biofeedback

A biofeedback device is anything that gives information on some biological aspect of your body and provides you with an option to take corrective action. So a thermometer can be thought of as a biofeedback instrument, as can EEG machines and stethoscopes. Examples of biofeedback measures are: heart rate as measured by your pulse, body temperature as measured by a thermometer, and brain states indicated by an EEG machine.

Biofeedback exercises play an important role in ACT because they demonstrate that people can do more than they think possible. And if they can control some aspect of their autonomic body functioning by applying the mind to a task, then what *else* can they do?

In one exercise, I provide participants with biodots, small thermometers in the form of a small paste-on plastic discs that change color with the temperature of the surface on which they're placed. By attaching one biodot on each hand, and referring to a color code, you can measure the temperature of each hand. Phase one of the exercise demonstrates the effect of different consciousness states on the body's skin temperature. Individuals take a guided fantasy that lowers the brain state from an alert beta state to a more relaxed alpha or theta state. Since skin temper-

Figure 8-11. Ned Taking Creative Advantage of his Morning Theta State

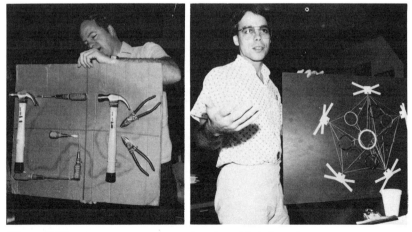

Figure 8-12. Personal Logo and Problem Modeling Examples

PHOTOS BY NEHDI

ature correlates directly with consciousness state, even beginners are able to demonstrate this relationship in biofeedback technique. Phase two of the exercise involves a more extended guided fantasy in which individuals are asked to change the temperature of only one hand. This is more advanced, but a good number of first-time participants can usually produce the desired results. In phase three of the exercise, participants are asked to practice changing the temperature of their hands at various times during the day-early in the morning, after getting up, at midday, and in the evening. Well over 50 percent of our participants are able to show significant temperature differences throughout the day. Many are also able to produce differences between one hand and the other.

Again, the question we pose is, What *else* can you do? If your mental processes are in such control of your body that you can "think" one hand warmer than the other, then to what extent can you influence your other mental and physical processes?

While the idea of biofeedback was considered "way out" in 1977 when I first proposed it as a learning technique for business participants, its effectiveness as a learning tool has won for it wide acceptance even from the tough-minded corporate audience.

Dreams and Theta States

In addition to creative visualization through guided fantasy, we create an awareness of the importance of dreams, both day and night. A largely metaphoric product of our right brains, dreams often contain elements of the answers we seek to our problems. However, to benefit fully from our dreams, we need to discipline ourselves to capture their fleeting messages and cultivate an appreciation for their meanings.

I problem-solve using dreams all the time. I especially appreciate the theta state—that wonderful time between sleep (delta) and wakefulness (alpha or beta). It's a delicious twilight zone: a creative, open place for developing ideas and coming up with insights and answers. Sometimes when I'm late for breakfast, my wife, Margy, will call up to the bedroom and I will often respond, "I'm working!" Indeed I am. The theta state is a wonderful place to do creative thinking. It can be evoked through the use of guided fantasies and special creativity tapes, and during ACT, participants begin to make valid use of this mode of mental processing.

Creative Materials:
The Personal Logo and Problem Modeling

What I call *creative materials* (and many people think of kindergarten things or junk) represent a significant resource in empowering individuals and groups. Most of us have been conditioned out of an appreciation for these materials, and we need to be reintroduced to their value and significance.

So in ACT and other whole-brain workshops, the leader always displays a generous assortment of creative materials, ranging from feathers and clay to wood, pieces of plastic, colored yarn, and wire. To help sensitize people to their nature and properties, item by item, the leader asks the group to describe the qualities and characteristics of each. For example, "it's colorful, it's soft, it's springy, it's light, it's flexible, it's smooth."

After this initial introduction, participants are invited to go into workrooms filled to the brim with such materials, and to pick out three or four they really like and one or two that turn them off. As the doors of the workrooms are opened, the excitement rises palpably. Especially at first glance, the materials present an impression of overwhelming richness. Attractively displayed and very accessible in open dishes or containers that allow people to touch and get acquainted with them, the materials include blocks of wood; squares of plywood; pieces of Styrofoam and cardboard; tubes, rods, dowels, hoops, and all manner of paper products, construction-type materials such as notched sticks, discs, and connectors; construction toys; bags of feathers, felt, fur, cloth, and ribbon; toy figures; different types of wire, string, and adhesives; pieces and parts of broken machinery, such as a washing machine pump, the dial from a broken thermometer, parts of small appliances; a great variety of felt pens, paints, crayons, pastels, watercolors, and numerous brushes; and much, much more.

Once people have selected their materials, we proceed to the two central exercises: (1) creating a three-dimensional personal logo; and (2) modeling a problem in need of a creative solution.

In creating their personal logo (a graphic or visual, sculptural model symbolizing themselves), the first of the creative material activities, participants are asked not only to include the creative materials they enjoy and have good feelings about, but also to incorporate and find redeeming value in some that they initially found unappealing. Part of the objective of this exercise is to stimulate people to find hidden value in things they normally pass over—in effect, to open their eyes to new possibilities. The logo exercise is itself a metaphor for becoming more attentive to the world around us. It is revealing that in a very high number of instances, people report that the materials they originally disliked helped them solve construction problems in making a logo or problem model. Often these represent warring factions within themselves.

In the second exercise, problem modeling, participants make a model of a problem so that they may see all aspects of it, and possibly find a solution in the process. This problem solving technique has proven itself to be unexcelled for its sheer power. More insights and potential solutions emerge from this exercise than almost any other I have seen or used.

Group Exercises in Communication

The exercises described to this point focus on helping people communicate across quadrant boundaries within their own heads. This next set of exercises assists in communicating across the brain quadrant boundaries that exist between us and others.

The first job is to help participants discover they're not communicating optimally—typically, they think they're communicating just fine. People tend to ignore voice inflection and facial expressions, which actually communicate more than words do. But have people pair up and say "yes" and "no" to each other in ten different ways, and suddenly they discover an awful lot of ways to convey meaning where they've been using only a few. Other communication exercises include: (1) speaking and writing from least-preferred quadrants; (2) communicating non-verbally by drawing interactively with partners with similar and different brain dominance profiles (see Chapter 6); and (3) observing a partner express feelings non-verbally through the manipulation of clay, and then emulating those feelings.

In leading people into communication experiences, instructors begin with homogeneous groups. The ease of solving problems and processing information with people of like preferences helps people experience affirmation in communicating and thus provides reassurance. Once the participants have experienced affirmation with like-minded others, the leaders gradually begin introducing differences, first in heterogeneous pairs, then in triads, and then in communities of six. Now participants encounter both the enhancements and challenges of having different mental modes at work in the same group. At first, people can be wary of, unbalanced by, and even hostile toward these differences. But that's only temporary, and they soon begin to understand the value of these different modes, as happened in the example that begins this chapter.

The unique combination of exercises included in ACT prepares participants to experience the creative process fully. In so doing, they enhance their understanding and acceptance of personal uniqueness, their respect for differences, and their ability to communicate across quadrant boundaries. This is most apparent when, at the end of the week-long experience, the heterogeneous six-person teams hit their stride. Most begin in a state of potential or virtual anarchy and move to an absolutely thrilling synergy, functioning in a more unified, powerful way than even the homogenous group did at the beginning.

COLORFAST BENEFITS: UNABASHED BRAGGING, TESTIMONIALS AND MIRACLES

Its effect will never be gone. That's the highest compliment I can give.*

If you find this section immodest, please indulge me. In case you haven't gathered by now, I'm inordinately proud of the ACT Workshops. It is a privilege to be a part of the wonderful breakthroughs, transformations, and healings that continue to take place in people's lives as a result of ACT. No one has ever felt dissatisfied to my knowledge, and I feel entirely free to tell anyone that it's a wonderful experience and that they would be the better and happier for taking it. So if this sounds like a sales pitch or bragging, it is, and I make no apology for it. I wish we could make the workshop available to every person who would like to attend—that's one of the reasons I wanted to write this book— so that as much of ACT as possible could reach as many people as possible.

There are several reasons I'm so proud of ACT. First, most training experiences fade with time, but because ACT concentrates on teaching in a whole brain way, rather than just intellectually, learners make genuine and permanent shifts in understanding and values. The most important of these shifts is in the ability to understand, accept, and celebrate their own uniqueness and that of others. The

many hundreds of people who have attended ACT share a common feeling of self-affirmation, a more complete understanding of answers to such questions as, Who am I? Why do I do the things I do? and What can I become?

What do ACT I graduates say about the experience a few months, a few years, and as much as five years later? Here are some examples of their feedback:

Homemaker/Executive Secretary
Three Months Later

"I went to ACT not knowing exactly what to expect. My husband had already been. I had seen some of the benefits at home of his going as they applied to some of the things we had been dealing with family-wise. Then I saw some of the positive aspects of his using it at work, and also got some very positive feedback for me. I think the most impressive thing for me at ACT was my going into a business-type workshop setting that reaches every spectrum of an organization, every thinking mode of every person from higher up, down to the lower levels, and to see how those interact and how they can be a value to one another, and how they function together. I discovered that creative problem solving is a really neat thing that you can apply on a personal level. I found I was also able to do that during my week at ACT."

Employee Relations Manager
A Year and a Half Later

"I went into ACT feeling that I knew myself and came out with the unique experience of discovering that I was someone a little bit different than I had thought. As I

---

*(Jane Coles, an analyst at GE's Steam Turbine Division, 1985, quoted in *Business Week*)

began to evaluate this new understanding of myself and really look at and challenge it, I found out that it really opened up some positive new awarenesses for me of who I really am. Then being able to take that back home to family and work settings and apply that new understanding to problem solving situations is very helpful. It's really a very powerful week to go through."

Corporate Training Manager
Four Months Later

"I went to ACT to find creativity again. I felt like I had been creative at one time, but had lost it. This unique ACT experience enabled me to find out again that it was okay to be creative, it was okay to take the risk. My creative side could come out without risking a lot at work and there was a way to do it without being too overpowering of others. In introducing it back home it helps to be calm and low profile about it."

Business Consultant
A Year and a Half Later

"What was impressive for me was actually seeing the effect of the whole brain—the four quadrants—working together as a creative problem-solving team. The special team exercise—in particular—seeing that evolve, has helped me in finding better ways of working with clients in structuring problem solving teams that include representatives of all four quadrants. Particularly a client situation where they have to create some really 'hot' new ideas."

Corporate Trainer
Four Months Later

"I came out of the ACT Workshop with a very pleasant feeling. A warm feeling that I want to hold on to forever. I like the way the workshop activities brought things together, brought people together. The approach was both stimulating and comfortable. I liked everything, but flying kites and interactive drawing were of particular interest."

Architect
One Year Later

"You may also be interested to know that since returning from ACT I, my practice has exploded. The dust is just beginning to settle, and through the clearing, I can see possibilities of larger and more exciting projects to design. A marvelous opportunity to continue to use my new-found ability to apply creative thinking."

Four Years Later

"I came to ACT to find out how a right-brain person can live in a left-brain world. The end result has been that it has awakened a lot of my left-brain functions and it has given me a great deal of confidence in continuing a whole-brain kind of approach to my profession of architecture. I always came away frustrated in the problem-solving dilemma, but ACT participation has given me more confidence toward positive, analytical solutions to problems. I am doing business at a higher level and more successfully than I was before ACT."

Communications Consultant
Six Years Later

"Creativity in advertising is a valued commodity—understanding what makes creativity happen is critical to success. ACT taught me that there are techniques for getting people to solve problems creatively. Because of that I have been able to apply a lot of those techniques and bring them back to a work environment where creativity is valued. ACT helps people to discover their own personal creativity and where and how to apply it. It has helped me greatly."

Marketing Consultant
A Year and a Half Later

"I went into ACT thinking everyone else was creative but me, but I learned that was not true. A powerful new idea from the many I came away with was the power of using a wide variety of creative materials in presenting ideas instead of always being verbal or using overheads. Going 3-D is so powerful in getting an idea across to a client."

Career Consultant
Four Years Later

"I went to ACT with the problem of how to get my doctorate and start my own business. I came away from ACT with a name, a logo, and three weeks later, I'm in business. Creativity works!

"I learned from ACT that what I used to think was only valid for playing is also extraordinarily valuable in business. I was turned on to playing and soon those around me were too. I just couldn't wait to get back to the real world and put it into practice."

Creativity Consultant
A Year and a Half Later

"I attended the ACT Workshop because it involved creativity. It was fun. My objective was to be more concrete in my goals—but I came away with quite the opposite. I decided to let go and now have more faith in the power of my own inspirations and intend to go on following my dreams, making things happen. I'm now a better speaker, philosopher—confident in whatever I set out to do."

Teacher/Trainer
A Year and a Half Later

"I was a right-brain person running away from a left-brain world. I was made to feel like I was 'weird.' ACT I made me realize that I really had something wonderful to offer the world. Creativity is for everyone. I came away revitalized, confident, and feeling more normal."

Manager, Financial Operations
Five Years Later

"ACT has helped me (a left-brainer) to learn to withhold judgment when dealing with creative people. It's not right or wrong; it's just right or left, being different. On a personal level, I've learned to trust my 'gut' more than I had in the past when I was dealing just from analysis. I'm still looking forward to more personal growth that will let me use some of those strengths I have out there somewhere in my right brain."

Technical Manager
Four Months Later

"You have established a remarkable environment in ACT. It cannot be an accident that all these engineers are so remarkably sensitive and caring. You have really done as incredible thing. Thank you. The learning environment enriched the experience for me greatly."

Technical Group Manager
Four Months Later

"ACT I was great! It gave me an awareness of creativity and risk and an understanding of myself. I came back convinced I could make a difference and am committed to try. I recommend you try it."

Senior Engineer
Four Months Later

"From a midweek skeptic, to a weekend believer, ACT I gave me some problem solving techniques that really work. Not only on paper, but in actual practice. A good opportunity to learn how others think and work in problem-solving situations, and how you can effectively interact irrespective of your brain orientation."

Technical Engineer
Four Months Later

"ACT I is the best week-long course I have ever attended. It offers you both personal and professional growth. You leave with some specific techniques that really improve your problem-solving capabilities. The group dynamics, the environment, and the instructors make for a very exciting and rewarding week. ACT I provides the participants with a significant and positive emotional experience to help them get out of their rut and apply the creative potential within them and among their associates and group managers."

Engineer
Three Months Later

"From the first moment we gathered as a group, there was no letup. Momentum began to build, and there was no let-up from 7:00 A.M. until after 7:00 P.M. each day and until Friday when we aborted the mission to return home. The people you meet and work with are top-notch, talented folk. If ACT II is any match for ACT I, then sign me up for it right now!"

Senior Engineer
Four Months Later

"A first-class program, well-organized, and flexible to meet the needs of the individual. It proved to me that I could be a creative thinker and that we all have that capacity. I believe that it will help me to be more positive in dealing with new ideas and as a side benefit, a better understanding of how others think about problems. I feel that this type of training is valuable to our organization and I strongly support sending others who are interested."

Design Engineer
Four Months Later

"It gave me some fresh insight on being creative and on being responsive to myself, my environment, and to others. This gives me a greater feeling of personal freedom than I have ever felt before."

Market Segment Manager
Four Months Later

"At the time, I was struggling to develop new strategies for two troubled product categories, and in the aftermath of ACT, a free flow of ideas and a new clarity of thought came forth."

Manager, Training Programs
Four Months Later

"Without exception, the recent ACT Workshop was superb in every respect. The course content, structure, presentation style, team sessions, and practical exercises were all excellent."

Homemaker
Six Months Later

"ACT I saved my life. I thought I was going nuts, but I was only different—creatively different."

Research Chemist
One Year Later

"Many ACT ideas are spreading—at least here at Corporate Research and Development. Many more people are aware of the basic premises of the program and I really believe the concepts are being used to the benefit of both the individual and the company. Of course, that is probably the best reward of teaching, isn't it?"

Artist
Six Months Later

"I learned more in one week than I've ever learned in my life."

Music Therapist
Four Months Later

"Insight after insight is unfolding for me in a wonderful flow. Both hemispheres are in action and I feel a sense of relief. This phase of life is really an idea whose time has come!"

Teacher/Trainer
Nine Months Later

"It was wonderful to let the wind blow through my brain for a week. A large stone was thrown into the pond. The splash and ripples were fascinating and fun. But, best of all, the level of the pond has been raised. Thanks again!"

Company President
Two Years Later

"In terms of impact on my management approach, ACT I was fully equivalent to my advanced degree in business. In the area of creativity, it started me down a road of self-discovery I am committed to pursue."

Think about yourself and how this book has changed your view of yourself. You might consider taking time out now to write down how you think you can improve or balance yourself now that you are aware of your personal preferences. Make it a letter to yourself. Seal it in an envelope and then open the letter a few months from now. We all tend to put off some of the things that we would like to change in ourselves even though they will improve us in the long run. Remember, the value of accomplishing those things you have avoided in the past. Put yourself in a safe, judgment-free environment when doing so.

Not only do these shifts people make at ACT last, they continue to happen, especially for people who carry out follow-up action plans. This is because the self-knowledge gained helps explain why things happened the way they did in the past, and how to influence them for the better in the future.

In addition to these profound interior shifts, graduates tell us of other specifically practical benefits. These benefits include improved abilities to: (1) use expanded problem-solving skills—analyzing alternatives, drawing and sculpting, modeling, visualizing, dreaming, to name just a few; (2) recognize and manage creative people better; (3) improve relationships with spouse, manager, peers, and friends; (4) make changes in work that increase productivity and fulfillment; (5) develop more meaningful and satisfying career plans; (6) diagnose similarities and differences in other people to improve communication and relationships; (7) be more successful as a parent; (8) better cope with interpersonal conflict; (9) overcome procrastination; and (10) improve the capture of good ideas.

I'm always particularly glad to hear that an ACT graduate is facilitating the "odd man in" syndrome back in the workplace—when members of a group discover that one person, who had been on the fringes if not "on the outs," has a profile quite different from those of the next. This "odd" person suddenly becomes more acceptable to the others, because they can see the differences in behavior derive from differences in mental preferences rather than from the deliberate perversity of a maverick who wants to disrupt the harmonious homogeneity of the group. Almost overnight, team relationships are improved, even transformed.

The workshop evokes the Aha! experience—the moment of sudden insight—but as we know, that creative flash must be applied in the here-and-now if it is to strengthen creative functioning longer-term. Here's how we assist in the application phase. Before arriving, each participant prepares for ACT by defining five business and personal issues he or she wishes to resolve. Issues run the gamut, from relationship problems to business or career dilemmas to artistic blocks. These problems and issues comprise the grist participants then feed through their own creative mill under the guidance of ACT instructors. ACT's last day is devoted to helping participants formulate specific steps to change their lives in regard to these or any other issues they choose. These steps could involve anything from writing a new resumé, to creating an elaborate program for time management, to planning a new product, or to writing a book. When they take those steps and experience the fruits of doing so, they close the loop of reinforcement that makes the experience complete.

We also coach people in the reentry process. For example, we point out through films and other media that new converts to any way of thinking can let themselves in for a hard time if they fail to pace the way they introduce these ideas to people who've not heard of them before. That goes for all settings—offices, families, friends, churches, and so on. For this reason, we encourage corporations to send more than one person if possible. A team of three or four is ideal. The mutual support helps strengthen commitment through the rather slow process of spreading the creative message.

Having the processes impact on their lives so very personally means that when they go home, participants have constant reminders associated with their expanded creative processing experience.

But there's more—much more, in fact—things anyone can do. Chapter 9 lays out a comprehensive approach that anyone can follow. Even if you're not yet ready to implement these ideas, do take some time to explore this next chapter.

"To be shaken out of the ruts of ordinary perception, to be shown for a few timeless hours the outer and the inner world, not as they appear to an animal obsessed with words and notions, but as they are apprehended, directly and unconditionally, but Mind at Large—this is an experience of inestimable value to everyone."

Aldous Huxley
from the Doors of Perception

"Music has an emotional quality akin to appeal of color. In the arts of painting, sculpture, architecture, and dance, form is vital, and intellectual interpretation is required. Beauty lies in the careful blending of many elements...But music and color require virtually no effort to be enjoyed: they have a primitive charm and flow readily over the dikes of the brain to inundate the emotions."

Faber Birren

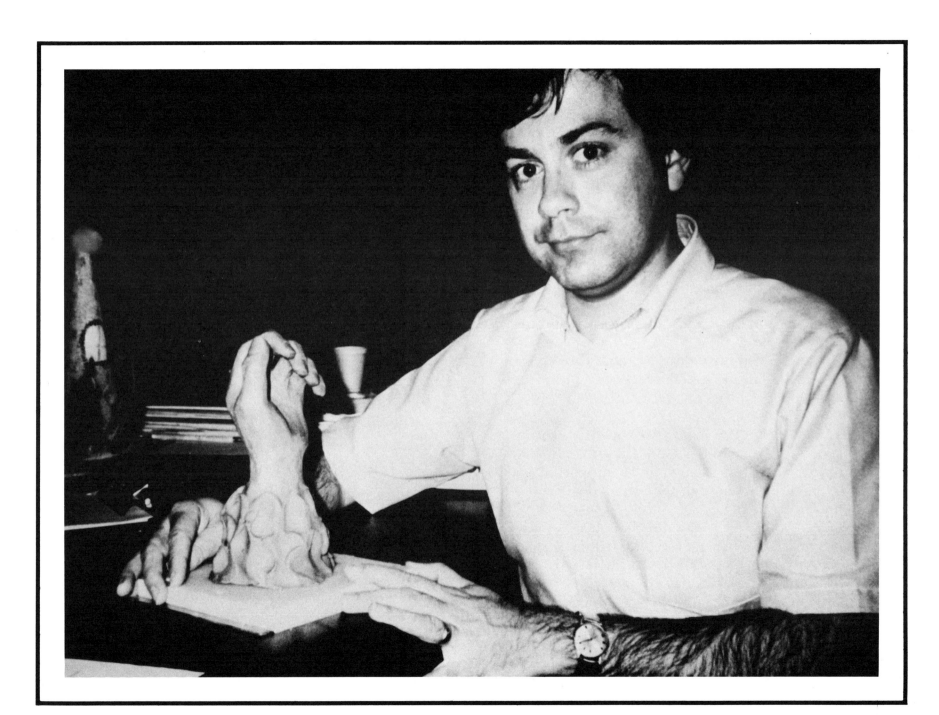

9

AFTER ACT – INTO ACTION

The biggest impediment many people will encounter on their road to creative functioning is their false belief that creativity is only for other creative people.

I recall vividly the moment when Richard LeBlanc, a GE quality control specialist, asked me whether we had any clay in our ACT supply room. The afternoon before, he had made a drawing of his hand with impressive realism. Now he had the urge to sculpt. It was a secret desire that he had suppressed for years, but his success in the drawing exercise gave him the confidence to try. In a few hours, he had created a sculpture of his hand that was so lifelike it touched his soul.

Here, in his own words, is Richard's account of the experience:

> I had tried to draw and sketch on many occasions, but was never really satisfied with the work. During ACT I, the final sketch of my hand gave so much encouragement, that for some reason, the clay was the next step—three dimensions. I piled clay on a base and started to sculpt with whatever tools I could find. I had never really tried to sculpt, but felt very comfortable doing what I was doing. I used one hand to sculpt while looking at the other as a model. What I was seeing was almost beyond three dimension—into the hand. I had to see the hand as bone formation with muscle and tendons covered with flesh with tension forming the image. I saw light and shadows, form and feeling, and could sculpt the hand. I was seeing beyond looking at my hand. The hand remains with me today as a reminder of what seeing can accomplish.

Figure 9-1. Richard LeBlanc (opposite)

I have used my experience with the hand on many occasions. I have not sculpted since that day—but I know I can. I have not seriously sketched since then, but I know I can. I have tried photography and the results are good. Getting on film what I can see (not always what is there) is very rewarding. Seeing a sunset at noon, creating a mood on film, or just the dew on a flower hanging on the edge capturing the image of the garden is beyond looking—*it's seeing*.

That happened three years ago and benefits are still evident. The limits of what we do, regardless of where we are, are self-imposed. We see what we allow ourselves to see; we challenge ourselves to self-imposed limits. Risk is required to really expand and risk is the step required to know if you can do it. Creativity is the breaking down of walls rather than the building of skills. I now know that I am really the one who controls how much I see by knowing how much I let go or am willing to risk. There is so much comfort with staying within the known, but so much excitement when you cross over to the unknown.

ACT has also provided the understanding that each problem can have many solutions. If a potential solution doesn't work, it doesn't mean that the idea was not good or the execution of the solution was bad. It may mean that the idea just has not reached its time. Trying a solution (the risk) and failing (the result) is not a loss—not trying is the loss. For every problem, try to find 5, 10, 50 solutions because if you run with the first idea you never used your full potential. I challenge more, I let go more, I see more than ever. I always share an idea, even if it's before its time. I try not to see the finish line because if I do, I know that I set my sights too low.

Monroe Barn

Thanks from the right side of my brain
    For enlightenment that surely will remain
A most enjoyable experience for me
    As I explore my enhanced creativity.

I will fondly remember your teaching
    And I hope you will go on reaching
For new heights of whole brain power
    So this will truly be your finest hour.

John R. Hanson
ACT I - 80
ACT II - 84

Figure 9-2. Barn and Poem by John Hanson

Figure 9-3. May and Leslie. Photos taken by Nehdi from the movie *May's Miracle*, from the Man Alive Series, Canadian Broadcasting Corporation

The whole-brain thought process has helped me attain the maximum benefits from relationships, whether social or at work. The understanding of that thought process, specialization by individuals, communication mismatch, and our own uniqueness has helped me every day since ACT. Every individual has restrained potential and the "letting go" of that potential is rewarding. The thoughts, ideas, and talents that may seem strange are that special uniqueness that makes us "one above the rest." There is little recognition, satisfaction, expansion, or full use of your potential if you are "one among the crowd." ACT taught me my uniqueness and the result is that I now want to show it.

ACT has taught me how to attain what I may want in the future because I set those goals and I set the limits. It all comes from within.

In an earlier session of ACT I, John Hanson, a GE engineering manager, applied his newly discovered drawing capability to capture one of the barns on the Monroe Institute property. He sent it to me a few years later mounted on a plaque with this poem of thanks (figure 9-2).

Our experience in working with thousands of people strongly supports the conclusion that most, if not all, are capable of finding some island of potential brilliance still hidden in their mental seascape. The true story of *May's Miracle*, a documentary produced by the Film Board of Canada, dramatically illustrates the reality of this seemingly implausible idea.

Mary Lempke, known by all as May, a tiny middle-aged woman with a grown family, felt challenged by the apparently hopeless plight of baby "Leslie," who was born not only blind, but also the victim of severe cerebral palsy. Doctors predicted death within months, but May was convinced that with her love and encouragement, the baby would survive. "Nothing ever dies that comes to me," she said. Convinced that her love would save the child, she adopted Leslie and nurtured him in an atmosphere filled with unconditional love and the firm expectation that he would eventually walk and talk. For the first eight years he was unable to do either, but she persisted, until one day he stood alone for about a minute before collapsing. It was another four years before he began to walk a few steps.

One day, in his early teens, while playing with a piece of string, Leslie moved his fingers in a rhythmic way and May instantly thought—music! She quickly acquired a used piano and assisted Leslie in banging on the keys. She began to fill the house with music from an old phonograph. One night, three years later, she awoke to piano music. Thinking she had left the TV on, she went into the living room to discover Leslie playing the piano. She couldn't believe it—real music! He was 16 at the time. His musical talent had incubated for 3 years before surfacing. Slowly, but surely, Leslie developed a musical repertoire. A few years later, he flabbergasted May when he began to sing. Eight years after beginning to sing, he began to talk. He was more than 25 years old before he spoke a single word.

By then, his musical skills were developed to the point where he began appearing in public concerts. In his late 20s, he was astounding audiences with his playing and singing abilities, including a show-stopping routine in which he played back music after hearing it for the first time—every note perfect.

Part of the drama of this story is that this boy's island of brilliance contrasted so sharply with his disabilities. While Leslie's left-mode capabilities were minimal, his selective right-mode musical capabilities were beyond smart—they were brilliant. Some people might think of

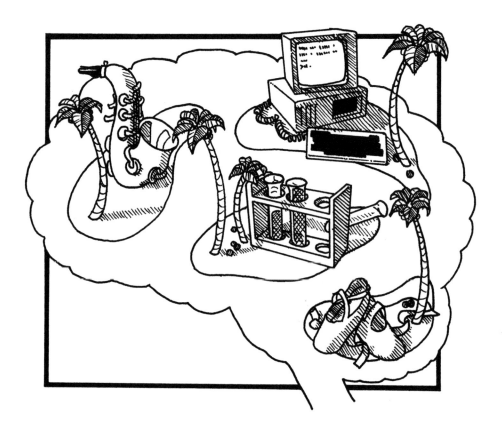

Figure 9-4. Islands of Brilliance

Leslie as severely retarded, describing him as an idiot savant. But that's a harsh judgment. Imagine, instead, what it would be like to grow up never seeing the light of day and occupying a body whose every limb was not only weak, but seemed to have a mind of its own—all going in different directions. But that's not the whole story. Another part of the drama is the extraordinary love, faith, and dedication of May, and most important, her positive assumptions about what he could become. There aren't many like her in this world. But you don't have to be disadvantaged to find your gifts, and you don't need a miracle worker like May to help you. The point is, May demonstrated that Leslie's hidden mental potential could be accessed and put to use. And if that's true for Leslie, I believe that the "island of brilliance" theory holds true for the rest of us. Every person, regardless of personality or occupation, has a brain in which there exists some particular area of optimal functioning—an area that, when accessed in the right situation, can provide the person with an experience of enormously fulfilling, competent, joyful activity.

People's talents vary greatly: Someone like Leonardo da Vinci seems to have had a whole continent of brilliance. Others of us have archipelagos. Some of us have gifts in language, mathematics, science, spatial relationships, or music. Your brilliance might be in raising plants or animals, or even earthworm farming. Your special ability might be to hear or see, taste, smell, or touch. Your talent might be useful to you at work or it might be simply a source of pleasure in play.

How great or numerous your talents happen to be isn't the crucial thing. What matters most is that exercising your gifts should feel terrific, provide a vehicle for personal growth, or even form the basis for a career.

So if we all have islands of brilliance and exercising them feels so good, why don't we always know about our own? There are several reasons. First, our islands of brilliance or giftedness sometimes come so naturally that we don't even know we have them or that they make us exceptional. Sometimes it takes an aptitude test or a challenge to spot them. For example, one friend took a battery of psychological tests and, at age 35, was told that her spatial aptitude was the kind that distinguished Frank Lloyd Wright from other architects. It was only then that she began to notice her mechanical aptitude and her interest in and awareness of spaces as anything out of the ordinary and to expand her use of that aptitude.

The second reason we may not be fully conscious of our islands is that we may not have had sufficient time, opportunity, or daring to follow our own inclinations. Raising children, working our way through school, applying ourselves to a career, or just keeping body and soul together can be a full-time occupation, and the courage to change can take time to develop. Even then, we may not be in the right environment to stimulate it. Often it takes an exciting job, a demanding problem, or a perceptive, understanding mentor to provide just the right stimulus to bring our gifts out in the open.

In spite of these obstacles, it's never too late for you to find new islands of brilliance for yourself or your loved ones. All you need is commitment. Every day, you make many small choices that determine how you spend your time; as soon as the commitment is there, you can begin to exercise your will in a new direction. A first step toward developing that commitment is to confirm and accept that you, like everyone else, have islands of brilliance and *can* find them if you are determined to do so. Once

"Capacities clamour to be used, and cease their clamour only when they are well used."

A.H. Maslow

"Creativity is the rightful heritage of every human being."

Michael F. Andrews

"A fair idea put to use is better than a good idea kept on the polishing wheel."

Alex F. Osborn

you have decided on this course, you will find that there are myriad possible paths to take.

When I addressed the subject of creativity in Chapter 7, I said you could increase your *commitment* to living the creative life if you followed one or more of four strategies: (1) learn from children; (2) practice affirming yourself; (3) learn to value your time; and (4) test different things that interest you until you find out what really turns you on. In Chapter 8, I described what "testing different things" is like for people who attend our ACT I workshop.

This chapter goes one step further and outlines how to integrate into your daily life ideas and activities that enhance your creative capabilities and experience. These activities further three main aims:

1. Strengthening the will to live creatively

2. Expanding mental preferences by changing frames of reference

3. Enhancing skills in the creative process.

STRENGTHENING THE WILL TO LIVE CREATIVELY

For most people, the prospect of living more creatively calls for significant changes in behavior, and, as we all know, old habits aren't always easy to break. Changing behavior, especially changing mental modes, takes willpower and persistence, particularly if you are expanding into an area of avoidance.

Strengthening your willpower will be easier if you first know what challenges you can expect to encounter so you can be prepared, and also if you have a list of tips on what you can do to maintain a positive attitude.

Challenges to Your Willpower

When you decide to expand preferences to include mental modes and activities you currently avoid, you can expect to encounter the following. *First*, expanding preferences is easier for some than for others. Generally, in terms of brain dominance, right-mode people who want to develop their left-mode capabilities have a somewhat tougher time than left-mode dominant people who want to develop right-mode capabilities. This is because left-mode activities are more knowledge-based and therefore require that the person learn specific language, facts, and techniques. Developing right-mode preferences is easier because it doesn't require such study. I'll explain what it does require shortly.

Second, you can count on running into resistance—old attitudes, "dragons"—which will drain you of energy when you expand into unfamiliar functions. This is only natural, no matter in which direction you're trying to shift. After all, you've been parented, taught, managed, and generally influenced by society for many years to value some things and deprecate, fear, or ridicule others. Consciously, you say you can't do something, or that you've tried it and you don't like it, or that it's too boring. Subconsciously, you may still be hearing old messages that invalidate what you want to do, or you may be remembering a traumatic experience, such as an embarrassment in school. Such habits won't disappear overnight, particularly if they're associated with identity (e.g., "real" men don't show pain, or "creative" people leave the finances to others, or "ordinary" people are not smart enough to handle big ideas). One common fear is the thought, "If I expand preferences into new areas, I will lose the gifts I now have." There's no need to worry. In fact, your strongest preferences and competencies can actually be reinforced and strengthened by exercising less preferred modalities. It may be, for example, that the experience of paying your bills and getting a better grasp of your financial position will provide the safety and security you need to take the next creative leap! Or that taking time to relax into imagery will refresh you and you will be able to return to work with renewed concentration on a detailed calculation.

Tips for Maintaining a Positive Attitude

You can be sure that if you make the commitment to expand preferences, enhance skills, and live more creatively, you will reach your goal. The key is a positive attitude, not only toward specific shifts, but also toward the entire change and growth process.

How do you go about developing this positive mental attitude? Here are some tips:

1. *Give yourself a few pats on the back* just for daring to try—most people never do.

2. *Count the profit up front.* Figure out what it costs

"Convince yourself that you are working in clay not marble, on paper not eternal bronze: let that first sentence be as stupid as it wishes. No one will rush out and print it as it stands. Just put it down; then another. Your whole first paragraph or first page may have to be guillotined in any case after your piece is finished: it is a kind of forebirth."

Jacques Barzun

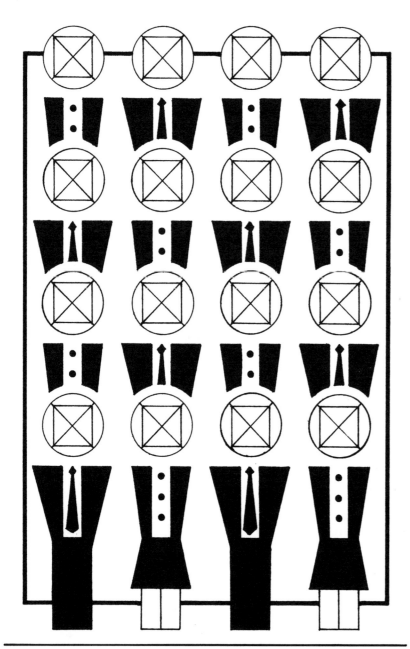

Figure 9-5. You Don't Have to be a 1-1-1-1

you *not* to have the skill you want to develop. For example, if you are an artist whose office, studio, and marketing activities are in desperate shape, you will never make it as a self-supporting painter. The profit of developing A and B preferences may well be having a successful career as an artist versus not having one.

3. *Regard learning as an exploration* or a scouting trip rather than as a painful chore. You aren't locked into any change, and so you are truly free to choose!

4. *Remember, you can choose freely.* You've already made it this far with your current talents and inclinations. Your survival doesn't depend on changing.

5. *Retain professionals to guide* you in learning how to function in those modes. These days, teachers abound for developing every modality, including intuition, body language, lateral thinking, bookkeeping, writing — there's no shortage of professional help.

6. *Get support from others.* Associate yourself with someone who thinks in the ways you want to think, and then work with that person on the solution to a difficult problem, using your own preferred modes, but also observing the other person's.

Or develop a support group. Instead of working solo, find other people who have the same growth needs and desires that you do, and do a group project in your quadrant of shared avoidance.

7. *Use skills you have to get skills you want.* For example, if you are an engineer who really wants to be more creative but doesn't know how, gather research about creative people, and then quantify, organize, process, and analyze the data to identify characteristic preferences common to people who behave creatively.

EXPANDING MENTAL PREFERENCES BY CHANGING FRAMES OF REFERENCE

It is not at all my recommendation that everyone strive to become a 1-1-1-1. That would prove inappropriate for many individuals and could deprive the world of some fascinating variety. However, I strongly recommend that everyone learn to access and situationally use as many quadrants and capabilities as possible for two important reasons: (1) an avoidance can keep us from getting what we want, and (2) the continuing pace and magnitude of change in our world demands creative responses, which calls for the ability to iterate among all quadrants.

One of the most powerful supports for shifting preference has to do with recognizing the value of less familiar modes. We've already spoken of attitudes opposing expansion of preferences. In this section, I want to propose some remedial thinking for those attitudes.

The concept of frames of reference is very useful in this connection, because it enables us to see the components

"You must play the fool a little if you would not be thought wholly a fool."
Michel de Montaigne

"Without going beyond his own nature, one cannot achieve ultimate wisdom."
Lao Tsu

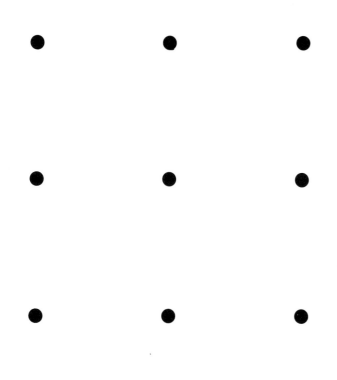

Figure 9-6. Nine-dot Puzzle

of the thought process of each quadrant. (You'll recall that the term *frame of reference* was introduced in connection with the B quadrant's focus on safekeeping in Chapter 5).

A frame of reference is a thought structure made up of values, reasoning, and decisions about something. Here's a frame of reference about physical fitness: "Physical exercise is good for one's health (value); I have what it takes to do that (reasoning); so I will stay physically fit (decision)." This is a good frame of reference to have if you want to get in shape. But what if your frame of reference about exercise is: "Physical exercise is a good thing, but it's too boring to bother with (value); it won't matter that much if I don't do it (reasoning); so I won't do it (decision)." With that frame of reference, you'd have a hard time getting yourself to do any exercise on a sustained basis. You'd need to change your values and reasoning before you'd be able to make a decision solid enough to stick to.

Keep in mind that frames of reference are quite individual and can be very complex. To detect your frame of reference about any quadrant for which you want to strengthen your preferences, write down your thoughts and feelings about the modes of that quadrant, then look at the list and tease out the values, reasoning, and decisions stated or implied in it.

Frames of reference can also be visual. Take the nine-dot puzzle shown in figure 9-6 as an illustration. The object of the nine-dot puzzle is to connect all nine dots with straight lines without: (1) taking your pencil off the paper or (2) going through any dot twice. If you aren't familiar with this puzzle, you might take a moment now to try it. (If you plan to do the puzzle, stop reading now, because here comes the answer.) Solving the puzzle is possible only by going outside the square space that the nine dots would define if straight lines connected the outside dots (See figure 9-7). Even though the lines aren't there, our minds tend to supply them anyway and thus create boundaries that we must then "go outside of" to solve the problem. Don't feel bad if you didn't figure it out, by the way—most people don't solve the puzzle at all or, if they do, it takes them quite a while.

I had a similar experience of shifting frames of reference in the course of developing the four-quadrant circular profile display. For graphing the intensity of preference for each quadrant, I established an arbitrary scale running from 0 to 100. It made sense to me at the time. After all, handedness was measured on a scale (zero to 100 percent), so why not measure brain dominance on a scale as well? Having set the minimum at zero and the maximum at 100, I then began to score the first batch of surveys and to plot the resulting profiles. After scoring about 500 instruments, it suddenly dawned on me that I didn't have to limit maximum quadrant scores to 100 if they went above that. I could draw profiles outside the circle. The numbers I was using for this scale, as opposed to the handedness scale, were not percentages, and in fact, staying within the circle was inappropriate and misleading. The scores went well beyond 100 to 125 or even 150. By limiting the maximum score to 100, I was simply cutting off—disregarding—the extremely strong preferences of the test takers. Despite these facts, my resistance to the change was considerable. I had already done 500 profiles the other way, and I had not truly let go of wanting to stay within the arbitrary limit of 100. Nevertheless, the logic was such that it overrode my attachment, and even while struggling mentally against this embedded thinking, I forced myself

"Every real individual is a creative person. This intrinsic creativity emerges, or is expressed, when the person is free to use his potentialities."

Clark E. Moustakas

"Every healthy and creative individual resists engulfment by custom and rigid habits."

Herbert Bonner

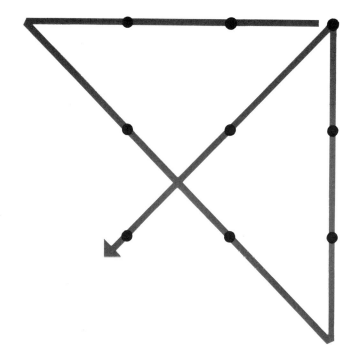

Figure 9-7.   Nine-dot Puzzle Solution

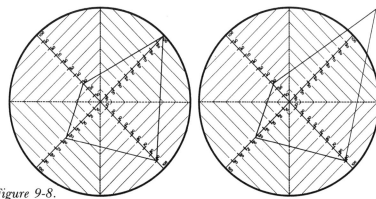

Figure 9-8.
100 pt. Maximum Profile Graph vs. Going Outside the Circle

to draw profiles that depicted scores beyond 100.

The moment I broke out of the constraining circle, I felt a great relief. Not only did I realize how much sense it made to validate those extreme scores, but also I was suddenly able to see much, much more. *First,* I saw and understood more completely the opposite of preference, which is avoidance. *Second,* I suddenly knew that those preferences that went outside the circle were so strong that they would be visible behaviorally—a person wouldn't be able to conceal them. *Third,* I understood that the equally strong avoidance was also publicly visible. Further, I realized that the combination of a preference in a quadrant that went outside the circle combined with an avoidance that was close to zero emphasized the strength of the preference all the more.

Expanding your own frames of reference can produce this same type of liberating effect, this sense of combined revelation and relief. As tenaciously as you hold your fixed ideas, going beyond them almost always feels better. For me, breaking out of the circle was another of the continuing reminders that we tend to constrain ourselves unnecessarily by imposing boundaries that don't really exist.

We develop frames of reference to cover almost everything, not only major issues, such as love, war, or religion, but all the humble things as well. Take this small incident that occurred a few years back. One of my peers at GE's Management Development Institute and I would occasionally meet in the parking lot and walk into the headquarters building together. He carried an executive-type attaché case (one of the fancy ones, with a combination lock and burnished cordovan leather exterior). I carried a suede tote bag, usually bulging with papers and "stuff." He would eye my tote bag occasionally, but it never came up in discussion. One day as we walked together, he suddenly stopped and said to me, "Ned, I want you to know how much I admire your using a tote bag like that. I couldn't do it. I admire the way you've taken a stand on carrying your papers the way you want to and not the way other people do, even though I'm sure you know that people joke about it." This very good man's frame of reference for proper dress did not include a suede tote bag. Although his practical logic might support carrying loose papers in this manner, it was simply outside his social frame of reference at the time.

Expanding Preferences for Specific Quadrants

We have seen that going outside our frames of reference is often required to expand mental preferences, to solve a puzzle, for example, or to express profiles accurately. In the same way, it is often necessary to go beyond our current frames of reference if we want to expand preferences in mental functioning.

The most difficult expansions of preference are those shifts that we make to the quadrant diagonally opposed to our strongest primary (A to C and C to A; B to D and D to B), so I will first discuss ways to effect such expansion. Then, because those who are double dominant have two primaries in adjoining quadrants, making them more cerebral than limbic or more left than right (or vice versa), I will go on to suggest ways to expand preference for other halves of the brain. These recommendations are summarized in the charts (figures 9-12, 9-13, 9-14, 9-15), which I encourage you to copy and post for easy reminders.

When I talk about shifting, by the way, I don't mean

"A person who never makes a mistake never tried anything."

unknown

"When you refuse to accept the obvious, you've taken your first giant step toward creativity."

unknown

"Intuition ... Intuition is something which you claim you had; after something you thought might fail is an unexpected success."

Ray Alvord

Figure 9-9.   Going from Calculating Logic to Teddy Bear Sensitive

substituting one preference for another. I mean *adding to* existing preferences by (1) relaxing dependence on one mode only; and (2) expanding the ability to operate in the diagonally opposed quadrant. We "shift" our mental center of gravity, but we lose nothing.

Expanding from A to C

People who strongly prefer A quadrant often consider it inappropriate to express or even feel certain emotions. Their frame of reference regarding feelings may go something like:

Value:	Feelings are not useful; in fact, they get in the way of clear thinking.
Reasoning:	I can shut off my feelings and it won't have any negative effect.
Decision:	Therefore, I won't feel; I'll just look at the facts and act accordingly.

To move beyond such a frame of reference, the A quadrant person needs to learn to appreciate several things. *First*, it is possible to think clearly and feel at the same time, although it may take some training and practice to learn how to do so. *Second*, beyond a certain point, you cannot turn off feelings without distorting thought.

Third, rather than obstructing thought, feelings can actually improve the quality of thought. Feelings are a different form of thinking. They involve neural activity in the context of the limbic system, just as cognitive thinking involves neural activity in the cortex of the cerebral hemispheres. Feelings provide enormous amounts of information and are therefore equal in value to other types of factual information. For example, if an A quadrant person suddenly feels nervous with an acquaintance, this can signal several possibilities: (1) the acquaintance is feeling fear and sending out signals of fear, and subconsciously the other person is picking up the cues and beginning to feel uneasy, too; (2) the acquaintance is feeling angry and is subtly threatening the other person; or (3) the person has noticed some kind of incongruity, usually words versus actions, that suggests all is not as it should be.

Conscious A quadrant thinkers will analyze a situation like the one described above, consider amending their attitudes about feelings, and then set a goal of learning to pick up and decipher emotional information. As they begin to value and respect feeling modes in others as well as in themselves, their new frame of reference tends to look more like this:

Value: Feelings provide important information for getting along in business and social situations.

Reasoning: In a situation involving both facts and feelings, facts alone will not provide enough information to act on. Feelings are of equal value to facts. I can feel without forfeiting my ability to think clearly.

Decision: It's appropriate and important for me to learn to detect and interpret feelings, seeking professional assistance if that's what it takes.

Expanding from C to A

People with strong C preferences who want to expand

further into A can follow a similar pattern. It's not uncommon for a C quadrant person to hold a frame of reference such as this:

Value: People who think and analyze too much are insensitive, and they use facts just to overwhelm and manipulate people.

Reasoning: I can't think analytically and feel at the same time. What my intuition doesn't tell me, I don't need to know.

Decision: I won't chase after facts. I won't analyze things. I'll follow what feels right.

To expand A quadrant thinking, the C quadrant person needs to learn several things about the relationship between feelings and analytical thinking. (1) Feelings alone are an unreliable source of guidance in highly charged situations, especially when other people are pressuring us to act in their interests rather than our own. (2) As a result, the decision to feel *rather than* to think logically may actually impede our ability to be compassionate toward ourselves and others. For example, people can't be fully caring and responsive to someone else's distress when they are confused and upset over their own money matters. (3) Feelings often change significantly in response to new facts, and it takes careful analysis as well as introspection to understand the source of our own feeling reactions and to respond appropriately.

Concentrating on thinking as well as feeling offers significant advantages, not only externally, but also internally. It can actually enhance our emotional life significantly by expanding the range of what we can react *to*. Some psychotherapeutic schools (not all) believe that all feeling

Figure 9-10.   Minister's Photo

proceeds from thinking, so the more creative and rich our thought life, the more creative and rich our feeling life will be. Einstein again serves as an example of a monumental intellect combined with soft, musical, emotional, interpersonal, spiritual attributes. He seemed to alternate between these contrasting modes, but history tells us he worked hard to attain his A quadrant competencies. His clear thinking facilitated his creativity rather than shutting it down.

Clear thinking also provides us with the psychic safety to experience our feelings fully without jeopardizing other cherished aspects of our lives. For example, if you are a C quadrant person and feel angry at another person, but are not in a situation where expressing your anger is a good idea, you can use the A quadrant mode to recall a principle for expressing feelings (Never hurt yourself in the process) and decide on a different option, for instance one of the following: The first involves several steps: (1) Ask yourself why the person is behaving in this way toward you; (2) if there seems to be a misunderstanding, check it out with the other person; and (3) clear up the misunderstanding. Another option involves a different approach: (1) Use the D quadrant mode and fantasize about your opponent's being tickled till he admits he's wrong and begs forgiveness; (2) move to B quadrant to do something simple and busy to give the feelings time to change; and (3) once the emotional charge is somewhat diminished, move back to C quadrant to renew your intuitive and feeling level functioning.

This kind of clear thinking about options allows C quadrant people to pay attention to feelings without responding in a way they might later regret, and is just one of the many examples of how they can enhance life through developing preferences for clear thinking as well as authentic feeling.

Once having expanded the A quadrant modes, the C quadrant's new frame of reference might look like this:

Value: Thinking clearly allows me to improve my understanding of why people act the way they do so I can respond in a way that's fully consistent with my humanitarian aims.

Reasoning: My thinking is simply unpracticed. If I give myself a little time to think, I'll be able to draw conclusions just like everyone else, and do so while I'm feeling.

Decision: I will learn to acquire and remember facts and principles, and to draw conclusions from them as a way to check my intuitions.

There are some wonderful examples of C quadrant people getting excited about the empowerment they feel when they give themselves permission and encouragement to think clearly. Here's just one. A minister, strongly dominant in the C quadrant, began a lay elders meeting by passing around a picture of a 102-year-old widow holding a photo of a handsome young man. He was her minister/husband who had died when he was only 32. The old lady's face in the picture was wonderful, full of love, peace, and thanksgiving. The church's national pension fund had paid her a pension for 70 years, through the raising of her 6 children, through the wars, through illness. Now in her last days, she had written a letter to the church news-

"'And the priestess spoke again and said: Speak to us of Reason and Passion. And he answered, saying:'

Your soul is oftentimes a battlefield, upon which your reason and your judgement wage war against your passion and your appetite.

Would that I could be the peacemaker in your soul, that I might turn the discord and the rivalry of your elements into oneness and melody.

But how shall I, unless you yourselves be also the peacemakers, nay, the lovers of all your elements?

Your reason and your passion are the rudder and the sails of your seafaring soul.

If either your sails or your rudder be broken, you can but toss and drift, or else be held at a standstill in mid-seas.

For reason, ruling alone, is a force confining and passion unattended is a flame that burns to its own destruction.

Therefore, let your soul exalt your reason to the heights of passion that it may sing.

paper expressing her profound gratitude for the loving embrace that her church home and family had supplied, financially and otherwise, for so many years.

The minister passed the picture around without comment because he considered its message obvious: In his mind, it evoked some of the good feelings people could have about the church's taking care of its own. The meeting moved on without his realizing he'd just allowed a major miscommunication to occur. Vestry members, headed by a person with strong A quadrant preferences, were quite irritated. The minister's own compensation/pension plan was always on the vestry agenda as a part of the budget review. So, without verbal information to clarify his purpose, they came to a variety of conclusions, ranging from, "I don't get it" to "Can you believe it—he's trying to soften us up and make us feel obligated to pay him enough to make him as happy as this woman."

Upon reflection, the minister knew intuitively that the picture had bombed, but couldn't understand what had gone wrong until weeks later, when he saw his own strongly C quadrant brain dominance profile. He suddenly realized why the mostly left-mode vestry members hadn't understood his attempt to communicate. The understanding brought instant embarrassment, followed by a sense of relief. He now knows how to prevent this kind of misunderstanding when he tells something to left-mode dominant people (A quad especially). He asks himself: First, what goal do I want to achieve by imparting this information? Second, what question am I attempting to answer? He then communicates the answers to his audience with an awareness of both the verbal and the non-verbal information he's giving. He now knows to save the old pensioner's picture, for example, for informal sharing during the coffee break, or for a future meeting on a different topic. To the vestry committee, on the other hand, he might say, "Since we will be discussing my pension arrangements today, I'd like you to know that I am very grateful to the church and to you, individually, for caring about what happens to me when I'm retired. I stand ready to provide any facts that you need from me to help you develop a plan."

Expanding from B to D

One of the most thrilling shifts is the one from the B to the D quadrant. When B dominant people choose to make that leap—and a leap into the unknown is definitely what it feels like initially—they can experience enormous liberation and power. The power comes because, having established an ordered, reliable base of operations as a foundation, they can often function with extraordinary effectiveness in intuitive and artistic modes. In the latter activity, particularly, B dominant people's attention to detail combined with D quadrant vision and sensitivity can produce work of extraordinary quality and elegance.

This shift relates to planning, and reminds me of a B dominant corporate planner who participated in a strategically oriented idea-generating session I was leading. As the process I was using moved toward the D quadrant mode and away from the more traditional A and B aspects of operational planning, he became less involved in the discussion, until he eventually fell totally silent. When, through a guided fantasy, he discovered his own intuition and conceptual capability, he blurted out the best strategic idea we had heard all day. Then, capitalizing on his B quadrant expertise, he backed up his strategic idea with an impressive string of details. The triumphant expression on his face said it all. A typical B frame of reference about D modes might go like this:

Value: The right way to do things is to use a proven method, to have a place for everything, and to have everything in its place. If there's no system, there's chaos. You won't know what works, you can't find what you need when you need it, and you waste a lot of valuable time. Change and new ideas will just mess up the already proven system.

Reasoning: Even with life's demands for change, life is constant enough so that there will always be a proven method for what I need to do, and a place that accommodates the different types of "everything" that I need. I can have some control over the rate of change.

Decision: I will use proven methods and keep my life orderly and secure so things don't get out of control.

In many places, especially in settings that are more functional than conceptual, this kind of frame of reference can work well for extended periods of time; but even there, problems arise when significant change occurs. On a personal level, for example, children grow up and their minds develop new capabilities, making it impossible for parents to relate to them as in the past. Or a husband or wife might decide to go back to school and that calls for changes in the distribution of work in the family. Suddenly *she* has to travel for her job; *he* has to cook. Broader societal

And let it direct your passion with reason, that your passion may live through its own daily resurrection, and like the phoenix rise above its own ashes.

I would have you consider your judgement and your appetite even as you would two loved guests in your house.

Surely, you would not honor one guest above the other; for he who is more mindful of the one loses the love and the faith of both.

Among the hills, when you sit in the cool shade of the white poplars, sharing the peace and serenity of distant fields and meadows— then let your heart say in silence, "God rests in reason."

And when the storm comes and the mighty wind shakes the forest, and thunder and lightning proclaim the majesty of the sky, then let your heart say in awe, "God moves in passion."

And since you are a breath in God's sphere and a leaf in God's forest, you too should rest in reason and move in passion."

Kahlil Gibran
excerpt from *The Prophet*

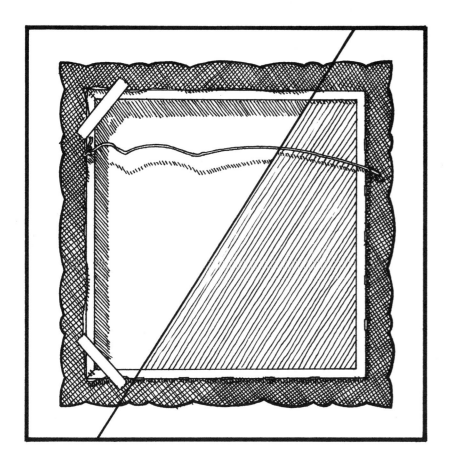

Figure 9-11. Improved Painting Packaging

changes demand similar attention. Years ago, most women didn't mind being called girls; today, a man calling a woman a girl can expect another kind of reaction—annoyance and even rejection. He used to pick up the dinner check automatically; now he often expects her to pay her own way.

In business life, change is the norm. When the market stops demanding a major product, for example, a company must respond creatively in order to survive—anticipating, even shaping, consumer desires rather than simply reacting to them. When a competitor introduces a new, superior product, the company must develop a new technology or a new business or it will die. When the company is bought out and new management that hails from a different industry comes in, it may hold different operating assumptions. Sticking by proven methods for the longstanding employees can lead to firing. The same holds true to a slightly lesser degree when a new supervisor is brought in.

Since such change is constant, B quadrant people need to develop ways to cope with it. For example, they can use their B quadrant talent and procedures, because there are processes and procedures for coping with change. Possible procedures include: (1) identifying the nature of the change at each state; (2) devising and assessing options for reacting to it; and (3) planning out how to implement those options. These procedures are learnable. There are also ways of dealing with emotional components: identifying and allowing them; then analyzing and accounting for long-range implications.

B quadrant people need to know that accessing other quadrants is possible and profitable, both in perceiving the nature of the changes and in incubating and illuminating creative ways to cope with them. Of particular value are D quadrant conceptualizing and visualizing capabilities, which, with practice, B quadrant people can learn to experience and translate into verbal expression. The power of these visual concepts is that they provide a broader conceptual framework within which the B quad's genius for organizing can allow for and accommodate change without sacrificing order.

In accepting these new abilities, the B quadrant person's new frame of reference might look like this:

Value: The *process* of coping with change effectively is an orderly one. One can learn to perceive changes in non-verbal terms without inviting chaos. One can keep order selectively. Change per se is not bad.

Reasoning: I can learn to be more open and creative and still pay attention to details as appropriate.

Decision: I will learn and follow proven procedures for accommodating change. I'll use my gift for order in a way that supports positive change. I will place a greater value on my intuitive modes and learn to access them so that I can accommodate change with greater comfort.

Expanding from D to B

The expansion from D to B can be very exciting as well. Consider the case of an artist friend, who was constantly in a mess with customers, sponsors, and suppliers.

"The open mind does not deny convention; it merely uses convention as a starting place for original exploration."
Bob Samples

"I use to think of it as an extraordinary act that produced something new and useful to mankind. I now see it as less cosmic and more common, an everyday affair, a mode of thought and action that is intimately associated with learning and changing not only oneself but one's situation."
unknown

"Do not the most moving moments of our lives find us all without words."
Marcel Marceau

"A man is not idle because he is absorbed in thought. There is a visible labor and there is an invisible labor."
Victor Hugo

CHART A
WAYS OF SHIFTING VALUES REGARDING YOUR MORE/LESS PREFERRED MODES

1. To move toward the Lower Right: Relax on need for proof by facts. **VALUE FEELINGS**

4. To move toward the Limbic Mode: Respect gut feeling. **VALUE BODY RESPONSE AND THE FORM OF THINGS, AND RELAX ON INTELLECTUAL AND CONCEPTUAL MODES.**

8. To move toward the Upper Left: Relax on intensity of feelings. **VALUE FACTS.**

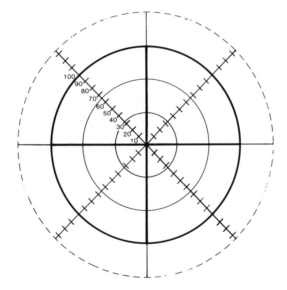

2. To move toward the Right mode: Respect intuition. **VALUE INSTINCTIVE, EXPERIENTIAL, HUMANISTIC APPROACHES**

7. To move toward the Left Mode: Respect logic. **VALUE PLANNED, ORGANIZED, RATIONAL APPROACHES.**

3. To move toward the Upper Right: Relax on tightness of form and structure. **VALUE SPONTANEITY**

5. To move toward the Cerebral Mode: Respect Cognitive Processes. **VALUE THE BALANCE OF RATIONAL AND INTUITIVE THINKING.**

6. To move toward the Lower Left: Relax on the need for absolute freedom. **VALUE FORM AND STRUCTURE.**

Figure 9-12.   Chart A. How to Expand into Quadrants not Currently Preferred

His paintings were wonderful and his work admired, but he never met his commitments. He was late, he delivered the wrong thing, he got the frame wrong, he charged the wrong amount, he never paid his bills. He won a lot of prizes, but he was so unreliable that he didn't sell much. Unaware of his own preferences and avoidances, he blamed others for his troubles. On one occasion when he was complaining about the way an art show was being run, I encouraged him to volunteer to run the next one instead of entering a painting. He immediately rejected the idea, but when I offered to help him form a committee and to support him throughout the project, he reluctantly agreed.

The experience was a metamorphosis. An art show is a complicated event to plan and run. The more he got into it, the more he seemed to accept the need for planning and organizing. While he didn't know how to do it, he began at least to try, and with the understanding and help of others, he managed to pull off a successful event. The rewards he received for his administrative leadership were equal to a blue ribbon. He ran another show. He was more successful. But what was even more impressive was the transformation in his own work. His paintings looked just as good as they always did, but their presentation was greatly improved. The mounting and framing were now professional. Protective brown paper covered the backs, and the screw eyes and picture wire were of the right size and securely mounted in the right place. This attention to detail sounds insignificant, but in reality it signaled a massive value shift that led to the rapid development of needed skills and behaviors and the eventual transformation of his professional relationships.

Prior to his metamorphosis, my friend's typical D frame of reference might have looked like this:

Value:	The most important thing is freedom to dream, to create, to live for the moment. Details, rules, and regulations are a drag: They're boring, they take too long, and they cramp a person's style.
Reasoning:	I can be free and fully creative without paying attention to details. Someone else is always around to pick up the pieces if necessary.
Decision:	I won't let anyone fence me into following rules or sweating out details.

Once we reach adulthood, freedom tends to be proportionate to the amount of order and discipline in our lives, whether we supply it ourselves or someone else does it for us (like a spouse or parent). Unless the artist disciplines himself to keep his paint brushes clean and paint containers covered, his paint is a loss. Unless we keep within our budgets, and do those humble things required to keep bill collectors from the door, the upset in our lives will drain us of the energy required for creative work and play. That's the penalty for not taking care of details.

But there's an up side. In addition to supporting life or keeping a workspace in order, taking care of detail also helps us function better in D quadrant because it improves our vision. D quadrant is where synthesis takes place, and the more clearly and fully we can see the parts, the more elegant and true will be the appreciation of the whole. Thus, discipline of detail and procedures not only makes creative thinking possible, it actually makes it better.

Learning this kind of truth experientially—especially for C and D dominant people who function in more expe-

CHART B

AT HOME ACTIVITIES — PERSONAL EXERCISES TO HELP ACCESS AND DEVELOP YOUR LESS-PREFERRED MODES

ACTIVITIES TO HELP ACCESS AND STIMULATE THE LEFT MODE

ACTIVITIES TO HELP ACCESS AND STIMULATE THE RIGHT MODE

UPPER-LEFT ACTIVITIES

Predict what will happen tomorrow based on what you know about today.
Find out how a frequently used machine actually works.
Take a current problem situation and analyze it into its main parts.
Review a recent impulsive decision and identify its rational aspects.
Convert your retirement dreams into a quantitative formula.
Join an investment club.
Engage in some logic games.
Learn to run a personal computer.
Play "devil's advocate" in a group decision process.
Write a critical review of your favorite movie.

UPPER RIGHT ACTIVITIES

Fly a kite the way a kite is meant to be flown.
Invent a "gourmet" dish and actually prepare it.
Play with clay and discover its texture and inner meaning.
Take a 15-minute "theta-break" before getting out of bed.
Drive to "nowhere" without feeling guilty
Run, don't jog.
Take "500" photographs without worrying about the "cost".
Create a personal logo or
Go "disco" dancing.
Allow yourself to daydream.
Imagine yourself in the year 2000

LOWER LEFT ACTIVITIES

Assemble a model kit by the instructions.
Develop a personal budget.
Prepare a personal property list.
Jog, don't run.
Organize your phonograph records in sequence according to categories.
Prepare a family tree.
Go "square" dancing.
Find a mistake in your bank statement.
Organize your home and garden tools.
Be exactly on time all day.
Organize your picture files.

LOWER RIGHT ACTIVITIES

Play with your children the way they want to play.
"Dance" without moving your feet.
Take a 10-minute "feeling break" every morning, afternoon, and evening.
"Love" a "pine cone", or any other natural thing.
Play the music you like when you want to hear it.
Allow tears to come to your eyes without feelings of shame or guilt.
Experience your own spirituality in a non-religious way.
Discover things your children have taught you, and find ways to thank them.

Figure 9-13. Chart B. Specific Activities for Strengthening the ability to use each quadrant

CHART C

A sampling of four types of every-day activities that, through regular practice, will help establish and reinforce a more whole brain, personal approach to work and life in general. (Modify, adapt, or change activities as required).

DAY 1 A. Review your financial status for the current week, past month and year to date.
B. Plan this week's priority activities.
C. Reveal your ability to understand recent events to someone in need of empathy.
D. Draw a metaphor of last week and have someone interpret the meaning.

DAY 2 A. Compare the results of last week's activities with your objectives for the week.
B. Experience a perfect day of "being there on time".
C. Discover something about your spiritual self.
D. Make an important decision based entirely on intuition.

DAY 3 A. Resolve a current problem by applying common sense.
B. Take a stack of personal papers and organize them.
C. Do something that will stimulate some strong personal feelings and make those feelings visible to others.
D. Take a "daydream" break.

DAY 4 A. Prepare an objective critique of an important project.
B. Identify something you are procrastinating about, and take action on it.
C. Touch a person you love and reveal your feelings for them.
D. Seek out a "unique" person and learn something of value from the experience.

DAY 5 A. Think about an important undertaking almost entirely in quantitative terms as expressed by numbers.
B. In exactly 10 minutes, straighten up, clean up, and rearrange your wallet/purse.
C. Explore the color and texture of a room you often use, but may not have noticed.
D. Meditate for 20 minutes.

DAY 6 A. In one short paragraph, state your current objectives.
B. Review the details of your will or other significant personal papers.
C. Take time out to listen to some favorite music.
D. Let an idea develop, enjoy the process of evolution and capture it.

DAY 7 A. Identify and prioritize ten key facts about yourself or your activities.
B. Arrange for your physical exam, security check, etc.
C. Achieve a pleasurable sense of your own body rhythm.
D. Take a risk by doing something very unusual.

Figure 9-14.   Chart C. A seven-day program for exercising all four quadrants every day

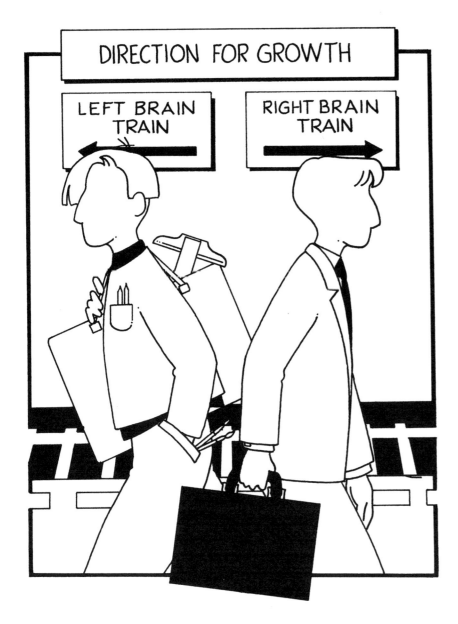

Figure 9-15. Left ⇄ Right Modes Subway Station

riential than intellectual modes—can be very helpful. For example, if balancing your checkbook for the last three months is a task that needs to be done, you should consider getting a supportive friend to come and help organize the task, and then encourage you through it. At the end of the task, you will more than likely experience a sense of accomplishment and strength—with more creative energy available than at the beginning of the task. This experience is powerful confirmation that expanding into B quadrant modes will improve the quality of life rather than making it a drag.

With such experiential understanding, the D dominant person who wants to be fully creative might change his frame of reference to look like this:

Value:	Tending to detail provides a secure foundation and that enhances creative functioning.
Reasoning:	If I take my time, I can master whatever necessary to handle the detail.
Decision:	I will take responsibility for attending to detail in my life, getting help to do so when the activity drains me instead of energizing me.

Expanding into Different Halves of the Metaphoric Model

As mentioned in Chapter 4, people's normal tendency to avoid opposing modes intensifies when they are double dominant in adjacent quadrants. This heightens their resistance to whole-brain functioning and thus may impair their ability to iterate among quadrants and function fully in the creative process.

This section presents ideas for effecting shifts between right and left and between upper and lower thinking modes. Refer to the charts listed below to combat any resistance you might have.

Chart A gives the essence of strategies for expanding into quadrants and into mental modes not currently preferred.

Chart B lists specific activities for strengthening the ability to use each quadrant.

Chart C presents a sample seven-day program for exercising all four quadrants every day.

Chart D summarizes how to access all thinking modes.

Right and Left Expansion

Resistance to the other half tends to be especially high for people whose two primaries fall in either the right or the left modes. In addition to the negative values concerning opposing modes, there is a disinclination to move out of the internal experience of pleasant, reassuring mental harmony that comes from staying with just one side of the brain. Shifting to include opposing modes disturbs that harmony by introducing thinking that feels out of sync or discordant, and that can take great effort to learn to integrate.

The good news is that shifting into opposing modes heightens creative power dramatically, because it makes full iteration—and therefore whole-brain creativity— possible. So although moving right or left can look like a great deal of work, it also makes mental life more varied and thus more interesting. Once the move is made, it can provide enormous pleasure. The overall strategy for mov-

"Inspiration is the impact of a fact on a prepared mind."
Louis Pasteur

"Enthusiasm is the most important single factor toward making a person creative."
Robert E. Mueller

"Serendipity or the happy discovery, happens only when you are actually seeking something."
M. O. Edwards

Figure 9-16.   Upper ↑↓ Lower Modes Escalator

ing from right to left is to learn how to use numbers; how to gather, organize, and analyze facts; and how to acquire self-discipline. This strategy advances through such activities as: (1) becoming computer literate; (2) practicing memory and concentration skills; (3) achieving number-processing competence; (4) learning administrative skills and techniques; (5) developing an ability to analyze; (6) gaining the discipline to recognize and capture important facts; and (7) acquiring and practicing time management skills. To give you a better idea on how to pursue one of these strategies, here are two discussed in detail.

Becoming computer literate. If you have decided to become computer literate, make it as easy for yourself as possible. Any computer will help you become more left-mode oriented, because all computers are quantitative, sequentially operated machines. Some, however, are more geared to upper-right thinking than others. So if you are a 3-2-1-1, don't choose the most user-*unfriendly* computers. Look at several, and before buying, make sure it has been designed with the right-brain, visually oriented person in mind. At the moment, the Macintosh™ is the most C and D quadrant-friendly personal computer available.

Achieving number processing competence. Some very innovative people have begun designing courses in accounting and finance that address right-mode needs by taking an experiential approach to the subject, rather than one that is didactic or lecture-based. The Accounting Game, offered by Quantum Educational Discoveries of Burlington, Vermont, is one such source. Others are offered at the Omega Institute, which operates in Rhinebeck, New York, every summer and has a week devoted specifically to business and financial learning.

Moving in the other direction, from left to right, calls

for relaxing the compulsion to verbally define and limit a thing, and instead to sense and feel it—its connection with everything around it, not only the thing itself. It means to experience, rather than to think logically *about*. It calls on a person's ability to imagine, to play with possibilities, to visualize what something might turn into, to tune in to an internal response to the thing.

For many A and B quadrant people, nurturing these "soft" abilities requires slowing down the mind, taking time to "lose" themselves in something. The intuitive and imaginative functions are too delicate to compete with busy-ness or business. You can't see fish in a lake on a windy day; the surface needs to become calm before you can become aware of their approaching the surface. Similarly, mental quietness allows natural rhythms, impulses, and images to surface. Biofeedback training is an effective path to this quieting. So are activities such as guided imagery, dreamwork, drawing, sculpting, or seeing pictures in a cloud.

Upper and Lower Expansion

Some people find shifting vertically between upper and lower modes poses fewer difficulties than does shifting to left or right. Those who have two primaries in either the upper or lower half already know how to iterate between left and right; this is the major part of learning to function in the quadrants synergistically. Others will find that quadrants on the same side of the metaphoric model have many similar values, making the frame of reference easier to expand north and south. For example, here's how you might expand appreciation for the upper or lower modes, taking one side at a time—first left, then right. In expanding from B up to A, you can use the verbal

"After all, most writing is done away from the typewriter, away from the desk. I'd say it occurs in the quiet, silent moments, while you're walking or shaving or playing a game, or whatever, or even talking to someone you're not vitally interested in. You're working, your mind is working, on this problem in the back of your head."

Henry Miller

"Inability to relax, to let go of a problem, often prevents its solution."

Eugene Raudsepp

"The soul never thinks without a picture."

Aristotle

LEARNING HOW TO ACCESS AND USE YOUR LESS PREFERRED MODES

IN MOVING FROM UPPER TO LOWER MODES

Learn how to trust your gut reaction, become more aware of your body, and use your senses more purposely.

This learning can be greatly aided by understanding the visceral nature of the brain's limbic system and developing confidence in your body reaction, emotional responses, sense of form and structure, and your primal instincts.

IN MOVING FROM LEFT TO RIGHT MODES

Learn how to sense, feel, visualize, play and trust your instincts.

This learning can be greatly aided by learning how to use creative materials, to draw, to sculpt, to model problems, to experience imagery, to develop biofeedback skills and to be open to change and personal risk.

IN MOVING FROM RIGHT TO LEFT MODES

Learn how to use numbers, how to gather, organize and analyze facts; how to acquire self-discipline.

This learning can be greatly enhanced by attaining computer literacy, acquiring memory and concentration skills, by achieving number processing competence, by learning administrative skills and techniques, and by practicing time management skills.

IN MOVING FROM LOWER TO UPPER MODES

Learn how to use both facts and insight, numbers and metaphors, rational and intuitive problem solving processes with situational effectiveness.

This learning can be aided by understanding the cognitive and iterative nature of the brain's cerebral hemispheres. Practicing personal decision making by moving back and forth between hard, fact-based positions and soft, insightful perceptions of the issue, and acknowledging the equal validity of both modes.

Figure 9-17.   Chart D. Whole Brain Development

and numerical skills of the left quadrants to explain, define, and demonstrate for yourself that using factually based, logical processes in solving problems has been very successful in the past. In expanding from A down to B, you can use those same verbal and mathematical skills to gather the facts. These facts would show the consequences of ignoring detail, quantify the value of those consequences, and point toward principles for following procedures consistently.

Generally speaking, moving to thinking modes of the upper quadrants involves learning how to integrate facts and insight, numbers and metaphor, rational and intuitive problem-solving processes. This iterative skill will increase with practice as you: (1) increase your understanding of the cognitive and iterative nature of the brain's cerebral hemispheres, and (2) practice making personal decisions using a deliberate technique of moving back and forth between concrete, here-and-now positions and more abstract, logical, and visual perceptions of an issue, and acknowledging the equal validity of both modes.

By contrast, moving to lower quadrant thinking modes involves learning how to trust gut reactions, becoming aware of body sensations, and using these senses more purposefully. By that I mean deliberately taking time out to check your body state in terms of relaxation, tension, irritation, etc., and using this awareness as feedback on which to base behavior change. This learning can be greatly aided by understanding the normally visceral nature of the brain's limbic system and developing confidence in your body reactions, emotional responses, sense of form and structure, and primal instincts.

Taking advantage of the similarity in modes provides access to moving vertically between right-mode quadrants.

"Latent abilities are like clay. It can be mud on shoes, brick in a building or a statue that will inspire all who see it. The clay is the same. The result is dependent on how it is used."

James F. Lincoln

"Creativity can be defined as both the art and the science of thinking and behaving with both subjectivity and objectivity. It is a combination of feeling and knowing; of alternating back and forth between what we sense and what we already know...

TO COMBINE THE TWO IS TO GAIN MORE THAN BOTH: A more natural and conscious balance between extremes. Such "creative" wholeness allows us to see ourselves from above. to both lead our way and to follow that way, to both determine our goal and to go: to both design the stimulus and to experience the response."

unknown

Both C and D quadrant people honor intuition: They know through experience that in order to understand something, sometimes all they need to do is focus attention on it until it becomes clear. Accordingly, in expanding into C from D, they can focus intuitive perception on discerning the value of functioning in emotional modes and develop a greater sense of the here-and-now. In moving from D to C, intuitive perceptions can also provide useful metaphors and strengthen your acceptance of new possibilities.

So there are myriad ways to access and develop less preferred modes, and they're not necessarily complicated. Take a look at Charts B and C. As you read these recommendations, you might even wonder what good such simple, ordinary activities could possibly do. In fact, they are excellent avenues to take for two reasons: (1) They easily access desired modes, and (2) simple and ordinary is actually the best way to begin because it feels safer. Exercising less preferred modes sometimes feels risky because our values so often exclude permission to use them. If we begin using those modes in low-risk situations—at home, alone, or with supportive friends, the risk diminishes.

It's important to persist in an activity until you know you've obtained full access to a given mode. Going through the routine once or twice will not work in your favor. Doing it systematically and persistently *will*. You will know you have arrived when you can do these simple tasks and feel satisfied rather than guilty, stupid, silly, abused, or dominated. For example, "driving to nowhere" provides excellent access to the D quadrant. However, if you are a B quadrant person, you probably can't just drive around without feeling a sense of waste and guilt while doing it. Full access to the D quadrant will be available to you only when guilt no longer arises.

The same idea goes for a D quadrant person moving toward B: If you are a D quadrant person, you will have full access to B quadrant capabilities for detail and orderliness only when your personal property list is prepared, not as a chore to be resented, but as a discovery process. You will know you have full access to the C quadrant when you've been able to play with your children the way *they* want to play without feeling ridiculous and wondering whether anybody is watching and passing judgment on your behavior. You will have fully accessed that mathematical, financial capability in A quadrant only when you find it personally stimulating and rewarding: You might recruit some like-minded people to join you in an investment club, or to celebrate the new-found freedom of taking charge of your financial life.

Beyond this, the best recommendation I can make is that you heighten the chances for satisfaction in your life by undertaking creative projects and by increasing specific creative skills in the creative process.

ENHANCING SKILLS IN THE CREATIVE PROCESS

The creative process requires certain skills, and mastering these can make an enormous difference. One skill involves laying the groundwork in the preparation phase. Another involves visualizing a metaphor and then zigzagging until the metaphor is fully expressed in nonmetaphorical terms that satisfy all quadrants. Yet another is allowing ideas to germinate and emerge without judgment until they have been captured in their entirety. This section offers suggestions in each of these critical areas.

Prepare: Define the Problem/Challenge/Opportunity

Creative insight is said to be preceded by hard work. "The prepared mind," we are told, "favors creativity." Einstein spent many years acquiring the facts and knowledge he needed for the base from which his two intuitive leaps could be made.

Preparation creates a point of departure and a direction for the subconscious mind to take. The old adage that "A well-defined problem is already half-solved" is true. The purpose of defining the problem is to develop a true understanding of it, which in turn becomes a part of or a directive toward the solution. A problem with an inaccurate definition is like a faulty compass, which may look like it's working, but isn't. If you follow the direction it points to, you may never get where you want to go.

Problem definition makes use of analysis, logic, and language. It demands precision and accuracy. It requires discipline and orderliness. It is wonderfully left-mode dominant. Defining a problem clearly and accurately requires the ability to "see" it for what it is, to discern its key features, distinguish between the significant and the trivial, and phrase the problem statement so it has the focus and clarity that provide direction for the rest of the creative process.

Think of this early work as a mystery, an adventure, or simply play. If you do, even the more structured, deliberate, and painstaking aspects of the creative process will become enjoyable—just more of a fascinating exploration. This approach helps the right brain to cooperate with the process rather than distracting from it.

"Our problem is to keep alive the powerful stimulant of individual thought at all levels and in every phase of our effort. Unless we do, we run the risk of making a displaced person out of the man with the big ideas."

Crawford H. Greenwalt

"The real mark of the creative person is that the unforseen problem is a joy and not a curse."

Norman H. Mackworth

Visualize: Look, See, Hear, Smell ...

Visualization is a skill that is helpful at every stage of the creative process. Although preparation tends to be more left-brain oriented, even here it can be helpful in reaching for intuitive comprehension of the problem.

Images don't have to be fully visual, by the way. They can be experienced non-visually: heard, felt kinesthetically, or even smelled. Somehow, the mind provides us with a sense of the image without necessarily showing us anything that looks like a "movie in the mind." So you don't have to be able to think in images to be creative. However, I believe the more visual you are, the easier your imagery is to translate into words, so it pays to develop and enhance your ability to think in images. There are many techniques for doing this. One is to use guided fantasy—a relaxing narrative, supported by appropriate music, can produce vivid mental images. Another is to take up photography—not as much for its own sake as to sharpen your visual skills. It's amazing how much will show up in the finished print that you never saw through the lens.

Incubate: Let Ideas Germinate

Incubation begins when the homework of preparation is near completion and everything needed to carry out the creative process lies within the mind of the individual. For some people, incubation can be disturbing. Productivity and efficiency are hard to come by; other people and things may distract or irritate; from the outside, it may look like nothing is happening—the person is goofing-off, playing around, twiddling, or simply staring out the window. During this time, people who press for more purposeful-looking behaviors can impede the incubating process and should therefore be avoided.

What helps the incubation process? Principally two things:

1. Being patient and trusting the process
2. Encouraging alpha and theta states of relaxation

You can nurture subconscious idea generation throughout the incubation phase by encouraging the relaxed alpha and theta states. These states occur naturally as you go through your daily cycles of mental activity, especially dreaming. Most people dream every 90 minutes during their sleeping hours, and also daydream every 90 minutes during their waking ones. You can also encourage these states by engaging in activities that evoke them, such as taking a bath or shower, relaxing in bed, dozing in a hammock, or, for many people, running and, particularly, freeway driving. You can even take a nap if you like (but only if you can do so without guilt). These less-than-focused, but fully conscious mental states are characterized by non-judgmental, non-critical, free-form, freeflowing modes of idea processing.

As the incubation stage gives way to illumination, try to keep this sense of relaxation because the best way to ensure a full harvest of ideas is to stay open. As the ideas begin to emerge, don't judge, simply capture them as they pop up.

Capture: Record All Ideas as They Pop

Creative individuals often produce many more ideas

than are actually required to solve a given problem. Like popcorn in an overloaded popcorn popper, ideas keep exploding and cascading around the problem. Let's look at this "popping" more closely. In the creative process, one idea leads to another, then to a third and a fourth, and every once in a while, whole clusters of ideas come together to form something totally new and different. As in a physical chain reaction, a mental chain reaction can "go critical," producing a big idea out of a lot of little ones. To use a physiological metaphor, the chain of ideas can be thought of as a chain of neurons firing in synaptic interactions. The more accustomed we become to this mode of thinking, the more often it occurs. The greater confidence we have that one idea will lead to a second and third—which might make the difference—the more likely it is to happen that way.

The flow of creative ideas can arise during conscious as well as unconscious times, when you are daydreaming or sleeping or simply going about your business. One of the values of defining a problem is that the process of doing so places it in your mental hopper as a task to be performed. Your mind then goes to work on it in its own way. Sometimes this work is done actively, consciously, and purposefully with our fully-conscious participation. At other times, it seems to "just happen." One way to encourage these modes is to trust your interests and follow them. As creative people know, that can reduce tension, increase enjoyment, and thus, refresh the mind.

Once the popping begins and ideas begin to flow, it's important to capture and record them without judgment. Avoid evaluating ideas in the early phases of the creative process, whether you're working alone or with others. Anyone whose ideas are criticized tends to hesitate before shar-

"If you have built castles in the air, your work need not be lost; That is where they should be. Now put the foundations under them."

Henry David Thoreau

"That in all of these sudden illuminations my ideas took shape in a primarily visual/spatial form without so far as I can introspect any verbal intervention is in accordance with what has always been my preferred mode of thinking. Many of my happiest hours have since childhood been spent absorbed in drawing, in tinkering, or in exercises of purely mental visualization."

Roger N. Shepard

Figure 9-18. Cerebral Iteration. Understanding the Facts > Synthesizing into the Whole > Analyzing the Results

ing them with others. But as you learn to assure yourself and others that you don't have to defend ideas from attack (your own or that of others), your energy is freed up for speculating and looking for new directions. In fact, the more kooky, far out, funny, or sexy the ideas, the greater the chance of coming up with solutions that are truly unique. Going "further out" gets you away from routine thinking patterns and helps break perceptual blocks. Take a "crazy" idea and look for ways to combine or build on it. You could produce the idea that leads to the electric car or the personal helicopter or the inkless fountain pen. Even if it's only a spaghetti twister, at least you'll enjoy yourself.

The best way to stay non-judgmental and open to ideas is to be experiential and playful. Play is safe to engage in for its own sake, without regard to production, efficiency, or fear of making a mistake. While playing, you can "fiddle" or "toy" with ideas without the adverse consequences of too much "seriousness." You needn't judge. You can let yourself be natural, give yourself time to reclaim your childlike nature—not according to a timetable, but naturally. This is the key to its success.

Zigzag With Gusto

Fact-based knowledge is accumulated in the analytical A quadrant, home of factbased knowledge, logical processing, and rational thinking. Imagination, on the other hand, takes place in the D quadrant, home of integration, intuition, and imagination. Settling on a creative response can therefore be described as the synthesis of knowledge and imagination. This is the synergistic "zigzag lightning" I spoke of earlier that the massively interconnected brain makes possible.

It works as follows: We accumulate knowledge and facts. We analyze them for meaning by breaking them down into their component parts. We then synthesize those parts into a whole from which we derive an essence of understanding. We return to an analysis of that essence. Did we put it together correctly? Does it fit? New facts and information and data surface as required. We analyze for meaning, synthesize an overview, and then reanalyze our new image. As we iterate back and forth between these two opposing modes of thinking, we create new understanding, new interpretations, new ideas. We "get it." When we get it, we know it. If we don't *know* it, we haven't gotten it yet.

This iteration is a wonderful and powerful phenomenon. And the best thing you can do is trust your uncertainty and keep pushing till it both feels right and looks so simple, you wonder what took you so long. Then it's time to give yourself a treat for hanging in till you got it!

Whatever the level of your creative capability, to make it pay off personally, organizationally, or corporately, you need to apply it in an environment that allows creativity to grow and flourish. It is to this vital area that we turn next.

"The creative mind is seldom bored."
Gordon A. Macleod

"There are certain things that our age needs. It needs, above all, courageous hope and the impulse to creativeness."
Bertrand Russell

"Nothing is as powerful as a good idea, but nothing is so powerfully sure-fire as a good idea whose time has come."
G. Herbert True

10

BUILDING YOUR CREATIVE ENVIRONMENT: BOTH INSIDE AND OUT

Creative space is a concept embracing the mental, physical, and emotional environments within which creativity operates. Neither managers nor partners nor spouses can give you the creative space you need to function as a unique person. Creative space is something you must carve out and claim for yourself. Here is how I did that for myself, both at home and at work, and what I learned in the process.

On first arriving at GE, I felt I was my own person: unique in education and experience, distinctive in appearance and motivation, and creatively active in many areas. For example, within two months of joining GE, I had invented a solution to the rotating coupling problem of the Underwater Object Locator—one of the General Engineering Laboratories' major projects at that time. Later I won acclaim as company "dean" of Effective Presentation, the company's most popular course in those days. I also set up a high-powered technical task force to deal with *unsolved problems in industry.* Off the job, too, I was creative, singing leads in the Schenectady Light Opera Company and acting principal roles in the Schenectady Civic Players. I also built our house with my own hands, using many innovative approaches, including a radiant

heating system installed in the ceiling. The Schenectady Junior Chamber of Commerce named me Young Man of the Year. The honors and attention I received included a recognition of my creative abilities and were satisfying to me.

However, as I began moving into more senior positions at GE, things changed. Pressure to constrict my behavior to conform to the needs of the bureaucracy intensified. When visiting the company's headquarters in those days, I had to first check out my ideas with a corporate consultant in order to get advanced approval to propose them. People perceived me as "different" and that had drawbacks—or so it seemed. I gradually yielded. As my responsibilities became ever more demanding, I took on the company colors and in my professional life I became more and more like one of the monogrammed crowd.

This conformity bothered me, for two reasons. First, I felt that I was losing my identity, my sense of wholeness. The split between my artistic self and the rest of me that began around my college years became sharper on the job, so much so that even my artistic endeavors couldn't fully compensate for it. Even worse, the kind of work I wanted to do at GE was either being neglected or farmed

Figure 10-1. Art Show at General Electric Headquarters, N.Y.C. (opposite)

out. Work requiring creative input went to outside "experts," as if a distance of 50 miles from headquarters qualified them as more creative than anyone employed on site. Even though I had been considered "creative" as a high-potential youngster, I wasn't considered at all once I became a mature professional. But I knew I wasn't less creative than before; the problem was in the way the corporate community perceived me.

The decision to fight back was made in 1968, when I said to myself right out loud, "Well, dammit, if they won't think of me as creative on the basis of my work, I'll have to make it happen on the basis of my art." That statement initiated a very deliberate strategy to change my image. At the time, the component of GE that I managed occupied the entire 27th floor of the headquarters building at 570 Lexington Avenue in New York City, and afforded me considerable space and freedom to take action. The next week, my reception room and inner office displayed 20 of my paintings that were slated to go into several upcoming art shows. I announced an art judging event. Anybody and everybody who had an opinion to give was invited to identify which of the paintings they felt should be exhibited at the 3 art shows that were pending. About 50 people participated, and over the course of the next week, I found ways to invite my senior managers in to see my informal show.

It worked. Initially, only verbal feedback evidenced the shift. "Gee, Ned, they're really great! I never knew you were so creative" and "Ned's work is really impressive —we need that kind of creativity down where I work." Then, Lindon "Lindy" Saline, a man who was to have a major impact on my life—as boss, mentor, and friend— dropped in and invited me to hold a one-man art show at the next Management Association Mother's Day cocktail party at GE's Management Development Institute. Over the next 12 years, that art show evolved into an annual company-wide event, involving over 100 artists, and exhibiting as many as 800 works.

As a result of all this, I became "officially" creative. Articles about me appeared in the GE's *Monogram Magazine*. People began to invite me to join task forces and project teams as the "creative" person. Outsiders were directed my way through GE channels to advise and consult on creative problems. In a short time, I was invited to join the staff of the Management Development Institute because of the creative contribution I could make. The man who invited me, believed in me, and protected me during the early stages of the brain research that gave rise to the HBDI, to ACT, and eventually to this book, was Lindy Saline.

In light of what I've learned since, I can now say that what I was doing was claiming and owning my creative space. That means I was:

1. Confirming my own belief that I was entitled to it, and developing a vision of what I wanted.

2. Demonstrating creativity to others.

3. Seeking and accepting creative assignments as they appeared and using them further to expand my own creative capabilities and potential.

In this chapter, I want to present my view of just what creative space is, and how to establish creative space for yourself and your children and for others, at home and at work.

WHAT IS CREATIVE SPACE?

Creative space is a concept that is rich in possibilities and opportunities. It is the sum total of what nurtures, supports, inspires, and reinforces our creativity. It thus includes ourselves, our families, our fellow workers, our reinforcing memories, our cuing systems, and our favorite places. My own creative space includes my house; the office; the lake where I daydream and dictate in my boat; the constant encouragement of my wife, Margy, my daughters, and my friends; the interaction with my colleagues; the mental and emotional attitudes and disciplines that I've developed over the years to confirm and support my own right to be creative; my commitment to living a creative life and the fruits of doing so; and last, but not least, the many people who have responded to my work.

The definition of creative space becomes more manageable when broken down into: (1) the individual; (2) the environment; and (3) the interface between the two. The "individual" is you. The environment is the total surround—physical, mental, and emotional. The crucial element is the interface between the two.

The interface between you and your environment has to have several characteristics if it is to stimulate your creativity.

A Good "Impedance Match." Impedance match is a technical term used in scientific fields. Very simply put, it refers to the balance of characteristics between two different items that are interconnected and through which there is a flow of energy from one to another. In audio electronics, for example, the electrical characteristics or

"There is always sunshine, only we must do our part: we must move into it."
Clara Louise Burnham (1854-1927)

Tsze-kung asked what constituted a superior man. The master said, "He acts before he speaks, and afterwards speaks according to his actions."
Confucius

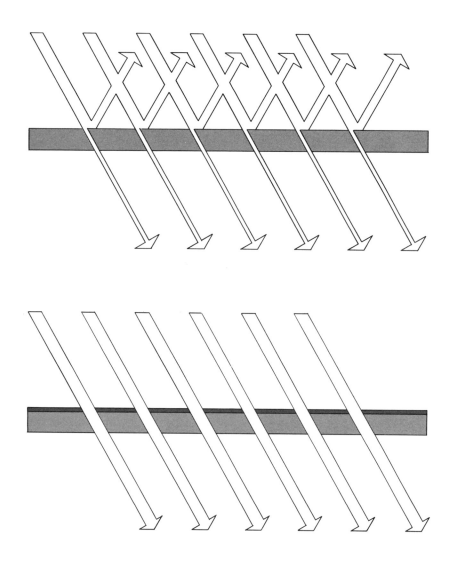

Figure 10-2.   Non-reflecting Glass: A good impedance match

impedance of a loudspeaker must be properly matched to the impedance of an amplifier to produce high fidelity. Another example: Non-reflecting glass results from an impedance-matching process. Normally, glass and air have impedances so different that when light passing through air hits the glass, it bounces back in reflection. By coating the glass with a transparent film of precise thickness, the manufacturer bridges the difference between impedances, and thus allows the light to pass from the air through the glass—largely *unimpeded*.

A good impedance match between an individual and his or her creative environment permits the interface to be "soft;" in other words, it allows a flow of energy to take place between the two that allows change and movement to take place in each. The creative process in human beings is delicate, so either the creative surround should be accommodating and pliable, rather than harsh or unyielding, or there needs to be an insulating bridge that protects the creative individual from meeting the environment directly.

Suitability for the Current Phase of the Creative Process. The interface also needs to be appropriate for the phase of the creative process in which the individual is involved at the moment. This means either that your creative environment must be adaptable and variable or, more likely, that you need more than one creative environment. You may need many. Writing this book involved using every room in the house—the studio, the loft, the living room, the gallery, the den, the deck, the lake, the ACS office, and every auto trip and plane ride. As the writing process called for different types of stimulation, I changed the environment accordingly.

Suitability is especially important for the verification and application phases. Remember, you need to *apply* your creative ideas to reinforce your creative process. If you have an idea for an incredible gourmet dish, it's important that you have a kitchen in which to prepare it and, preferably, people around to eat it. If you want to model an idea, you need the creative materials to work with. If you have an idea for a painting, you need a place where you can use paints, have good lighting, etc., a place where you can actually *produce* a painting without uncomfortably interrupting other aspects of your own life or the lives of others. Ideally, your creative environment allows you to stop in mid-process with everything spread all over, go away without cleaning up, and come back to pick up exactly where you left off.

Personal Renewal. The interface between you and your creative environment needs to be personally renewing. In my experience, that renewal is most easily and powerfully supplied by nature—the outdoors, sounds of wind and water, flowers, trees, birds, lots of nature vistas, and living, growing things around. It's especially important to have plenty of light and air available. Other things besides nature that provide for personal renewal are music, books, toys, and stimulating people when you need them.

Mutual Nurturing. The interface should also allow for mutual nurturing. This means that the environment should stimulate and nurture you and you, in turn, should replenish the environment's stores of what may have been withdrawn in the creative process.

Portability. You shouldn't have to leave your creative space behind. Elements of it should mentally follow you to nurture your process wherever you are, so that in every situation you have encouragement. In this sense, my studio and Pat's sculpture traveled with me on the commute to New York City and back. In this sense, my house and Lake

"Ideas won't keep. Something must be done about them."
Alfred Narth Whitehead

"After investigating a problem in all directions, happy ideas come unexpectedly, without effort, like an inspiration. So far as I'm concerned, they have never come to me when my mind was fatigued, or when I was at my working table.... They came particularly readily during the slow ascent of wooded hills on a sunny day."
H. L. Von Helmholtz

"Into every corner, into all forgotten things and nooks, Nature struggles to pour life into the dead, life into life itself."
Henry Beston
"The Headlong Wave"
The Outermost House

CLAIMING CREATIVE SPACE EXERCISE

Indicate *your* creative space in the four quadrants below by drawing a shape that will "enclose" that space in the appropriate portion of a / or several quadrants. Then, on the lines provided within the quadrants, write a description of the "turn on" work that will establish your ownership of that space.

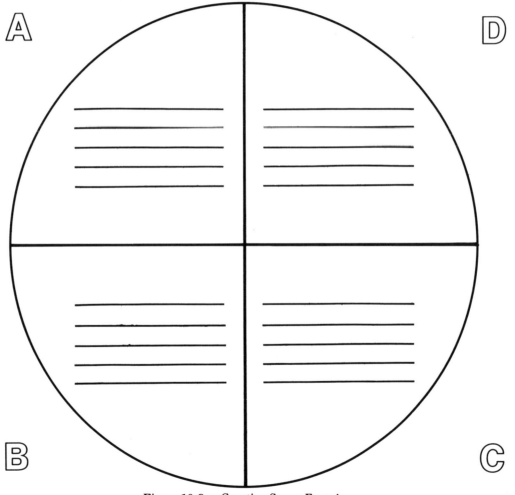

Figure 10-3. Creative Space Exercise

Lure surrounded me as I wrote parts of this book in cars, planes, or between workshop sessions. Frequently, my time in church has been a rich source of creative ideas.

The creative space that you carry around in your head is the most important of all. All the external richness in the world won't help you be creative if the creative space in your head is too small or tight.

Initially, creative space will develop as a result of your earliest mental and emotional environment, especially the permissions and encouragement you received from your parents and other teachers and caretakers. Later, when you have that environment established in your own minds, you will tend to work from the inside out, translating your inner space as best you can into the external environment you have created for yourself and others. How this is done varies: Translating inner space into the external environment may mean building a physical space that gives freedom to create; it may also mean deciding to pursue a project at work and developing a deliberate and clear strategy for winning permission and support to do it.

To live a creative life, everyone needs positive creative space, an expansive sense of creative possibility. The purpose of this chapter is to help you make your own creative space into what you want it to be. As a first step, I invite you to begin to claim your own creative space by completing the creative space exercise in figure 10-3.

This chapter devotes relatively little time to describing the specific physical characteristics of the creative environment, because what stimulates one person can differ so markedly from what excites another. For example, the environment I create for myself might be far too cluttered for someone else. ACT I provides a creative environment that works for most people because there is truly something

for everyone—the number of options is overwhelming. But it would hardly be practical to suggest gathering such an immense collection of options/materials in every home or workplace.

What if there *were* an ideal creative environment—one that worked for everyone? I'm hoping and planning to create one for myself, my family, my friends, and my clients—my ultimate creative space. It's still a dream, but I own the site and the dream is beginning to take shape. My ideal creative environment would be a physical metaphor of the whole-brain creative process and would appeal to all four quadrants of the brain. It would include a building that was like a live-in sculpture, with a variety of small private rooms for individual activities and great big rooms for movement, lights, films, group meetings, and music—and not just any music, but on special occasions, music translated into color and motion by audio lights, dancing optical fibers, and lasers. You would see sculptures and paintings in progress, inviting others to partake, and photographic projects underway. In the workrooms, creative materials of all kinds would be always available. Other rooms would be stocked with tools, toys (plenty of toys), and machines (computers, copiers). A multimedia library would overflow with books, tapes, videos, and posters. Outdoor extensions of the space would include a sculpture garden, fountains, a tree house, wooded paths, and a number of viewing places to provide a variety of different perspectives to help in adopting different viewpoints. It would be a place where creative expression was normal for everyone involved. I anticipate interested people visiting Lake Lure some day when the dream has become a reality.

So your own physical creative environment is something you'll need to evolve. I can—and do—make suggestions in this chapter, but it will be your own research and experimentation that tells you what works for you. As you read on, keep your own inclinations and resources in mind, and develop a list of options to try out for yourself. When you've found some that work for you, you'll have moved a significant way toward a fuller creative life.

A good first step in traveling the distance—no matter what your age—is to learn about how to establish creative space for children.

CREATIVE SPACE FOR THE CHILD

It's appropriate to start with parenting, for whether or not we have biological children, we always have the child within us who needs nurturing and encouragement as much as we ever did when we were little.

In fact, the parent/child metaphor offers another way of understanding our internal iterative process—which can be negative or positive. Unfortunately, too often it's negative: Most of us spend too much time admonishing ourselves rather than allowing ourselves the freedom to express ourselves fully. For example, we scold ourselves as childish or immature when we stray from a task, or play when we should be working, or are irreverent. We berate ourselves for ignorance, for honest mistakes, for unavoidable delays. Then, like children reacting against this inner tyranny, we also rebel—harboring contempt for authority, disdaining the painstaking research required for certain artistic activities, deriding proven procedures as "old and boring." This negative internal tug-of-war depresses us mentally and physically, and seriously interferes with our ability to cope with situations requiring innovative response.

A positive form of the parent/child iteration contrasts with this negative internal tug-of-war by affirming *all* kinds of creative endeavor and modes—left, right, upper, and lower. When childlike spontaneity or irreverence occurs, the parental response is positive, e.g., "What an interesting idea" or "Gee, that didn't work, but I'll bet we can figure out what will" or "Why not" or "Try something else instead" or "Good for you for trying." Other positive messages would include, "It's okay to be whatever we prefer, because our mental preferences are good" and "We can also learn what we need to know, and needn't punish ourselves in order to do that."

These messages are congruent with my belief that preparing children to live satisfying lives in this fast-changing, highly technical, exciting world of ours means helping them:

1. *Maximize the number of mental options* they have for responding to a given set of circumstances.

2. *Follow their natural inclinations* toward dominance in one or more quadrants.

If I had it to do over again with my own children, I would do many things differently: Rather than the three R's, I would concentrate on the four P's—permissions, praise, play, and personal uniqueness.

Permission

Permissions include free rein to do mainly what comes naturally—what our children's tastes and curiosities incline them to at the time that they choose to follow them. We give several important permissions.

You Can Try It All

Children want to try a wide variety of things: Curiosity is built into them to encourage just that kind of experimentation so they can learn about their world, themselves, and others. We give permission for such experimentation by making the opportunity abundantly available—that is, by providing stimulation that covers a full range of experience: visual, auditory, tactile, olfactory, kinesthetic, and gustatory, as well as emotional, physical, imaginative, and intellectual.

An important part of providing a broad range of stimulation is using a range of modes to communicate. Given the chance to do it over again with my daughters, I would remind myself that the way I connect with them has enormous impact, and that I need to make sure our communication takes place in more than one quadrant. Accordingly, I would learn whatever was necessary to do that, opening up areas of my own avoidance to make sure that I didn't miss precious moments of understanding in my children's own languages. For example, in addition to introducing them to factual reality, my communication would also include metaphors, stories, and fantasies. My children and I would share and spend time processing our dreams. I would also learn more about how to express feelings—not just glad and mad, which tend to feel safest for men, but *all* the feelings. I would share the learning of a simple procedural task like mixing paint, or the how-to's of putting together a puzzle.

"Our children can begin to experience fulfillment as soon as we choose to create environments permitting them to do so."

Bob Samples

"Parents should play much more with their children. Because people who can't play can't be much good at their work either."

Boy (11)

Figure 10-4.

You Can Follow Your Own Favorite Way

At the same time that I provided a full range of experiences, I would also take care to notice and support my daughters' preferences for particular ways of knowing, trusting that their own inner direction was healthy and valid for them. To make sure that a preference for one quadrant didn't produce a crippling avoidance of another, I would also be sure to provide complementary developmental opportunities, and gently guide them into becoming comfortable with those quadrants.

You Can Take Your Time

Another important permission is the right to develop at one's own pace. The brain grows in stages and spurts, just like the rest of the body, and asking a child to appreciate something or perform at a high skill level before that child's brain is ready engenders considerable anxiety. It can also engender unhealthy competition, mostly to satisfy the parent's ego needs. To avoid this, I would keep learning about the developmental stages and how to recognize them, and match my expectations and requirements to the stage each child had reached.

Praise

Permission and praise are very closely linked. All human beings gravitate toward doing what they get love and attention for. If I had to do it over again, I would praise my children lavishly, not only for those things I wanted them to do or that society approves of, but for all their advances in all of the quadrants. I would praise them not only for spelling or learning to add and multiply, but for these things:

- Learning to "see,"—to notice things: the beauty of a line or color, the way it interacts with other colors, the exquisite texture of a piece of stone or cloth

- Recognizing smells and tastes, trying new ones, and expanding their list of acceptable items

- Moving the body in dance and sports, and expressing ideas in movement

- Understanding a person's emotions in the face of a new or conflicted situation.

Rewards, an extension of praise, need to be given in forms that the child perceives as positive. I would make sure to delight and reward progress in all quadrants, and I would check with each child to make sure I wasn't unconsciously withholding rewards or otherwise pushing them for performance in one mode over another.

I would also make sure to praise and reward my daughters simply for *being*, and not only for performing. Knowing that we can simply be alive and have someone glad for that alone reduces anxiety, increases energy, and liberates us to choose freely. I would make sure my children knew that my love didn't depend on their performance.

Play

Play is the essential business of children. It's the means by which they learn how to live in their world. It's also a lifelong source of joy. Much of the unhappiness and lack of imagination people experience in their lives springs from their having forgotten how to play.

"Play so that you may be serious."
Anarcharsis, 600 B.C.
quoted in Aristotle's *Nichomachean Ethics*

"It is a happy talent to know how to play."
Emerson, *Journals* 1834

"It is a great sign of mediocrity to praise always moderately."
Vauvenargues

"Children's playing should be deemed as their most serious actions."
Michel de Montaigne

To help my children retain a freshness of spirit and outlook in later years, I would spend a lot of time playing with them—not so much on my terms, but the way *they* wanted to play. It would take a high priority as part of my conscious intention to complement school learning rather than just reinforcing it. However, our playing would be a permanent part of our lives together, not simply a pre-school duty.

In line with this, I would remind myself of the need to spend as much quality time with my children as my wife does.

Personal Uniqueness

As children mature and begin to make decisions about their education and careers, it is vitally important that they feel safe in following their own desires. Doing what they think someone else wants or just following in another's footsteps usually doesn't work, and it often takes them years to regain their own personal sense of purpose.

One of the things we parents do unconsciously is to ask our children either to become replicas of ourselves or to live out the lives we would like to have lived but didn't. Sometimes these unconscious desires are extremely strong, and we express them very powerfully without even knowing it.

It's not bad to have dreams for our children, but we need to combine those dreams with a very firm commitment to let our children follow their own stars, and honor their personal uniqueness. For them to follow their own inclinations and yearnings rather than the ones others have laid out for them, they need specific reassurance that doing so won't shake the love or closeness they need and want

Figure 10-5.   You Don't Have To Be Like Me

from us.

Our children need us to love them for their uniqueness, and not only for the ways in which they can demonstrate that we are good parents—genetically or otherwise. They provide a little bit of immortality for us—a name, familiar features in a younger form—but we earn our greatest accolades when our children are able to choose, happily and freely, to follow their personal interests.

As my children grew old enough to understand, I would want to say things like this:

"I've got good news for you. You don't have to be like me or your mother. You don't have to take the same subjects in school, follow the same careers, or marry the same kind of people. You don't have to marry at all, although I recommend it. You don't have to do any of it our way. We want you to be your own person, unique and different.

"This doesn't mean that I don't have some dreams and preferences about what I'd like to see you do, or that part of me won't be disappointed if you go another route. What you need to know is that those preferences of mine represent just one part of me and my disappointment is my problem, not yours.

"I would be even more disappointed to learn that you did what I wanted rather than what makes you happy and satisfied. As much as I love you and as well as I know you, my view of you is imperfect. Even my view of myself is imperfect, so how can I tell what will work for you?

"It makes me feel very good to tell you all this, because my parents grew up in a different time, when people thought 'Father knows best,' and most kids didn't have the kind of choices I'm giving you. It would be great if we could go back to do it over again, but we can't. What I can

"If a child lives with approval, he learns to live with himself."
Dorothy Law Nolte

"To dream anything that you want to dream. That is the beauty of the human mind. To do anything that you want to do. That is the strength of the human will. To trust yourself to test your limits. That is the courage to succeed."
Bernard Edmonds
American Writer

"Be thine own palace, or the world's thy jail."
John Donne (1573-1631)

do is offer you the freedom of choice that I wish I and all those of my generation had had. But it's never too late. I can be more of a whole-brain parent now. You may want to be one in the future."

CREATIVE SPACE FOR ADULTS

Once childhood is behind you, the responsibility for your creative space becomes entirely your own. Others can encourage, model, and exhort, but you are the one who must decide which influences to allow and what to do with them.

In general terms, three main guidelines for establishing creative space apply:

- You have to *claim* space for yourself—in many cases that calls for a declaration of the intent to exercise and expand your creative self.

- You don't actually *own* it till you *use* it; that is, begin to allow it to change you and vice versa, and accept responsibility for its quality and character.

- Others who share the same space must participate in the decision-making process.

You can carve out creative space in your own home perhaps more easily than anywhere else—most people have more control in the home and at least a few physical areas they can truly call their own. Here are some samples to show options for both small and large creative spaces.

Figure 10-6. Stamford Art Studio

Studios and Corners

The process of changing my image and claiming my creative space at work was preceded by a similar change at home. This wasn't too long after my heart block black-outs. (If you'll remember, they cut short my singing career and I took up painting.) Shortly thereafter came my transfer to corporate headquarters in New York City and the associated move from Cincinnati, Ohio to Stamford, Connecticut.

After experiencing the pain of losing one outlet for my creative urges, I resolved never to be without such an outlet again, and I was obsessed with having a studio in our new house. So was Margy: In Cincinnati I was painting in the family room, which adjoined the kitchen, and she was terribly allergic to the oil paints I was using. But so great was my drive to paint that to deny it would have produced frustration beyond my ability to cope. For this reason, Margy and I chose for our new home a converted stable, with a 12-by-20 foot tool shed that became my artistic domain for the next 17 years.

The studio looked, before too long, as if a cyclone had moved through it, but to me it was heaven. It had a huge drawing table, on which were piled stacks of paper plates (I used them for palettes and saved them for color reference after finishing a painting). Files overflowed with interesting inspirational material. Cabinets bulged with painting supplies. Next to a television set and various projectors, pedestals for sculpting and miniatures of Michelangelo's sculptures competed for the shrinking space. Dabs of clay and cold-cast bronze dotted the floor, giving its already exuberant, paint-splattered surface a three-dimensional richness. In addition, as I moved into

"The artist is not a different kind of person, but every person is a different kind of artist."

Eric Gill, Philosopher

"Oh, you're looking for that special paintbrush? Don't worry, I put it in a safe place."

C. H.

"Creative Imagination Defined: I put the first brush stroke on the canvas. After that, it is up to the canvas to do at least half the work."

James Brooks, Painter

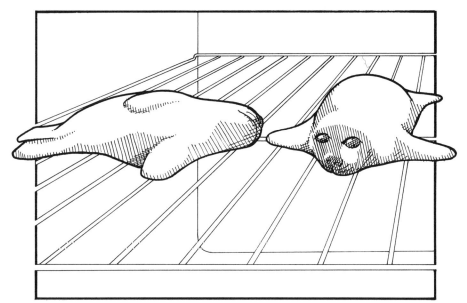

Figure 10-7. Baking Bronze Sculptures

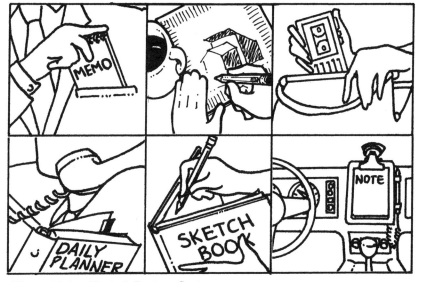

Figure 10-8. Typical Capture Systems

using cold-cast bronze, the place took on a distinct chemical aroma from the molding material. (To this day, my daughters remember the harsh odor of the baby seal bronzes baking in the kitchen oven.) To add to the excitement, each of the girls had her own cabinet for whatever art projects she had in progress. In short, the studio soon contained anything and everything that I could possibly fit into it that might inspire or support my creative endeavors.

While for me and many others the creative process is fundamentally messy, it doesn't always require the appearance of chaos; nor is a separate room always necessary. In fact, there are only a few minimums that a fixed physical environment should have to serve the creative process:

1. *Capture system.* Whether illumination comes in bits and pieces or all at once, it's important to collect the pieces until they begin to fall into a completed pattern. Capture systems can be simple—a pencil and pad, a journal, or a dictating machine. The main requirement is they be where you are at the moment of illumination.

2. *An incubation display.* It's important to have a work table or bulletin board for displaying materials accumulated in the preparation process. For example, while deciding what to paint, I might spread out examples of scenes that are close to what I want but not just right. The stuff on the table would "talk" to me over a period of time until something clicked (illumination), and I was ready to actually paint.

3. *A place to create.* That can be the same work table as in item 2. It can be a typewriter or drawing

table, a piano or tape recorder. The main requirement is that it afford enough space to accomplish the task at hand and where work can be left in mid-process without having to be cleaned up. One option, if you have only a small space in a larger room, is to erect a waist-high room divider—low enough not to evoke claustrophobia and high enough to hide the mess and give a sense that the space is separate. Another option is to find some friends with similar tastes and rent a loft or studio together to help share the costs and add to the creative stimulation.

4. *Affirmative messages for the individual*. An affirmative message can be a sign on the wall that says, "Writer in residence" or "My creative corner" or "I claim this creative space." It can be a bulletin board on which you write notes to yourself and stick up interesting thought starters to help get your mind into gear. It can be a letter from a respected mentor saying, "Your writing is a smash." It can be an interesting headline or news story. Or it can be a much-loved painting or poster—anything that takes your mind into your own creative realm, encourages and strengthens you, and makes you feel good.

What you'll find is that the act of setting up a nourishing, physical environment for your creativity is in itself a creative process, complete with all six stages. Moreover, at the end of that process, the interaction between you and the external environment will also be reflected in a richer interaction between you and your internal environment. This was very much the experience Margy and I had when

"No one has ever had an idea in a dress suit."

Sir Frederick G. Banting

"Every composer knows the anguish and despair occasioned by forgetting ideas which one has not the time to write down."

Hector Berlioz

(Of all said words of the writer's pen, saddest are these, "I didn't jot it when!")

"Creation is always preceded by Chaos"

Holmes, the Guardian Angel

we built our Lake Lure home.

A Whole-Brain House

Margy and I, being equally committed to living in a whole-brain, creative way, chose to design our entire home as a creative space. It was without a doubt the biggest and one of the most profound creative events I've been through yet, and it had a wonderful effect on my own inner creative space. It also illustrates some important aspects of and options for thinking about creative space—the importance of communication, the use of creative processes/materials to develop comprehension, and the rewards of persistence. Take from the story whatever speaks to you. Here goes.

When Margy and I were planning our post-GE lives, we agreed we wanted to build a whole-brain environment in which both of us could claim our work and nonwork creative space and have our creativity enhanced, both individually and in partnership.

Creating such an environment required us to communicate with one another more clearly and deeply than we had in years. Since we both wanted that, we prepared ourselves to be particularly conscious in the process of creating our ideal space.

Fairly early in my evolving understanding of the impact of personal brain dominance on behavior, I was reminded of my own forcefulness by a comment from Margy. She said, "Ned, it's impossible to win an argument with you. Your logic is so relentless, the tone of your voice so intimidating, the endless stream of words so overwhelming that I never have a chance to get my point across. Often, I go along with your ideas to keep from getting worn down."

Perhaps I should have known, but I didn't. But in the context of the whole-brain model, I suddenly got Margy's point. My logical, rational, verbal expression was so compelling to me at certain times that I couldn't appreciate the intuitive, sensitive feeling-oriented modes of expression she often prefers. It wasn't that she couldn't be logical, rational, and verbal or that I couldn't be intuitive, feeling, and non-verbal. It's just that we would periodically get stuck in opposing modes—A and C, and B and D. And in the absence of clear feedback from each other, neither of us could understand what we were doing that blocked the communication. The differences between us had always been part of our attraction to each other, but until we began to understand the source of these differences and to honor them fully, we couldn't translate them into a synergistic partnership.

It hasn't been easy for either of us to change a lifetime of habit, but we've made remarkable progress in moderating our behaviors. I, for one, became much more conscious of my own forcefulness and found it occasionally excessive. I've realized that expression of verbal logic often carries a certain arrogance, albeit unintentionally so. This arrogance, coupled with a booming bass voice and a performer's gestures and expressions, forms the basis of true intimidation. The information had been around for years, but until I saw it in the context of the brain model, I never got the point. Today, I try to listen to others openly, without simultaneously formulating arguments. Equally important, I listen to myself and the feedback allows me to make continuous adjustments in my behavior. The understanding that came from my four weekend seminars at Esalen Institute, Big Sur, California, opened me up to the feeling and the expression of genuine emotions.

Margy, for her part, has changed also. Rather than allow my delivery to overwhelm the content of my message, she allows my occasional excesses to roll past her and responds instead to the verbal meaning. This is very helpful to both of us because it helps us experience being allies rather than adversaries. As a result, we've discovered we really need each others' mental differences to supplement our own lack of preferences or avoidances. We are becoming more and more effective and fulfilled partners in our life together. And we are doing it with high good humor, which is inextricably intertwined with creativity.

This kind of learning is not age dependent: It's a lifelong opportunity for personal development, not only for us, but for anyone in a committed relationship. That is a message of hope for all of us, particularly those who, like I, are growing older everyday.

This communication learning continued throughout the house project and helped us make very good decisions. For example, we'd originally planned to settle in Grafton, Vermont, which we both loved and where I'd done the majority of my landscape painting. However, after spending time there in winter and spring as well as in the colorful fall, we knew that for too much of the year, Vermont was simply too wet, muddy, cold, and remote to meet our combined needs. Without knowing the name for it, we were practicing a key step in the creative process—verifying the appropriateness of our proposed solution—and it didn't pass the test.

Thus began a five-year search in which I painted my way down the Appalachian Trail, to find a warmer, easier "Vermont," a place with four distinct seasons, mountains, water, lots of trees, privacy; a jetport, and a metropolitan center within an hour's drive. Of all the places I

"Be obscure clearly."
E. B. White

"Communication is something so simple and difficult that we can never put it in simple words."
T. S. Mathews

"To think justly, we must understand what others mean: to know the value of our thoughts, we must try their effect on other minds"
William Hazlitt, "On People of Sense", *The Plain Speaker* 1826

"Sculpture is a kind of architecture."
Stevenson, *The Wrecker, III*

"The great requisite for the prosperous management or ordinary business is the want of imagination."
William Hazlitt

"Anyone who by his nature is not his own man, but is another's, is by nature a slave."
Aristotle (384-322 B.C.)

Figure 10-9. Lake Lure House Site in Bronze

Figure 10-10. Sketch of the Property

traveled in the United States, the one that best satisfied all these needs and wants was the resort community of Fairfield Mountains in the beautiful little town of Lake Lure, North Carolina. This was the land that so impressed the architect in the story told at the beginning of Chapter 6. We both love the mountains, and for Margy there was a bonus—she was going home!

Once the Fairfield Mountains site was selected, the first order of business was getting to know the environment and learning about the soul of the land. We did this in several ways. First, since we both loved small planes, we took a series of photographic aerial survey flights to verify our choice of property. The area was so heavily wooded that it was the only way to get a sense of how the ground lay or what the views might be. It passed the aerial test. Later, when we had purchased enough of the property to know that the building project could be completed, I followed my artistic instincts by modeling the topography of the land in two cold-cast bronze sculptures, and also creating a series of 12 sketches and 6 full paintings of various views from different perspectives. This was a new kind of preparation for me and an extraordinarily useful experience. After completing those projects, I felt the land and its natural vistas fully belonged to me, that I knew, in a deep way, its character, foibles, and inner secrets.

Designing our home really stretched my visualization skills. The site was too heavily wooded to see exactly where the best views of the lake and the mountains would be, so I had to conjure them up in my mind. This was especially important in thinking about the upper stories of the house. My visualizations had revealed that to capture the view from at least two floors, we would need to build a three-story house. To think through the general design and the location of windows, I "beamed" myself up as much as 20 feet above the forest floor, visualized what the view would be like from there, and based on that, did a series of painting sketches of various design possibilities. I had practiced for this challenge by painting an aerial view of the town of Grafton Vermont, from the perspective of being 200 feet up in a hot air balloon. What fun!

We wanted the house to have a good impedance match with its magnificent natural environment. We thought of it as an inside/outside house: It should let in the outside with all of the nature that was available and, at the same time, let the inside out, meaning it should enable us to pass easily out into the natural surroundings—as if the outdoors were simply an extension of the interior. A good impedance match also meant at least one place in the house from which one could see in all directions. To achieve this inside/outside character, I put together in my mind the location of every single window, skylight, and door in the house. Whenever I got stuck, I would just take another airplane ride and that would start the mental juices flowing again.

Even before the house was designed, Margy and I decided to install an active solar-heating system. In such a climate, we thought it simply inconceivable not to. Experimenting with unconventional heating wasn't new to me. In 1949, I designed and built a very effective hot water radiant heat system imbedded in the ceiling of the house in Schenectady. It had worked perfectly, so I was very confident.

Others weren't anywhere near as comfortable with the idea of a solar-heated home. The architect, while enthusiastic, had never done a heating system like this and felt less than fully competent to design it into the house.

"Every bird likes its own nest best."
Randle Cotgrave

"We shape our buildings; thereafter they shape us."
Winston Churchill, *Time*
September 12, 1960

"It is the marriage of the soul with Nature that makes the intellect fruitful, and gives birth to imagination."
Thoreau, *Journal*

Figure 10-11. View of the House from Downhill

The local builders were even more leery. They did have some cause, for there were some challenges. First, to take advantage of the view and still have an effective collector, the collector system would need to be separate from the house, which meant transporting the solar energy 35 feet; nobody considered this practical. Second, solar technology had developed unevenly, with storage systems' technology lagging behind that of collector and air-handling mechanisms. Even the most promising storage system, which was originally designed by MIT and involved the use of eutectic or "glaubers" salts, had never worked properly.

But I had high hopes that the technical problems of storage would be solved. They were. So was the problem of piping the solar energy 35 feet into the house, which I found could be done with essentially no loss in energy! A key player in this process was Richard Pratt, a young man in the area who as an environmentalist had become enthusiastic about the future of solar energy and made himself available as a consultant on the project. It was he who converted my dream into a technically sound plan and supervised the construction of the collector storage system and the installation of the air handling equipment. Today, after 5 years' operation, we have fully verified the system—it really works—as I was certain it would.

But I'm getting ahead of my story. We had the property but hadn't yet found an architect whose work seemed appropriate for the visualizations I had in my head. And had we been looking! During 10 years of searching and dreaming, we had pored over hundreds of house magazines and sent away for dozens of house plan books, which now filled an entire shelf in our bookcase. Then one day, thumbing through a house magazine, I found a design that I really liked. It fitted neither the site nor our needs, and the architect lived in Oregon, but I liked it. I kept trying ways of modifying the design, but nothing worked. It didn't dawn on me consciously that a house could be designed by somebody who wasn't local, but in my frustration, I picked up the phone and called the Oregon designer—Lou Bruinier of Portland to complain about his living so far away. My conversation went something like this: "I really like your design of the house I saw in the house plan magazine. And I'm just sorry that you can't design a house in North Carolina." He said, "Why not? If you'll buy me a coach ticket, I'll be there whenever you want and I can design the house long distance." Bingo! It sounded crazy, but because of my own previous house-building experience, it also sounded possible.

Lou Bruinier's initial reaction to the site, described in Chapter 6, was followed by an extended exchange among the three of us. As we walked about the site, Margy and I spoke to Lou of our dream, gesturing to convey a sense of the space we felt we needed. Only 10 percent of our time went into describing the outside space—the rest was spent on the inside, so the house was essentially designed from the inside out. The central core of the house was to be our kitchen. That way, no matter what kind of event was taking place in the house, this room would be the natural gathering place; we wanted none of the isolation the typical homemaker suffers in conventionally laid-out houses. Accordingly, both horizontally and vertically, the inside spaces were arranged around that central kitchen. In addition to seeing and being in on the activities taking place with people in other rooms in the house, Margy wanted prime views, not only of the outdoors, but of the inside as well: From the center of the kitchen, she wanted

to be able to enjoy the fireplace in the living room, the television and wood-burning stove in the family room, and the magnificent rock-faced mountain rising above the lake and across the valley.

The rest of the house was to extend from this core concept out to and through the windows. Windows, windows, and more windows. We wanted a vaulted living room with the spectacular view of the valley, lake, and mountains to provide a sense of openness and space. We wanted the master bedroom/bathroom suite on the third floor, separate from the dual-purpose guest rooms/break-out rooms on the bottom floor, to be a "tree house." Through visualizing, I had positioned the windows to provide not only a view of the lake by day and the stars at night, but also the first glimpse of the sun in the morning. We wanted extravagant two-story windows encasing the stairwell to connect us visually with the natural world outside each time we went up and down the stairs. And Lou gave us windows. The enormous number of windows in the house have made it what it is and have contributed immeasurably to our enjoyment of the total space.

What happened after that meeting with Lou comprises a long, delectable series of successful solutions to design and construction problems. For example, after Lou had produced the initial plans, we wanted a still clearer sense of how the house would work. Margy, who is marvelously creative and has a sense of color, form, and style that far exceeds my own, pressed for a more concrete way to verify our mental construct of the internal space. To provide that, I decided to build a scale model of the house, using the architect's preliminary plans. It took about four sets. I simply pasted the exterior elevations and floor plans on shirt cardboards, cut them out, and assembled them

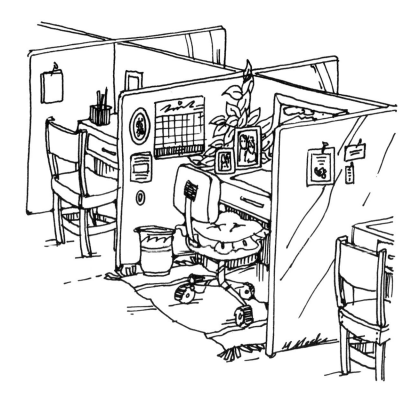

on a base that replicated the contours of the site. It was terrific! By removing the roof and interior floors, we could see both the inside and the outside of the house three-dimensionally. We discovered some hidden opportunities this way: Two roomy closets, for example, were made available simply by cutting doors in two walls. The scale model not only helped us, it also helped others understand what we had in mind. I was delighted on one visit during the construction of the house to discover that the workers had built a little protective shed for the model. Whenever they ran into a problem in interpreting the plans, they would gather around the model and see visually how the plans translated into the rooflines and interior space.

To me, the completed house is a live-in sculpture. It's also a smashing success, with universal appeal. Margy and I are very proud of it as a metaphor of the work I'm doing. We are also grateful to have been able to build the house, because doing so has enormously strengthened, confirmed, and enlarged our personal internal creative environments. No matter what the scale, your own external work on establishing a creative environment can do the same for you. It's worth the effort.

I generally recommend that people start flapping their creative wings at home before doing so at work, first because for most it feels safer, and second, because they usually have more room to experiment with different media and behaviors.

However, although exercising one's creativity at home is wonderful, I didn't think anything satisfies over the long term like functioning creatively on the job—working in a whole-brain way that honors the humanitarian values of C quadrant, the vision of D, the logic of A, and the prac-

Figure 10-12.   A Creative Cubbyhole

ticality of B. Ultimately, I wish for everyone the chance to develop creative space for themselves at work.

Creative Space at Work

It's important to remember that creative space on the job cannot be established by anyone other than the person who will be using it. Why not? The reasons are obvious when you think about them. *First*, since your creative space comprises so many internal as well as external factors, no one else can possibly know all the things that are going to stimulate you to creative work. (This is the same reasoning that led me to make the HBDI a self-administered instrument.)

Second, others' mental preferences and priorities may impair their judgment of what will work for you. For example, an administrator wrestling with a budget crunch imbalance will naturally consider his budgetary needs first, even when laying out options. It's not that he shouldn't, but such constraints need to be considered later in the decision-making process, rather than right in the beginning, narrowing the range of alternatives. The idea that is too expensive may be just the spark needed to bridge to another option that is affordable.

Even though creative space cannot be imposed, company managements repeatedly try to do so, but they don't get what they want. A common mistake they make is to confuse the idea of a creative space (frequently known as the R & D facility) with the control room of the *Enterprise* of "Star Trek" fame; creative spaces simply aren't space ships, and the sterility of a space vehicle control room doesn't go far in nurturing creativity.

Let me give you what I hope is an extreme case of

"It is a blessed thing that in every age some one has had the individuality enough and courage enough to stand by his own convictions."

Robert G. Ingersoll

Figure 10-13. Changes in Appearance

this confusion. It stands as a classic example of what not to do when designing creative space for others. I visited one company that had just spent nearly $100 million converting unused factory space into a new creative center. It could have been wonderful, but they built the wrong kind of environment and the people who worked there hated it. They had no private space. They were constrained from personalizing their workspace. Meeting spaces were small, inconvenient, and windowless. The colors were gray and black. Even more damaging was the demand for neatness: No work or resource materials could be left out, no messy products could be brought in. Creative materials were unavailable. The building was run like a military base, complete with dress codes and fixed work schedules. To compound their original mistake, management focused attention on the enormous investment they'd made and announced a "research efficiency" drive. Company groups that had formed their own private skunkworks were advised to close down those messy and inefficient quarters and consolidate their efforts within the new creative center.

What a heartbreaking waste! Imagine what that company could have done if management had assigned the creative groups a budget and the charter to design their own space from the inside out. Instead, through ignorance, insensitivity, and the arrogance of logic, they created a costly monster, and destroyed or limited the opportunity for creative expression so desperately needed by the company. That's not money lost this year. That's money lost forever.

Much as I know about the creative process and much as I may have desired to help my staff, I couldn't hand them their creative space on a platter. At GE, the closest I could come to establishing their creative space for them was to: (1) demonstrate commitment to functioning creatively myself; (2) let them know I expected it of them; (3) encourage, praise, and reward them when they did it; and (4) give them more exciting, creative tasks to perform.

So establishing creative space on the job is very much each person's own responsibility, but at the same time, other people are inextricably involved. Even when you're the president and chairman, you can't make a creative space for yourself without at least the tacit agreement of others (only an owner can act with impunity). Therefore, to win and maintain the right to function creatively in our chosen professions, most of us need to persuade others that letting us do so is in their best interests.

It is, at least in part, a public relations job and involves projecting an image that is consistent with being creative in that profession. I urge people to change clothing and hairstyles when they want to change their image. It's a visible signal of intent to change and I've proven personally that it works. Mind you, it's important to recognize each profession has its own range of acceptable behavior and appearance, especially for males, who are so rigidly uniformed in our society. A banker handling millions of dollars of corporate money rightly feels he can't afford to blemish his traditional image of conservative, meticulous prudence. Even in the face of such stringent normative demands, however, opportunities exist to enhance the appearance of one's dress. Even a banker can wear an attractive shirt, an exquisite tie, and a contemporary, well-cut suit. Even a banker can wear his hair slightly more flowing.

By comparison with the banker, the engineer and the administrator can have a field day: They can move toward more color in their wardrobes, wear sweaters, relax a little on conservatively cut suits and formal shoes. Women have even more latitude, and many are taking advantage of it. The old stereotype of the business-suited female executive was too often simply a euphemism for dowdy. Lovely colors and fabrics and a flowing scarf are never out of place on a woman, no matter what her position.

The story that introduces this chapter tells how I deliberately set out to change the way I was perceived at GE. Changing my appearance was only the first piece of a deliberate four-part strategy.

1. *Changing appearance.* I revised my personal appearance by changing my hairstyle and wardrobe, letting sideburns and hair grow a half-inch longer than previously. I bought colored shirts and softer, less structured ties with patterns that were organic rather than geometric.

2. *Demonstrating ownership.* I demonstrated that I considered my office fully mine by holding an art show in my office area. I created a huge wall display providing a visual status report of my organization projects.

3. *Introducing and encouraging creative approaches.* I deliberately stimulated my staff to use creative approaches in carrying out the everyday work of the various departments. I introduced new activities into the development program for which I was responsible. I convened meetings with my clients and colleagues to solicit ideas and information about their needs and involved them in my creative problem solving.

4. *Publicizing the changes.* I arranged for my department managers and corporate officers to visit my office area to see what I had done, not only with

the space, but with the activities carried out in the space. I devised fresh and novel ways of reporting our results to senior executives. In so doing, I not only claimed the space, but also claimed credit for its effective use.

Perhaps the most important thing I did was to invite others to join in the fun. Because it *is* fun, and when people have fun, their creative juices start to flow, and then they usually become much more valuable as employees. *Nobody loses* and *everybody wins*. Let me give you an example:

My office here in Lake Lure is often filled with laughter. Even in the midst of a potential disaster, we have all had fun trying to come up with inventive solutions, and frequently do. Marie Crisp, a key staff member who administers creative workshops, often brings a smile to the faces of those who work with her. By approaching problems from the funny side, she improves her chances of opening up new alternatives that would be blocked by being overly serious. I encourage all around me to find humor in their work, because I feel it is a legitimate and necessary part of a creative environment.

Many of the well-received visuals used in my public presentations are the result of finding humor in the highly technical, serious aspects of my work. I frequently use cartoons, news clips, and jokes to lighten my presentations to business audiences. A while ago, I asked Nehdi, a professional photographer who is my staff specialist on visuals, to add a series of cartoons to my presentation kit for a major national conference. Instead of providing me with a literal translation of my request, he incorporated a hilarious cartoon on each of the several dozen title visuals. I was delighted. When I asked him how he came up with the idea, he said the titles seemed too boring by themselves, and since I used humor all the time anyway, he felt he could use some humor, too—after all, my visuals were also *his* creative space. Not only did the audience love it, but he invented a new art form in the process. These humorous title visuals have now become standard.

Many of the materials my staff creates are the result of their being turned on to this work and the climate in which they perform it. I can model it. I can give permission to pursue it. But it's up to them to create it.

It's a turn-on for me every time it happens. Like the time that Angie Conner, a key staff member who assists me on major projects, had a problem to solve. What to do to support a major client who was mounting a "Creativity Fair" for company employees and wanted to promote our ACT Workshop. Angie asked a few people for their opinions and this led to a total staff brainstorming session. Ideas began to pop. How about an ACT photo album and participant quotes? A continuous video of an ACT workshop in progress? A newsletter? Hey, how about a special newspaper with the client's name on the masthead! Angie was off like a shot. That idea appealed to her and quickly became hers. She started claiming her creative space immediately. Angie had never created a newspaper, but she did all the writing, headlining, picture selection, and layout work on a "crash" basis, and got 500 copies to the client on time, along with a dozen other creative items. The client loved it and even decided to stimulate more company interest by shipping the ACT exhibit around to a number of their plant sites. It was exciting to see her grab the idea and follow through on it. Everybody else got excited helping her succeed, and during those few days she claimed half the office building as her creative space.

It should be clear to you by now that establishing creative space on the job, but also anywhere else you go, is essentially an inside job. No one else can do it for you. *You* have to do it yourself, and that's true no matter what your organization level. It's a job worth doing from everybody's viewpoint—especially your own, and also the boss's. By providing the environment conducive to your claiming your creative space, the boss allows the miracle of self-motivation to manifest itself. Nobody's power is relinquished—rather, it is placed into the hands of the one who can use it best—the turned-on worker.

DOOR TO NORMALCY

ALL WHO
ENTER HERE
BELONG

Z. NEZZILL 1988

11

MESSAGES OF HOPE FOR THE FUTURE

We used to think of the brain the way most of us do about "black boxes"—mysterious things that make other things go, but that are so far beyond our capacity to understand that it's senseless to try to figure out how they work. The brain was a subject reserved for scientists buried in laboratories, working on obscure and esoteric chemical experiments and theories. Today that era has clearly passed. Where ten years ago I was called aside and advised not to speak of the brain in public, today I am welcomed into boardrooms, invited to kick off annual corporate meetings, selected to give keynote addresses at national conferences, treated with respect on college campuses, and called and written to by hundreds of people in the general public.

The era of the personal brain has arrived. By that I mean the brain and its functioning is now out of the laboratory; it is a subject to which we can all relate *personally*. We can now infer the way our own brains function from observing our daily lives in brain dominance technology. What's more, we can *influence* that functioning. Brain dominance technology can help us open up doors we didn't even know we'd closed.

Of all doors we can open, none is more liberating than the one with the sign reading THE DOOR TO NORMALCY—ALL WHO ENTER HERE BELONG.

Figure 11-1. Door To Normalcy (opposite)

REDEFINING NORMAL: ALL WHO ARE DIFFERENT BELONG

In my work, redefining what normal means is a central theme—in fact, *the* central theme. Brain dominance technology gives us some new ways to look at normalcy and define it more appropriately than we have to date. Two of these new definitions are: (1) normal means belonging to a tribe of similar people; and (2) being normal includes being unique.

Tribal Normalcy

"Normal" is a comparative concept, usually defined in terms of culture. We are normal if we are like everybody else in our school or in our community. We are even more normal if we are like everybody in our social group, our gang, or our tribe. People who aren't like the rest of the tribe "aren't normal," a phrase that carries a very negative connotation because it says, "that person doesn't belong

Figure 11-2. Technoid Dave and His Tribe

to our group." He or she doesn't share our goals, language, and expectations—all of which define our normalcy.

In the context of the four-quadrant model, normal means having one of the profiles, behaving in accordance with it, and thus becoming a member of the homogeneous tribe composed of people with that profile. If you prefer one quadrant over the others, you should know that you are not alone. In a room full of Weird Johns, Weird John is just John—normal. Just as Straight Sally, Careful Henry, and Emotional Mary are normal in their own tribes—simply Sally, Henry, and Mary. Normal ranges across the entire brain dominance spectrum.

That being true, somewhere in this composite whole-brain world each uniquely different person is indeed normal. Someone once said that the purpose of a tribe is to exclude people who don't fit the tribal norms. If so, then it's also true that the purpose of a tribe is to *include* people who *do* fit these norms. Our data sample shows that, taken as a whole, people in the world make up a composite whole brain, with relatively equal distribution in all four quadrants. So for every person displaced from one tribe, there's another tribe with norms that he or she does fit.

Learning this truth has transformed many lives at a very deep level. People have written to me or have told in person, with tears in their eyes, that as a result of understanding the whole-brain concept and learning their profiles, they now feel okay about themselves. They have discovered that their overwhelming feelings of isolation—of being abnormal—resulted from simply being different from their local tribe. They had felt displaced from that group and therefore lacked the sense of belonging that we all need and search for. But they now realize there are others like themselves. They belong.

Unique as Normal

While brain researchers debate many theories, none of them argues that any brain is just like any other. Brains are like snowflakes: Every one differs from every other one, and so do the complex mental patterns and behaviors associated with each. It's normal to be different, *because no one is just like anyone else.*

But how different is different? Where does one draw the lines between unique, eccentric, abnormal, and ill? That debate has raged on for centuries and certainly won't be settled to anyone's satisfaction in my lifetime.

My purpose is not to lay out who should be *excluded*; rather, it is to widen the definition of who should be *included*. Why? Because inclusion works better, as any graduate of ACT will joyfully certify.

Using the broader definitions of normalcy available through the four-quadrant model opens up several additional ideas. These are messages of hope that I like to think will help people who intend to live more creatively. Here they are:

1. Differences are not only normal, but also positive and creative.

2. Appreciating and using these mental differences makes change easier to deal with because it makes us more creative.

3. As we appreciate the full spectrum of mental gifts—ours and those of others—we can make better choices in our lives, especially in selecting educational and career directions.

4. If those who manage others will acknowledge and honor personal preferences and give people the chance to match their work with their preferences, they will be able to tap tremendous productivity gains.

5. As we learn to value and, above all, *affirm* one another's mental gifts, we can participate in the formation of true community—perhaps our best hope for survival in this strife-torn world.

When personally applied, these ideas can supply profound affirmation and release enormous power. They have done so in my own life, and they can in yours.

REDEFINING DIFFERENCES: WE CAN LEARN TO SEE THEM AS POSITIVE AND CREATIVE

If we accept that mental differences are normal, it is only a halfstep further to the perception that they are also generally positive and specifically important to creative functioning:

Positive because all quadrants are necessary, so nobody's profile is undesirable in the right setting.

Creative because, for both individuals and groups, using all the quadrants situationally and playing off the differences between them is what advances the creative process.

These facts are especially important to remember when we consider male/female relationships.

Vive Les Différences!

As it happens, the majority of physiological differences among brains cluster into two major groupings, which correlate with gcndcr: malc and female. So do the acquired mental preferences associated with these physiological differences. Men generally lean toward the analytic upper left, women toward the emotional lower right. Now, as you've seen, the problems between people with diagonally opposed preferences can be significant, so it's not surprising that as a group, men and women tend to polarize in their opinions. But, as you've also seen, in a creative environment, the potential for enhanced functioning is also enormous.

Valuing Differences Exercise

Imagine what's possible between two people who not only provide creative space for themselves but also love one another and are committed to functioning creatively together! To get a sense of that potential, try the following exercise. It's a very powerful and potentially important one for you personally, so I urge you to spend enough time to gain benefit from it.

Name _____ Date _____

First, make copies of this exercise for yourself and for a person with whom you have an intense connection. Each of you should respond to the following sections by answering the questions as objectively and openly as possible.

PART I

A. What do I value about my logical, analytic, rational self?

_____

B. What do I value about my planned, organized, procedural self?

_____

C. What do I value about my emotional, interpersonal, feeling self?

_____

D. What do I value about my insightful, synthesizing, imaginative self?

_____

PART II

A. What do I value about the other person's logical, analytic, rational self?

_____

B. What do I value about the other person's planned,

organized, procedural self?

_____

C. What do I value about the other person's emotional, interpersonal, feeling self?

_____

D. What do I value about the other person's insightful, synthesizing, imaginative self?

_____

PART III

Think about what the other person could do for you if he or she decided to affirm, assist, or instruct you. Looking at the differences between your positive qualities and those of the other person, reflect on the ways in which you could: (1) *encourage and praise* that person for the value you see in what he or she already has; (2) help that person with your skills; and (3) teach that person to acquire your skills if they wanted to learn. With these things in mind, complete these five items about yourself and the other person:

Major differences between us:

_____

Positive qualities between us:

_____

Things I can do to affirm myself:

_____

Things I can do to help the other person affirm himself

or herself:

_____

Opportunities for positive synergy between you:

_____

PART IV

When you have both completed the exercise up to this point, share your responses with each other by exchanging the written forms completed in Parts I, II, and III. After talking over your responses to each others' satisfaction, complete Part V of the exercise *by entering your responses on the other person's form.*

PART V

Here is how I feel, now that we have had a chance to share and discuss our responses:

_____

_____

These are the actions I feel we could take:

I can: _____

You can: _____

Both of us can: _____

PART VI

When both of you have completed Part V, return the

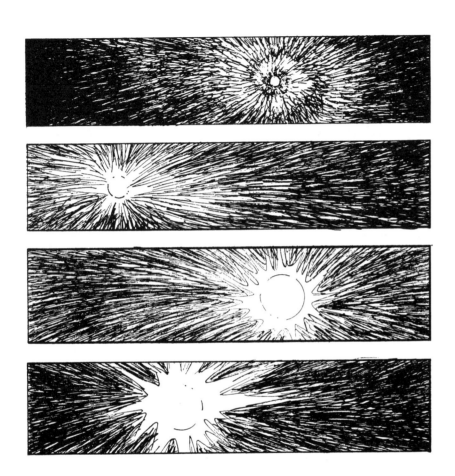

Figure 11-3. The Birth of a Star Metaphor

forms to the original person. Before you talk with each other about your feelings and your action plans, take time to consider the importance of the communication opportunity you now have with each other. When you are both ready, begin to talk.

When you've finished this exercise, you'll have identified ways in which you and the other person can contribute significantly to one another's well-being and creativity. In fact, just thinking this way may have begun that contribution already. You may already feel more affirmed about who you are, more excited about who you might become, more prepared to make that happen, and more potent in your ability to make a difference in someone else's life.

If this was the first time you've tried thinking in just this way, the power and possibility of it may seem a little overwhelming! Making use of differences, as opposed to arguing about them truly leads to a positive outcome. Given this kind of potential, it's little wonder that opposites attract! You and the other person may now be more prepared to form a synergistic, creative partnership between you.

I think it's fair to say that appreciating and using different modes of thinking, no more and no less, is the single most reliable and important signal that a person has moved from ordinary to creative functioning. This is true not only in our partnerships, but in *all* relationships, including the one we have with ourselves. Creativity is possible only as we let down our defenses against differing visions, understanding, and methods, and allow in the richness that these other perceptions offer. The fact that we are able to let down those defenses offers us significant hope for dealing with change in this world.

MASTERING CHANGE: WE CAN LEARN TO "GO CREATIVE"

Astrophysics theory, when used to describe the birth of a star, provides the basis of a fascinating metaphor for the whole-brain creative process.* The universe consists of uncounted billions of stars—200 billion in our Milky Way galaxy alone—so many in fact, that each person on earth can claim as many personal stars as he or she likes. Just as each person is unique, so is each star different from all others. Just as all of us have a life of our own, so do stars—they are born, live, and die. A star is "born" out of a rich mixture of gases and cosmic dust. A nucleus forms out of these particles and grows in size as it sweeps up surrounding matter by gravitational attraction. Ultimately a globe forms out of this cosmic material and this over time eventually grows into a dull red protostar—the first major milestone towards stardom. As the protostar globe continues to gain mass, gravitational forces pack the cosmic matter tighter and tighter in the core region, where the pressure, density, and temperature steadily climb. Eventually, the temperature becomes hot enough to ignite the protostar's nuclear furnace, and it then matures into a brilliant *main sequence star*. When the core temperature is

---

*My apologies to people who are particularly knowledgeable about astrophysics. I'm using the birth of a star as a metaphor, over-simplified, because I feel it helps clarify the profound transformation that takes place in people and organizations when they begin using their whole brain.

"The natural world is dynamic. From the expanding universe to the hair on the baby's head, nothing is the same from now to the next moment."

Helen Hoover
"The Waiting Hills" *The Long-Shadowed Forest*

hot enough to trigger the nuclear furnace, the star "goes critical."* Its energy ignites, and it attains its second major milestone toward stardom. It will now shine brightly both night and day for billions of years.

Going critical for a star means attaining the highest possible internal energy state. When this energy is released, the fusion process becomes self-sustaining and no further input of external energy is required to keep it going. Instead, as the energy of fusion is released, the process takes on a life of its own. It shifts into a whole new dimension of activity arising out of its own core and the star system achieves a sustained state of balanced high energy—a true star has been created, perhaps even a life-giving sun.

In the creative process, we can "go critical" at the moment of illumination—the Aha! moment of the birth of an idea. Ideas are made up of attracting fragments that are swept together as mental momentum builds toward the critical state. Prior to that, facts, needs, opinions, and perceptions collide with each other and also bump up against our established ways of thinking about a subject, just as the cosmic particles crash into each other as fusion takes place in a star's core. For some of us, this may be greatly perturbing, for others, less so, depending on how open we are—how able we are to deal with the coming together of our internal differences. When the Aha! occurs, these rise up from deep within our minds, a power that is released in the form of a new vision—a fresh perspective that lifts us beyond our old perceptions and shifts us into a whole new realm of understanding. In that new vision, our old perceptions are both included and transcended and a new idea is created.

*The term *going critical* refers to a transition point at which some character or property undergoes a finite change.

The metaphor embracing the nuclear fusion in a star and the creative process in humans, holds true in that both fusion and creative energy, when released, can be used either positively or negatively. To be used positively, the energy must be balanced, controlled, and harnessed so that it flows in constructive directions; otherwise, it will simply undo the existing structure—just as an uncontrolled star can become a supernova and explode, or expend its energy so fast that it shrinks and dies a quick death. How does one control creativity? The energy contained in the star's core is controlled through system balance. The star's fusion process is both controlled and sustained through system equilibrium. In the creative process, we can control mental energy by achieving whole-brain equilibrium both before and after the moment of illumination: (1) before, by carefully defining our purpose in the preparation phase, and (2) after, by subjecting our ideas to rigorous examination in the verification phase and by applying the ideas in fruitful ways in the application phase. To put it another way, we keep our creative energy relevant, safe, and usefully applied by using our whole brain in the process rather than just an unbalanced part of it. The core √ of a protostar must go critical if a star is to be born. In the same sense, our mental process must go critical if an idea is to be born. When this happens, we "go creative."**

As we hurtle toward the year 2000, this ability to harness our mental energy through fuller creative functioning becomes more and more important. The pace of change is accelerating so rapidly that humans will be able to handle

**The term "go creative" refers to a transition stage in the mind in which the specialized modes necessary to the creative process become situationally available for application to a task in response to a felt need.

it with nothing short of their whole brain.

Learning to go creative improves our ability not only to come up with new ideas, but also to cope with change on both individual and group levels.

Going Creative as Individuals

The individual response to change is one of the factors that differentiates one human from another most markedly. Some of us find change easy, and we respond with enthusiasm. A move to another location is an adventure, a reorganization opens up possibilities. Others of us find change disruptive and upsetting, even terrifying. It interferes with getting things done the way we know how to do them, so it may threaten things we value about ourselves and our work: our competence, the quality and magnitude of our work output, the way we are viewed by our colleagues. Both at work and beyond, change interrupts established relationships, thus opening up our carefully repressed loneliness and fears of the unknown, and often closing off options we used to view as avenues of escape.

Although some of us handle change better than others, there isn't one of us who can't benefit from learning ways of doing it better. Even the most adaptable people resist certain types of change, and we all have a limit on how much we can tolerate at a time. Approaching or exceeding that limit activates our instinctual urge to seek safety and security. How intensely we respond to that instinctual urge depends on the magnitude and speed of the change and how much of a surprise it is to us.

Although I, too, have much to learn in this area, I believe I've got one technique down to a science: Whenever big changes hit, I "go creative." For me, that means going

"There is nothing permanent except change."
Heraclitus (540-475 B.C.)

"Change your thoughts and you change your world."

"Our business in life is not to get ahead of others, but to get ahead of ourselves — to break our own records, to out-strip our yesterday by our today, to do our work with more force than ever before."
Stewart B. Johnson

"One change always leaves the way open for the establishment of others."
Niccolo Machiavelli

"I wonder if I can send this computer back."

"How could I have lived without it?"

Figure 11-4. The Joy/Trauma of Change

into a preparation mode using all quadrants. First I go left, laying out and analyzing facts, defining processes, and tracking events where appropriate. I then move right, to my C and D quadrants, to activate my intuitive and visionary capabilities for brainstorming alternatives, then back to B quadrant for capturing those ideas. Then I move into incubation and turn to other work, secure in the knowledge that my homework is done and my subconscious is busily at work on the changes while I'm taking care of other business. When illumination hits, I immediately record it and begin iterating between B and D, clarifying the solution's definition and verifying its appropriateness for the situation.

Going creative like this can help anyone cope with change because it does three specific things:

1. *It initiates movement in us internally, which makes it easier for us to perceive constructive ways to react to the changes going on externally.* Unless we are in an active, moving mode, the challenge to change finds us simply mired in our resistance, stuck in an attitude of "Never!" or "You can't make me," rather than "What if...?"

2. *It activates in us those intuitive faculties that best equip us to accept and respond to change.* It's the compulsion to establish control that gets in our way when change hits. If we persist in trying to impose our established procedural and factual thinking on a new situation, accommodating change is very taxing. But the very nature of the intuitive modes involves appreciating and flowing with change, so there's relatively little strain involved.

3. *It tends to lower our anxiety because it is an active mode which feels pleasurable.* When we're afraid, we become self-protective: We contract our muscles, tighten down mentally, and hold on to what we know has worked in the past. Our bodies produce enormous amounts of adrenalin—energy which, because we hold it back, creates enormous tension in us. By contrast, becoming mentally active instead of just reactive allows all that energy to move—we can breathe again. In the simple act of concentrating on a moving process—even a very focused one—we release the vise of fear constricting our minds and bodies.

I believe that in this creative approach to change lies enormously good news for those of us who are increasingly aware of our mortality. The myth has been that as we age, we lose our mental elasticity and become increasingly unable to deal with even the smallest disruption to our routine. The truth is, this frightening rigidity needn't set in at all. If we learn to go creative in response to change, the years can simply add to our expertise.

Nor does any age group have an edge in learning to go creative. Using whole-brain classroom techniques, our faculty members enjoy the everyday experience of having people aged 65 and 70 learn the same material in the same classroom with people 40 years younger. All are equally motivated, responsive, and successful. None of the common barriers of age seem to exist.

When Organizations Go Creative

What applies to individuals seems to hold true for

"All serious daring starts from within."
Eudora Welty, *One Writer's Beginnings* (Harvard University Press)

"It's the most unhappy people who most fear change."
Mignon McLaughlin

"No matter how old you get, if you can keep the desire to be creative, you're keeping the man-child alive."
John Cassavetes

Figure 11-5. An Organization Goes Creative

organizations as well. The more creative an organization, the better it copes with change.

Making an entire organization creative is not as easy as initiating creative functioning for one's own self, but some similarities exist: (1) In both cases, accessing creativity also accesses the part of us that either gladly accepts change or empowers us to cope with it; (2) In both cases, creativity can be learned, provided individuals are willing to recognize and honor diverse styles, both in themselves and in others; (3) In neither case can either change or creativity be legislated by an outside influence—it's a process that arises from within, in each person's own decision to honor his or her personal experiences and creative desires.

As an organization evolves toward creative functioning, it tends to pass through a number of stages. In the first, which is where most organizations remain, creative individuals may operate in the organization, but they are either isolated or working at subdued levels on the job and expressing their creativity elsewhere. The move toward creative functioning begins in the second stage, as soon as two or more individuals have begun to collaborate creatively. When that happens, a chain reaction begins that may reach toward a critical mass. If management is savvy about creativity, it will issue creative challenges, in the form of needs, and then harness the resulting energy with careful capture and verification procedures. When that happens, the organization will go creative, which is the third stage.

Because of the way this happens, you can think of creatively active people in the organization as "change agents." They promote creative functioning in the rest of the organization.

This has important implications for any organization that has decided to promote creativity. It's absolutely imperative to make sure the individuals responsible for that effort have learned to be effectively creative themselves. A person who has not yet learned to produce change in his or her own life through creativity can hardly lead an organization to do so. That person needs to understand the creative process, appreciate human differences and build on them, lead without dominating, and speak all the languages of the brain, not only one or two. Under the direction of such a person, truly marvelous changes can take place, even in organizations that many consider incurably hidebound, such as manufacturing companies, banks, law firms, military organizations, insurance companies, and the like.

One of the thrilling things you see when watching an organization go creative is that people's sharpness and ability to focus on a problem seem to increase immensely. They're not getting more intelligent; they're just showing what they can do. The reason they can is that in a whole-brain team functioning in a creative environment, a person will gravitate naturally to what he or she does best, and because others are doing what they do best, this person can leave those modes to others without losing the benefit of the iteration between them. This brings up these questions:

1. How do we measure intelligence? Are people more gifted than we give them credit for?

2. How can we arrange for people to do work that allows them to use their preferred modes of knowing?

The next two sections of this chapter provide some of the answers.

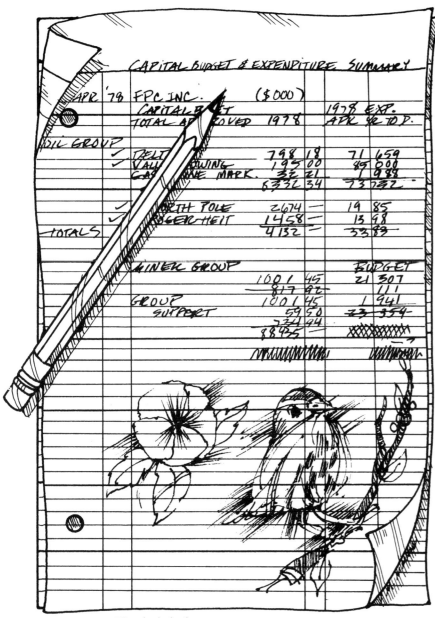

Figure 11-6. The Artistic Accountant

REASSESSING INTELLIGENCE: WE CAN IMPROVE CHOICES OF COLLEGE, MAJOR, AND CAREER

Observing and participating in creative work in organizations, one begins to see that conventional measures of intelligence and creativity are skewed, if not irrelevant. As our survey data prove, intelligence comes in at least four different forms. Typical tests of intelligence, however, measure only two thoroughly (A and B), and disregard the other two (C and D) almost completely.

This bias is even more pronounced when it comes to college entrance criteria. By far the greatest proportion of learning, both in preparation for and as a result of attending higher educational institutions, appears to be defined almost exclusively in left-brain terms.

When we assess talent without considering the entire spectrum of intelligences, we mismatch education, careers, and jobs. The consequences are particularly painful when loving but uninformed parents attempt to help their children make educational choices.

Now I'm not advocating that people learn only in their preferred modes—far from it. Living in this world is less problematic if we balance our abilities. So someone with C and D preferences probably *should* take a personal finances course, for example. A strongly A quadrant individual probably *should* take an experiential course in human relations.

But to expect the right-mode person to *major* in accounting or the A quadrant person to become a social worker makes no sense at all. Nevertheless, just that type of choice is made every day. The innkeeping profession requires a strong people-orientation, which demands a preference for C. The single dominant A quadrant person who attends a premier hotel school to follow the family innkeeping tradition may be able to pursue a career in the financial end of the business, but may never achieve superior competence and satisfaction in the critical people-services. The youngster who strongly prefers the C quadrant and enters the medical profession to please his well-meaning parents will have a very difficult time surviving the educational process, to say nothing of the brutal internship that follows. The less we know about our preferences, the more likely we are to mismatch, which is expensive, demoralizing, and wasteful.

The tragedy isn't that these people learn something they don't prefer, although the emotional and psychic cost can be considerable; it's that they—and we, society at large—forfeit the benefits of their achieving truly remarkable levels of performance and satisfaction. And they forfeit the joy and satisfaction of building competence in an area they really love.

Compared with governmental and academic bureaucracies, business and industry have a better track record in matching jobs and preferences if only because a company's survival demands a certain competence level, which tends to correlate with preference—but even business has some glaring exceptions. One of the most costly is the job-rotation form of fast-track programs for high-potential managers. Such programs put promising individuals through a series of very different jobs and give them a

"Treat people as if they were what they ought to be and you help them to become what they are capable of being."
Johann W. von Goethe (1749-1832)

"One of the saddest experiences which can come to a human being is to awaken, gray-haired and wrinkled, near the close of an unproductive career, to the fact that all through the years he has been using only a small part of himself."
V. W. Burrows

pass or fail depending on whether they do equally well at all of them. Those few who are equally brilliant in each of many different jobs requiring different competencies are clear candidates for a presidency, but the great majority fall by the wayside because they cannot star at certain jobs that call on their less developed mental preferences and, therefore, competencies.

MATCHING WORK WITH PROFILES: WE CAN HARNESS TALENT AND INCREASE PRODUCTIVITY

If most of us are not well-prepared to make decisions about our education, we are even less ready to make decisions about careers. Ideally, we should choose "turn on" work in the area of our strongest preferences and greatest competency. While it's not reasonable, or even ideal, to expect to land a job where we do nothing but our favorite things, it is reasonable to expect that most of us can do our favorite things at least some of the time. In fact, it is not only reasonable, but also critically important. Work is a central component of human existence, not only in the material sense—food, shelter, etc.—but also in terms of human satisfaction and well-being.

Another reason why doing our favorite thing is so important stems from the nature of work itself. Most work—even physical labor—is largely mental. It stands to reason, then, that we will be most productive if we are doing work that calls for the mental modes we most strongly prefer. To make that kind of match possible, we

need to know enough about our mental selves to choose not only the right career, but the right job within that career. Here's what I mean by that. The category of medical doctor, for example, usually calls for a left-mode A quadrant orientation. The mental requirements of specific disciplines within that profession, however, vary greatly, as mentioned in Chapter 4. May none of my family ever have a pediatrician or psychiatrist with a profile suited to a pathologist or radiologist! The enormous variations in doctors' competencies and satisfaction levels often result from such mismatches: Physicians who are less competent and/or dissatisfied might be the same ones who made decisions based on family aspirations or tradition (as I did), economics, or other factors rather than on the crucial issue of true preference. One day, I believe that we will learn responsible ways to match mental modes and work as the technology for doing so develops, and that the productivity gains from doing so will be enormous!

How does one match mental profiles with specific work? Even though we've learned a great deal about work and mental preference, we are still only at the beginning. For that reason, *please note*: I do *not* recommend instituting a policy of considering or not considering someone for a given job just because that person's profile does or does not match the job's brain-dominance characteristics.*

---

*I want to mention two other reasons that the HBDI shouldn't be used in a formal matching process as a hard-and-fast determinant of a person's eligibility for a job. First, just like all instruments, the HBDI is a snapshot that measures preference for mental modes at a given point in time. It does not measure competence, nor does it measure other important decision factors (strength of character, personal loyalty, effectiveness under pressure, ability to complement another important executive, influence as a catalyst for the management team, or motivation to grow and change). The second reason is

Encouraging that match, however, is advisable and I do recommend the following specific ways this can be accomplished:

1. *Design jobs with mental preferences in mind.*
   a. Analyze jobs into work elements according to the quadrant they call for.
   b. Set priorities to identify the primary elements of that job, and make sure the bulk of time the person spends in that job involves activities that call on the same mental modes as the most important work.
   c. Refrain from simply adding responsibilities to that position, even for administrative convenience, if they *unbalance* the mental tilt of the job, i.e., shift it away from the quadrant required to achieve the job's basic purpose.

2. *Encourage work and preference matching on an ongoing basis.*
   a. Educate employees at all levels about how brain dominance relates to their job effectiveness and satisfaction.
   b. Train managers and supervisors in job counseling techniques and instruct them to cooperate with subordinates' efforts to adjust job assignments (consistent with getting done the job that's got to be done).
   c. Measure resulting productivity gains.

---

that when people do their own job-preference matching, the results are generally what company management wants anyway. There's no need to go through the cost and trouble of institutionalizing preference matching, because, given the opportunity, most people gravitate naturally to work they like best, and they do so in a way that few managers could improve on.

"Let us train our minds to desire what the situation demands."

Seneca (4 B.C. A.D. 65)

"Our minds need relaxation, and gives way/ Unless we mix with work a little play."

Moliere, *The School for Husbands* (1661) 1.3, tr Donald M. Frame

"With a good heredity, nature deals you a fine hand at cards; and with a good environment, you learn to play the hand well."

Walters C. Alvarez, M.D.

"At bottom, every man knows well enough that he is a unique being, only once on this earth; and by no extraordinary chance will such a marvelously picturesque piece of unity as he is, ever be put together a second time."

Friedrich Nietzche (1844-1900)

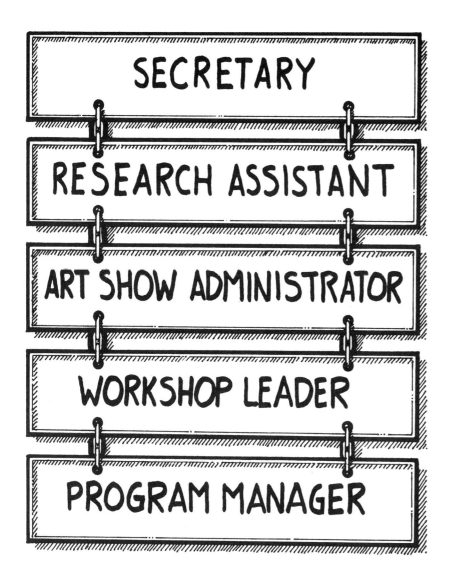

Figure 11-7. Naomi's Title

Delegating job-matching initiative to the incumbent is only common sense when you think of it. In the final analysis, most of us know more about our own work and our own preferences than anybody else does. Moreover, when we feel we've regained a measure of control over our work lives, we release a great deal of positive energy that can then be turned to productive work.

Like most good management techniques, this relieves the management burden in the long term, but instituting the approach in the first place is not a minor effort for an organization to undertake. Changing mind sets and upgrading necessary skills requires considerable commitment, education, time, and courage. However, I believe the benefits are so great that the effort will seem insignificant by comparison. Such a program should more than pay for itself in reduced stress and productivity gains alone. Let me give you a few examples of the kinds of situations it can help resolve.

In 1974, when I was manager of management education at GE's Management Development Institute, I had the good fortune to have Naomi Steinberg as my secretary. Naomi, who had completed several years of college and was an outstanding performer, really wanted to work at a professional (exempt salary) level, so whenever opportunities arose, I added independent professional level work to her job assignment to give her more experience. Her secretarial role expanded enormously when I rediscovered the brain for myself and initiated the related research effort. Naomi became my research assistant and collaborator, and we both started to enthusiastically gather information about the brain from the many sources that had opened up during that period. To many people, the extra load would have been quite overwhelming and unmanageable. Within a few months, however, Naomi had set up a research system in which significant information was entered on 5 X 7 cards, sequenced, then clustered under appropriate headings.

As she began to accumulate information for her own knowledge base, she began to acquire books on the brain, read them, and direct my attention to important references she felt I should be aware of. With only general direction from me, she maintained a steady flow of information, including key contacts, professional meetings, and presentation opportunities, which taken together, represented a major new priority in my work life. On her own initiative, she took work home at night and came in the following day with summaries of materials that she had read on my behalf and recommendations of actions that I should take. What I later learned to be her strong B quadrant preferences had developed into motivations and competencies that matched my needs perfectly.

But that's not all. During this same period, I was chairman of the Elfun Art Show, which was held annually at the Institute. As my secretary, Naomi became the administrative focal point for the art show, but she went way beyond the nominal duties of a support person. She became personally involved with up to 100 artists—who submitted as many as 600 or 800 separate works—and took the initiative to handle the myriad strange and wonderful issues that arise in putting together such a huge art show. On the weekend of the show itself, she did whatever was needed and handled many items that I knew nothing about entirely on her own.

As Naomi's capabilities became more and more obvious, I decided to respond to her preference for independent professional work by having her trained as a work-shop leader, and, as a result, she soon became a member of the faculty at the Management Development Institute, even though she was still my secretary. In the middle of all of this, Naomi decided to go back to school nights and weekends and get her degree. In the few years she took to accomplish this, she continued to perform all of her other normal and special assignments at an outstanding level. When the opportunity came up in my own department to promote Naomi to a program manager position, I selected her without hesitation (not without some twinges of loss). In her new role, she continued to perform as a course leader, doing so well that she was soon training other course leaders. Within four years, Naomi leapt from secretary to program manager, and substantially increased her salary, to say nothing of her sense of personal satisfaction. Her energy and motivation seemed almost limitless. The more high-quality work I made available to her, the more responsive she became. She was "turned on" to her work in all respects. Since then, Naomi has continued to grow and, even today, occupies a position of responsibility on the corporate technical education staff. She enjoys the admiration and respect of everyone who works with her.

Engineer Charles Brown offers another example of someone whose productivity rocketed when he had the chance to do work he preferred. Assigned to the production engineering component of a large technical business, he had all the talents required to perform his job as assigned; he also had other capabilities and interests. What was not known at the time, but is now obvious, was that Charles had an upper-right D quadrant preference just as strong as his upper-left A quadrant preference. Therefore, his A quadrant work continually sparked his D quadrant imaginative ideas. Under past management, he had been discouraged from experimenting with the product itself, because that responsibility was not in his job description and was therefore assigned to individuals in another component. But a new manager took over and quickly sensed Charles' other interests and potential capabilities. Instead of opposing the design improvements Charles volunteered, he encouraged them. Charles responded with a geyser of ideas and improvements in all areas, and ultimately provided the basis for a brand new product.

Everybody wins when this kind of thing happens. Naomi and Charles both redesigned their own jobs. All they needed was the chance to do so. Ultimately, everyone profited: they, their managers, and their company included.

The same could be said for every member of my Lake Lure staff. They are like helium-filled balloons of energy tugging at the job constraints that get in the way of even higher performance and personal satisfaction. I feel blessed and so do they.

Job-matching also helps solve the problem of the golden cage. It's quite common, particularly among highly paid professionals, for people to reach a plateau of effectiveness—and interest—and stay there because the job calls on mostly their secondary preferences. At first, the excitement of promotions and a sharp learning curve keep them interested. They do acceptable, even excellent work. But at some point, often at the point where they've "made it"—whatever that means in their vocabulary—all that excitement and striving gives way to the realization that if they had their druthers, they'd be doing something different. Unfortunately, such professionals are caught in a golden cage. Having advanced to their current level, financially, there's nowhere to go but down, and they've geared their life-styles and obligations to a high income level.

This situation engenders tremendous stress, in some ways more difficult to handle than the stress of someone who clearly and consciously hates what he or she is doing. For the person in the golden cage, stress is generalized over the whole work situation: high pay, but little satisfaction; high seniority, but almost no chance for significant promotion; lots of "dog work," but no thrills of achievement; gainful employment, but no chance for self-actualization on the job. The individual may try a number of solutions: a second profession, non-work-related hobbies, or community service. Many engage in physical fitness programs, and some companies facilitate it by providing wellness programs. But these solutions don't tackle the central issue and the stress persists.

But watch what happens when people match their mental preferences to the nature of the work being done! Careers that have plateaued, take off. Colorless performance on the wrong job gives way to effortless expertise in the right work. Self-actualization off the job is replaced with self-actualization on the job. Everybody wins!

AFFIRMING ALL MODES: WE CAN LEARN COMMUNITY

The power of community. It's something I've experienced for years in this work but hadn't labeled until helped along by M. Scott Peck's brilliant new book, *The Different Drum.* Community may be one of the most significant outcomes of applying the whole-brain concept, and Peck defines it as "a group of individuals who have learned how to communicate honestly with each other, whose relationships go deeper than their masks of composure, and who have developed some significant commitment to rejoice Y together, mourn together, and delight in each other, make others' conditions our own."

Forming community goes far beyond my conscious initial purpose, which was to create optimum learning groups where each member, by his or her very nature, contributes to the learning of other members. And that is part of the power of a composite group when it becomes a community. But there's much more. As you'll remember from Chapter 4, homogeneous groups form easily and reach consensus quickly. Although heterogeneous groups form slowly and reach consensus with difficulty, tremendous bonding, affirmation, and power come out of that struggle. In ACT I, the transformation is obvious when, at the end of the week, the six-person team operating as an organism can create lasting community.

What's even more thrilling to me is that the bonding doesn't seem to be confined to specific individuals in a particular ACT group or even to all ACT I graduates, although one can clearly see the bonding when reunions bring several ACT alumni groups together. Rather, the sense of community expands to include members of any composite community that has learned to accept, celebrate, and capitalize on differences. In other words, the *idea* of the whole-brain group itself, combined with the experiential knowing, motivates individuals to bond into a new group with incredible ease and speed. We have seen this happen on numerous occasions, even though the initial ACT I community experience occurred three to five years earlier with different people.

Each of the more than 1,000 people who've graduated

"I really felt I could call any of the participants today about anything (not just workshop related) and receive their help.

"It seems incredible to me that even though we each had a personal experience and this goal was not team building per se. I feel closer to those people from that week's experience than some of my own colleagues."
Doreen Kereysik (Workshop participant)

"No man is an island, entire of itself; every man is a piece of the continent."
John Dunne, *Devotions* (1624)

Figure 11-8. Community

from ACT I to date says that their group was the best "learning community" that they have ever experienced. I am absolutely certain that if we brought all those people back together again, but recombined them into different groups, they would feel the same toward their new communities.

Here are some reasons I think this happens in the composite whole-brain communities we create:

1. The differences in the group highlight the personal uniqueness of each member, so people can behave authentically as unique individuals and still feel normal.

2. People see that individual differences are actually resources for learning; everyone is a course enricher.

3. As a result, people recognize, appreciate, and acknowledge one another's contributions. That positive feedback provides enormous nourishment, which feeds energy back into the group process.

4. Because individual differences are so stimulating and fun, whole-brain groups are simply more interesting.

5. Whole-brain designs foster learner behaviors that lead to high levels of participation, involvement, and personal care for each other.

6. Participants begin to teach each other the things that they are motivated to learn, and, therefore,

the very process of learning is made more personal and interactive.

With careful facilitation, these same benefits of a composite whole-brain learning community can be made available outside the classroom—in the family, in work communities, in all manner of organizations, and at all levels. Our intellectual understanding of community is in its infancy. As Peck says, it's a phenomenon—like electricity—that is larger than we are and therefore beyond our embrace. But its creative power—to motivate, enliven, accomplish, and heal—manifests itself again and again in our whole-brain learning communities!

Brain dominance technology has been accompanied by a dramatic change in our frame of reference. The fancy term for this is paradigm shift. Ordinary people are becoming interested in the brain, ready to understand it. And through that understanding, make better use of this most vital personal resource. In doing so, we've gone outside the limiting boundaries that culture has inadvertently drawn around us. We have broken through the arbitrary circle that limits our view of self, and have made the human brain a subject to teach, apply, and celebrate. The brain has become the focus of my life's work. For you, it may be the beginning to understanding your creative self. Come join the whole-brain parade and go creative!

APPENDIXES

THE VALIDITY OF THE HERRMANN BRAIN DOMINANCE INSTRUMENT

by C. Victor Bunderson, Ph.D.*

Abstract: The Herrmann Brain Dominance Instrument (HBDI) provides a valid, reliable measure of human mental preferences when applied in a professional way, interpreted in conformity with the four-quadrant model, and scored with the approved scoring method.

This appendix was prepared to answer questions that both lay users and professionals in measurement might ask about the Herrmann Brain Dominance Instrument (HBDI). Does the HBDI actually measure what it purports to measure? Is there defensible evidence based on accepted measurement standards that the scores produced by this instrument provide a reliable and valid guide to a person's profile? Are preferences for different types of thinking, feeling, and doing (expressed through responses to the instrument) an outward manifestation of an underlying reality in the brain as this book suggests? Under what circumstances does the HBDI maintain its validity? These types of questions boil down to three basic ones:

1. Is the four-fold or quadrant model of brain dominance supported by research data?
2. Is the instrument a good way to quantify and thus make evident the underlying preferences for different ways of using the brain?
3. Is a particular application of the scores appropriate and valid?

The short answer to these questions is that on the basis of the investigations reported in this appendix and elsewhere, there is good evidence that:

1. Four stable, discrete clusters of preference exist.
2. These four clusters are compatible with the model explained in this book.
3. The scores derived from the instrument are valid indicators of the four clusters.
4. The scores permit valid inferences about a person's preferences and avoidances for each of these

---

* C. Victor Bunderson has collaborated with Ned Herrmann for almost 10 years. He has a background in educational measurement and psychometric methods, computer applications in teaching, learning, and testing, and has long-standing interests in biographical self-report information. At the time the validity studies reported herein were conducted, he was President of the WICAT Education Institute, a non-profit research and development organization studying computers in education, and also Chief Scientist of WICAT Systems, a computer company specializing in educational systems. He left WICAT in 1984, and has served since 1986 as Vice-President of Research Management at Educational Testing Service in Princeton, NJ.

clusters of mental activity.

5. Furthermore, the use of the instrument meets high professional standards as it has so far been applied in learning, teaching, counseling, and self-assessment settings.

More detailed answers are considered under the following headings:

- *Professional Standards for Using the HBD Instrument: Relationship to Validity* (This section discusses the circumstances under which validity can be maintaincd.)
- *Understanding Validity: The Kinds of Evidence to Support Validity.* (Construct-related evidence is the most important. Constructs are the set of ideas or concepts in the quadrant model about how people prefer to use different brain processes, or avoid them. This section discusses internal and external construct validity.)
- *The Constructs Measured by the HBD Instrument* (This section defines the constructs and the assumptions underlying their measurement. It reports some descriptive statistics from a study of 8000 cases.)
- *Review of Six Studies Dealing with Internal and External Construct Validity.* (This is the longest, most technical and detailed section of the appendix. The studies all used the statistical method of factor analysis to validate inferences about how the items *internal* to the HBDI group together and how the scores from the HBDI relate to *external* scores of both similar and different constructs.)
- *Future Research* (Three areas of future research are discussed: (1) refining the scoring and improving the scaling of the HBDI, (2) validating inferences about how people with different profiles activate their brains differently, and (3) validating inferences about how people with different profiles behave differently, that is how do they do such things as learn, teach, communicate with one another, work together in teams, and select occupations.)

PROFESSIONAL STANDARDS FOR USING HBD INSTRUMENT: RELATIONSHIP TO VALIDITY

Major test publishers of quality measurement instruments all subscribe to a set of professional standards for the construction, evaluation, and use of tests. Standards are published in *Joint Standards for Educational and Psychological Testing*, promulgated by the American Educational Research Association, the American Psychological Association, and the National Council on Measurement in Education (Joint Standards, 1985). Some organizations publish their own standards, which expand on but generally refer to the Joint Standards (e.g., ETS, 1986). The

Joint Standards list validity as the first item of concern, but also deal with reliability, sound methods of test development and revision, scaling, norming, score comparability, and the quality of manuals and user's guides.

For a small organization that is not a major test publisher, Applied Creative Services, Ltd., has done an exceptional job of establishing high professional standards for test development, validation, and appropriate use. This book, with its appendix, is the most detailed presentation to date of the concepts and methods on which brain dominance measurement and its uses are based. Documentation has been provided and research has been supported throughout the entire history of the development of the HBDI, and research continues today. High standards of instrument interpretation and use are maintained by requiring certification of those who would score and use the HBDI. Regularly scheduled certification workshops have been given at least 4 times each year since 1981 to maintain these high standards.

Certified users know that the HBDI is not a "test." The Joint Standards also recommend against using the word "test" to describe questionnaires dealing with personality, interest, attitude, and the like. It is a preference profile derived from evidence about the varieties of mental processes evident in the human brain, and refined on the basis of practical application and continuing empirical research over a period of about 11 years.

Standards for use of a measurement instrument really depend upon the uses for which the instrument was intended. In selecting from the various professional standards and codes for quality, fairness, and professional use of measurements, the following stand out as being most applicable to the HBDI:

1. *To Communicate Clearly With all Intended Audiences.* The materials and instructions associated with the use of the HBDI should avoid technical jargon and explain the relevant brain preference constructs and the profile scores clearly. This book augments and replaces earlier materials but does not replace the certification experiences.

2. *To Supply Evidence of the Quality and Usefulness of the Measurement Instrument.* The materials associated with the HBDI should represent accurately the quality and usefulness of the instrument and base such statements on empirical evidence (e.g., the data cited in this appendix). Another kind of evidence is provided to users during certification workshops and management education workshops where the instrument is used.

3. *To Help Users Interpret Their Scores.* Users must be informed of how to interpret their scores. At a certification workshop considerable effort is expended in providing full explanations of the scales used for reporting the scores and how these are related to the brain preference constructs. Information can be provided about different subpopulations and their profiles. Questions are given to help instrument users avoid over-interpreting and misinterpreting scores. Users are told about other sources of information in addition to the profile scores to help them make the kinds of inferences appropriate to the four-fold brain dominance model.

The communication of proper instrument interpretations of the HBDI goes beyond what can be written in a book like this or in a test manual. Much of the attitudinal, emotional, and interpersonal information that assures the proper use of the HBDI can best be communicated non-verbally. This is done through the establishment of "learning communities" in a properly conducted workshop or learning situation involving the HBDI.

The best insurance against misuse of the instrument is to avoid the evaluation of different profile categories as being good or bad. The modeling demonstration by good teachers through both verbal and nonverbal means occurs in certification and other workshops where proper instrument use is taught. These teachers develop a positive and creative climate in which all participants' profiles are seen as good and where authenticity is valued. If a teacher or group leader with a Lower Left preference made disparaging remarks and created a climate where being "right-brained" was seen as being somewhat "flaky" or undesirable, or if a right-brained person in authority designated the lower left as boring, or stereotyped left-brained people as "Nerds", the climate for the appropriate use of the profile scores would be damaged.

The means to promote growth rather than a bland acceptance of everyone as different and wonderful is provided through the "whole-brain concept." Groups can aspire to function together in a more "whole-brained" way, valuing the contributions of the disciplined managers and analytical left-brained people within the group, as well as the interpersonal facilitation of those people who prefer the activities in the Lower Right quadrant and the intuitions of those people who favor the activities of the Upper Right quadrant. In addition to fostering acceptance of the contribution of different people within a group, the whole-brained concept leads individuals to aspire to greater situ-

ational access to less preferred quadrants.

Because of the need for a subtle and frequently non-verbal climate that honors all profile differences, yet strives for greater completeness, certification workshops are desirable. Such workshops epitomize proper use of the HBDI. This is why it has been seen as so important by Ned Herrmann and his associates to offer certification and other workshops to provide the level of understanding required for professional application of the HBDI.

Coachability and Fakeability

As with other questionnaires dealing with interests, attitudes, and preferences, the validity of the HBDI depends upon honest responses from each respondent. While studies have not been conducted, it is probable that a coached person (a reader of this book, for example), could greatly influence the scores if he or she knew that selection to an important job, promotion, or reduction in force were at stake, and had information about what profile was desired.

The instrument is probably less subject to faking than to coaching because without some coaching about the nature of the brain dominance constructs, providing information about the descriptive adjectives, work situations, and so on for each quadrant, a person trying to fake answers may not know how to do it. The resulting profile might still reveal the primary patterns of dominance and avoidance.

Appropriate Uses of the HBDI

Appropriate uses for the HBDI include, but are not limited to the following areas:

1. *Better Understanding of Self and of Others.* To learn about one's own brain dominance profile and to understand how that profile compares to that of other people and other occupational groups.

2. *Enhanced Communication.* To be able to understand and predict the way different profiles might affect communication which leads to problems or to enhancement of interpersonal relationships on the job and at home.

3. *Enhanced Productivity Through Teamwork.* To learn how to increase the productivity and enjoyment of interpersonal associations in work, at home, and elsewhere. This can be accomplished through honoring and building upon the great advantages of differences in enhancing the effectiveness of teamwork in problem-solving, teaching and learning, etc.

4. *Work Climate for Creativity.* To identify inhibitors to creativity, productivity, and a positive work climate, and to establish the conditions for a positive work climate that will foster creativity.

5. *Authenticity.* To foster a climate of authenticity among groups of people who must work together.

6. *Enhanced Teaching and Learning.* To improve the effectiveness of learning and teaching and to achieve greater enjoyment in learning and teaching.

7. *Better Management.* To improve management of human activity in a variety of jobs ranging from supervision of work groups at lower levels to executive functioning at the highest level.

8. *Counseling.* To relate a person's profile to the profiles of others in college major fields, occupational groups, work groups, or families as a guide to clarifying and improving current relationships or making wise decisions.

9. *Building Composite Learning Groups.* To organize, in advance of a group learning activity, heterogenous or homogenous pairs, triples, sextets, etc. in order to promote understanding of interpersonal communications and of "whole-brained" teamwork in creative problem-solving and design.

Experience exists in the professional use of the HBDI in all of these applications. The conditions for validity and proper use can be maintained in each of these applications.

Uses of the HBDI Where Validity Cannot be Assured

The HBDI was not validated for use in clinical or diagnostic testing, nor in medical or psychological classification. It was not validated for use in admissions testing prior to educational or training programs nor for placement at different levels within these programs. (Using a test score as a condition for admission is an application distinctly different from the use of the HBDI to assemble optimal seminar groups.) It was not validated for use in selection testing for employment, for professional and occupational licensure and certification, nor for making a decision about a person that is beyond the control of that person.

While validity studies have not been performed for these uses, such studies could be done. Because of the strong cross-situational applicability of the instrument, demonstrated later in this appendix, it is likely that some such studies would show high predictive validity. For example, a study which used the HBDI to select people for jobs would likely show that people selected using the HBDI would be more satisfied and successful in that job. Nevertheless, the continued validity of such an application would be suspect for two reasons:

1. In common with other questionnaires of its type, the validity of the HBD instrument depends on honestly and freely given responses by the individuals who take it. This in turn depends on the climate of trust created by the persons in authority who require the instrument. It would be difficult to maintain conditions under which respondents would continue to believe that "honesty was the best policy."

2. Preference questionnaires like the HBDI are inherently coachable. In the employment selection example, word would inevitably get out about what type of profile the employment office favored. Respondents could then learn to produce that profile without authenticity.

More validity studies are indeed needed to guide the users of the HBDI in the many applications in which the conditions for authentic responses and proper follow-up can be maintained. The areas of using profile scores in teaching and learning, in academic, vocational and interpersonal counseling, in work redesign, and in managing work groups are especially promising for future research.

Having considered the conditions of proper use under which validity can be maintained, we will now consider the topic of validity itself and the evidence for the validity of inferences drawn from the profile scores produced by the HBDI.

UNDERSTANDING VALIDITY: THE KINDS OF EVIDENCE THAT SUPPORT VALIDITY

Validity is generally recognized to be the most important consideration in evaluating a test or questionnaire instrument. The concept refers to the appropriateness, meaningfulness, and usefulness of specific inferences made from test scores. It is not the scores themselves that are valid or not valid, but rather the specific inferences we might make from those scores and from the scales underlying the scores. The test validation process is designed to accumulate evidence to support a given type of inference. Different studies are needed for different types of inferences. The studies cited herein focus on inferences about four clusters of mental preference and how different profiles may be interpreted. Other studies would be needed to validate predictions about occupational satisfaction, management effectiveness, the different effects of teaching treatments for different profiles, etc.

There are several types of evidence used to support the validity of different inferences. These include content-related evidence, criterion-related evidence and construct-related evidence. Constructs are concepts or ideas about what an instrument measures. Construct validity is what this appendix is all about and is discussed in detail later.

Content-related Evidence of Validity

Content validity or content representativeness refers to the closeness of the match between the content categories involved in some description of a content domain and the content of the items in the instrument. For example, the terms and tasks sampled by test items in an insurance agent certification exam should match and sample well from the terms and tasks used by knowledgeable and competent insurance agents. Since the Herrmann Brain Dominance Instrument is designed to measure preferences, and is not a test of knowledge, content validity is not an important issue here.

Criterion-related Evidence of Validity

Criterion-related evidence requires additional measures besides the HBDI scores. These additional measures serve as criteria for judging that certain people are good at something or are possessed of some valued quality. High grades are a criterion of academic success. Publications and patents are criteria of professional productivity. Scored responses to a questionnaire may serve as a criterion of marital or job satisfaction. The HBDI scores may be correlated with such criteria to validate inferences about which profiles are related to academic success, professional productivity, marital or occupational satisfaction, etc. The HBDI scores themselves may be used as a criterion to select groups of people of distinctly different profiles in order to validate inferences about how these people will react or perform on some other measure of interest.

Criterion-related evidence of validity is important to this appendix. It is a part of most of the studies cited herein. This kind of evidence, however, is really most appropriately viewed as evidence to support the construct validity of an instrument. A recent scholarly and complete treatment of the entire topic of validity by Samuel Messick of Educational Testing Service (Messick, 1989) argues that construct related evidence of validity is the only fundamental and necessary type of evidence. All other kinds of evidence for validity are supportive in confirming or disconfirming inferences about the construct validity of an instrument. Before turning to this topic, let us consider first the older idea of face validity.

Face Validity

The topic of face validity is of particular relevance to a preference questionnaire. Face Validity means that an instrument, the scores, and their explained meaning "look or feel right" to the persons who will use them.

While the terms "Face Validity" and "Self-Validation" are not found in the section on validity of the latest Standards for Educational and Psychological Testing (Joint Standards, 1985), these concepts are highly pertinent to instruments such as the HBDI, which is dependent on honestly given preference judgments and forthright biographical reports.

Word of mouth recommendation is one major way that information about the HBDI has been spread. The recommendation of trusted others influences the attitude with which a person first fills out the instrument. Thus, "self-validation" is of the utmost importance. Self-validation may occur when a new user has an experience in a workshop, at home, or on-the-job that may be interpreted using information about his own or other people's profiles.

Experiential validation means that such users interpret the inferences drawn from their scores as valid and relevant to their own, and other people's communication, thought processes, work, and personal creativity. Situations where self-validation can occur are sought by Ned Herrmann and his colleagues in all applications of the HBDI. Self validation is not an attempt to gather selected testimonials, but to offer each user the opportunity to develop his/her own testimonial from personal experience with the instrument.

Face Validity to Users

The face validity of the HBDI to most individual users appears to be very high. They find the four-fold model easy to understand and to visualize, perhaps because it is not complex, perhaps because they are familiar with the bilateral symmetry of their body parts and with known personal preferences for hand, foot, eye, side of face, ear, and presumably, with parts of their brain. This concept of dominance is also exemplified by handedness. This conceptual familiarity is an aid to face validity. So is the ready agreement of users with their own profile: "That's me alright." The user's personal profile is defined using the very adjectives the user picked to describe himself or herself. This ready understanding and acceptance is claimed by HBDI advocates to be one of the strongest advantages of the instrument.

Evidence for this form of user acceptance of their profiles could be validated empirically. Such evidence was collected by questionnaire in 1979 and 1980, but these data have not been published. After that face validity was monitored for a time in groups by show of hands. Since

so few exceptions to the face validity of the quadrant model and of an individual's own profile were found using these methods, use of the HBDI continued without furthur efforts to collect empirical evidence of user acceptance. Instead, considerable effort is made to provide users with experiences which are self-validating. Exercises such as describing the "work I do best," followed by contrasting the responses of people representing dominance in the different quadrants offer users the opportunity to validate their own profile in contrast with others in a group. These activities both demonstrate and enhance the understanding and acceptance of a person's own profile. This understanding and acceptance is what we have chosen to call "face validity". These activities also meet high standards for instrument use related to clear communication, and assistance to users in interpreting their scores.

Face Validity to Professionals

It is also useful to consider the face validity of the concept of brain dominance measurement to experts in scientific fields associated with the brain. Here it is safe to say that the very idea of left brain-right brain dominance remains somewhat controversial. For reasons mentioned (i.e., bilateral symmetry and selective dominance of body parts), the idea of dominance and avoidance within different recognizable "areas" of the brain is easy to grasp by the public. Such ideas can have considerable face validity. This has led to a surge of popularizations in advertisements, cartoons, articles, and demonstrations and claims by consultants, lecturers, and writers that may oversimplify and erroneously interpret research on brain lateralization, specialization, and dominance.

This background of popularization of brain concepts has occurred before our rapidly changing scientific understanding of the brain has even begun to stabilize. In reaction to the oversimplification, it is easy to overlook those applications which have been tried and tested over many years, and for which serious attempts have been made to provide evidence of validity. The HBDI stands out in this respect, for it has been studied and improved over a period of 11 years before the publication of this book. Some claims have been validated. Others claims are replicable and can be demonstrated reliably in group settings, but have not yet been systematically quantified, confirmed or disconfirmed, and published.

Most professionals within a discipline ignore or quickly dismiss the work of those not certified in their own discipline. Some professionals, however, have taken the time to investigate the HBDI, and their articles, letters, and comments regarding the HBDI indicate that there are many more who support than detract. The increasing use of the HBDI in published articles, theses, and dissertations is evidence of acceptance by professionals.

As a colleague who has investigated the validity of his work. I have been asked by Ned Herrmann to evaluate the relevancy of the occasional attacks he has received. He has sent two, a letter and an article. These two detractors based their criticism on their impression that the model is making a statement about the geographical location of functions in specific areas of the brain. Despite impressions these writers may have formed, the four quadrant model explained in this book depends fundamentally on preference clusters and the idea of dominance or avoidance of these clusters for individuals, not on ideas about the localization of brain function.

Since preference and avoidance are the fundamental constructs of the HBDI, we will turn now to the topic of construct validity.

Construct Validity

Of the several types of validity, evidence of construct validity is the most general and the most relevant to the HBDI. The word *construct* is a term frequently used by behavioral scientists to refer to a theoretical concept about some kind of human trait, capability, kind of process, etc., that is not directly observable. The ideas of left and right brain dominance are theoretical constructs, as are the four quadrants of the brain dominance model.

Internal Construct Validity. Internal construct validity refers to the number of distinct constructs measured by an instrument, often referred to as the "dimensionality" of the instrument. It also refers to the match of the scores to the dimensions; thus, it is concerned with the validity of the scoring key. There are four distinct constructs, but two pairs of them seem to fall along the opposite ends of two underlying dimensions of preference or avoidance.

Internal construct validation studies tell us which kinds of mental processes cluster together (e.g., logical and mathematical), and those which are negatively related or unrelated. Internal construct validity does not tell us anything about other important constructs not measured by the HBDI, or how important the four brain dominance constructs are as compared to others.

External Construct Validity. External construct validation enables us to assess the validity the entire four construct theory of brain processing by comparing the measures of the constructs internal to the HBDI to measures

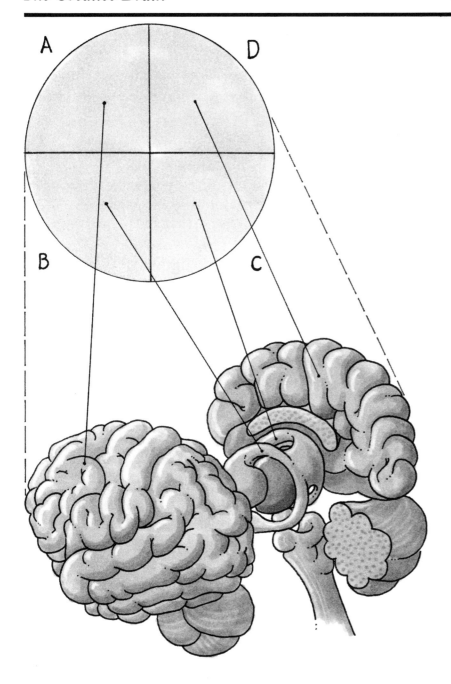

of constructs external to the HBDI. These external constructs can be either similar to or different from the constructs underlying the HBDI. We are able to predict whether external constructs should be positively or negatively related, or unrelated, to the HBDI scores. These predictions can be validated.

The constructs underlying the four-quadrant theory are very general. They were formed on the basis of observations of men and women in many important life situations; at work, at home, and at play. Thus, the constructs should relate to many important actions and decisions that can be observed (and sometimes measured) in situations other than that of responding to biographical and preference items on the HBDI.

Evidence of external validity can validate inferences drawn from the quadrant model of multiple brain dominance. It can help show how general and how useful the four constructs of brain dominance are in a variety of life situations. Construct validation is an unending process in this case because there are so many predictions or inferences that can be made from a model of preferences in brain processing. The existence of the HBDI scores makes it possible to confirm or disconfirm many of these predictions—doing so in the quantitative and replicable manner demanded by scientists.

THE CONSTRUCTS MEASURED BY THE HBD INSTRUMENT

The constructs measured by the HBDI are summarized metaphorically in reference to Ned Herrmann's

Figure A-1. Everything You Need to Know About the Brain. Figure 2-12 with the addition of the four quadrant concept.

insightful image of the rotated triune brain, seen from the back of the head, with emphasis on the dual cerebral and limbic hemispheres. Figure A-1 is a redrawing of Figure 3-12. Chapter 3 to emphasize the four keys constructs. The picture in Fig. A-1 helps us to see four major parts of the brain and reminds us that there exist four major clusters of preference or avoidance. Tracing along the intercommunication lines in Fig. A-1 can also suggest the great distance between the processes of A vs. C and B vs. D. These pairs are least often found preferred by the same individual, and dissonance is produced when the two opposites are widely divergent. The illustration also embodies the idea that the two left quadrants (upper left and lower left) and the two right quadrants (upper right and lower right) are "closer" than their opposites in the opposing hemisphere. Thus, the AB and CD pairs are found together and are more compatible. Figure A-1 suggests geographic location of function. Thus it is perhaps the source of some criticism. The strong communication lines between the parts of the brain offset this criticism because they suggest that functions are typically distributed, not localized.

Definitions and Assumptions

There are several assumptions and definitions upon which brain dominance measurement is based:

1. Common words can be used to describe the many different information processes available for use in the normal human brain. These nontechnical words can be found in the brain specialization/ lateralization literature. These terms and descriptions are relevant to the application areas described in this book. The terms are understandable to persons of average education when used on the instrument and in communicating about its interpretation.

2. Individuals prefer a subset of the many brain processes potentially available to them. This preference is analogous to their preferences for the right versus the left hand, right versus left eye, etc. A strong preference for a particular subset of processes is called dominance of that subset. A tendency not to use a set of processes is called an avoidance.

3. Information-processing functions in the brain need not be considered one at a time because there are several major clusters of information processes. People tend to prefer one or two clusters more than the others. They may avoid one or two.

4. A person's characteristic preference pattern of dominance and avoidance can be determined from honestly given responses to questions about educational focus, career choice, work elements, inner self perception through free and forced adjective choices, values, and use of discretionary time. The questions involve the terminology discussed in 1 above. These preference responses, when combined according to a fairly complex scoring protocol, are strongly related to the person's characteristic dominance pattern, which manifests itself in perception, thinking, learning, communicating, and interpersonal relationships.

5. A person's Brain Dominance Profile is a model

using numbers and a graphic which refers to that characteristic pattern of preference and avoidance.

The Constructs and Their Scores

Although the main independent constructs are the four quadrants plus Introversion/Extroversion, there are nine main scores derived from the HBD Instrument; Left and Right Dominance, the four quadrant scores, Cerebral and Limbic preferences, and Introversion/Extroversion. There are also several minor scores useful in making certain inferences, and a construct of balance referred to as being "whole-brained." Ranges and means are derived from the scores of 7989 individuals analyzed as a part of the doctoral dissertation work of Kevin Ho. About one third of these were women. These score means do not include any weight from college major or occupational choice, which would add up to 14 points to the sum of the two left vs. right score means and to the sum of the four quadrant score means.

1. **Left versus right brain dominance.** It is useful to measure an overall left versus an overall right brain dominance without making the cerebral/limbic distinction. Two overall scores are given by the instrument, one for left and one for right. The left and right score means are summarized in table A-1.

TABLE A-1
Breakdown and Summary of Left and Right Scores.

	LEFT SCORES			RIGHT SCORES		
	Low	High	Mean	Low	High	Mean
Men	18	151	95.2	17	165	86.0
Women	27	141	81.0	32	173	102.3
Combined	18	151	91.0	17	173	91.0

2. **The four quadrant constructs.** These constructs are the fundamental constructs in the four-fold model of brain dominance.

A. *Upper left*—This construct implies a cluster of processes related to the preference for mathematical, technical, analytical, and logical thinking. These preferences express themselves in school, in work, in interpersonal relationships and in hobbies. See Table A-2.

TABLE A-2
Summary and Breakdown of Upper Left Scores

	LOW	HIGH	MEAN
Men	14	138	75.1
Women	11	128	53.3
Combined	11	138	68.6

B. *Lower left*—The construct of lower left refers to preferences for those processes which deal with an organized, planned, orderly, and step-by-step approach and avoidance of risk and novelty. See Table A-3.

TABLE A-3
Summary and Breakdown of Lower Left Scores.

	LOW	HIGH	MEAN
Men	9	140	68.1
Women	18	129	68.8
Combined	9	140	68.3

C. *Lower Right*—This construct refers to a class of processes described as a concern for emotions, interpersonal warmth, and feelings, and as an interest in music and communication through speaking, writing, and reading. See Table A-4.

TABLE A-4
Summary and Breakdown of Lower Right Scores.

	LOW	HIGH	MEAN
Men	8	128	55.5
Women	23	126	74.9
Combined	8	128	61.2

D. *Upper Right*—This construct refers to the synthesizing and intuitive modes of thought: holistic, visual, imaginative thinking. See Table A-5.

TABLE A-5
Summary and Breakdown of the Upper Right Score.

	LOW	HIGH	MEAN
Men	15	179	73.9
Women	17	164	79.1
Combined	15	179	75.5

In addition to the four quadrant scores described above, adjective pairs scores are often singled out as reflections of preferences for the four quadrants. These are generally highly correlated with the overall scoring and indeed form a part of it. However, they show which quadrants are preferred when one is forced to make a choice.

3. **Cerebral versus Limbic scores.** Even though there is more evidence for an overall left versus overall right dominance mode, it is sometimes useful to look at the balance in a particular individual or group between cerebral (upper) and limbic (lower) processing. Two scores are provided which statistically combine the left and the right cerebral for an overall cerebral score, and the left and the right limbic for an overall limbic score. See Table A-6.

TABLE A-6
Summary and Breakdown of the Cerebral and Limbic Scores.

	CEREBRAL (UPPER)			LIMBIC (LOWER)		
	LOW	HIGH	MEAN	LOW	HIGH	MEAN
Men	40	156	99.04	33	153	82.1
Women	37	136	87.91	36	148	95.4
Combined	37	156	95.74	33	153	86.0

4. **Introversion/Extroversion.** This bipolar dimension is an old standby in personality theory. It refers to the extent to which an individual prefers to look within (introvert) for information about the world versus looking outside, especially to other people (extrovert). This dimension is mea-

sured in the Myers-Briggs Type Indicator, an instrument for classifying types of personalities based in the theories of the psychologist Carl Jung. The HBDI I/E score has been correlated with the Myers-Briggs Type score and is highly related. Introversion/Extroversion is rated on one 9-point scale in the HBD instrument, and other items also reflect this distinction. The introversion/extroversion scores for the men and women combined range from 1 to 9 with a mean of 5.5. The introversion/extroversion scores for men ranged from 1 to 9 with a mean of 5.4. The introversion/extroversion scores for women ranged from 1 to 9 with a mean of 5.7.

5. **Minor scores.** The consolidated score sheet, generated when the HBDI is scored, breaks out several of the different components that go into the overall quadrant scores. This breakout sometimes provides additional diagnostic information. For example, Ned Herrmann has observed that a higher score in motion sickness, especially for a left-brained individual, is an indication that the individual may be more receptive to experiences which will broaden his or her acceptance of a less preferred quadrant, and thus move him/her toward being more "whole brained."

6. **The "whole-brained" construct.** This construct is a key one for personal growth. A person's preferences for different types of thought are not seen as inexorably fixed. While each dominance pattern is good and valuable in its own right, being characteristic in many cases of whole occupational groups with demonstrable social value, it is of adaptive value for an individual to utilize brain processes situationally. The circular profile grid displays a graphic metaphor of "being whole-brained." While only a small fraction of the population is quadruple dominant, an individual can benefit from recognizing areas of avoidance and can practice less predictable and less stereotyped modes of thought, depending on the situation.

Reliability of the Scores

The "whole-brained" construct acknowledges that a person's brain dominance scores can change over time (e.g., an avoided quadrant may become more used through conscious effort). Despite this, the overall pattern appears to be fairly stable. Empirical data on test-retest stability has not yet been collected systematically. However, Kevin Ho found 78 repeated measures of the same persons in a large data set, and calculated the test-retest reliabilities (see Table A-7).

TABLE A-7
Test-Retest Reliabilities for 78 Repeated Measures.

Left	.96
Right	.96
A Quadrant	.86
B Quadrant	.93
C Quadrant	.94
D Quadrant	.97
Cerebral	.93
Limbic	.91
Intro/Extroversion	.73

Classes of Construct Validity Studies

A good program of construct validity for the HBDI would include the following types of studies:

1. *Internal construct validity studies* to determine the dimensionality of the instrument and the relationship of those dimensions to the four brain dominance constructs and to the scoring key. Two such studies are included in this appendix.

2. *External construct validity studies* to determine how general and pervasive the brain dominance constructs are across other domains of human traits that have been measured, such as personality, cognitive abilities, and learning and thinking styles and strategies. Those studies also validate specific predictions made from constructs of brain dominance. Three such studies are reported here, and an increasing number of new ones are beginning to appear in the thesis and dissertation literature and in journals.

3. *Generalizability studies.* Generalizability refers to the validity of the HBDI scores across different situations or contexts. The scores should be construct valid for either sex and for different cultures. Generalizability studies answer the question: Is the HBDI scoring valid for different languages, genders, and age groups, or do different keys need to be developed? There is evidence, not reported here, that it is generalizable.

4. *Experimental manipulation* is required to validate some inferences, such as what portions of the brains of people with different profiles are activated when they perform different tasks. A few studies are referenced herein, but this appendix is not the place for a thorough review of either these studies or the numerous studies of the HBDI that bear on other aspects of external validity.

Construct validation must be an ongoing process. When it stops, a set of constructs like the four-fold model of brain dominance has stopped being useful, and an instrument like the HBDI has grown static. This appendix is thus only one response among many in an ongoing program of construct validation being conducted by numerous collaborators and users of the HBDI.

SIX STUDIES DEALING WITH INTERNAL AND EXTERNAL CONSTRUCT VALIDITY

While Ned Herrmann was still head of manager education at General Electric, his organization contracted with the WICAT Education Institution and later with WICAT Systems for a series of studies to determine the construct validity of his instruments and methods. Together with my colleague, Dr. James B. Olsen and a series of research assistants, we conducted several studies. These will be listed and discussed briefly in this section. A more detailed examination of each of the studies follows in a later section.

Study 1. A literature review. A literature review was conducted in 1979 spanning multiple measurement domains, including cognitive aptitudes, personality, thinking styles, learning styles, and learning strategies. The objective was to develop a battery of measures against which the HBDI scores could be compared and contrasted. This work is reported in a WICAT Technical Report (Olsen and Bunderson, 1980a).

Study 2. External Construct Validation. The first factor analysis of the 1979 version of the instrument used a battery of measures selected as a result of the first study, applied against a set of scores derived from the current Participant Survey and Twenty Questions Instruments. At this time the four-fold model of multiple brain dominance as described in this book had not been fully articulated, so the construct validation at that time was aimed primarily at two scores: an overall left and an overall right score. The results of the first factor analysis indicated that there was promise in the brain dominance scores, but that the instrument should be analyzed item by item and a better scoring procedure developed. This study is reported in a WICAT technical report (Bunderson and Olsen, 1980b).

Study 3. Internal Construct Validation. An item factor analyses of 439 cases, which included both GE and non-GE participants in management education workshops, was performed to establish internal construct validity of the existing scores. Ned Herrmann's holistic scores were found to be valid. New scoring procedures were developed as a result of this analysis. Bunderson and Olsen factored all of the items in both the Participant Survey and the Twenty Questions Instruments, developed a set of subscores, factor analyzed these, and obtained a remarkable construct validation of the four clusters of preference. The study was not published at the time, but is summarized below. The revisions resulting from this study were: (a) combining Participant Survey and Twenty Questions into one instrument; (b) adding a more balanced set of adjectives and work elements; (c) adding adjective pairs; and (d) introducing the circular quadrant graph. This new instrument and scoring procedure are now taught in the Certification Workshops conducted by Ned Herrmann.

Study 4. External Construct Validation. A second factor analyses used the old instrument but the new scoring procedure and applied to the same data set described in Study 2 above. It produced evidence of external construct validity and was documented in a WICAT Technical Report (Bunderson, Olsen, and Herrmann, 1982).

Study 5. External Construct Validation. The third factor analysis was performed by Olsen and Bunderson in 1982 using the new instrument, a battery of cognitive ability tests, several instruments measuring personality dimensions and learning and thinking styles and strategies. Subjects were 205 students at Brigham Young University. This study was not published at that time, but is summarized below.

Study 6. Internal Construct Validation. This study was conducted in connection with Kevin Ho's doctoral work in Instructional Science at Brigham Young University (Ho, 1987). Ho analyzed the items from about 8,000 HBD Instruments obtained through a variety of workshops conducted by Ned Herrmann and his colleagues during 1984, 1985, and 1986. One part of

Ho's dissertation (which dealt with the use of the quadrant scores for occupational profiling) was to replicate the earlier internal construct validation study (Study 3 above). Some of Ho's results are summarized below.

A variety of theses and dissertations (several dozen) at a number of universities have used the HBDI, and senior investigators have employed it in studies, providing evidence for external validity related to other behaviorally measured constructs. In addition, some studies have been conducted to validate inferences about actual brain processing of persons with different HBDI profiles. It is beyond the scope of this appendix to summarize these.

Validity Study Summaries

Studies 2 through 6 will now be examined in detail.

Study 2. The First Factor Analytic Study of the 1979 Versions of the Participant Survey and the Twenty Questions (143 Cases)

Factor analysis is a multivariate statistical method commonly used in both internal and external construct validation studies. A factor analytic study starts with multiple variables (scores) on a large number of persons. It results in a reduced number of dimensions, called "factors." The idea is that although there may be many separate scores dealing with a large number of processes that go on in the brain, there are only a few major constructs that deal with related clusters of processing activity. The idea is also that these constructs will, if all goes well, be apparent in the factors that result from the analysis. The first Factor Analytic Study involved 31 scores derived from 15 instruments.

Six of these scores were derived from *Participant Survey* and *Twenty Questions*. These consisted of:

- An overall right and an overall left score.
- A "left center" and a "right center" score.
- A right Twenty Questions and a left Twenty Questions score.

Herrmann had been using the Twenty Questions scores prior to this study and had developed two numerical scores, one for right and one for left. The *Participant Survey* was originally scored holistically to obtain overall "primary and secondary dominance" in four categories: left, left center, right center, and right. It was necessary to develop numerical scores for each of these four constructs, specifically for this study. The other tests in the battery were selected from several broad categories of human trait measurement: personality, cognitive abilities, learning styles, and learning strategies. These are discussed below in some detail since they were used not only in this study but also in two others.

Tests of Personality. Four scales were used from the Myers-Briggs Type Indicator, highly regarded as a measure of personality type. These included:

- **Intuition/sensing.** *Sensing* individuals are said to obtain information from the five senses (according to the Jungian theory on which the Myers-Briggs is based). These individuals look for "hard" facts and tangible information. The *intuitive* individuals obtain information from inferences, insights, and the search for relationships. They experience "gut" level perceptions about the meaning of information.

- **Thinking/feeling.** The *thinking* individual thinks through problems and decisions analytically, objectively, and logically. The *feeling* individual weighs the implications of problems and decisions in terms of the feelings and values of the persons involved. This information is usually processed subjectively.

- **Judging/perceiving.** The *judging* person wants to make decisions and judgments in an orderly, planned way. Once decisions are made, this individual will follow through with the decisions. He has deep beliefs about how the world is organized and would like to modify or change the world to better meet his needs. The *perceiving* individual wants to see, experience, and understand the world as it is. This individual wants to view every side of a question or issue and may avoid making decisions.

- **Introversion/extroversion.** *Extroverts* gain information from the environment, from people, activities and objects. The extrovert prefers to work with others. The introvert gains information from self-referent thoughts, concepts, and ideas. The introvert prefers to work alone.

Tests of Cognitive Ability. Seven tests of cognitive ability were selected. Five were chosen from the ETS Kit of Factor Reference Tests (Ekstrom, French, Harman, and Derman, 1976). These five were Necessary Arithmetic Op-

erations, Gestalt Completion, Street Gestalt Completion, Paper Folding, and Hidden Figures. Two tests, Necessary Arithmetic Operations Test and the "Similarities" subtest from the Wechsler Adult Intelligent Scale (1958) were chosen after telephone communication with neuropsychologists indicated those as good markers for cerebral left processing. The Gestalt Completion Test from the ETS Kit and the Street Completion Test (Street, 1931) were chosen to be related to holistic synthesizing abilities, supposedly of the right cerebral hemisphere. The Paper Folding Test from the ETS kit was also selected as being related to right hemispheric abilities. The Hidden Figures test from the ETS kit and a score derived from the Ravens Progressive Matrices, were selected as markers for integrated hemispheric abilities. Because of time limitations, only the eighteen even-numbered items were used from the Ravens Progressive Matrices, Advanced Set II (Ravens, 1962). These require both reasoning and visual abilities.

Tests of Cognitive Styles. Correlates for cognitive and learning styles came from four sources:

- The *Hill Individual Difference Questionnaire* (Hill, 1976), supplied four subscales: (1) the verbal linguistic preference (VL); (2) verbal quantitative preference (VQ); (3) qualitative auditory (QA); and (4) qualitative visual (QV).

- The *Paivio Individual Differences Questionnaire* (Hitchcock, 1978), an indicator of learning style, supplied two subtest scores—a verbal score (Verb) and an imagery score (Imag).

- The *Word/Shape Sorting Test* (Galin and Johnstone,

n.d.) consists of 60 items, each of which contains three shapes. Given these shapes, each with a word in it, subjects are asked to cross out one, leaving two related shapes or two related words.

- Not a commonly recognized cognitive style test, *Face Recognition* (Benton, Van Allen, Hamsher, and Levin, 1975) was included because of its presumed relevance to the supposed right hemisphere ability to recognize faces.

Tests of Learning Strategies. Based on some early work by Claire Weinstein, James B. Olsen developed an instrument called *Learning Methods and Activities*. This consisted of 35 scale items measuring how frequently a student used various learning strategies. Olsen performed a factor analysis from which he developed five subscores mentioned below.

1. Verbal learning strategies
2. Visual learning strategies
3. Selection of parts (keywords and main ideas)
4. Purpose oriented learning strategies
5. Personal experience oriented learning strategies.

Individuals Tested. The 143 participants all completed the 15 instruments using a self-administration procedure involving a cassette tape of instructions. The group included fifty-two General Electric employees, mainly managers, who had participated in workshops conducted by Ned Herrmann and 91 college students and graduates from Brigham Young University. The college sample was distributed between the following majors and graduates:

social science (15)
organizational behavior (12)
mathematics (11)
electronics technology (10)
accounting (9)
art and design (7)
honors (6)
life sciences (5)
business management (4)
engineering (2)
education (2)
foreign language (1)
physics (1)
computer science (1)
various college graduates (5)

The test battery took approximately 3 1/2 hours to complete and yielded 31 different profile scores.

Method. A largely exploratory, partly confirmatory factor analysis was conducted. It was partly confirmatory because several hypothesis which had been developed as a result of the literature review (Study 1) were examined in this study. It was determined by the appropriate tests that 10 factors should be extracted.

In factor analysis, the factors first extracted rarely correspond to constructs of interest to investigators. The first factors are mathematical abstractions that pick up the most variance in the correlations among the variables, 31 in this case. Such factors need to be rotated into a different configuration that will reveal constructs of greater interest. For example, if we correlated a variety of measures such as height, weight, shoe size, waist measurement, etc., we might extract two factors. The first one might look like generalized bigness, but we could rotate the two to define the two more meaningful dimensions or constructs of height and weight.

Using the principal factors method, 10 factors were extracted from the correlations among the 31 scores. These were rotated using a promax rotation program prepared by Gorsuch (1976). Some factor analysts recommend using orthogonal (uncorrelated) factors. We selected the promax rotation because we expected the factors to be correlated with one another to some degree. It is our assumption that the brain constructs are related, due to the many interconnections discussed in this book. There is no reason to expect that clusters of preference for different kinds of information processing will be totally uncorrelated; indeed, the correlations between factors are also of interest in the construct validation process.

Results. The salient factor loadings from the factor structure for nine of the ten factors are presented in Table A-8. (The tenth factor was not interpreted.) These factor loadings are correlation coefficients between the original score and the underlying dimension or construct. If a correlation is close to 1.0, the relationship is very strong and positive. If close to -1.0, the relationship is strong and negative. If close to 0, the variable or score has no relationship to the construct defined by the factor. The first factor accounts for the greatest portion of common variance, the second next most, and so on.

The factors in Table A-8 list only the scores with loadings greater than .29 or .30. You may assume that scores not listed were so close to 0 as to have no important relationship to that factor. In interpreting factor A, Intuition, Right 20 Questions and Right Participant Survey scores all have high loadings of .64 to .69. These are considered to represent a strong relationship to the factor in question, which we named "Innovative vs. Safe-Keeping Preference." This factor is bipolar, that is, it has two opposite poles. At the negative end we find Left Participant Survey and Left 20 Questions, also with high correlations of -.60 and -.62 with the underlying factor. We can infer that there is a construct of preference for certain ways of thinking, and that the intuitive, holistic, modes of the Right scores are at one end and the logical, linear modes of the Left scores are at the other. The existence of a bipolar factor dimension does not mean that the Left and Right modes are opposite ends of the same thing, but that if you prefer the one, you are likely to neglect or even avoid the other.

The reader can examine the other factors in Table A-8 to see what scores cluster together in the same factors, which factors are the strongest (listed in order), and which variables cluster together. One example of clustering that was not expected is Necessary Arithmetic Operations (a "Left" process) as factor B, which included the "Right" processing scores of Paper Folding, Gestalt Completion, etc. This shows that the kind of test (speeded ability test) is more important than the kind of process in this factor. In general, considerable variance from the type of test is evident; speeded ability test, preference inventory, and self-reported use of learning strategies. This produced a larger number of factors than would be expected in a more homogeneous battery. Factors A, D, and I are composed of preference measures, B of cognitive tests, and C and H of learning strategies. The exceptions are E and F, which mingle preference with cognitive ability. Factor G mingles a behavioral measure, word-shape sorting, with visual learning strategies.

TABLE A-8
Salient Factor Loadings for Learner Profile Measures.

Variables	Loading
Factor A—Innovative vs. Safe-Keeping Preference	
Intuition vs. Sensing (Myers-Briggs, Intuition High)	.69
Right Twenty Questions	.68
Right Participant Survey	.64
Perceiving—Judging (Myers-Briggs, Perceiving High)	.61
Imagery on Paivio Test	.40
Personal Experience L.S	.34
Visual L.S.	.29
Verbal on Paivio Test	.29
Verbal Quantitative	-.37
Left Participant Survey	-.60
Left Twenty Questions	-.62
Factor B—Speeded Cognitive Ability	
Paper Folding Test	.74
Raven Matrices	.63
Necessary Arithmetic Operations	.64
Hidden Figures	.57
Card Rotation	.55
Verbal Quantitative Style (Hill)	.36
Gestalt Completion	.32
Street Gestalt Completion	.31
Factor C—Use of Learning Strategies to Capture Information	
Verbal on Paivio Test	.65
Verbal L.S.	.58
Imagery on Paivio Test	.63
Selecting Parts L.S.	.60
Personal Experience L.S.	.52
Visual L.S.	.44
Purpose-Oriented L.S.	.37
Introversion-Extroversion (Introversion High)	-.46
Factor D—Feeling vs Thinking Preference	
Right Center Participant Survey	
Thinking/Feeling (Myers-Briggs, Feeling High)	.56
Intuition/Sensing (Intuition High)	.42
Qualitative Auditory (Hill)	.34
Left Participant Survey	.33
	-.40
Factor E—Verbal Quantitative Thinking Style	
Verbal Linguistic (Hill)	.62
Verbal Quantitative (Hill)	.41
Left Participant Survey	.40
Necessary Arithmetic Operations	.39
Thinking Feeling (Feeling High)	-.39
Right Participant Survey	-.42

Variables	Loading
Factor F—Holistic Non-Verbal Thinking Style	
Right Participant Survey	.65
Gestalt Completion Test	.54
Qualitative Auditory (Hill)	.38
Card Rotations	.27
Word-Shape Preference Test (Word High)	-.35
Left Participant Survey	-.57
Factor G—Visual vs. Verbal Learning Preference	
Visual Learning Strategies	.66
Qualitative Visual	.60
Imagery on Paivio Test	.48
Verbal on Paivio Test	-.34
Word Shape Preference (Words High)	-.36
Factor H—Learning Expansion Strategies	
Purpose Oriented L.S.	.69
Personal Experience L.S.	.49
Similarities Test	.27
Factor I—Dominant Intellectual Preference (Tentative)	
Left-Center Participant Survey	.54
Left Participant Survey	-.41
Verbal Quantitative Preference	-.34

The intercorrelations among these nine factors were:

	A	B	C	D	E	F	G	H	I	J
A	1.00									
B	-0.21	1.00								
C	0.20	0.10	1.00							
D	0.14	-0.05	0.06	1.00						
E	-0.28	0.32	-0.05	-0.06	1.00					
F	0.26	0.05	0.08	0.04	-0.31	1.00				
G	0.05	0.19	0.11	-0.18	-0.12	0.12	1.00			
H	0.06	-0.08	0.12	0.30	0.00	0.07	-0.05	1.00		
I	0.11	-0.38	0.01	0.09	-0.21	0.16	-0.20	-0.01	1.00	
J	0.19	0.27	0.30	0.23	0.03	0.20	-0.02	0.05	-0.07	1.00

Lessons Learned From the First Factor Analysis Study

The evolving brain dominance constructs and their new quantitative scores took a big step forward as a result of the first factor analysis. The Right and Left Participant Survey scores were strongly involved in factors A, E and F. The new Right Center participant survey score anchored factor D and could be interpreted as being closely related to the *feeling* side of the Myers-Briggs Thinking vs. Feeling score. The opposite of the Right Center Score was found to be the Left *Participant Survey*.

The Left and Right *Participant Survey* scores had the highest communalities in the entire battery. Communality is a measure of common variance accounted for by a given score. Variables with a high communality are related to many other variables. Right and Left Participant Survey had communalities of .78 and .77 respectively and were followed by the Paivio scores with .72 and .70. Communality is also a lower bound estimate of reliability, indicating that these Participant Survey scores were quite reliable. The Right and Left Twenty Questions scores had about average communality, but the left center and right center scores were very low, indicating that they shared less reliable variance with other measures, or were themselves less reliable.

From a construct point of view, Factor A showed the right and left scores to be polar opposites, with the right side reflecting Intuition and Perceiving from Myers-Briggs, Imagery from the Paivio, and preference for Personal Learning Strategies. On the left side, the verbal quantitative learning style combined the left *Participant Survey* and left Twenty Questions.

Of considerable interest are Factors E and F, which show that the left and right scores are related to different kinds of cognitive ability. The left Participant Survey went with the Necessary Arithmetic cognitive test as well as the linguistic and verbal-quantitative cognitive styles. Factor F showed that the right participant survey combined with the visual cognitive tests; Gestalt Completion, Street Gestalt, and Card Rotation. The Right score was also related to the Hill Qualitative Auditory Cognitive style. Thus an aspect of the right and left constructs relate to cognitive abilities and cognitive styles in the expected directions.

External construct validation helps us infer the meaning of an otherwise obscure construct from its relationships to other constructs we know something about. The *Right construct* (factors A and F) is seen as related to Intuition as a personality orientation, visual abilities like Gestalt Completion and Card Rotation, and preference for personal experience learning strategies. The *Left construct* (the negative side of A, and factor E) is shown as converging with verbal quantitative and verbal linguistic thinking styles, the Necessary Arithmetic cognitive test, and preference for words over shapes. The *Right center construct* (factor D) is shown in this study to converge with feeling as a personality orientation, somewhat less with intuition, and with the qualitative auditory cognitive style.

Discriminant validation is seen in the polar opposites of these scores and in the unrelated factors. The important Factor B, Speeded Cognitive tests, contains all of the cognitive tests (except for the Similarities Test which did not function as expected). Factors C, G and H were all learning strategies factors of one type or another and are clearly discriminated from the brain construct scores, except for secondary relationships.

Note that the extroverted personality type as measured by the Myers-Briggs is discriminated from the brain dominance scores, but is strongly related to the learning strategies factor C. This active learning is in accord with the interpretation of extroversion as a tendency to look to the external world for information versus the introverted way of looking inward. Based on our understanding of the constructs before this study, Olsen and I had hypothesized a correlation of introversion with the right brain and extroversion with the left brain. We had to correct our thinking on this, because the correlation was in the opposite direction. In a series of studies, we have found Introversion to be somewhat correlated with the A quadrant and Extroversion with C, but it will separate as its own factor if other introversion or extroversion measures are in the battery.

Study 3. Item Factor Study (439 cases, old instrument)

Despite indications of construct validity and reliability of the right and left scores, the two center scores were functioning poorly. Thus it was decided to obtain another larger data set and conduct an item factor analysis to see if the four scores left, left center, right center and right could be further discriminated. This became the first major study dealing with internal construct validation.

Methods. In late 1980, Ned Herrmann provided 439 Participant Survey and Twenty Question forms which had been administered to workshop participants at General Electric Workshops. Many of these were GE managers and engineers but many were from interested professional groups from a variety of other companies who had participated in GE's open education offerings. The following list shows how many people we had in each of several occupa-

accounting	10
finance	9
sales	13
marketing	8
general business	19
personnel	10
public relations	16
computer programming	12
engineering	39
chemistry	12
physics	14
art	23
industrial design	15
management training	27
teaching	19
educational administration	19
management	30
students	13
manufacturing	19

tions. This list does not include many other occupations with fewer cases.

A broad range of college majors was also represented in the sample.

Item scores were obtained by using dichotomous scores (either 1 or 0) for every adjective, hobby, and work element in the instrument. Five point scale scores were assigned to each of the twenty questions, and scores were assigned to different aspects of handedness, rankings of preferred college subjects, motion sickness, and introversion vs. extroversion.

The first step was to perform a principle factor analysis and promax rotation of the item intercorrelations (Pearson). The item intercorrelation matrix consisted of

TABLE A-9

Item Factors from Participant Survey and Twenty Questions Listed in Order of Greatest Common Variance.

Factor 1. *Safekeeping Preferences versus Creative Synthesis*
Positive loading items involved preferences for specific instructions, step by-step methods, detailed planning, administration, organization, and avoidance of uncertainty.

Negatively related items involved conceptual thinking, dealing with creative aspects, and desire to synthesize and express ideas.

Factor 2. *Analytical Problem Solving versus Interpersonal/Empathetic*
Positive loadings involved analytical, logical, technical and mathematical problem solving.

Negative loadings were for items involving interpersonal aspects, dealing with emotion, intuition, and liking to make decisions based on first impressions and hunches.

Factor 3. *Creative Making of Things*
These items involved self-descriptions as creative, artistic, getting ideas from daydreaming, and enjoyment of arts and crafts.

Factor 4. *Active Outdoor Pastimes versus Reflective Introversion*
These items involved preference for outdoor activities like boating, fishing, swimming, diving, tennis, camping, and woodworking and being more competitive with others than with self.

The negative loadings were for being an introvert, reading, and spending a day alone with one's thoughts.

Factor 5. *Intuitive Preferences vs. Orderliness*
These preference items were chosen by persons who like to rely on hunches, enjoy breaking rules, and get ideas from daydreaming and first impressions.

At the negative pole were items for being reliable rather than imaginative, taking a step-by-step method, and controlling things by thorough planning and organization.

Factor 6. *Hobbies Preferred by the Non-Mathematical*
These items dealt primarily with hobbies, including cooking, reading, music listening, sewing, and gardening. Math was not liked as the best subject.

Factor 7. *Dominant Management*
Preference items for managing, leading, organization, ability to anticipate solutions, and being dominant were positively related. Avoided were preference items for emotions, music, or introversion.

Factor 8. *Preference for English Over Math*
This was a weak factor dealing with English and Foreign Language as "best subject" over math, and by preferring more detail and less creative aspects.

Factor 9. *Creative Writing*
Items showing a preference for English as a best subject, also for creative writing, expressing ideas, being a writer and reading. Disliked were math, home improvements, and being logical and technical.

---

the intercorrelations between ninety-one items, twenty from Twenty Questions and seventy-one from the Participant Survey. This step was used to obtain information to produce subscores for a second factor analysis.

Results. Nine factors were extracted, three of them were bipolar; that is, items loading on one end of the factor were negatively related to items loading on the other end of the factor. Those types of items that had the more significant loadings on the nine item factors are summarized in Table A-9.

Because these items were based primarily on dichotomous item scores of unknown stability, no serious attempt was made to interpret these nine factors as stable constructs. Rather they were used to develop "item parcels" consisting of subsets of 5 to 15 items. Each item in a parcel was given one point, so a score of 0 to 15 or so was possible in each parcel. Both positive and negative ends of Factor 1 (safekeeping vs. creative), Factor 2 (analytical problem solver vs. interpersonal/ empathetic), and Factor 4 (active outdoor pastimes vs. reflective introversion) were scored separately. The two ends were seen as separate preference constructs. This transformed the nine scores into twelve scores.

When these twelve subscores, now much more stable than the original individual item scores, were factor analyzed, they produced a clean two-factor solution. The first factor was what we have come to know today as upper right versus lower left (D vs B). People preferring the "D" end of this factor describe themselves as holistic, creative, synthesizers, intuitive, artistic, and spatial. People with opposite preferences choose controlled, detailed, and dominant. This factor was well measured by the Twenty Questions Items with the right brain preferences dealing with day-dreaming, hunches, getting a kick out of breaking rules, and getting best ideas when doing nothing. The "B" quadrant preferences, on the other hand, dealt with liking step-by-step processes, being reliable versus imaginative, disliking uncertainty, having a place for everything, planning and organizing, and preferring specific instructions.

The second factor was also bipolar, but did not involve many Twenty Question items. It was produced largely by the adjectives, work elements, and best/worst subjects. The two opposite ends of this factor were the two dominant

types that today we call Upper Left (A) and Lower Right (C). "A" people prefer the adjectives "logical," "analytical," "mathematical"; and the work elements "technical", "analytic" and "problem solver". They generally like math as their best subject. Lower Right items were "like to rely on first impressions," emotional, intuitive, interpersonal, expressing ideas, teaching and training.

These two bipolar factors were slightly correlated so that A and B, and C and D were closer together than A and D or B and C. A correlation between two second order factors can produce a third order factor. It did in this case; a third order factor emerged which was a strong bipolar left-right dominance factor. (Since the two bipolar factors were obtained from item parcels developed from a first-order factorization of the items, they could be thought of as second-order factors.)

The two bipolar factors and the overall right/left higher-order factor provided a better definition of the four constructs than we had hoped. At that time Olsen and I were most interested in defining *left-center* and *right center* as constructs. We sought to learn how to score those clusters of preferences that Ned Herrmann had observed in people and called "left-center" and "right center."

The two bipolar factors validated the existence of these clusters in a convincing manner. They showed *right center* to be the preferred or avoided opposite of tough-minded upper left thinking: the *feeling* side of the thinking-feeling dichotomy we had first seen in Study 2 in relationship to the MyersBriggs Thinking vs. Feeling scale. The second bipolar item factor showed the elusive *left center* to be the preferred or avoided opposite of holistic, intuitive upper right thinking—risk-avoiding through control and organization vs. the risk-taking appeal of new ideas, intui-

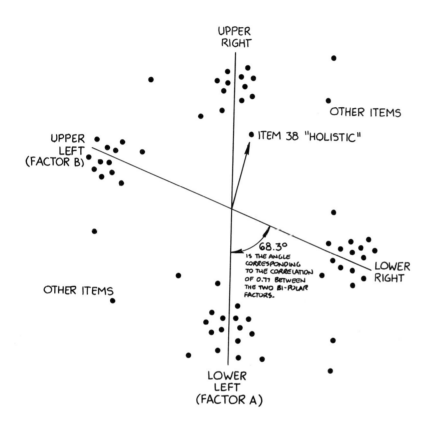

UPPER
RIGHT

OTHER ITEMS

• ITEM 38 "HOLISTIC"

UPPER
LEFT
(FACTOR B)

68.3°
IS THE ANGLE
CORRESPONDING
TO THE CORRELATION
OF 0.77 BETWEEN
THE TWO BI-POLAR
FACTORS.

LOWER
RIGHT

OTHER ITEMS

LOWER
LEFT
(FACTOR A)

Figure A-2

Four Clusters of Items From Participant Survey and Twenty Questions
Defined Two Bipolar Factors

tions, and alternate visions.

Moreover, the strong third-order factor validated the existence of the overall right-left distinction as a pervasive dichotomy in human thought, observed by many thinkers and scientists from Hippocrates to Sperry.

The study also validated Herrmann's holistic "Primary" Scores as the loadings in Table A-10 show. Assigning scores to each holistic primary score produced the correlations from which the extension loadings in Table A-10 were derived. (Factor extension makes it possible to obtain loadings on scores not included in the main factor analysis).

Table A-10 shows that Ned Herrmann's intuitive idea of one Left-Right dimension with two "center" scores, is supported by the preference clusters which exist in the item data from Participant Survey and Twenty Questions. This construct is validated by Factor L vs R, the higher-order bipolar factor. Right is the positive end, Left is the negative end, and the two "center scores" fall midway on the positive and negative sides. The two second-order factors A vs C, and D vs B, provide a better description of the item data and lead to a two-dimensional instead of a one-dimensional model. The holistic left and right "primary" scores, scored personally by Ned Herrmann, show considerable convergent and discriminant validity against the internal dimensions. The two "center" scores should have had loadings of about -.50 on B and about .50 on C, respectively, to have been as strong. Table A-10 shows that the loadings were in the right direction on B and C but were weak, indicating lower reliability or validity of the original holistic "center" scores. The new quantitative B and C scores helped clarify the constructs of B and C and improved their reliability and validity.

TABLE A-10
*Validation of Holistic "Primary Scores" Against the Left vs. Right
Factor and Two Bipolar Preference Factors*

Herrmann's Original "Primary" Scores	3rd-Order L vs R (Left Negative)	2nd-Order B vs D (B Negative)	2nd-Order A vs C (A Negative)
Primary Left	-.51	-.22	-.47
Primary Left-Center	-.12	-.24	.08
Primary Right-Center	.14	.02	.18
Primary Right	.54	.52	.20

The data tables from this study were reported with some excitement to Ned Herrmann, who served as the technical coordinator of the study as well being a mentor in brain dominance constructs. We were all pleased that we could now develop stable scores for right and left center, and differentiate the items representing the four preferences from the overall left-right score. These numbers, plus the metaphor of factor analysis which used the concept of vectors, provided "left-brained" input to Ned Herrmann's creative thought processes that soon resulted in the theoretical constructs of "Lower Left and Lower Right" and the quadrant plot of the four-fold profile.

Factor analysis uses a mathematical model based on vector algebra. A vector can be depicted geometrically as an arrow drawn in relation to coordinate axes. For two dimensions, such as we found, the vectors can easily be plotted on a piece of paper. In the item factor study, factors are axes, items are vectors. Generally the first, most impor-

tant factor is drawn as the vertical axes (see Figure A-2). The second factor is correlated with the first one, so it is not drawn at right angles. A correlation coefficient has the geometrical interpretation of being the cosine of the angle between two vectors (or two axes). Thus a correlation of 0 corresponds to 90 degrees, and a correlation of 1.00 corresponds to 0 degrees (e.g., item vectors are colinear). The single correlation between the two major factors gives rise to a second order factor, over-all right-left brain dominance. This factor, which requires a third dimension, is not depicted. The groups of small circles in Figure A-2 represent the clusters of some items from Participant Survey and Twenty Questions. Each circle represents the endpoint of a vector corresponding to the position of each item in relation to the two factors. One item (38, Holistic) is drawn as an arrow to provide an example.

Factor analytic results communicate quite well to technically trained individuals, but less well to others. Nevertheless, Figure A-2, taken in relation to Figure A-1, is an attempt to communicate with readers of all the profiles that Ned Herrmann developed in the four-fold model and describes in this book. Figure A-2 shows that there is indeed a simple, powerful clustering of preferences and avoidances that shows itself in the empirical data. The quadrant model does deal with important clusters of preference for statements that people regard as being more or less descriptive of themselves. The HBDI does have internal construct validity.

The item factor analysis and some other analyses Olsen and I conducted led to recommendations which Herrmann incorporated into a revised HBD Instrument. It included both Participant Survey and Twenty Questions and some new adjectives, work elements, and adjective pairs. New scoring protocols and a new consolidated score sheet were developed.

Study 4. Refactorization of the 143 Cases

Methods. The old (1979) Twenty Questions and Participant Survey Instruments for the 52 General Electric employees and 91 college students were rescored using the new scoring procedure developed from the understanding of the four item clusters. This resulted in the first set of quadrant scores. The Introversion/Extroversion score from the HBDI was also included in this analysis. However, to avoid the strong clustering of speeded cognitive tests, only three were left in the battery; Street Gestalt Completion and Gestalt Completion as markers for holistic synthesizing cognitive processes, and Necessary Arithmetic Operations as a marker for analytical, mathematical, cognitive processes. Similarly, to reduce and simplify the learning styles and learning strategies instruments, only two of the Hill scales, verbal linguistic and qualitative visual, were left in. The two Paivio scales for verbal and imagery were left in, along with the two learning strategies, verbal learning and visual learning. The intent was to produce a factor structure based on personality, learning strategies, learning styles, and cognitive processing, and the four quadrant scores in order to determine the convergent and discriminant relationships of the four quadrant scores to these other constructs.

Results. Table A-11 presents the names associated with the variable labels. Only variable labels are given in Table A-12, which contains the promax factor structure (correlations of variables with factors) for the reduced battery with the new fourfold dominance scores. Factor loadings greater than .33 are statistically different from zero at the .05 level.

TABLE A-11
List of Variables and Their Labels.

Label	Description
INTRO	HBD Introversion vs Extroversion
GC	Gestalt Completion
NA	Necessary Arithmetic Operations
SGC	Street Gestalt Completion
WS	Word-Shape Preference (Words)
SI	Weschler Adult Intel. Similarities
I	MBTI Introversion vs. Extroversion
N	MBTI Intuition vs. Sensing
F	MBTI Feeling vs. Thinking
P	MBTI Perceiving vs. Judging
VL	Verbal Linguistic (Hill)
QV	Qualitative Visual (Hill)
VERB	Verbal Paivio
IMAG	Imagery Paivio
VLS	Verbal Learning Strategies
VILS	Visual Learning Strategies
L	HBD A
LL	HBD B
LR	HBD C
R	HBD D

TABLE A-12
Promax Factor Structure for Learning Profile Variables and Hemispheric Dominance Scores

Factor Structure Matrix

	A	B	C	D	E	F	G
INTRO	0.01	0.82	-0.19	-0.12	0.05	-0.31	0.08
GC	0.08	0.14	0.13	0.09	0.57	0.07	0.10
NA	0.11	0.04	-0.19	-0.16	0.20	0.10	0.37
SGC	0.17	0.04	0.01	0.03	0.64	0.09	0.11
WS	-0.06	-0.30	-0.12	0.27	-0.26	0.24	-0.01
S	0.26	-0.05	0.04	0.01	0.17	0.05	0.11
I	0.05	0.82	-0.21	-0.24	0.17	-0.37	0.13
N	0.70	-0.14	0.12	0.23	0.15	0.28	-0.23
F	.20	-0.11	0.52	0.17	0.00	-0.02	-0.22
P	0.63	-0.03	0.15	0.20	0.09	-0.06	-0.23
VL	0.13	0.00	-0.44	-0.12	0.13	0.14	0.06
QV	0.28	0.08	0.15	0.46	0.34	-0.23	-0.07
VERB	0.31	-0.31	0.09	0.09	0.19	0.84	-0.02
IMAGE	0.31	-0.24	0.32	0.75	0.21	0.28	-0.02
VLS	0.12	-0.19	0.24	0.28	0.04	0.38	-0.01
VILS	0.18	-0.15	0.18	0.80	0.06	0.02	-0.10
L	-0.14	0.12	-0.34	0.10	0.04	-0.05	0.68
LL	-0.33	-0.03	0.07	-0.15	-0.03	0.03	0.45
LR	0.29	-0.25	0.61	0.13	0.22	0.32	-0.27
R	0.59	0.11	0.27	0.22	0.37	0.10	0.08
V*	17	10	10	8	7	6	6
CV*	17	27	37	45	52	58	64

V = Percent Variance
CV = Cumulative percent variance

The intercorrelations among the seven factors were:

	A	B	C	D	E	F	G
A	1.00						
B	0.00	1.00					
C	0.12	-0.17	1.00				
D	0.24	-0.11	0.35	1.00			
E	0.35	0.19	0.17	0.23	1.00		
F	0.04	-0.44	0.15	0.05	0.07	1.00	
G	-0.14	0.13	-0.15	-0.08	0.23	-0.01	1.00

Factor Interpretations

- **Factor A:** *Lower Left vs. Upper Right*
  Factor A cross-validates the organized vs. creative synthesizer factor (B vs. D) found in the large sample of 439 persons. Positive loadings were found for the creative synthesizer preference (D) and the Intuition and Perceiving scales of the Myer's-Briggs Type Indicator (MBTI). Negative loadings were found for the organized, controlled preference (B) and for the Sensing and Judging scales of the MBTI.

- **Factor B:** *Introversion vs. Extroversion*
  Factor B has high loadings on the Herrmann and Myers/Briggs Introversion-Extroversion scales (the simple correlation between the two was .73). Negative though non-significant correlations were found for the Lower Right construct indicating that it may be associated with extroversion. Negative correlations were also found on the word score of the Word Shape Sorting test and the Verbal and Imagery scales of the Hill IDQ. The correlation of verbal preference with extroversion is not surprising since extroverts like to communicate verbally with other people.

- **Factor C:** *Upper Left (A) vs. Lower Right (C)*
  Factor C cross-validates the HBD A vs. C factor found in the larger sample of 439 persons. Positive loadings were found for the HBD C, and the Feeling scale on the MBTI, (thus the MBTI "thinking" scale is highly related to the Cerebral Left Construct). Negative loadings were found for the HBD A score and the Hill Verbal Linguistic Preference scale.

- **Factor D:** *Visual Learning Preference*
  Factor D includes significant positive loadings on all three visual learning style and strategy scales. A negative loading was found for the Word score of the Word Shape Sorting Test, indicating a preference for shapes over words. It is interesting that visual vs. verbal preference discriminated from one another in Factor D and F, rather than the three different instruments producing three instrument factors.

- **Factor E:** *Visual Closure and Upper Right*
  Factor E has positive loadings on the two gestalt completion tests, the qualitative visual preference, and the upper right construct(D). The Word Shape Sorting Test also signaled a shape preference. The new upper right score was thereby shown to be related both to cognitive spacial ability and to behaviorally measured preference for shapes over words.

- **Factor F:** *Verbal Learning Preferences*
  Factor F has positive loadings on the Verbal scale of the Hill Individual Differences Questionnaire, the Verbal Learning Strategy score, HBDI C score, and the Word Shape Preference Test. Negative correlations were found for the two Introversion scales.

- **Factor G:** *Analytical, Mathematical Processing*
  Factor G has positive loadings on HBDI A, HBDI B, and the Necessary Arithmetic Operations Test.

In summary, the new brain dominance scores were still found to be pervasive in cutting across a number of domains. Personality type was the strongest domain, seen in relation to the Myers-Briggs intuition and perceiving scales (HBDI D) and feeling vs. thinking scales (HBDI D vs. HBDI A). But HBDI A also relates to a speeded cognitive test of logical mathematical processing, while HBDI D relates to cognitive tests of visual closure, so these constructs are more than personality. Also, HBDI D is related to visual learning styles and strategies. The correlations could almost be predicted from knowledge of the constructs alone.

The intercorrelations among the four Myers-Briggs Scales were consistent with results found in the construct validation literature on this well-researched instrument. Thus, we judge that the Myers-Briggs Scales were functioning properly in this study. One difference in the two theoretical models (Myers-Briggs and Herrmann) is that the Myers-Briggs assumes a person must be characterized by one or the other end of each of their four scales, while the Herrmann constructs allow a person to express preferences for activities at both of the poles in a single profile.

The data from the HBDI shows strong negative correlations in the population between the polar opposites, A vs. C and B vs. D. The Myers-Briggs Scales are also polar opposites. The Brain Dominance constructs permit a person to have an individual brain profile in which a person might prefer to be both a "thinker" and a "feeler" or both a "risk avoider" and a "risk taker" at the same time. According to personal comments made to the author by users or reported by Ned Herrmann, these personal dichotomies are felt strongly by the people with these less common profiles. They know they have these personal inconsistencies to live with. The subgroup of people with strongly bipolar profiles constitutes an interesting group for future research.

Study 5. The First Factor Analysis with the New Instrument

Even though the refactorization of the 143 cases was quite interesting, it was based on the old Participant Survey and Twenty Questions. The item factor analysis (Study 3), led to a new scoring protocol and a revised instrument with 120 instead of 91 items.

An analysis was designed and data collected in 1982 to determine whether the new Brain Dominance scores as measured by the new instrument would continue to have the cross-situational applicability and convergent and discriminant validity found with the old rescored Participant Survey and Twenty Questions. These data are currently being reorganized for publication.

The completed Promax Analysis is of interest to the quest for evidence of convergent and discriminant validity, so it is reported here for the first time. As in the second factor analysis, the study design involved a battery consisting of the four HBDI scores, personality measures, learning strategies, learning styles, and tests of cognitive style and processing. The sample consisted of 182 BYU students drawn from a wider cross section of college major fields than in the earlier analysis.

The Test Battery. The test battery consisted of the following types of tests:

1. *Brain Dominance Profile Scores, A, B, C, and D*
   The revised HBD Instrument was scored with the new key to produce the four quadrant scores.

2. *Cognitive Tests*

The battery included a wider variety of cognitive tests. It included all of the tests in the first factor analysis except WAIS Similarities and Ravens Matrices, plus two new tests:

a. The Remote Associates Test—claimed to be a test of creative thinking based on difficult and remote verbal associations.

b. The Metaphor Triads Test—is a group-administered test with color slides showing three objects. Two of them can be related in a concrete fashion and a different pair in a deeper metaphorical fashion. The deeper metaphorical response was the one scored.

3. *Personality Type Tests*

a. The Myers-Briggs Type Indicator was included.

b. A personal style instrument developed by Kolb was included. It has frequently been used in management education activities. It had four scales: Concrete Experience, Reflective Observation, Abstract Conceptualization, and Active Experimentation as personal styles.

4. *Thinking Style Tests*

a. All of the Hill thinking style scales were included. In addition to the Verbal Linguistic, Verbal Quantitative, and Qualitative Visual scales employed in the previous analysis, the Qualitative Empathetic, Rule Orientation, and Purpose Orientation scales were added.

b. The Word-Shape Sorting Test was included.

5. *Learning Strategies*

a. All five of the learning strategy scales developed by Olsen were included: verbal, visual, purpose oriented, personal experience, and structured learning strategies.

The Relation of the Brain Dominance Constructs to High-Order Factors. Before presenting selected results from this study, it is useful to observe that the bipolar A vs. C and B vs. D factors often appear in higher-order factors. The constructs of brain dominance have become much clearer since 1982, when this factor analysis was conducted. Moreover, the ways that measures of these constructs should behave in external validation studies have become much clearer. The two bipolar factors that give rise to the four quadrant scores have now been shown in several studies to be pervasive and general. This is as it should be, because these constructs purport to describe generalized preferences for complex, interrelated, and intercommunicating processes of thought and action mediated in the human brain. Thus, the expectation should be that these bipolar factors will emerge in higher order factors because these are the most general. In the internal validity analysis of the 439 cases, the item parcels were derived from first order item factors, and thus the two bipolar factors were second order. The overall left vs. right dominance was a third order factor. Correspondingly, we should look for manifestations of these two bipolar factors among the higher order factors in batteries of preference and biographical information that cut across many types of instruments. Cognitive tests can be included too, so long as they do not constitute a very large percentage of the battery, or else the prediction does not hold. In these cases we may get familiar "G" factors of cognitive ability among the higher-order factors.

Results of The Higher-Order Promax Analysis. The Gorsuch program used in studies 2, 3, and 4 was again used with the scores from the battery of tests.

The Gorsuch program executes a Schmid-Leiman Solution. This statistical procedure shows the status of the original variables on first-order and all higher-order factors. The analysis produced four second order and two third order factors. The two third order factors are listed in Table A-13, defined by the most significant scores loading on these factors. The first and most important third-order factor is most strongly marked by the upper Left/Lower Right dichotomy with extroversion also manifesting itself, perhaps due to its correlation with lower right. The measures that load on this bipolar factor are in accord with the constructs behind the upper left/lower right distinction. Necessary Arithmetic Operations is related to Cerebral Left as it was in the earlier study.

The second third-order factor is weakly consistent with the upper right vs. lower left dichotomy. The Myers-Briggs Perceiving and Intuition dimensions mark the positive end of this factor along with the Remote Associates test of creative thinking. The upper right loading is not strong on this weak factor but is in the relationship predicted by the quadrant model. The lower left score marks the negative end along with rule oriented, structure oriented, and purpose (main idea) oriented learning strategies and the verbal learning strategy.

Study 6. Selected Results of the Kevin Ho Study (7989 cases)

TABLE A-13

Salient Loadings on Third Order Factors Derived from a Cross-Instrument Analysis of Personality, Thinking Style, Learning Style, and Cognitive Tests With Four HBD Scores

	Factor I (Third Order)	Factor II (Third Order)
Herrmann Brain Dominance		
HBD A	-41	
HBD B		-22
HBD C	44	
HBD D	22	18
Extroversion	32	
Myers-Briggs Type Indicator		
Extroversion/Introversion	35	
Perceiving/Judging		27
Intuition/Sensing		20
Kolb: Concrete Experience	31	
Paivio: Imagery	31	
Olsen: Learning Strategies		
Group	33	
Personal Experience	30	
Visual	23	
Verbal	24	-20
Purpose (Main Idea)		-22
Structured		-22
Hill Individual Differences Questionnaire		
Kinesthetic	25	
Qualitative Empathetic	23	
Rule-Oriented		-20
Cognitive Tests		
Necessary Arithmetic	-21	
Remote Associates Test		20

Methods. As one step in his dissertation study of occupational preferences and their relationship to brain dominance as measured by the HBDI, Kevin Ho analyzed the HBDI scores from 7989 subjects. The scores were derived from responses to the revised HBD instruments taken by participants in many workshops, individual consultations, and public presentations by Ned Herrmann in 1984, 1985 and 1986. Instead of the 91 items Bunderson and Olsen had analyzed in the earlier study of 439 cases, Ho analyzed 120 items from the instrument current through 1986. Until this time no internal construct validation had been undertaken using this revised instrument.

Some of the 120 items were transformed into dummy types of variables to make interpretation of the factors easier. This resulted in having 127 variables for the factor analysis. In the interest of being consistent with the original validation studies by Bunderson and Olsen, a principal factors method of factor extraction was used in the factor analysis.

The appropriate tests indicated that either five or seven factors could be extracted. Both of these solutions had many similarities to the earlier study with the 439 cases. After examining both sets of results (five and seven factors), it was decided that in the interest of interpretability and simplicity, the five factor solution would be used.

Of the five factors extracted, three were strongly bipolar; that is, these three factors had a number of both strongly negative as well as positive loadings. This is similar to the results of the previous validation studies. The following is a listing of the five factors in order of the greatest common variance accounted for, along with those types of items that loaded strongly on each of the factors (see Table A-14).

TABLE A-14
Five Factors and Those Types of Items That Loaded on Them

Factor 1. *Safekeeping vs. creative*
Positive loadings included preferences for order, planning, administration, organization, reliability, detail, and a dislike for uncertainty.
Negative loadings include preferences for holistic thinking, conceptualizing, synthesis, creating, and innovating.

Factor 2. *Interpersonal, people-oriented vs. technical, analytical*
Positive loadings include preferences for interpersonal, verbal, people oriented, emotional and musical types of activities and style.
Negative loadings include preferences for analytical, technical, logical, and mathematical types of activities and style.

Factor 3. *Female, emotional vs. rational, logical*
Positive loadings include preferences for emotional, spiritual, musical, artistic, reading, arts and crafts, introvert and feeling types of activities and style. The gender item(female) also loaded positively on this factor.
Negative loadings include preferences for logical, rational, mathematical types of activities and style.
Note: Although similar to factor 2, this factor is subtly different. The gender item (female vs. male) is very strong. Notice the emotional, spiritual, introverted aspects of factor 3 as opposed to the interpersonal aspects of factor 2. Both factors 2 and 3 appear to share the same negative pole; that is, those items that are negatively correlated with factors 2 and 3 are those which are logical, analytical, mathematical and technical in nature.

Factor 4. *Creative, innovative*
The loadings for this factor include preferences for innovating, conceptualizing, creating, imaginative, original and artistic types of activities and style. A small number of negative loadings occurred: controlled and conservative.

Factor 5. *Handedness factor*

This appears to be loaded positively by left hand items and negatively by right hand items. This factor is at least partially an artifact of the small number of items measuring handedness in the HBDI and the way they were scored.

Because this initial factor analysis dealt with items, and the results from item factor analysis tend to be unstable, factor scores were generated for each subject on each factor. These factor scores can be thought of as being construct or scale scores. They are similar to the item parcel scores in the first internal construct validation study with 439 cases. These five factor scores for each of the subjects were factor analyzed again using a principal factors method of extraction.

Results. The Promax solution produced two bipolar factors. The two factors and the loadings of each of the five factor scores on the two factors appears opposite in Table A-15.

Factor A vs. C appears to be the now familiar interpersonal and emotional vs. analytical, and logical factor. It is interesting to note that factor 4 (the creative factor) also loads slightly on factor A, thus indicating that adjacent quadrants are more likely to be correlated than opposite quadrants. Creativity is seen by Herrmann to be a function of more than one quadrant, especially of D combined with A or with C.

Factor B vs. D appears to be the familiar creative (upper right) vs. safekeeping (lower left) factor. The bipolar nature of these factors is more clearly seen in the positive and negative loadings of individual items in these two factors, not shown here.

As was expected, the handedness factor (factor 5) did not load significantly on either factor A or B.

A higher order factor was also produced. It appears to be the familiar overall left vs. right factor. The Schmid-Leiman solution showing the correlations between the five factor scores and the higher order factor (I) as well as the two primary bipolar (a and b) factors can be found in table A-16.

TABLE A-15
Promax Factor Structure Matrix

	Factor A vs. C	Factor B vs. D
	(A negative)	(B Negative)
Factor 1 Safekeeping vs. creative	-.14	-.59
Factor 2 Interpersonal vs. analytical	.59	.22
Factor 3 Emotional vs. rational	.61	.25
Factor 4 Creative	.39	.65
Factor 5 Left handedness	.06	.05
eigen values	1.77	1.12
cumulative variance	35.42%	57.79%

The correlation between these two factors was .37.

TABLE A-16
Correlations of Variables With Higher Order and Primary Factors

Primary Factor	Higher order factors		
	I	a	b
Factor 1 Safekeeping vs. creative	-.33	.07	-.49
Factor 2 Interpersonal vs. analytical	.36	.47	.00
Factor 3 Emotional vs. rational	.38	.47	.02
Factor 4 Creative	.46	.13	.47
Factor 5 Left handedness	.05	.04	.03

The higher order factor (I or the overall right vs. left factor) accounted for 39% of the common variance, while the primary factors ("a" or the emotional, interpersonal vs. rational factor and analytical factor and "b" the creative vs. safekeeping factor) accounted for the other 61% of the common variance.

The Schmid-Leiman solution above, shows that the higher order factor does indeed appear to be a general right vs. left factor. The extension loadings of the items into this 3-factor space confirmed the placement of items in clusters that were found in the previous internal validation study.

The new items added after the previous internal construct validation functioned well according to the predictions of the quadrant model. Thus, the scoring key for the HBDI, taught in the certification workshops, was validated by this study. The results suggested, however, that a refined scoring key with differential item weights would offer a further refinement. A weighted key would, however, be impractical except through computer scoring.

Discussion. The results of this factor analysis substantiate the internal validation results of the earlier Bunderson and Olsen studies in relation to the items common to both the old and new instrument. The results also showed that all new items functioned properly. The two bipolar factors were found again and the higher order "right/left" factor was again extracted. This strengthens the evidence for construct validity of the four clusters of brain dominance in the HBDI.

FUTURE RESEARCH

Refining the Scoring and Improving the Scaling of the HBDI

This book recounts how the HBDI Instrument has been improved over a period of years based on a combination of research and feedback from practical applications. That process is continuing today. Ned Herrmann and his colleagues are supporting a research program which has several aspects. One activity is to develop a data base of HBDI scores balanced in terms of occupations and gender. Given such a data base, internal construct validation studies such as that of Kevin Ho could lead to several improvements in the instrument:

- A weighted scoring scheme could be developed to better reflect the A-C and B-D factors and the third-order Left-Right factor.
- Scaling of the four quadrant scores to a common standardized metric could be accomplished so that comparisons between quadrant scores would be more accurate.
- A set of standard occupational profiles could be developed.
- Generalizability studies could be conducted to determine whether gender-specific keys would be desirable.

Such a balanced data base with weighted and rescaled scores would also support a variety of cross-tabulation studies to show the joint occurrence of different preferences or avoidances in a balanced sample reflective of the larger population. Generalizability studies to different cultures would require a data base appropriate to each culture.

Intercorrelations Among the Four Construct Scores

As the meaning of the four quadrant constructs evolve, the definitions of each quadrant cluster in relation to the others should explain the inter-correlation among the HBDI scores.

The intercorrelations among quadrant scores found in Kevin Ho's sample of 7989 cases (Study 6) can be seen in Table A-17. These correlations are generally in line with the factor structure, but show some departures that could be corrected by a more refined weighted scoring scheme.

Note that the two left quadrants, A and B, and the two right quadrants, C and D, are positively correlated. This fact, along with the negative correlations between A and D (-.53) and B and C (-.20), lead to the higher-order Left/Right factor. Note also that scores for processes which fall on the opposite ends of bipolar factors are strongly negative. A vs. C is -.77, B vs. D is -.68, and Left vs Right is -.91. Recall that the constructs are seen as representing separate clusters of brain functions, not different ends of a single process. The negative polarity between the opposites must be explained as part of the construct. A possible explanation lies in the concepts of preference and avoidance. These concepts require item types that involve some selecting of one descriptor and rejecting of another, which contributes to but does not fully account for the polarity.

TABLE A-17

Correlations Between the 4 Quadrant Scores, Left and Right Scores, and Cerebral and Limbic Scores.

	A	B	C	D	Left vs Right
A	1				-.91
B	.08	1			Cerebral vs Limbic
C	-.77	-.20	1		-.78
D	-.53	-.68	.38	1	

The research now going on can lead to a refined set of intercorrelations. Both weighted scoring and a balanced sample could affect the correlations. The six intercorrelations between the four scores should ultimately be explainable by the quadrant model. Thus, it is desirable to learn what these correlations would be in a balanced sample with weighted scores. We would expect the A-B correlation to be positive and of the same magnitude as the C-D correlation (.08 seems too low). We would expect the A-D correlation to be negative and of the same magnitude as the B-C correlation (-.53 seems too large in absolute value).

With scores scaled to a common standard, the summary scores (1 = dominant preference, 2 = available for situational use, 3 = avoidance) could be made more precise in order to support more precise inferences about the nature of avoidance and its occurrence in the population and in different subgroups. A summary score of 3 is probably sufficient as a rule of thumb for its current applications, but the concept of avoidance, and its measurement, needs further definition. The research now underway may lead to further advances.

Validating Inferences About How People with Different Profiles Activate Their Brains Differently

While inferences about the location within the brain of different sorts of mental activity are not important to the uses of the HBDI discussed in this book, such inferences could be validated or confirmed experimentally.

A variety of hypotheses could be tested. For example, the well-known neuroscientist, Karl Pribram, stated in a public lecture that creativity, or as he describes it, the "guts" to take a risk and follow an intuition, is mediated in the frontal limbic and hippocampal systems. He contrasts this with risk avoidance, which he says is mediated in the posterior convexity. Experiments could be conducted using subjects dominant in B quadrant, subjects dominant in the D quadrant, and subjects dominant in both the B and D quadrants to find out whether people of the opposite dominance would use these parts of their brains differently when confronted with tasks offering the use of safe-keeping or intuitive/risk-taking processes.

When attempting to validate inferences about the identification of any of the four quadrant constructs with a particular brain system, it is better to use the neutral descriptors A, B, C, D, rather than the cerebral or limbic designators, which prejudge location.

A variety of measurement techniques, including EEG recordings and Positron Emission Tomography (PET) Scans could be used to determine which parts of the brain are active while performing different tasks. One could also compare these measures for people with different profiles. The emphasis on the brain as the source of the four preference clusters is an interesting and motivating aspect of Herrmann's theory of brain dominance. It is easier to visualize having a preference for certain clusters of mental processes we control within our own brains than to imagine what it is about us that is our "super-ego," or our tendency towards "psychasthenia," or some other purely psychologically defined construct.

Research to validate inferences about brain functioning in relation to different profiles would broaden external construct validation in an interesting way. It would provide us with explanations of how different brain systems mediate processes identifiable within each preference cluster.

Some such studies have been conducted. It is beyond the scope of this appendix to review all of these, but the following studies are representative of the kinds of questions that have been asked.

The Schkade Study of EEG Differences in Accountants and Artists

Lawrence Schkade, Professor and Chairman of the Systems Analysis Department at the University of Texas at Arlington used the HBD Instrument to select 12 clearly left-brained senior accounting students and 12 clearly right-brained seniors in studio art. He took brain waves (Electro-encephalogram readings) from these students and computed the Fourier transforms of the brain waves. He looked at the alpha frequency (8-13 cycles per second). He computed the ratio of the power of the EEG waveforms of the left hemisphere to that of the right for each subject and computed the mean ratio for each occupational group.

The results indicated that accountants and artists differ not only in their HBDI scores, but in their brain waves as well. A ratio of the power of the left hemisphere to the right would be 1.0 if both were used equally. The mean power ratio for accounting students was .77 (more alpha from the right, from which we may infer more active processing in the left.) The mean power ratio for art students was 1.2 (more alpha from the left than the right hemisphere). The results were statistically significant with a probability less than .001 that they could have resulted by chance (Schkade and Potvin, 1981). Doktor and Bloom (1977) have also observed that different occupational groups show different amounts of alpha in the two hemispheres.

Studies of Lateralization of Cognitive Style

The account that finally emerges from the research relating cognitive styles measured behaviorally to activity measured directly from the brain is not likely to be simple. For example, consider the cognitive style Field Independence vs. Field Dependence, developed over three decades of research by the renowned psychological scientist Herman A. Witkin (Witkin, Dyk, Faterson, Goodenough and Karp, 1962; Witkin, 1977). The field independent person (also called analytical field mode) is able to analyze the feelings of the vertical sensed from the body and separate these from the appearance of the vertical in a visual field. Thus the field independent person will move a rod more accurately to the vertical when distracted by a tilted frame when in a darkened room where both rod and frame are lighted. The field dependent person (also called global field mode) will move the bar closer to the apparently vertical axis of the tilted frame. The Hidden Figures test is another measure of Field Independence (high scores) and Field Dependence (low scores).

This cognitive style, like the HBDI scores, is very pervasive, cutting across performance in perceptual tasks, cognitive problem-solving tasks, and ways of relating to people in the world. Witkin's description of the two cognitive styles is sufficiently similar to the A-C dichotomy that it is tempting to hypothesize them as related.

Field Independent	Field Dependent
Analytic	Global
Autonomous of others	Highly sensitive to others and influenced by them
Keeps other at "arms length"	
Sometimes demanding, inconsiderate	Seek physical and emotional closeness
Better at restructuring to solve complex problems	
Good at breaking set	Warm, friendly, tactful
Better at spacial tests of perception and reasoning	Slow at restructuring to solve problems
Technical, mathematical occupations	More functionally fixed
	Better at verbal fluency tests
	Social, Intrapersonal occupations

Field Independence-dependance is a Bipolar Dimension. The hidden figures test is negatively correlated with C, positively correlated with A and D. Witkin's hypothesis was that field independence was a more differentiated and less global state and that this would be reflected in the lateralization, or separation, of functions within the two brain hemispheres. Research with right handed males confirmed this. Oltman, Semple, and Goldstein (1979) used EEG recordings to show that males who were field independent were more likely to use one or the other hemisphere, but not both together, in performing different tasks that have been associated with either the right or the left brain. The EEG recordings for field dependent men were more correlated between the two hemispheres. They were less correlated, indicating greater lateralization, in field independent man.

In another study, Zoccolotti and Oltman (1978) used a tachistoscope to present letters and faces to either the right visual field (linked to the left brain) or the left visual field (linked to the right brain). This study showed that right handed males who were field independent did significantly better in recognizing letters when presented to their right visual field (left brain) and better with faces when presented to their left visual field (right brain). Field dependent men did equally well with either hemisphere, showing less differentiation of function.

Summary of Needed Brain Research

These studies show that inferences about the relationship of pervasive cognitive styles to the activation of the brain in different ways can, with some effort, be validated. There are substantial individual differences in characteristic patterns by which the brain is activated. It is likely that different patterns of activation will someday be shown to be correlated with high level cognitive styles, of which the two bipolar HBDI factors are prime candidates because of their internal and external construct validity. It is also likely that the patterns of activation will prove to be complex and hard to isolate, measure, and interpret.

Validating Inferences About How People with Different Profiles Behave Differently

A wide range of workshop activities conducted by Ned Herrmann and associates have repeatedly provided experiences that are self-validating for the participants. These "experiments" could be quantified and tested statis-tically. Some examples follow. Assume that people are arranged in the room in a continuum from left to right as they would be arranged by rank on the 3rd order Left-Right factor.

- **Answering questions.** People on the left raise their hands to questions like "I like order and organization." People on the right to ones like "I depend on hunches in solving problems."
- **Style of presentations.** Teams from the left come back with a leader, a flip-chart with 3 organized points to present, and are right on time. People from the right struggle in late with no leader, no organization, and a lot of hand-waving and global statements.
- **What work turns me on.** The list from the left is distinctly different from the list from the right. In addition, each side considers the opposite work either as "flaky" or "boring."
- **Occupational choice.** The profiles of different occupations, based on the average profiles of people who are successful in that occupation, are quite different from one another. Such profiles could be used for counselling persons contemplating entering each occupation. Profiles could also be used to help students choose their college majors.
- **Interpersonal communication.** Through interactive drawing, people learn that nonverbal communication with a person who has a different profile can be difficult; with someone who has a similar profile, a matched person, wordless communication can be easy.

- **Preferred mode of learning.** The ACTAL workshops present ways to match presentations and practice activities to different profiles. For example, C quadrant people seem to do well in group discussions. Each such guideline is an hypothesis subject to confirmation or not.
- **Improving group functioning.** Ways are presented to enhance authenticity and teamwork in families or work groups. Principles are given to value diversity and improve productive functioning. Each principle could be confirmed or not.

The demonstration of these phenomena in the workshops, like the physics or chemistry demonstrations given in excellent science classrooms, are compelling to the participants. These demonstrations could be replicated under standardized situations and validated or disconfirmed as general principles for dealing with differences.

SUMMARY

Evidence for the internal and external construct validity of the HBDI has been presented in this appendix. The following statements can be made with confidence that they are supportable by replicable validation studies.

Internal Construct Validation

1. There are four distinct clusters of preference and avoidance measured by the HBDI.
2. The four clusters are consistent with the descriptions given in this book of the quadrant model of brain processing.
3. The scores derived from the instrument are reliable.
4. The internal factor structure consists of two bipolar 2nd order factors (A vs. C and D vs. B) and a single bipolar third order factor (Left vs Right Dominance).
5. Avoidance is most often found in the end opposite to a preferred end of one of the bipolar factors.

External Construct Validation

1. The Left vs. Right Score and the four quadrant scores are involved in a pervasive and a predictable way with the mental processes involved in measures of other constructs:
   - personality type
   - cognitive style/cognitive abilities
   - learning style

2. The bipolar factors internal to the HBDI are also found in first, second, and third-order factors in batteries of instruments that cut across these different instrument types. The quadrant constructs thus have explanatory and predictive power well beyond the HBDI item types.

3. While the HBDI scores share variance in predictable ways with speeded cognitive ability factors, introversion/extroversion and the tendency to use different learning strategies, these are all different factors which separate as distinct factors in properly constructed test batteries.

4. By contrast, the Myers-Briggs Type Indicator and other high-order measures of pervasive personal styles load on the same bipolar factors with the HBDI scores. They appear to be different rotations of item clusters which, while developed based on different theoretical models, may ultimately be explainable by a common set of constructs.

Future Construct Validation Research

1. There is a small amount of tantalizing evidence that the brain dominance constructs are related to the selective activation of certain functional subsystems in the brain. While no simplistic geographical model is expected to be valid to explain the four pervasive HBDI construct and the Left vs. Right factors, research with EEG recordings,

PET scans, and other methods for measuring brain functioning may reveal stable correlations between different brain activation patterns and different HBDI profiles.

2. A variety of self-validating experiences in learning, teaching, communicating, counselling, and occupational choice are commonplace for users of the HBDI. Criterion-related evidence of the reliability and validity of these predictable relationships with different profiles could be readily obtained, extending the research base for new valid applications of the HBDI.

Conditions for Validity Depend on Professional Standards and Use

A number of standards for proper use, and conditions under which validity has been established were presented. A brief summary is that the HBDI scores can be used with the assumption of validity in those situations where the respondent has confidence in the professional use of the resulting scores and has not been coached to effect some outcome.

Through observing standards, holding certification workshops, and supporting research to continually validate and improve the HBDI and refine its uses, Ned Herrmann and his associates have met high standards for professional use of the HBDI.

References

American Educational Research Association, American Psychological Association, National Council on Measurement in Education. (1985). *Standards for educational and psychological testing.* Washington, D.C.: American Psychological Association, Inc.

Benton, A.L., Van Allen, M.W., Hamsher, K. de S., & Levin, H.S. (1975). *Test of Facial Recognition, Form SL.* Iowa City, Iowa: Department of Neurology, University of Iowa Hospitals.

Briggs, K.C., & Myers, I.B. (1977). *Myers Briggs Type Indicator, Form G.* Palo Alto, Ca.: Consulting Psychologist Press.

Bunderson, C.V., & Olsen, J.B. (1980). *A factor analysis of personal profile measures related to cerebral hemisphere specialization.* (Scientific and Technical Report #4: prepared for General Electric). Orem, Utah: WICAT Incorporated Learning Design Laboratories.

Bunderson, C.V., Olsen, J.B., & Herrmann, W.E. (1982). *A fourfold model of multiple brain dominance and its validation through correlational research.* (Scientific and Technical Report #10: prepared for General Electric). Orem, Utah: Wicat Incorporated Learning Design Laboratories.

Doktor, R., & Bloom, D.M. (1977). Selective lateralization of cognitive style related to occupation as determined by EEG alpha asymmetry. *Psychophysiology, 14,* 385-387.

Ekstrom, R.B., French, J.W., Harman, H.H., & Derman, D. (1976). *Kit of Factor Referenced Cognitive Tests.* Princeton, N.J.: Educational Testing Service.

ETS standards for quality and fairness. (1986). Princeton, N.J.: Educational Testing Service.

Galin, D., & Johnstone, J. (n.d) *Word Shape Sorting Test.* Langley Porter Neurological Institute.

Gorsuch, R.L., & Dreger, R.M. (1979). Big Jiffy: a more sophisticated factor analysis and rotation program. *Educational and Psychological Measurement, 39,* 209-214.

Hill, J.E. (1976). *Cognitive Style Mapping Instrument.* Bloomfield Hills, Michigan: Oakland Community College.

Hiscock, M. (1978). Imagery assessment through self report: What do imagery questionnaires measure? *Journal of Consulting and Clinical Psychology, 46,* 223-230.

Messick, S. (1989). Validity. In R. Linn (Ed.), *Educational Measurement,* Vol. III.

Olsen, J.B. (1980). *General Learning Methods and Activities* non published instrument developed from *Learning Activities Questionnaire* (Weinstein, et. al., in press).

Olsen, J.B., & Bunderson, C.V. (1980). *Toward the development of a learner profile battery: Theory and research.* (General Electric Technical Report No. 2). Orem, Utah: WICAT Incorporated Learning Design Laboratories.

Oltman, P.K., Semple, C., & Goldstein, L. (1979). Cognitive style and interhemispheric differentiation in the EEG. *Neuropsychologia, 17,* 699-702.

Ravens, J.C. (1962). *Advanced Progressive Matrices, Set II.* London, Great Britain: Silver End Press.

Schkade, L.L., & Potvin, A.R. (1981). Cognitive style, EEG waveforms and brain levels. *Human Systems Management, 2,* 329-331.

Street, R. (1931). *A Gestalt Completion Test.* (Contributions to Education No. 481). New York: Columbia University Teachers College.

Wechsler, D. *The measurement and appraisal of adult intelligence.* Baltimore: Williams and Wilkins.

Witkin, H.A., Dyk, R.B., Faterson, H.F., Goodenough, D.R., & Karp, S.A. (1962). *Psychological differentiation*. New York: Wiley. (Reprinted: Potomac, MD: Erlbaum, 1974.)

Witkin, H.A. (1977). *Cognitive styles in personal and cultural adaptation*. Volume XI. Heinz Werner Lecture Series, Clark University Press.

Zoccolotti, P., & Oltman, P.K. (1978). Field dependence and lateralization of verbal and configurational processing. *Cortex, 14*, 155-163.

GENERIC PROFILE DESCRIPTIONS

1-3-3-2

 This profile is a singular dominant profile, the most preferred quadrant being Upper Left A, characterized by logical, rational, mathematical, and analytical processing. The secondary of this profile occurs in Upper Right quadrant D, whose characteristics are functional, yet clearly secondary to those processing modes of the Upper Left quadrant A. The holistic, creative, and synthesizing processing modes of Upper Right D would be used, but the logical, rational, and quantitative modes of quadrant A would visibly be the most preferred. The two remaining quadrants, both Lower Left B and Lower Right C, are tertiaries. The characteristics of controlled, planning, and organizing of Lower Left B coupled with the interpersonal, emotional, and intuitive modes of Lower Right C would clearly be lacking or may even be avoided modes of processing. These tertiaries would tend to visibly reinforce the prominence of the primary and this person would be seen as singularly dominant in the Upper Left A quadrant. Occupations are varied, including engineering, chemistry, those in technical fields, legal and financial work, and some in the technical middle management positions.

1-2-2-3

 This is a singular dominant profile, the most preferred quadrant being the Upper Left quadrant A, with the characteristics of logical, analytical, rational, and quantitative processing. The Lower Left B and Lower Right C quadrants are secondaries. Therefore, this person would typically be functional in the processing modes of control, organization, structure, and planning of Lower Left B, as well as interpersonal, emotional, and spiritual in Lower Right C. The fourth quadrant (Upper Right D) is a tertiary and the characteristics of holistic, creative, and synthesizing in this quadrant would clearly be lacking or even avoided. This person would clearly be seen as logical, rational, and analytic, with some capabilities for administrative and detailed activities along with some interpersonal and emotional characteristics. The occupations typical of persons with this profile are technically, mathematically or financially based, with some working in the scientific, legal and middle management professions.

1-2-3-2

 This profile is a singular dominant profile, the most preferred processing mode occurring in Upper Left A quadrant with characteristics of logical, analytical, rational, and quantitative. The secondary in the Lower Left quadrant B and the Upper Right quadrant D are functional in terms of controlled, conservative, and organizing modes of processing (in the Lower Left B), and holistic, creative, and synthesizing modes (in the Upper Right D). The fourth quadrant, Lower Right C, is a tertiary and it's characteristics would clearly be the least preferred—the more interpersonal, emotional, and spiritual modes of processing. This person's most visible preferences would be logical, analytic, rational, quantitative, and technical processing with some secondary abilities for organizing and synthesizing. The lack of preference for the more interpersonal aspects would reinforce the strength of the primary in Upper Left A. Occupations would include those in the technical, legal and financial areas, including accounting and tax law, engineering, mathematics, and some middle management positions that require little Human Resource involvement.

1-2-2-2

 This profile is the profile of a clearly logical, analytical, mathematical, and rational person. It is a singular dominant profile, the most preferred quadrant being in Upper Left A. To a lesser extent, but still functional in processing, are the controlled, organized, planned modes of thinking in the Lower Left B quadrant, the interpersonal, emotive modes of the Lower Right C quadrant, and the holistic, creative, and synthesizing modes of Upper Right D quadrant. Individuals with this profile would typically be capable of functioning in the three secondaries, quadrants B, C, D, but the clear preference and preferred processing mode would be that of Upper Left A. Occupations that would be typical of this profile include chemists, mathematicians, technicians, engineers, and financial and technical managers.

1-1-3-3

 This profile is a double dominant profile, with two strong primaries occurring in the Upper Left A and Lower Left B quadrants. The two contrasting tertiaries of this profile are in the Lower Right C and the Upper Right D quadrants. This profile is characterized by the distinct lack of preference, even avoidance, for the characteristics of the right modes of C & D. This individual would be rational, logical, analytic, and quantitative, coupled with controlled, planned, organized, and struc-

tured. There would be an extreme lack of preference for the emotional, interpersonal, and spiritual aspects of the Lower Right C quadrant, as well as the same lack of preference for the holistic, creative, synthesizing and integrative modes associated with Upper Right D. The preferences for the left modes of processing would be even more pronounced in this profile as they are reinforced by the extreme lack of preference for the right mode. Occupations would include professional contributors in technical, accounting, and financial occupations, manufacturing, and a variety in the management areas where "facts and form" rather than "people and concepts" are the primary focus.

1-1-2-3

 This profile is double dominant with primaries occurring in Upper Left A and Lower Left B quadrants. The profile has a secondary in Lower Right C, and a tertiary in Upper Right D. This would indicate a strong preference for the analytic, rational, and logical processing of the Upper Left A, and an equally strong preference for the controlled, structured, and organized modes associated with the Lower Left B quadrant. The Lower Right C quadrant, characteristic of interpersonal, emotional, and intuitive thinking modes, would be functional, yet secondary. The Upper Right D quadrant, characteristic of holistic, imaginative, synthesizing, and integrative processes, would be tertiary or of low preference. Occupations for this profile would include technical managers, manufacturing managers, financial positions including accountants and bookkeepers, and operational and production oriented engineers.

1-1-3-2

This is a double dominant profile with the two most preferred modes of processing occurring in the Upper Left A and Lower Left B quadrants. The characteristics of this profile would be logical, analytical, and rational in Upper Left A and controlled, conservative, and organized in the Lower Left B. The secondary of this profile is in the Upper Right D quadrant, in which the characteristics of imaginative, holistic, and synthesizing modes would be functional, yet clearly secondary in comparison with the primary left hemisphere modes. The characteristics of the Lower Right C quadrant — emotional, interpersonal, and spiritual, would be visibly lacking or even avoided as this is expressed as a tertiary. The distinct secondary/tertiary position of the two right quadrants would reinforce the strength and preference of the left modes and this person would clearly be seen as logical, rational, controlled, and organized. Occupations would include professional contributor positions in the technical and engineering professions, the financial occupations, and some in middle management positions.

1-1-2-2

This is a double dominant profile with primaries in the Left mode—Upper Left A and Lower Left B quadrants. It is the second most common profile in the general population, representing 15 percent, and the most common profile for males, representing 21 percent. The profile is characterized by a logical, analytic, technical orientation, and is effective in rational problem solving from the Upper Left A quadrant. Lower Left B quadrant preferences include planning, organizing, implementing and administrative activities. In this profile, the processing modes of Upper Left A and Lower Left B would clearly be the most preferred, and the interpersonal, emotional, and spiritual modes of Lower Right C and the holistic, creative, and synthesizing modes of Upper Right D would be at the secondary level, yet functional. This profile is typical of those occupations in technical fields, such as engineering and manufacturing, financial positions, middle managers, and in general, those positions for which left mode processing is clearly most important, and the right mode processing being necessary, yet secondary.

2-1-2-2

This profile is a singular dominant profile with the most preferred being the Lower Left B quadrant. The person with this profile would be characterized by strong preferences in the controlled, planning, organizational, and structured modes of processing. This person would tend to be a perfectionist in terms of detail and the implementation of activities. The secondaries in the remaining three quadrants represent the interpersonal and emotional modes of thinking of the Lower Right C quadrant, the holistic, creative, and conceptual modes of the Upper Right D quadrant, and the logical, analytic, and rational modes of the Upper Left A. While these processing modes are relatively well balanced and functional, the singular preference for quadrant B would represent the primary mode of thinking for this profile. Occupations of people with this profile typically include secretaries, foremen, office managers, bookkeepers, manufacturers and business administrators - occupations that typically require highly planned, organized, structured, and detailed work activities leading to specific results.

1-1-1-3

This is a triple dominant profile, with the three primaries occurring in Upper Left A, Lower Left B, and Lower Right C quadrants. The profile would be characterized by a relative balance between the modes of logical and analytical processing in Upper Left A, the control and planning in Lower Left B, and the interpersonal and emotional aspects associated with the Lower Right C quadrant. This profile would be further characterized by the lack of preference for the holistic, conceptual, and synthesizing modes of processing found in the Upper Right D quadrant, which is expressed as a tertiary. As a result, the Upper Right D characteristics would be relatively invisible, and the three primaries would impact the person's mental preferences with a fair amount of balance. Occupations typical of individuals with this profile would include human resource professionals, technical administrators, foremen, legal and technical secretaries, and some in middle management positions where the work requirements for D quadrant competencies are very low.

1-1-1-2

This profile is a triple dominant profile, featuring two primaries in the Left mode, both Upper Left A and Lower Left B quadrants, and a third primary in Lower Right C. The secondary is in Upper Right D quadrant. Characteristics of this profile would be analytical, rational, and quantitative processing of Upper Left A, with controlled, conservative, structured, and organized processing modes of Lower Left B. Coupled with this would be the interpersonal, emotional, and spiritual aspects of Lower Right C. Distinctly secondary, but usually functional, would be the integrative, creative, and holistic

characteristics of Upper Right D. This profile is relatively well balanced, yet clearly the descriptors of the Upper Right D quadrant are secondary. Occupations that are typical of individuals with this profile include professionals and managers of a technical nature, such as engineering, chemistry, and manufacturing managers, and managers with a high administrative content to their work, such as hospital administrators.

1-1-2-1

This profile is a triple dominant profile with two primaries in the left mode, both Upper Left A and Lower Left B, and the third primary in the Upper Right D quadrant. The secondary, or less preferred mode, occurs in the Lower Right C quadrant—the more interpersonal, spiritual, and emotional mode. This profile is characterized by its multi-dominance, yet, in a relative sense, it lacks a level of "personal touch" that would be present if the Lower Right C quadrant was also a primary. Descriptors for this profile would include logical, analytical, and rational in the Upper Left A quadrant, and planning, organizing, and administrative preferences in the Lower Left B quadrant. This more conservative, safe-keeping preference of Lower Left B would be contrasted with the primary in the Upper Right D quadrant which would be characterized as conceptual, holistic, creative, and "risk oriented" in it's mode. Occupations with this profile would be those requiring a combination of logical and analytical problem solving coupled with imaginative and innovative thinking along with administrative and managerial duties. Such occupations would include technical positions such as design engineers, researchers, and those making both conceptual and quantitative decisions.

1-1-1-1

This profile is a quadruple primary that is multi-dominant in all four quadrants (A,B,C,D) with relatively equal preferences in all four. This profile occurs in 3% of the population. Individuals with this profile would be characterized by being well balanced and having sufficiently strong preferences in all four quadrants to develop the understanding and the ability to use each of the processing modes of the four quadrants. This person is often a "multi-dominant translator", that is, acting as a "translator" for others in order to facilitate communication and understanding between the various modes. In the ideal case, they would be able to move back and forth between the quadrants on a situational basis. This can, however, lead to many conflicts within the individual—the "fact"—"feeling" dichotomy of the Upper Left A and Lower Right C diagonal, or the "form"—"futures" pull of the Lower Left B and Upper Right D diagonal that are evident in this profile. Ultimately, it can lead to a very well integrated person. Occupations with this profile are those that require effective processing in all four quadrants. Examples would be chief executive officers, chairmen of the board, executives with multi-functional responsibilities, and often times, executive secretaries.

1-3-3-1

This profile is double dominant with two primaries in both the cerebral quadrants, A and D. It would feature the logical, analytic, and rational processing of Upper Left quadrant A and the holistic, creative, and synthesizing modes of Upper Right quadrant D. The two remaining quadrants are expressed as tertiaries. The characteristics of the Lower Left quadrant B, the more controlled, conservative, and structured modes of thinking, coupled with the interpersonal, emotional, and spiritual aspects of the Lower Right quadrant C, would visibly be lacking or even avoided. This lack of preference for the two limbic quadrants (B & C) would reinforce the strength or preference for the two cerebral quadrants (A & D). Occupations typical of this profile would include researchers, particularly physicists, financial consultants or advisors, design engineers and many in top executive positions in technical or financial business where futures - oriented strategic thinking is a major work requirement.

1-2-3-1

This profile is double dominant featuring two primaries in the cerebral quadrants, A and D. Individuals with this profile prefer the more cognitive processing modes associated with these cerebral quadrants compared to the more visceral characteristics of the limbic mode (B and C quadrants). In particular, preferences for logical, analytical, quantitative modes of thinking in the Upper Left A quadrants along with integrative, synthesizing, imaginative, and holistic aspects of the Upper Right D quadrant are exhibited. This profile also indicates a clear secondary preference in the Lower Left B quadrant. Lower Right C is a tertiary or the least preferred quadrant in this profile. The interpersonal, emotional, and spiritual characteristics associated with this quadrant would situationally be avoided. Individuals with this profile frequently exhibit the ability to switch back and forth between the two cerebral modes A and D as the situation demands. Occupations typical of this profile would include those in technical fields, computer design, finance analysts, physicists, or research and development.

1-2-2-1

This profile is double dominant with the two primaries in the cerebral quadrants, A and D. Individuals with this profile would exhibit strong preferences for logical, analytic, quantitative modes of thinking in the Upper Left A quadrant, and in contrast would also have a preference for the integrative, synthesizing, creative, and holistic aspects of Upper Right D. This profile indicates a clear secondary preference for the emotional, interpersonal processing of Lower Right C as well as a clear secondary for the controlled, conservative, organized processing modes of the Lower Left B quadrant. Individuals with this profile frequently exhibit the ability to switch back and forth between the two cerebral quadrants, as the situation demands. Occupations typical of this profile include design engineers, financial consultants or advisors (those involved with forecasting financial trends), and research and development scientists, particularly physicists. It is also typical of senior executives in operating and strategic positions in technical organizations.

1-2-1-2

This is a double dominant profile on the diagonal axis between the Upper Left A quadrant, and the Lower Right C quadrant. The diagonal of Lower Left B, and Upper Right D, is at a secondary level. This profile is characterized by individuals who are very logical, analytic, and rational in the thinking styles of Upper Left A, but also is strong in the intuitive, interpersonal, "feeling" aspects of the Lower Right C quadrant. This person would show a very distinct preference for the

"facts"—"feelings" axis, compared with a clearly secondary preference for the "form"—"futures" axis. It is quite possible for the primaries in Upper Left A and in Lower Right C to create an inner conflict for this person because of the quadrants' differing characteristics. Occupations would include positions that would be technically or financially oriented with a strong preference for people interaction or an interpersonal focus, such as investment counsellors, technical trainers, or social service lawyers.

2-1-2-1

This is a double dominant profile representing a cross relationship between preferences. The two primaries occur on the diagonal axis between the Lower Left quadrant B and the Upper Right quadrant D. The opposite diagonal of Upper Left A and Lower Right C is at the secondary level. This profile is characterized by its distinctly opposing thinking processes—the Lower Left B quadrant being characterized by "safe-keeping" and the Upper Right D quadrant as experimental or "risk-taking". The Lower Left features control, structure, planning, organizing, and conservative modes of processing. The Upper Right is holistic, conceptual, creative, holistic, and synthesizing. The person with this profile would feel this distinct difference in their approach to work, communications, decision making, and life experiences. On one occasion, they may be quite controlled and structured and in another situation, quite loose and free-wheeling. The combination of these two preferences can be very powerful if the Lower Left B is able to stand aside and permit the more imaginative, creative Upper Right D to make its special contribution. Occupations typical of this profile are not clearly evident, although positions requiring capabilities in both evaluation and design such as: program administrators, quality control leaders, movie producers, some entrepreneurs, and occasionally market researchers exhibit this profile. It appears in many fields.

2-1-1-2

 This profile is a double dominant profile with the two primaries in the Lower Left B and Lower Right C quadrants. It is a double primary in the limbic area. The profile is characterized by very strong preferences in conservative thinking and controlled behavior with a desire for organization and structure as well as detail and accuracy from the Lower Left B quadrant. Persons with this profile tend to worry about details. The primary in the Lower Right C would equally show itself by emotional and interpersonal preferences, an interest in music, and a sense of spirituality. It would also show in an intuitive "feelings" sense of this person. The two limbic primaries could represent an important duality for the person to resolve within themselves. The opposing qualities of control and structure, of "form"—and the emotional and interpersonal "feelings" can cause internal conflict. The clear secondary preferences of the cerebral modes, both Upper Left A and Upper Right D, are also characteristic of this profile, with logical and analytical in the Upper Left A quadrant and holistic and creative thinking of Upper Right D quadrant. Occupations typical of those people with this profile include nurses, homemakers, secretaries, and other members of the "helping" profession, particularly those requiring a heavy administrative load.

3-1-1-2

 This profile is a double dominant profile featuring two primaries occurring in Lower Left B and Lower Right C quadrants. The characteristics typical of this profile would be the controlled, organized, and structured processing modes of the Lower Left B and the interpersonal, emotional, and spiritual modes of the Lower Right C quadrant. The secondary in the Upper Right D quadrant would make the characteristics of holistic, artistic, and conceptual modes of processing functional, yet secondary in preference. This profile is further characterized by absence or avoidance of the logical, analytic, and rational processing of the Upper Left A quadrant. The tertiary in Upper Left A, coupled with the secondary in Upper Right D, make this profile clearly one with limbic mode preferences, which express safe-keeping, feeling and visceral processing. Occupations typical of people with this profile would include trainers, secretaries, nurses, social workers, and homemakers.

3-1-1-1

 This profile is a triple dominant profile, with the three most preferred quadrants occurring in the Lower Left B, Lower Right C, and the Upper Right D quadrant. A person with this profile would be characterized by a fair amount of balance between the organized and structured processing modes of the Lower Left C quadrant, coupled with the interpersonal and emotional modes of the Lower Right C, and finally, the Upper Right D aspects of holistic, synthesizing, and creative modes of processing. The lack of preference or even avoidance of the logical, rational, and analytical processes of the Upper

Left A would also typify this profile. This tertiary expressed in the Upper Left A would tend to strengthen and make more visible the other three primaries. Occupations typical of this profile include teachers, social workers (particularly in heavy case-load positions), trainers, human resource professionals, and those in artistic professions requiring planning, organizing, and detailed administrative duties.

2-1-1-1

 This is a triple dominant profile with two primaries in the right mode, Lower Right C and Upper Right D quadrants, and the third in Lower Left B. It is the most common of all profiles, with 16 percent of the population exhibiting this multi-dominant array of preferences. It is the clear majority for the female population, 24 percent exhibiting this profile. The 2-1-1-1 profile is characterized by its multi-dominant and "generalized" nature, and fairly balanced amount of understanding and ability to use the three primary quadrants — the preferred processing modes being creative and holistic in Upper Right D, interpersonal and feeling in Lower Right C, and planning and organizing in the Lower Left B. The Upper Left quadrant A is least preferred, but still the person is typically quite functional in their use of the logical and analytical aspects of this quadrant. This profile is typical of many personnel and human resource professionals, including teachers as well as those whose occupations require an understanding and ability to function on many levels, such as social workers, executive secretaries, and supervisory nurses.

1-2-1-1

 This profile is triple dominant, with three preferred quadrants. These primaries occur in Upper Left A, Lower Right C, and Upper Right D quadrants. This is a multi-dominant profile that would be characterized by well balanced processing modes of Upper Left A — the analytic, logical, and rational processing; the interpersonal, emotional, and intuitive thinking modes of Lower Right C, combined with the artistic, creative, and holistic processing modes of the Upper Right D quadrant. The Lower Left B secondary quadrant would be functional, yet clearly of less preference in terms of organizing, control, structure and conservative thinking styles. This profile is also double dominant in the cerebral modes, both left and right. This individual would be more experimental than safe-keeping and more emotional than controlled. Occupations would involve those with less administrative detail and more attention to broad concepts, strategic planning as compared to operational planning, and those occupations tending towards a more "generalized" nature. Positions involving technical innovation and future planning fit this profile along with human resource and development professions.

2-2-1-2

 This profile is a singular dominant profile with the most preferred quadrant being the limbic right quadrant C. The person with this profile would clearly prefer the interpersonal, emotional, musical, and spiritual aspects of this quadrant. The three remaining quadrants are functional, yet distinctly secondary to the limbic right characteristics. This person would thus be quite visibly "feeling" and people-oriented, but still well balanced in the logical, analytical, factual thinking styles of cerebral left A, and the organized, administrative and controlled qualities of limbic left B, and finally the creative, synthesizing, holistic modes of processing in cerebral right D. Persons with this profile are typically nurses, social workers, musicians, teachers, counselors, or in the ministry.

2-2-1-1

This profile features two primaries in the right mode, quadrants C and D, and two secondaries in the left mode, quadrants A and B. It is the third most common profile in the population at large, at 14 percent, and with only a relatively slight difference in the male and female populations — respectively 11 percent and 17 percent. Typical characteristics would include the ability to be creative, holistic, and synthesizing in the Upper Right D quadrant, and interpersonal, emotional, and spiritual in the Lower Right C quadrant. The left mode secondaries with logical, analytical, and mathematical thinking styles from Upper Left A, and the organizational, planning, and structure from Lower Left B, would be functional, yet clearly secondary to the preferred right modes of thinking. Those with this profile often have the occupations of teaching or facilitating. Other occupations include the arts, such as writers, musicians, artists, and designers, as well as those in the "helping" fields — psychologists and counselors. This profile could also support entrepreneurial behavior, since it features the imaginative, innovating, and "risk" oriented behavior of the right mode, quadrants C and D without the control or preference of the structured, logical, and conservative modes of the left quadrants A & B.

3-2-1-1

This profile features double dominant profiles in the right mode with the most preferred quadrants being the Lower Right C quadrant, and Upper Right D quadrant. The secondary preference appears in the Lower Left B, while the least preferred quadrant, expressed as a tertiary, is in the Upper Left A quadrant. The Upper Right D primary quadrant would express itself in creative, holistic, synthesizing, and artistic modes of thinking. The Lower Right C primary, is characterized by interpersonal, spiritual, and emotional aspects. Together, these would express themselves in intuitive, insightful thinking, both in the feeling and problem solving processes. The secondary in Lower Left B quadrant, would typically be functional in terms of organization, administrative responsibilities, and control, yet is distinctly secondary to the right modes. The tertiary in Upper Left A quadrant, is characterized by the lack of, or even avoidance, of logical, analytical, mathematical, and rational modes of thinking. This profile is frequently that of professionals in the human resource area, sales persons, teachers, social workers, nurses, entrepreneurs and artists.

3-3-1-1

This is a double dominant profile in the right mode, with the two primary preferences in the Lower Right C quadrant and the Upper Right D Quadrant. The tertiaries occur in the two left mode quadrants, Upper Left A and Lower Left B. This profile is characterized by the Upper Right D primary aspects of imaginative, artistic, holistic, and conceptual processing and the Lower Right C aspects of interpersonal, emotional, and spiritual modes of thinking. These right mode primaries become visible in the absence of strong left mode qualities — those being the lack of, or even avoidance of, the logical, analytical, or rational thought of the Upper Left A quadrant and the controlled, conservative, structured, and organized modes of the Lower Left B quadrant. A person with this profile would exhibit very creative, imaginative, intuitive, emotional, and interpersonal qualities without any strong inclinations for rational thinking or organized implementation. For example, a person who has the imagination to create a new business, but is not well suited to operating it or maintaining it over the long term. Occupations with this profile are typically non-technical and include entrepreneurs, artists, and those in the teaching and "helping" professions.

2-3-1-1

This profile is a double dominant profile, with the two most preferred modes of processing occurring in Lower Right C and Upper Right D quadrants. Characteristics of this profile would include interpersonal, emotional, and spiritual aspects of the Lower Right C quadrant and the holistic, creative, and conceptual processing modes of the Upper Right D quadrant. The Upper Left A quadrant is expressed as a secondary, with the modes of processing including logical, analytic, and rational being functional, yet secondary in preference to the right modes. The tertiary in the Lower Left B quadrant would indicate an avoidance or lack of preference for control, planning, organization, and structure. The general lack of preference in the two left hemisphere quadrants, A & B, would reinforce the strength of the primaries in the right quadrants, C & D, and this person would clearly be seen as

intuitive, holistic, interpersonal, creative, and imaginative. Occupations that would be typical of persons with this profile would include artists, sales representatives, entrepreneurs, human resource professionals, and teachers or trainers.

2-3-3-1

This profile is a singular dominant profile, with the most preferred mode of processing occurring in the Upper Right D quadrant. This profile is characterized by strong preferences in holistic, conceptual, artistic, and synthesizing modes of processing. The secondary in the Upper Left A quadrant would make the characteristics of logical, analytical, and rational thought functional, but secondary in nature. This profile is also typified by the lack of preference or even avoidance of the Lower Left B quadrant and the Lower Right C quadrant, with both expressed as tertiaries. The ability to organize, plan, or pay attention to detail and the interpersonal, emotional, and spiritual modes of processing of the limbic mode would clearly be the least preferred. This lack of preference or avoidance would emphasize and strengthen the primary preference of Upper Right D and this person would be viewed as artistic, creative, imaginative, and holistic. Occupations typical of persons with this profile would include artists, futurists, strategists, and some top level executives.

2-2-2-1

This singularly dominant profile prefers the Upper Right D quadrant. Characteristics associated with this quadrant include creative, imaginative, holistic, and integrative processing.

Synthesizing would likely be the most preferred thinking style. The three remaining quadrants are functional, yet distinctly secondary. This permits the person to be quite visibly imaginative, intuitive, experimental, and innovative—yet situationally functional and farily well-balanced in terms of the logical, analytical, factual modes of thinking from the Upper Left A quadrant; organized, administrative, and controlled in terms of the Lower Left B quadrant; and finally, interpersonal and emotional from the Lower Right C quadrant. Persons with this profile are typically entrepreneurs, facilitators, advisors, consultants, sales-oriented leaders, and artists.

3-2-2-1

This is a singular dominant profile with the most preferred quadrant occurring in Upper Right D. It would be characterized by holistic, creative, synthesizing, and artistic modes of processing. The Lower Left B and Lower Right C quadrants are expressed as secondaries, and the characteristics of control, planning, and organizing of quadrant B, coupled with the interpersonal, emotional, and spiritual processing modes of the Lower Right C quadrant, would typically be functional yet secondary to the singular preference of the Upper Right D quadrant. The Upper Left A quadrant is expressed as a tertiary. The characteristics of logical, rational, and analytical processing are therefore avoided or of low preference. This tertiary in quadrant A, coupled with the secondaries of the two limbic quadrants, reinforces the strength and primary preference of the Upper Right D quadrant. This person would likely be seen as imaginative, holistic, conceptual, and synthesizing in their thinking style. Occupations typical of people with this profile would include entrepreneurs, those in top level management or executive positions, business advisors and consultants, and those in the more aesthetic/artistic occupations.

FINANCIAL OCCUPATIONS

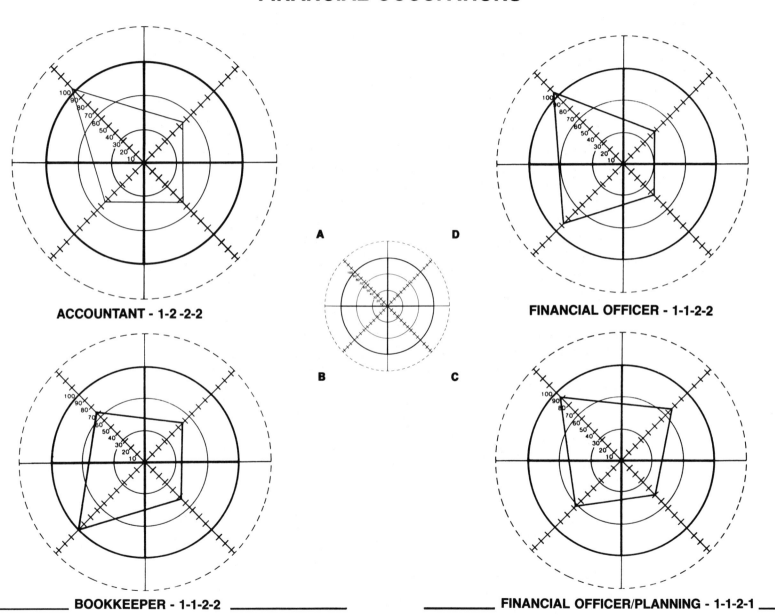

ACCOUNTANT - 1-2 -2-2

FINANCIAL OFFICER - 1-1-2-2

BOOKKEEPER - 1-1-2-2

FINANCIAL OFFICER/PLANNING - 1-1-2-1

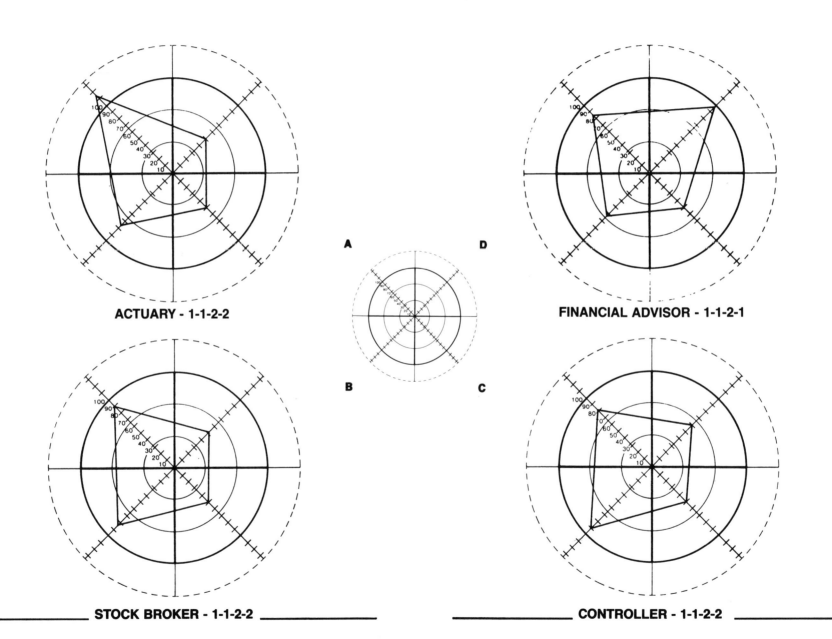

ACTUARY - 1-1-2-2

FINANCIAL ADVISOR - 1-1-2-1

A   D

B   C

STOCK BROKER - 1-1-2-2

CONTROLLER - 1-1-2-2

MEDICAL OCCUPATIONS

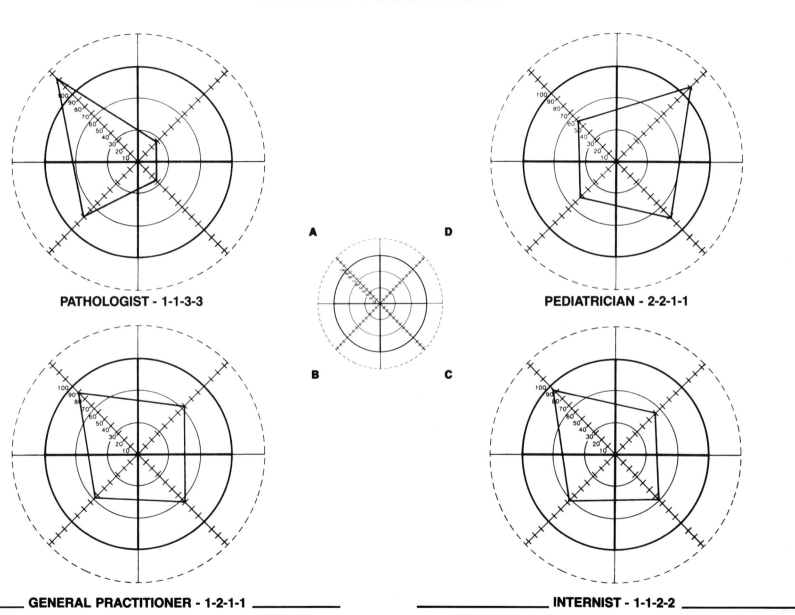

PATHOLOGIST - 1-1-3-3

PEDIATRICIAN - 2-2-1-1

A   D

B   C

GENERAL PRACTITIONER - 1-2-1-1

INTERNIST - 1-1-2-2

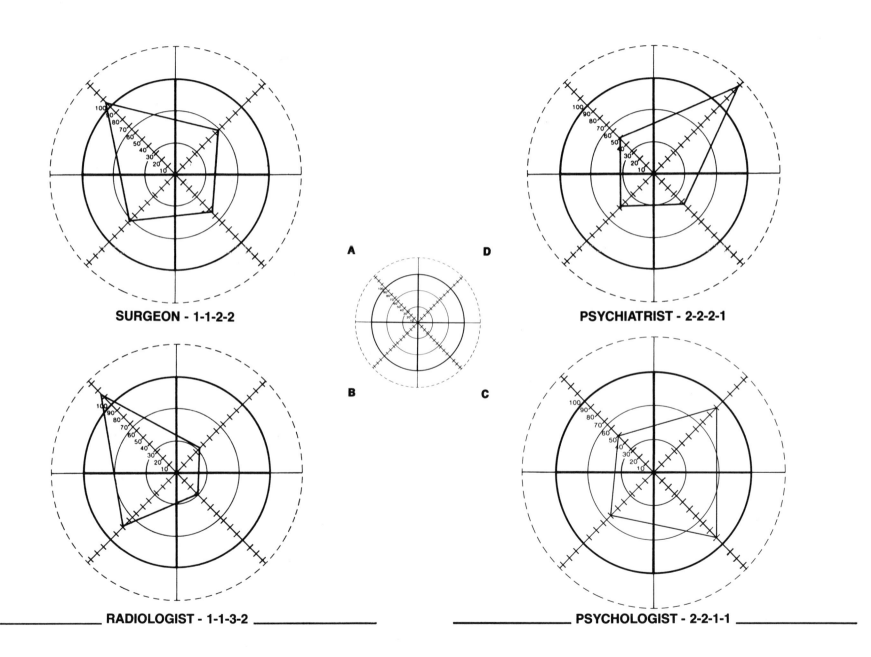

SURGEON - 1-1-2-2

A   D

B   C

PSYCHIATRIST - 2-2-2-1

RADIOLOGIST - 1-1-3-2

PSYCHOLOGIST - 2-2-1-1

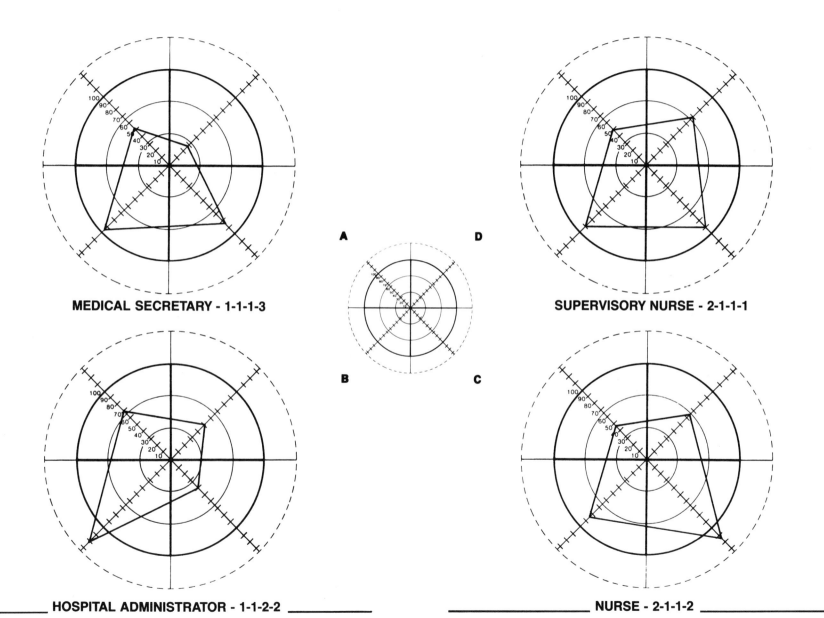

MEDICAL SECRETARY - 1-1-1-3

SUPERVISORY NURSE - 2-1-1-1

HOSPITAL ADMINISTRATOR - 1-1-2-2

NURSE - 2-1-1-2

HUMAN RESOURCE DEVELOPMENT OCCUPATIONS
ALL PROFILES SHOWN ARE GROUP AVERAGES

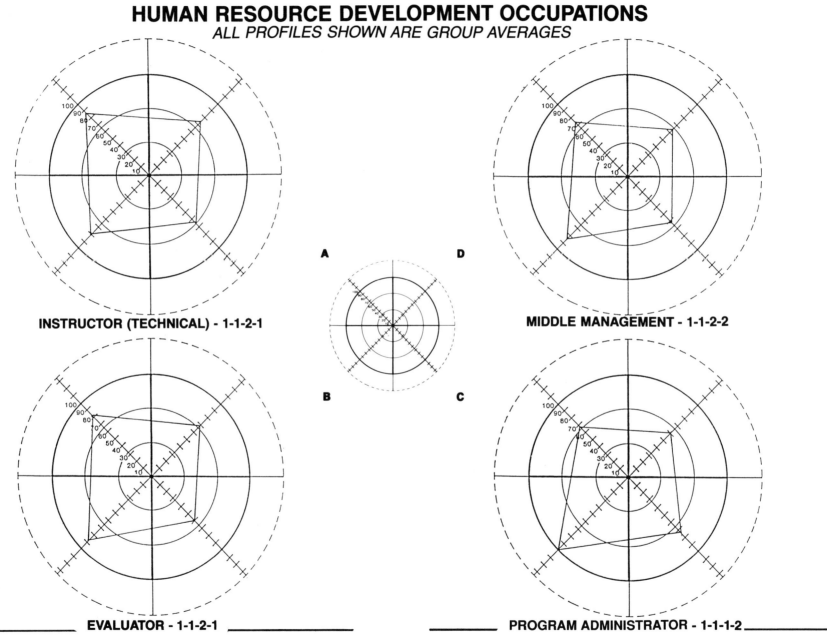

INSTRUCTOR (TECHNICAL) - 1-1-2-1

MIDDLE MANAGEMENT - 1-1-2-2

EVALUATOR - 1-1-2-1

PROGRAM ADMINISTRATOR - 1-1-1-2

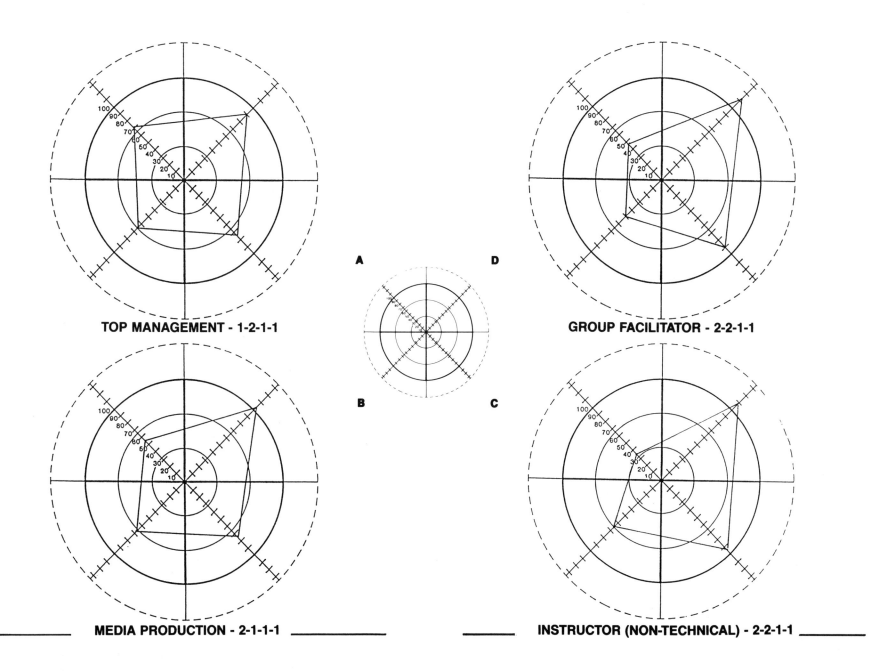

TOP MANAGEMENT - 1-2-1-1

A   D

B   C

GROUP FACILITATOR - 2-2-1-1

MEDIA PRODUCTION - 2-1-1-1

INSTRUCTOR (NON-TECHNICAL) - 2-2-1-1

ORGANIZATIONS

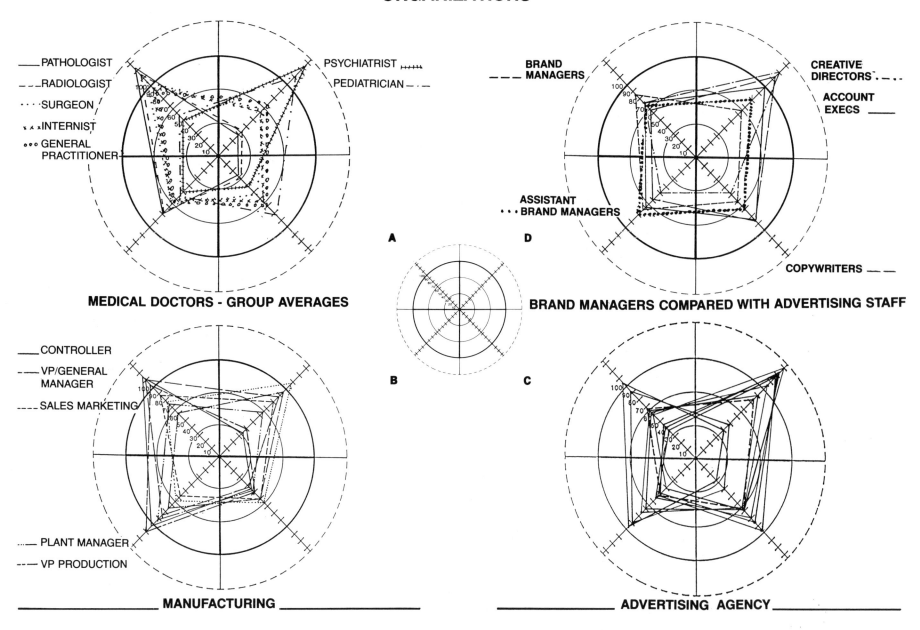

PATHOLOGIST
RADIOLOGIST
SURGEON
INTERNIST
GENERAL PRACTITIONER

PSYCHIATRIST
PEDIATRICIAN

MEDICAL DOCTORS - GROUP AVERAGES

BRAND MANAGERS

CREATIVE DIRECTORS
ACCOUNT EXECS

ASSISTANT BRAND MANAGERS

COPYWRITERS

BRAND MANAGERS COMPARED WITH ADVERTISING STAFF

A

B

C

D

CONTROLLER
VP/GENERAL MANAGER
SALES MARKETING

PLANT MANAGER
VP PRODUCTION

MANUFACTURING

ADVERTISING AGENCY

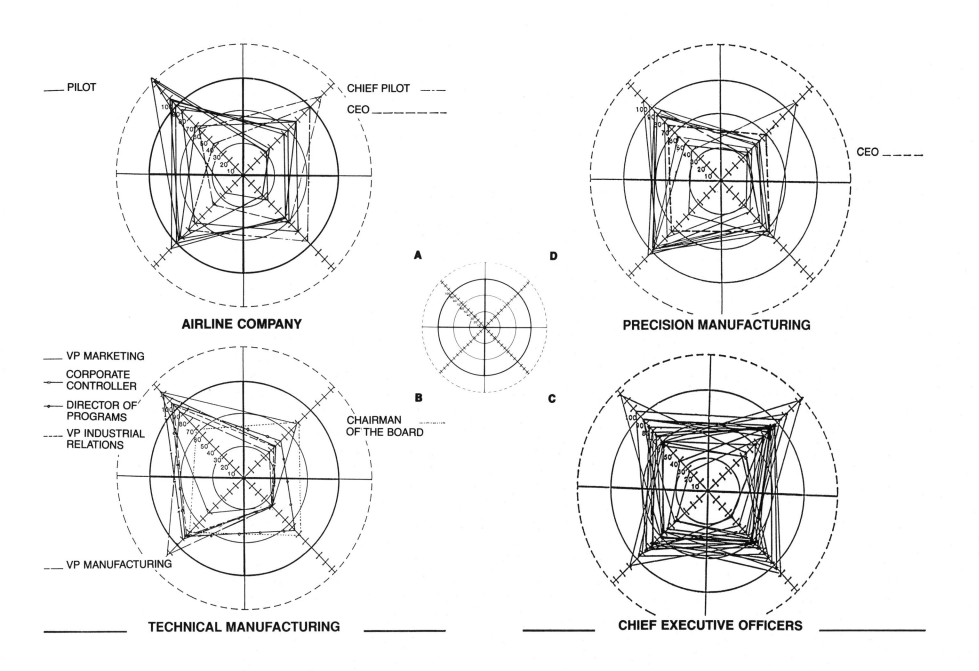

PILOT ——

CHIEF PILOT —— ·——

CEO —— —— ——

AIRLINE COMPANY

A

D

CEO —— ——

PRECISION MANUFACTURING

VP MARKETING ————

CORPORATE
CONTROLLER

DIRECTOR OF
PROGRAMS

VP INDUSTRIAL
RELATIONS

CHAIRMAN
OF THE BOARD

VP MANUFACTURING

B

C

TECHNICAL MANUFACTURING

CHIEF EXECUTIVE OFFICERS

CORPORATE STAFF

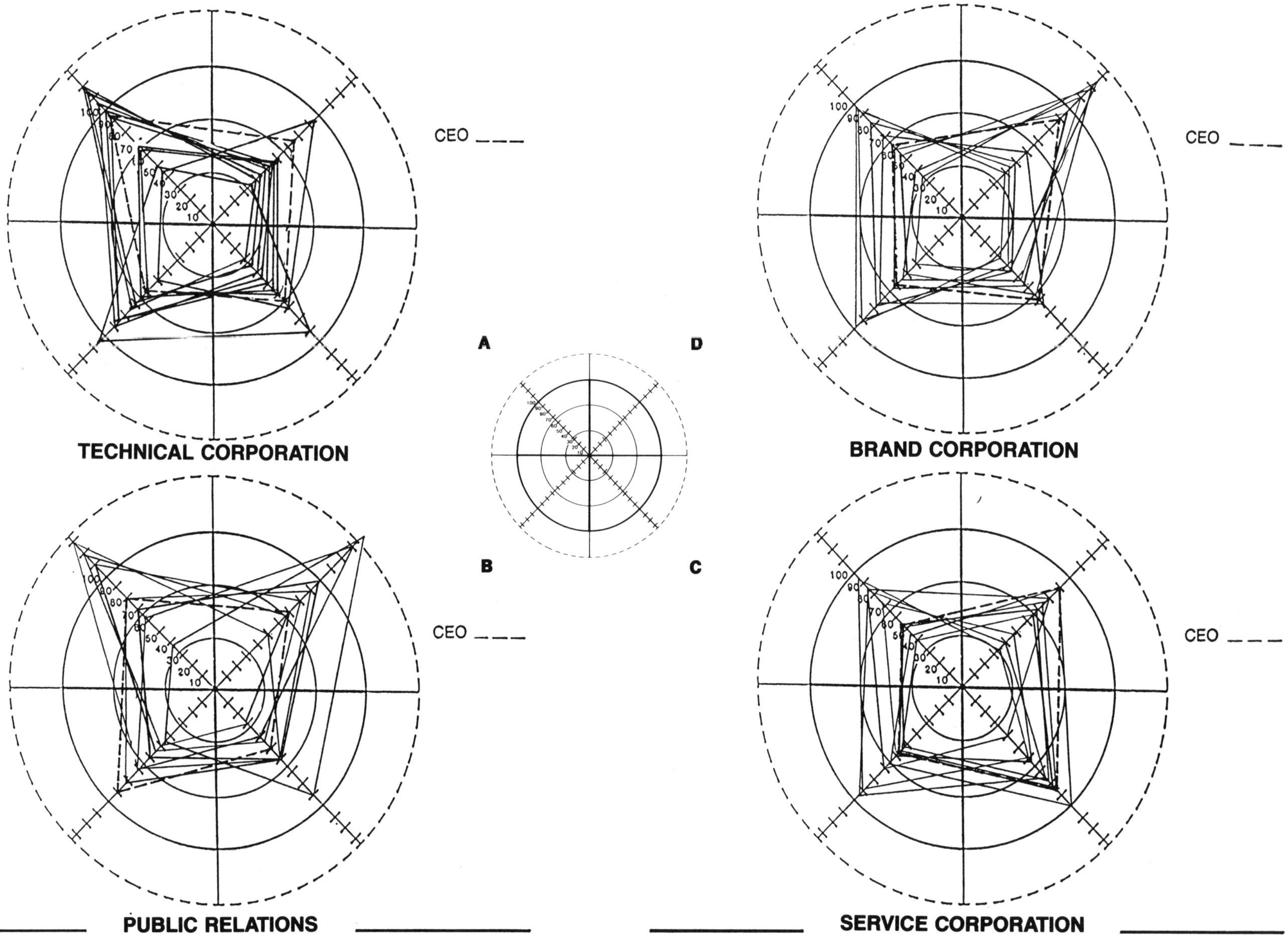

TECHNICAL CORPORATION

CEO ___

BRAND CORPORATION

CEO ___

PUBLIC RELATIONS

CEO ___

SERVICE CORPORATION

A

B

D

C

SELECTED PROFILES

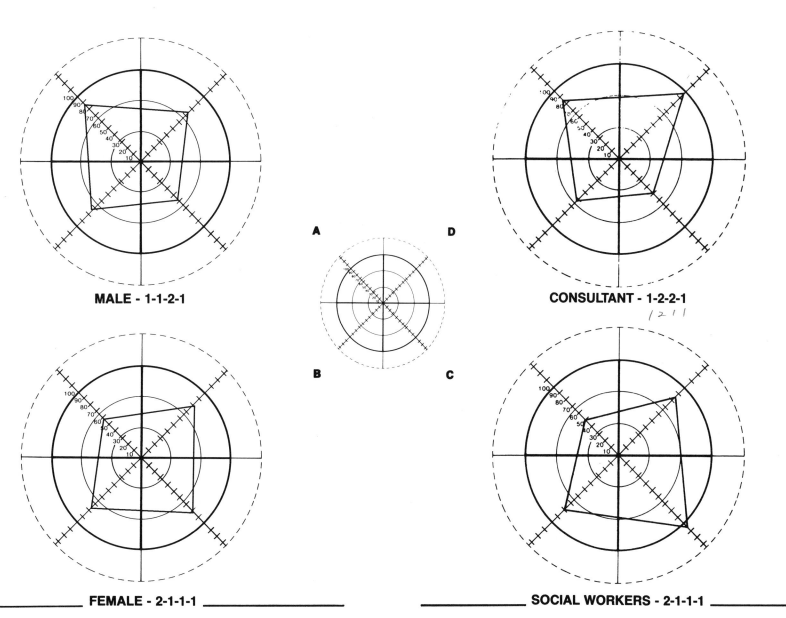

MALE - 1-1-2-1

A   D

B   C

CONSULTANT - 1-2-2-1

FEMALE - 2-1-1-1

SOCIAL WORKERS - 2-1-1-1

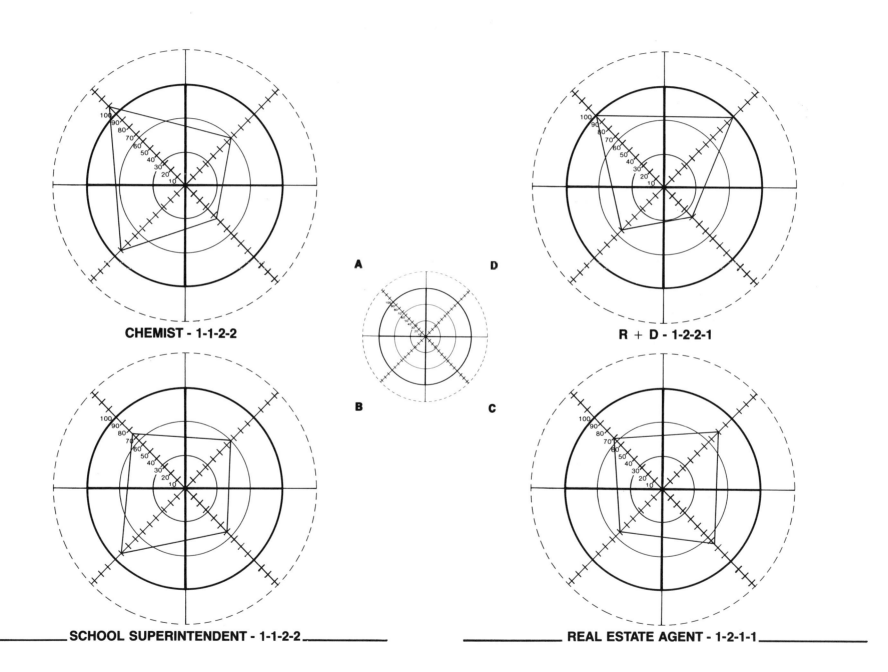

CHEMIST - 1-1-2-2

A

D

B

C

R + D - 1-2-2-1

SCHOOL SUPERINTENDENT - 1-1-2-2

REAL ESTATE AGENT - 1-2-1-1

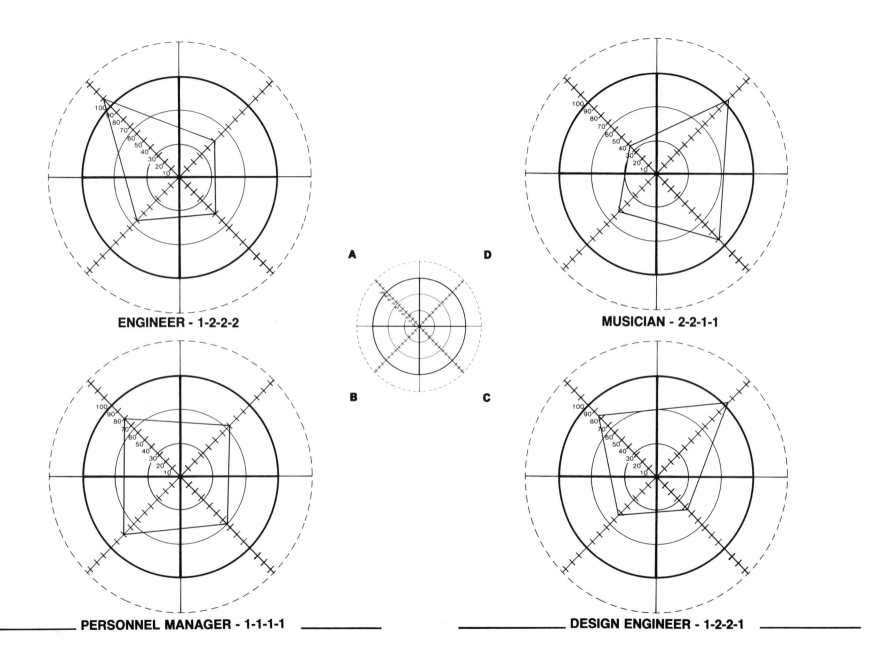

ENGINEER - 1-2-2-2

MUSICIAN - 2-2-1-1

A

D

B

C

PERSONNEL MANAGER - 1-1-1-1

DESIGN ENGINEER - 1-2-2-1

Proforma Profiles

Great Brains in History

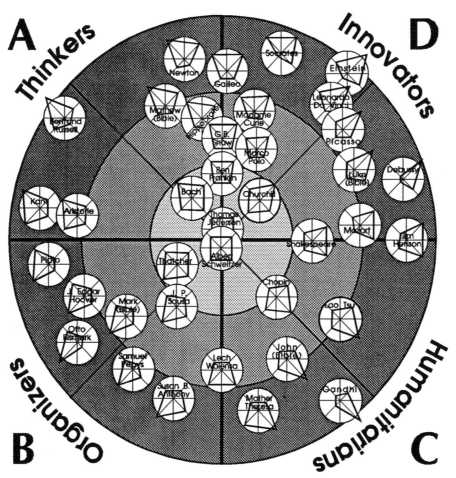

© 1990 Ned Herrmann

LIFE Magazine's 100 Most Important Americans of the 20th Century
Herrmann Brain Dominance Circular Continuum

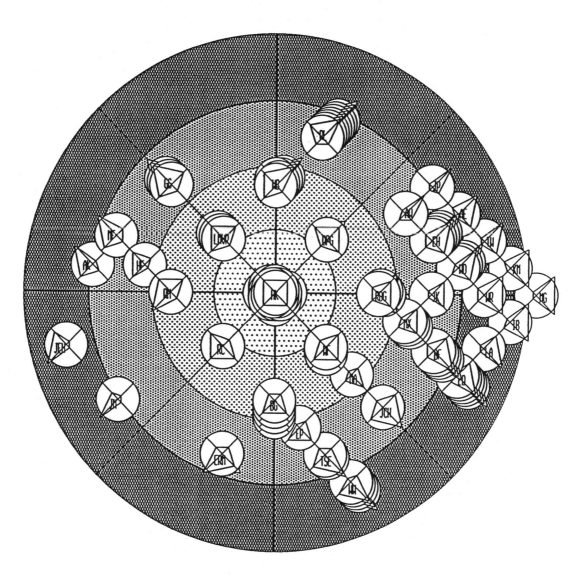

LIFE Magazine's 100 Most Important Americans of the 20th Century
Herrmann Brain Dominance Proforma Profiles

Name	A	B	C	D
Jane Addams	3	1	1+	2
Muhammad Ali	3	2	1	2
Elizabeth Arden	2	2	1	1+
Roone Arledge	2	1	1	1+
Louis Armstrong	3	3	1+	1
George Balanchine	1	1+	1+	2
John Bardeen	1	2	2	1+
Irving Berlin	3	2	1+	1+
Edward L. Bernays	3	2	1	1+
Leonard Bernstein	2	2	1+	1
W.E.B. Du Bois	1	1	1	1
Marlon Brando	3	2	1+	1
Wernher Von Braun	1	2	2	1+
Wright Brothers	1	1	2	1+
Dale Carnegie	2	2	1+	1
Wallace Carothers	1+	1	2	1
Willis Carrier	1	2	2	1+
Rachel Carson	1	1	1	2
Bing Crosby	3	1	1+	2
Clarence Darrow	1	1	1	1
Eugene V. Debs	3	2	1+	1
John Dewey	1	1	1	1
Walt Disney	3	2	1	1+
Allen Dulles	1	1	2	1
Bob Dylan	2	1	1+	2
Albert Einstein	2	3	1	1+
T.S. Eliot	2	1	1+	2
William Faulkner	2	1	1	1
Abraham Flexner	1	1	1	1
Henry Ford	1	1	3	2
John Ford	1	1	2	1+
Betty Friedan	2	2	1+	1
Milton Friedman	1+	1	2	2
George Gallup	1+	1	2	1
A.P. Giannini	1	2	1	1
Robert De Graff	2	2	1	1
Martha Graham	3	3	1+	1+
Billy Grahm	2	1	1	2
W.D. Griffith	1	1	1	1+
Joyce C. Hall	2	1	1+	1
Ernest Hemmingway	2	2	1	1+
Oliver Wendell Holmes	1	1	1	1
J. Edgar Hoover	1	1+	3	3
Robert Hutchins	1	2	2	1
Helen Keller	1	1	1	1
Jack Kerouac	3	3	1	1
Billie Jean King	2	1	1	2
Martin Luther King Jr.	3	2	1+	1
Alfred Kinsey	1+	1	2	3
Willem Kolff	1	1	1	1
Ray Kroc	2	1	1	1+
Edwin Land	1	1	2	1+
William Levitt	2	1	1	1
John L. Lewis	3	1	1+	2
Charles Lindberg	1	2	2	1+
Raymond Loewy	1	2	2	1+
Henry Luce	1	1	1	1
Douglas MacArthur	1	1	1	1
George C. Marshall	1	1	1	1
Louis B. Mayer	1	1	1	1
Claire McCardell	2	2	1	1+
Joseph McCarthy	2	1+	3	3
Frank McNamara	1	1	2	1
Margaret Mead	1	1	1	1
Karl Menninger	2	3	1+	1+
Charles Merrill	2	2	1	1
Robert Moses	1	1+	2	1
William Mulholland	1+	1	2	1
Edward R. Murrow	2	1+	1	2
Ralph Nader	1	1	1+	1+
John Von Neumann	1	2	2	1+
Reinhold Niebuhr	2	1	1	2
Eugene O'Neill	3	2	1	1
J. Robert Oppenheimer	1	2	2	1
William Paley	1	1	1	1
Jackson Pollock	3	3	2	1+
Emily Post	3	1	1	2
Elvis Presley	3	2	1+	1
Jackie Robinson	2	2	1	1
John D. Rockefeller Jr.	2	2	1+	1
Richard Rogers	1	1	1	1
Will Rogers	2	2	1+	1+
Ludwig Mies Van der Rohe	1	1	2	1
Eleanor Rosevelt	3	2	1+	1
Babe Ruth	3	2	1	1
Jonas Salk	1	1	1	1
Margaret Sanger	3	2	1	1+
Alfred P. Sloan Jr.	1	1	2	1+
Benjamin Spock	2	2	1	1+
Alfred Stieglitz	1	2	2	1
Roy Stryker	2	1	1	2
Bill W.	1	2	1+	1
Andy Warhol	3	2	2	1+
Earl Warren	1	1	1	1
James D. Watson	1	2	2	1
Thomas J. Watson Jr.	1	1	1	1
Tennessee Williams	3	3	1	1+
Walter Winchell	3	1	1+	2
Frank Lloyd Wright	1	2	2	1+
Malcolm X	3	2	1	1

WHOLE BRAIN MODEL

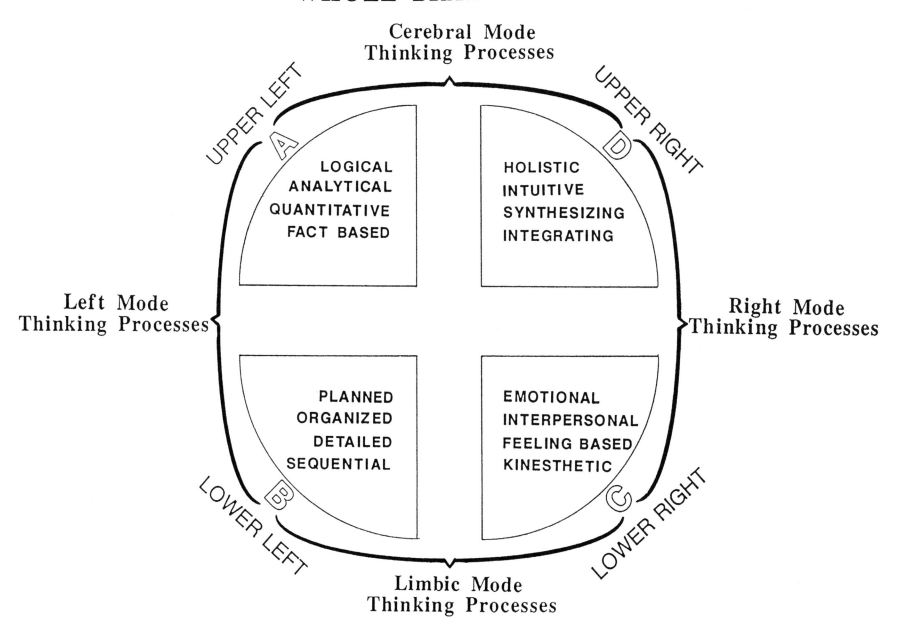

Cerebral Mode
Thinking Processes

UPPER LEFT

UPPER RIGHT

A

LOGICAL
ANALYTICAL
QUANTITATIVE
FACT BASED

D

HOLISTIC
INTUITIVE
SYNTHESIZING
INTEGRATING

Left Mode
Thinking Processes

Right Mode
Thinking Processes

B

PLANNED
ORGANIZED
DETAILED
SEQUENTIAL

C

EMOTIONAL
INTERPERSONAL
FEELING BASED
KINESTHETIC

LOWER LEFT

LOWER RIGHT

Limbic Mode
Thinking Processes

THE INTERCONNECTED BRAIN SYSTEM

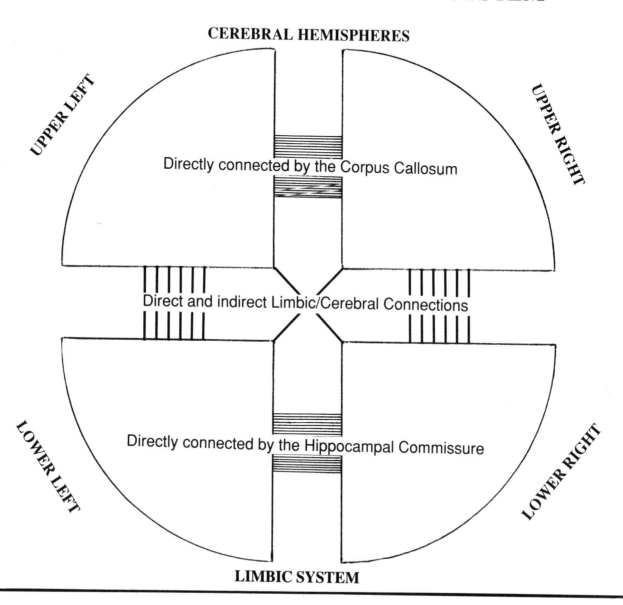

CEREBRAL HEMISPHERES

UPPER LEFT

UPPER RIGHT

Directly connected by the Corpus Callosum

Direct and indirect Limbic/Cerebral Connections

LOWER LEFT

LOWER RIGHT

Directly connected by the Hippocampal Commissure

LIMBIC SYSTEM

ARCHITECTURE

FOUR INTERCONNECTED CLUSTERS OF
SPECIALIZED MENTAL PROCESSING MODES

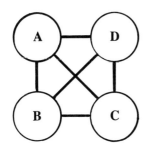

THAT FUNCTION TOGETHER SITUATIONALLY
AND ITERATIVELY, MAKING UP A WHOLE BRAIN
IN WHICH ONE OR MORE PARTS BECOME
NATURALLY DOMINANT.

THE ORGANIZING PRINCIPLE

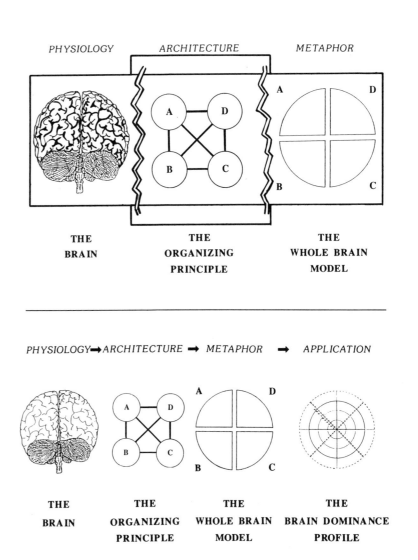

PHYSIOLOGY   *ARCHITECTURE*   *METAPHOR*

THE   THE   THE
BRAIN   ORGANIZING   WHOLE BRAIN
                   PRINCIPLE   MODEL

PHYSIOLOGY ➡ *ARCHITECTURE* ➡ *METAPHOR* ➡ *APPLICATION*

THE   THE   THE   THE
BRAIN   ORGANIZING   WHOLE BRAIN   BRAIN DOMINANCE
             PRINCIPLE   MODEL   PROFILE

RELATIONSHIPS MODEL

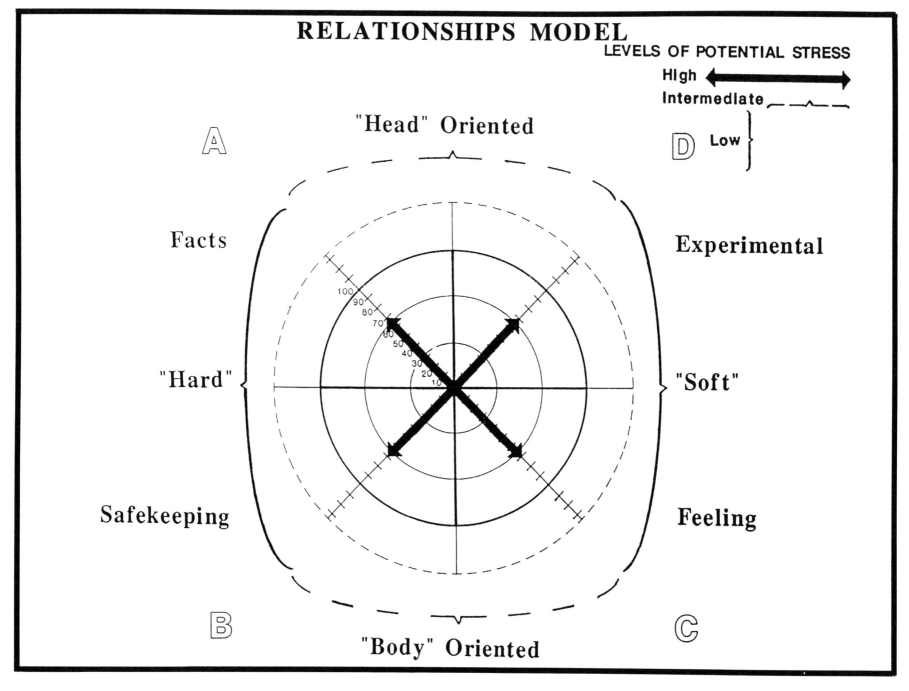

LEVELS OF POTENTIAL STRESS

High

Intermediate

Low

A

"Head" Oriented

Facts

Experimental

"Hard"

"Soft"

Safekeeping

Feeling

B

"Body" Oriented

C

D

THE UNIVERSE OF THINKING STYLES

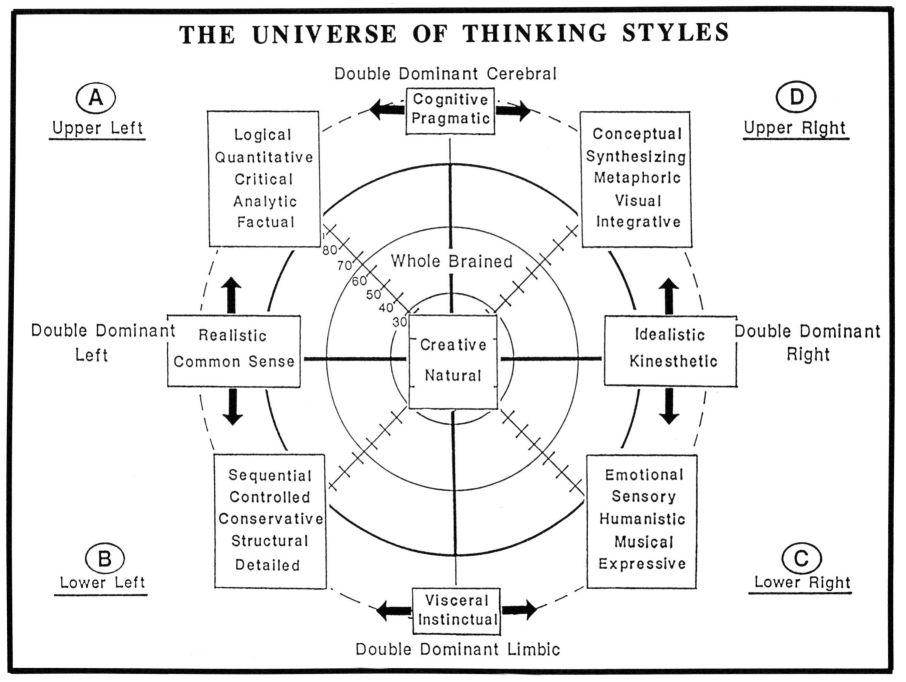

Double Dominant Cerebral

(A) Upper Left

(D) Upper Right

Cognitive Pragmatic

Logical
Quantitative
Critical
Analytic
Factual

Conceptual
Synthesizing
Metaphoric
Visual
Integrative

Whole Brained

80
70
60
50
40
30

Double Dominant Left

Realistic
Common Sense

Creative
Natural

Idealistic
Kinesthetic

Double Dominant Right

Sequential
Controlled
Conservative
Structural
Detailed

Emotional
Sensory
Humanistic
Musical
Expressive

(B) Lower Left

(C) Lower Right

Visceral
Instinctual

Double Dominant Limbic

EXPANDED WHOLE BRAIN CREATIVE PROCESS MODEL

THE SURROUNDING ENVIRONMENT IN WHICH CULTURE EXISTS
(Physical, Geographic, Economic, Temporal)
INTELLECTUAL

A

PERFORMANCE
FINANCE DRIVEN
STOCK EXCHANGE

D

PLEASURE
RISK DRIVEN
SKUNKWORKS

THE CULTURE IN WHICH PROCESS IS APPLIED
(Ethnic, Family, Social, Managerial)

"URBAN"

MATERIALISTIC
AUTHORITARIAN
"WESTERN CULTURE"
"INDUSTRIAL"

EXPLORATIVE
ENTREPRENEURIAL
"EASTERN CULTURE"

WHOLE BRAINED CREATIVE PROCESS

PREPARATION / VERIFICATION / INCUBATION / ILLUMINATION

A | INTEREST

APPLICATION | D

CEREBRAL

LOGICAL THINKING
ANALYSIS OF FACTS
PROCESSING NUMBERS

VISUALIZATION
IMAGINATION
CONCEPTUALIZATION

UPPER LEFT | UPPER RIGHT

TIME CONSCIOUS

PREPARATION & VERIFICATION

LEFT MODE

RIGHT MODE

INCUBATION & ILLUMINATION

"SOCIAL"

SPACE CONSCIOUS

LOWER LEFT | LOWER RIGHT

PLANNING APPROACH
ORGANIZING FACTS
DETAILED REVIEW

GUT REACTION
SENSORY RESPONSE
INTERPERSONAL

DOMINANCE PROFILE

B

LIMBIC

C

ITERATIVE MODEL

BUREAUCRATIC
TRADITIONAL

HUMANISTIC
SPIRITUAL

"RURAL"

B

FACTORY
PRODUCTION DRIVEN
RELIABILITY

C

FELLOWSHIP HALL
VALUE DRIVEN
SATISFACTION

PHYSICAL

EXPANDED WHOLE BRAIN TEACHING & LEARNING MODEL

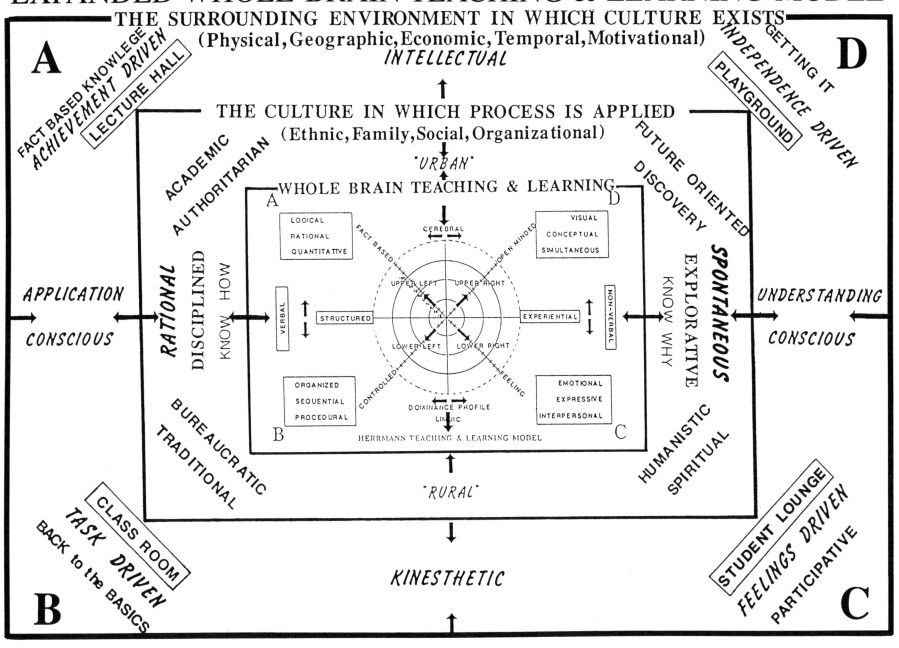

THE SURROUNDING ENVIRONMENT IN WHICH CULTURE EXISTS
(Physical, Geographic, Economic, Temporal, Motivational)

INTELLECTUAL

A   **D**

FACT BASED KNOWLEGE *ACHIEVEMENT DRIVEN* LECTURE HALL

GETTING IT *INDEPENDENCE DRIVEN* PLAYGROUND

THE CULTURE IN WHICH PROCESS IS APPLIED
(Ethnic, Family, Social, Organizational)

"URBAN"

ACADEMIC AUTHORITARIAN   FUTURE ORIENTED DISCOVERY

WHOLE BRAIN TEACHING & LEARNING

A   D

| LOGICAL RATIONAL QUANTITATIVE | | VISUAL CONCEPTUAL SIMULTANEOUS |

CEREBRAL

FACT BASED   OPEN MINDED

UPPER LEFT   UPPER RIGHT

VERBAL   STRUCTURED   EXPERIENTIAL   NON-VERBAL

LOWER LEFT   LOWER RIGHT

CONTROLLED   FEELING

| ORGANIZED SEQUENTIAL PROCEDURAL | | EMOTIONAL EXPRESSIVE INTERPERSONAL |

DOMINANCE PROFILE

LIMBIC

B   C

HERRMANN TEACHING & LEARNING MODEL

RATIONAL DISCIPLINED KNOW HOW   *SPONTANEOUS* EXPLORATIVE KNOW WHY

APPLICATION CONSCIOUS   UNDERSTANDING CONSCIOUS

BUREAUCRATIC TRADITIONAL   HUMANISTIC SPIRITUAL

"RURAL"

CLASS ROOM *TASK DRIVEN* BACK to the BASICS

STUDENT LOUNGE *FEELINGS DRIVEN* PARTICIPATIVE

KINESTHETIC

B   **C**

WHOLE BRAIN TEACHING AND LEARNING
OBJECTIVES AND STRATEGIES

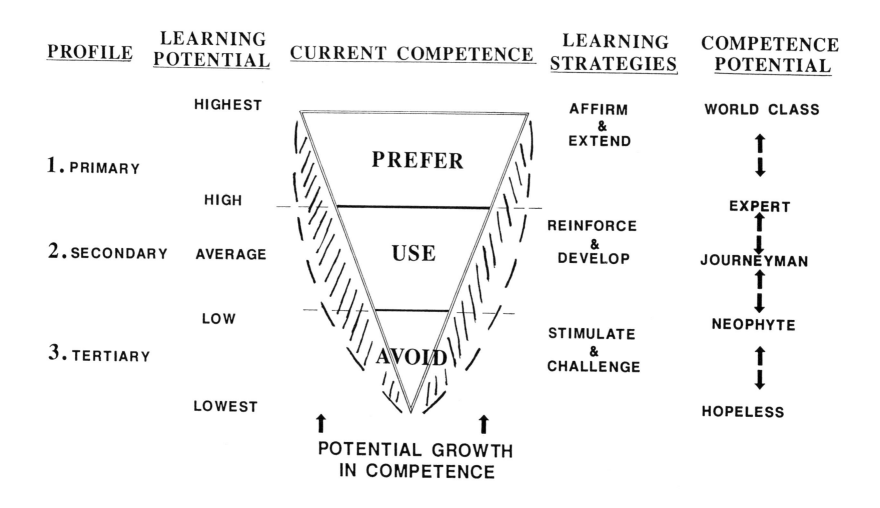

PROFILE	LEARNING POTENTIAL	CURRENT COMPETENCE	LEARNING STRATEGIES	COMPETENCE POTENTIAL
	HIGHEST		AFFIRM & EXTEND	WORLD CLASS
1. PRIMARY		PREFER		
	HIGH			EXPERT
2. SECONDARY	AVERAGE	USE	REINFORCE & DEVELOP	JOURNEYMAN
	LOW		STIMULATE & CHALLENGE	NEOPHYTE
3. TERTIARY		AVOID		
	LOWEST			HOPELESS

POTENTIAL GROWTH
IN COMPETENCE

WHOLE BRAIN LEARNING AND DESIGN CONSIDERATIONS

A-UPPER LEFT

LEARNS BY:

ACQUIRING AND QUANTIFYING FACTS
APPLYING ANALYSIS AND LOGIC
THINKING THROUGH IDEAS
BUILDING CASES
FORMING THEORIES

LEARNERS RESPOND TO:

FORMALIZED LECTURE
DATA BASED CONTENT
FINANCIAL/TECHNICAL CASE DISCUSSIONS
TEXT BOOKS AND BIBLIOGRAPHIES
PROGRAM LEARNING
BEHAVIOR MODIFICATION

D-UPPER RIGHT

LEARNS BY:

TAKING INITIATIVE
EXPLORING HIDDEN POSSIBILITIES
RELYING ON INTUITION
SELF DISCOVERY
CONSTRUCTING CONCEPTS
SYTHESIZING CONTENT

LEARNERS RESPOND TO:

SPONTANEITY
FREE FLOW
EXPERIENTIAL OPPORTUNITIES
EXPERIMENTATION
PLAYFULNESS
FUTURE ORIENTED CASE DISCUSSIONS
VISUAL DISPLAYS
INDIVIDUALITY
AESTHETICS
BEING INVOLVED

B-LOWER LEFT

LEARNS BY:

ORGANIZING AND STRUCTURING CONTENT
SEQUENCING CONTENT
EVALUATING AND TESTING THEORIES
ACQUIRING SKILLS THROUGH PRACTICE
IMPLEMENTING COURSE CONTENT

LEARNERS RESPOND TO:

THOROUGH PLANNING
SEQUENTIAL ORDER
ORGANIZATIONAL AND ADMIN. CASE DISCUSSIONS
TEXT BOOKS
BEHAVIOR MODIFICATION
PROGRAM LEARNING
STRUCTURE
LECTURES

C-LOWER RIGHT

LEARNS BY:

LISTENING AND SHARING IDEAS
INTEGRATING EXPERIENCES WITH SELF
MOVING AND FEELING
HARMONIZING WITH THE CONTENT
EMOTIONAL INVOLVEMENT

LEARNERS RESPOND TO:

EXPERIENTIAL OPPORTUNITIES
SENSORY MOVEMENT
MUSIC
PEOPLE ORIENTED CASE DISCUSSIONS
GROUP INTERACTION

CORRELATIONS MODEL

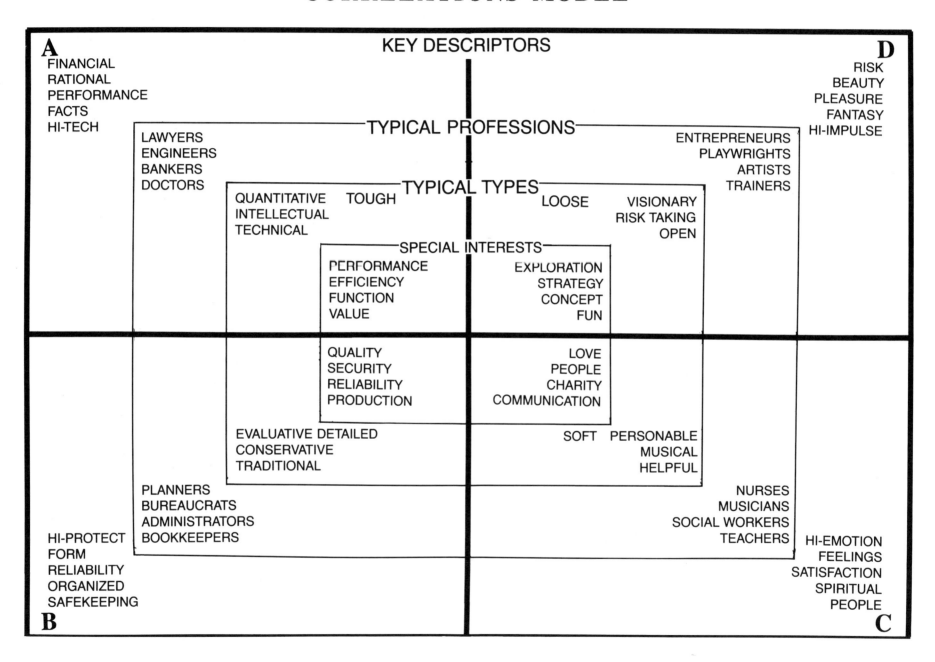

KEY DESCRIPTORS

A

FINANCIAL
RATIONAL
PERFORMANCE
FACTS
HI-TECH

D

RISK
BEAUTY
PLEASURE
FANTASY
HI-IMPULSE

TYPICAL PROFESSIONS

LAWYERS
ENGINEERS
BANKERS
DOCTORS

ENTREPRENEURS
PLAYWRIGHTS
ARTISTS
TRAINERS

TYPICAL TYPES

QUANTITATIVE   TOUGH
INTELLECTUAL
TECHNICAL

LOOSE   VISIONARY
RISK TAKING
OPEN

SPECIAL INTERESTS

PERFORMANCE
EFFICIENCY
FUNCTION
VALUE

EXPLORATION
STRATEGY
CONCEPT
FUN

QUALITY
SECURITY
RELIABILITY
PRODUCTION

LOVE
PEOPLE
CHARITY
COMMUNICATION

EVALUATIVE DETAILED
CONSERVATIVE
TRADITIONAL

SOFT   PERSONABLE
MUSICAL
HELPFUL

PLANNERS
BUREAUCRATS
ADMINISTRATORS
BOOKKEEPERS

NURSES
MUSICIANS
SOCIAL WORKERS
TEACHERS

HI-PROTECT
FORM
RELIABILITY
ORGANIZED
SAFEKEEPING

HI-EMOTION
FEELINGS
SATISFACTION
SPIRITUAL
PEOPLE

B

C

DIFFERENT LANGUAGES OF THE BRAIN

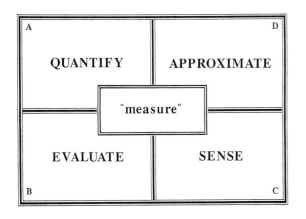

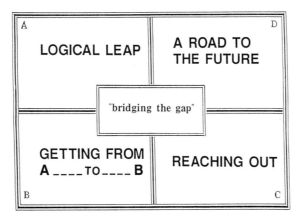

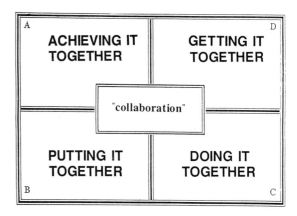

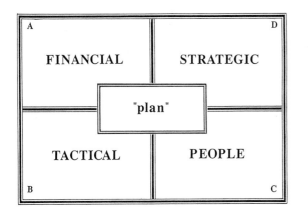

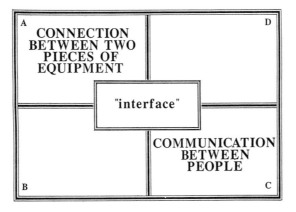

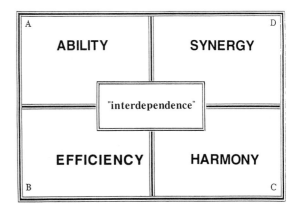

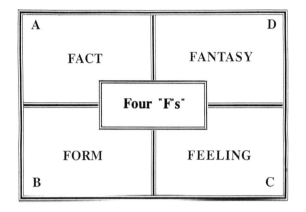

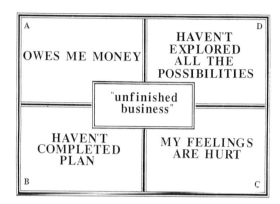

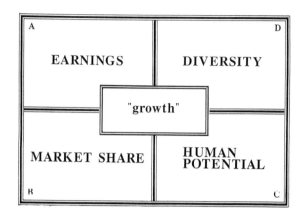

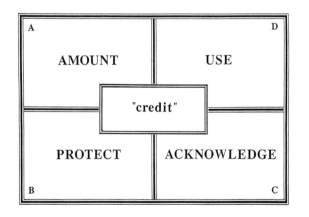

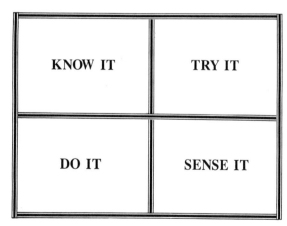

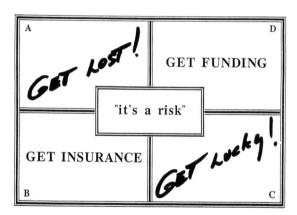

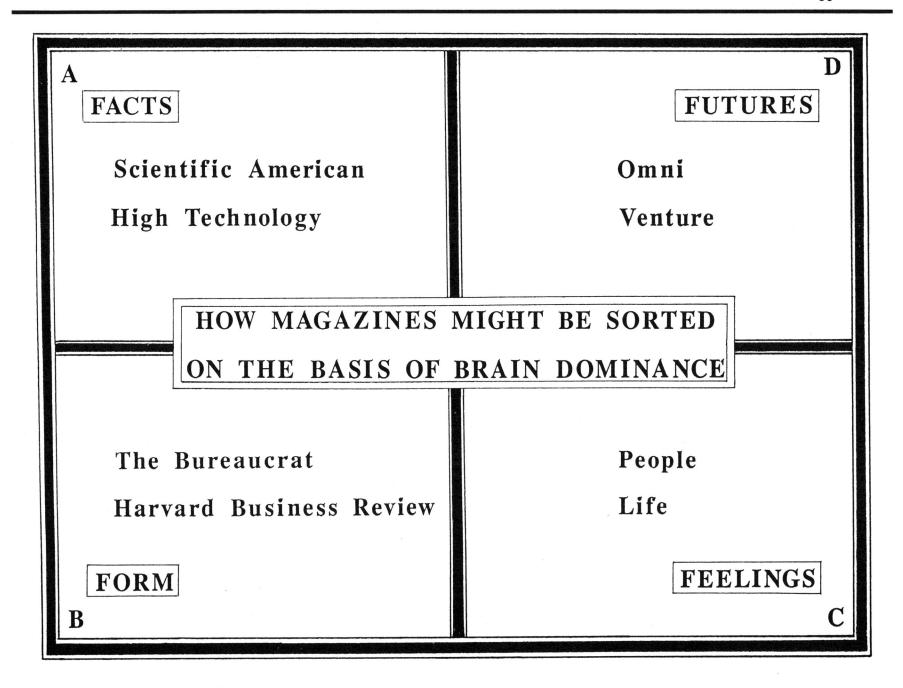

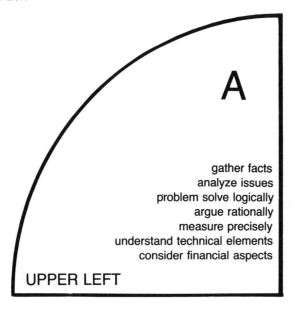

A

gather facts
analyze issues
problem solve logically
argue rationally
measure precisely
understand technical elements
consider financial aspects

UPPER LEFT

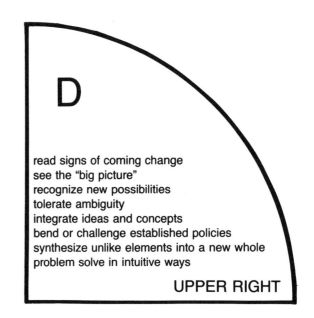

D

read signs of coming change
see the "big picture"
recognize new possibilities
tolerate ambiguity
integrate ideas and concepts
bend or challenge established policies
synthesize unlike elements into a new whole
problem solve in intuitive ways

UPPER RIGHT

HOW THE SPECIALIZED BRAIN PROCESSES EVERYDAY BUSINESS ACTIVITIES

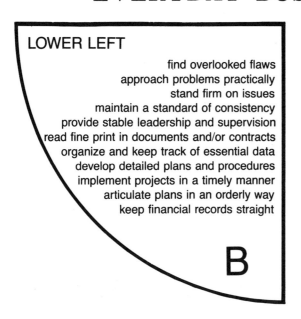

LOWER LEFT

find overlooked flaws
approach problems practically
stand firm on issues
maintain a standard of consistency
provide stable leadership and supervision
read fine print in documents and/or contracts
organize and keep track of essential data
develop detailed plans and procedures
implement projects in a timely manner
articulate plans in an orderly way
keep financial records straight

B

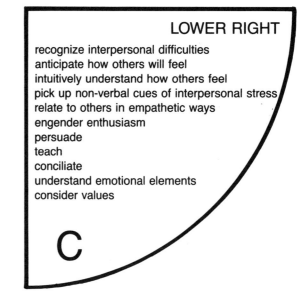

LOWER RIGHT

recognize interpersonal difficulties
anticipate how others will feel
intuitively understand how others feel
pick up non-verbal cues of interpersonal stress
relate to others in empathetic ways
engender enthusiasm
persuade
teach
conciliate
understand emotional elements
consider values

C

©ACLS

DIFFERENCES IN PROCESSING MODES

	Upper Left A	Lower Left B	Lower Right C	Upper Right D
Descriptors	logical factual critical rational analytical quantitative authoritarian mathematical	technical reader data collector conservative controlled sequential articulate dominant detailed	musical spiritual talkative symbolic emotional intuitive (re- garding people) reader (personal)	creative/innovative intuitive (regard- ing solutions) simultaneous synthesizer holistic artistic spatial
Skills	problem solving analytical statistical technical financial	planning supervising administrative organizational implementation	expressing ideas interpersonal writing (cor- respondence) teaching training	creative innovative integrative causing change conceptualizing strategic planning
Typical phrases used	"Tools" "Hardware" "Key point" "Knowing the bottom line" "Take it apart" "Break it down" "Critical analysis"	"Establishing habits" "We have always done it this way" "Law and order" "Self discipline" "By the book" "Play it safe" "Sequence"	"Team work" "The family" "Interactive" "Participatory" "Human values" "Personal growth" "Human resources" "Team development"	"Play with an idea" "The big picture" "Cutting edge" "Broad-based" "Synergistic" "conceptual blockbusting" "Innovative"
Typical derogatory phrases (zingers) used by others	"Number cruncher" "Power Hungry" "Unemotional" "Calculating" "Uncaring" "Cold fish" "Nerd"	"Picky" "Can't think for himself" "Unimaginative" "Stick-in-the-mud" "Grinds out the task"	"Bleeding heart" "Talk, talk, talk" "Touchy-feely" "A push over" "Soft touch" "Sappy"	"Reckless" "Can't focus" "Unrealistic" "Off-the-wall" "Dreams a lot" "Undisciplined" "Head in clouds"

GLOSSARY

A

Alpha - The band of EEG Brain wave patterns in the range of 8 to 13 cycles per second (Hz.), usually taken to indicate the absence of arousal, and therefore, a more relaxed state.

Amygdala - A set of nuclei in the base of the temporal lobe; part of the limbic system.

Analytic - Breaking up things or ideas into parts and examining them to see how they fit together.

Anterior Commissure - Axonic fiber tract that joins the temporal lobes of the left and right hemispheres.

Anxiety - A generalized term which covers clinical states varying from fear of a particular situation or object to so-called "free-floating anxiety" which has no special object.

Aphasia - Defect or loss of power of expression by speech, writing, or signs of comprehending spoken or written language due to injury or disease of the brain.

Artistic - Taking enjoyment from or skillful in painting, drawing, music, or sculpture. Able to coordinate color, design, and texture for pleasing effects.

Association Fibers - The most numerous of three categories of white matter within the brain; nerve fibers which link together all regions of the cortex within the same cerebral hemisphere.

Auditory Cortex - A region of the cerebral cortex, lying mostly within the temporal lobes, where sounds are received and processed.

Axon - A long fiber extending from the cell body of a neuron which conveys impulses to neighboring neurons.

B

Beta - A band of EEG brain wave patterns in the range of 13-30 cycles per second (Hz), indicating an aroused state such as when actively thinking.

Biofeedback - The technique in which an attempt is made to consciously regulate a bodily function thought to be involuntary such as heartbeat, blood pressure, and brain-wave states by using an instrument to monitor the function and to signal changes in it.

Brainstem - The primitive structures that form the central core of the brain, running from the top of the spinal cord into the middle of the brain.

Broca's area - The region within the left frontal lobe that controls the flow of words from brain to mouth.

C

Cell Body - The main portion of a neuron, containing the nucleus.

Cerebellum - The major structure of the hindbrain specialized for motor coordination.

Cerebral Cortex - The layer of gray matter on the surface of the cerebral hemispheres composed of neurons and their synaptic connections that form four to six sub-layers.

Cerebrum - The large, upper portion of the brain consisting of the left and right hemispheres.

Cognitive - The mental process of knowing something through perception, reasoning, or intuition.

Commissure - A bundle of axonic fibers connecting corresponding points on the two sides of the central nervous system. The major commissures are: The corpus callosum, the hippocampal commissure, and the anterior commissure.

Commissural Fibers - Bundles of axonic nerve fibers that link both cerebral hemispheres and the two halves of the limbic system.

Commissurotomy - The surgical cutting of the corpus callosum, the hippocampal and anterior commissures which constitute the three connecting link s between the two brain halves.

Computerized Axial Tomography (CAT) - A technique for diagnosing brain disorders. As an X-ray beam passes through a thin section of the head, detectors record how much radiation the slice absorbed, then relay the information to a computer. The computer mathematically reconstructs the data and projects an image onto a video screen.

Conceptual - Able to conceive thoughts and ideas—to generalize abstract ideas from specific instances.

Controlled - Restrained; holding back; in charge of one's emotions.

Conservative - Tending toward maintaining traditional and proven views, conditions, and institutions.

Creative - Having unusual and original ideas and imaginative thoughts. Able to put things together in new and novel ways.

Critical - Judging the value or feasibility of an idea or product. Looking for faults.

D

Delta - A band of EEG brainwave patterns in the range of .05 to 4 cycles per second (Hz) indicating deep dreamless sleep.

Dendrite - A short, fine branch extending from the cell body of a neuron which receives impulses through synaptic contacts with nearby neurons.

Detailed - Paying attention to the small items or parts of an idea or project.

Disconnection - Severing by damage or by surgery of the

fibers that connect two areas of the brain such that the two areas can no longer communicate; also, the condition that results.

Dominance - The condition or fact of one member of a paired organ being the one principally used to carry out a task, i.e., hand, foot, eye, brain.

Dominant Hemisphere - The condition or fact of one hemisphere controlling the processing of information involved in a particular mental task. Often used to refer to the hemisphere controlling speech.

Dyslexia - Impaired reading and word and number processing often associated with children, particularly left-handed boys.

E

EEG (Electroencephalograph) - A recording of electrical brainwave patterns taken from electrodes placed on the scalp, which are connected to an electronic EEG device.

Emotional - Having feelings that are easily stirred; displaying those feelings.

Empathetic - Able to understand how another person feels and able to communicate that feeling.

Entrepreneur - A person, independent and imaginative, who starts a new business, offering innovative products and/or services.

Epilepsy - A neurological condition characterized by recurrent seizures of various types associated with a disturbance of consciousness.

Extrovert - More interested in people and things outside of selfinternal thoughts and feelings. Quickly and easily exposes thoughts, reactions, feelings, etc., to others.

F

Financial - Competent in monitoring and handling of quantitative issues related to costs, budgets, and investments.

Forebrain - Term used in this book for the cerebral hemispheres—basal ganglia, thalamus, amygdala, hippocampus, and septum.

Frontal Lobe - One of four regions of the cerebral cortex. The frontal lobe lies directly behind the forehead. The hindmost part of this lobe contains the motor cortex.

G

Glial Cell - "Nerve glue;" special cells that surround each neuron, providing support and nourishment.

Going Creative - A transition stage in the mind in which the specialized modes necessary to the creative process become situationally available for application to a task in response to a felt need.

Going Critical - A transition point at which some character or property undergoes a finite change.

Gray matter - Cortical tissue in the brain and spinal cord consisting of the cell bodies of neurons. In the brain, gray matter is located on the surface; the gray matter of the spinal cord is interior.

Gyrus - A convolution of the cortex of the cerebral hemispheres.

H

Hemisphericity - The tendency for one hemisphere to be dominant independent of the task.

Hindbrain - A region of the brain that consists primarily of the cerebellum, medulla, pons, and fourth ventricle.

Hippocampal Commissure - The axonic fiber connecting link between the two halves of the limbic system, smaller, but similar in function to the corpus callosum.

Hippocampus - A U-shaped cortical formation in the limbic system known to play an important role in learning and short-term memory.

Holistic - Able to perceive and understand the "big picture" without dwelling on individual elements of an idea, concept, or situation.

Holography - A photographic technique in which a three-dimensional image is produced from interference patterns created by a split laser beam. Holography has been proposed as a model for memory and perceptual processes.

Hormones - Chemical substances produced by endocrine glands which stimulate the activity of certain organs.

Humanistic Psychology - A school of psychology that emphasizes the uniqueness of human beings and their potential for self-fulfillment; it holds that each person is responsible for his own actions.

Hypothalamus - A part of the limbic system known as the "Brain's Brain;" a small neuron cluster at the base of the forebrain, essential in coordinating central nervous system functions and involved in nearly all behavior, including the regulation of body temperature, sex drive, thirst, and hunger. It also controls endocrine activity and plays an important role in emotions of pain and pleasure.

I

Imaginative - Able to form mental images of things not immediately available to the senses or never wholly perceived in reality; able to confront and deal with a problem in a new way.

Implementation - Able to carry out an activity and ensure fulfillment by concrete measures and results.

Intrapreneur - An innovative leader who organizes, manages, and assumes the risks of a business activity.

Innovating - Able to introduce new or novel ideas, methods, or devices.

Integration - The ability to combine pieces, parts, and elements of ideas, concepts, and situations into a unified whole.

Intellectual - Having superior reasoning powers. Able to acquire and retain knowledge.

Interconnected brain - The physiological result of the proliferation of association, projection, and commissure fibers distributed throughout the brain. This vast network of up to 500 million fibers connect together all major structures of the human brain.

Interpersonal - Able easily to develop and maintain meaningful and pleasant relationships with many different kinds of people.

Introvert - Directed more toward inward reflection and understanding than toward people and things outside of self. Slow to expose reactions, feelings, and thoughts to others.

Intuitive - Knowing something without thinking it out—having instant understanding without need for facts or proof.

Iterative - The repetitive process carried out by the brain's interconnections of moving back and forth between specialized brain modes in order to accomplish a desired mental result.

L

Laterality - Side of the brain that controls a given function; hence, studies of laterality are devoted to determining which side of the brian controls various functions.

Limbic System - A major neural complex of the brain, referred to as mammalian, consisting of a richly interconnected double ring of cortical and sub-cortical structures, each half of which is nestled in one of the cerebral hemispheres with these separate halves joined together by the hippocampal commissure. The limbic system is strongly involved in emotional reactions and behaviors, storing and transforming memories, learning processes and dealing with survival issues such as feeding, fighting, fleeing, and sexual reproduction.

Logical - Able to reason deductively from what has gone before.

M

Mathematical - Perceiving and understanding numbers and being able to manipulate them to a desired end.

Medulla Oblongata - Part of the brainstem linking the spinal cord below with the pons above; controls respiration and blood circulation.

Metaphorical - Able to understand and make use of visual and verbal figures of speech to suggest a likeness or an analogy in place of literal descriptions, e.g., "heart of gold."

Midbrain - The short segment between the forebrain and hindbrain including the tectum and tegmentum.

Modes of Knowing - The specialized ways in which knowledge is acquired and used. Examples include factual, intuitive, visual, kinesthetic, emotional, sequential, verbal, etc.

Musical - Having an interest in or talent for music and/or dance.

Myelin - The fatty white cells forming an insulating sheath around certain nerve fibers including the axonic fibers comprising the corpus callosum and hippocampal commissure and aid in the transmission of electrical impulses.

Myelinization - Formation of myelin on axons. Considered as an index of maturation. Occurs at a younger age in girls compared to boys.

N

Neocortex - Newest layer of the brain, forming the outer layer or "new bark;" has four to six layers of cells. In this book, term synonymous with cortex.

Nerve Impulse - Movement or propagation of an action potential along the length of an axon; begins at a point close to the cell body and travels away from it.

Neuron - The basic conducting unit of the nervous system (also called the nerve cell), consisting of a cell body and threadlike projections that conduct electrical impulses. The axon, a single long fiber, transmits the impulses while shorter extensions called dendrites receive them.

Neuropsychology - The study of the relation between brain function and behavior.

Neurotransmitter - A chemical; one of approximately thirty messenger molecules that transmit impulses from neuron to neuron. Stored in axon terminals, this chemical substance is released into the synaptic gap when a neuron fires and locks onto a receiving cell's dendrites.

NMR - Nuclear Magnetic Resonance. An imaging procedure in which a computer draws a map from the measured changes in the magnetic resonance of atoms in the brain.

Nucleus - A spherical structure in the soma of cells; contains DNA; also, a group of cells forming a cluster that can be identified histologically.

O

Occipital Lobes - A general area of the cortex lying in the back part of the head.

Organized - Able to arrange people, concepts, objects, elements, etc. into coherent relationships with each other.

P

Paralimbic Cortex - A term for areas of three-layered cortex that is adjacent to the classically defined limbic cortex and has a direct connection with limbic cortex, e.g., cingulate cortex.

Parietal Lobe - A region of the cerebral cortex located between the frontal and occipital lobes; the receiving area for touch sensations and information about spatial orientation.

Perception - A cognition resulting from the activity of cells in the various sensory regions of the neocortex beyond the primary sensory cortex.

Phrenology - The study of the relation between the skull's surface features and mental faculties. Long discredited.

Planning - Formulating methods or means to achieve a desired end in advance of taking actions to implement.

Pleasure Centers - Nerve circuits within the hypothalamus and other limbic system sites where pleasurable feelings are thought to originate.

Pons - A portion of the hindbrain composed mostly of motor fiber tracts going to such areas as the cerebellum and spinal tract.

Positron-Emission Transaxial Tomography (PETT) - A tool which produced images of body metabolism used to diagnose brain functions and disorders. The PETT scanner traces radiation through body tissue, following the injection of a radioactive isotope. Analyzing information recorded by the scanner, a computer transforms the data into a color video image of the body's biochemistry.

Preferred Cognitive Mode - Use of one type of thought process in preference to another, e.g., visuo-spatial instead of verbal; sometimes attributed to the assumed superior function of one hemisphere over the other.

Prefrontal Lobe - Part of the frontal lobe lying directly behind the forehead. Its function may be related to the ability to plan and to make choices.

Problem Solving - Able to find solutions to difficult problems by using logical reasoning.

Projection Fibers - One of three types of white matter, they convey impulses between the cerebral cortex and other parts of the nervous system.

Q

Quantitative - Oriented toward numerical relationships and inclined toward measurement of amounts, proportions, and dimensions.

R

Rational - Making choices on the basis of reason as opposed to tradition, emotion, intuition, or speculation.

Reader - One who reads often and enjoys it.

Reticular Formation - A dense web of neurons in the brainstem that regulates consciousness and channels the brain's attention.

Rigorous Thinking - Having a thorough, detailed approach to problem solving.

S

Sequential - Dealing with things and ideas one after another or in order.

Simultaneous - Able to process and make sense of two or more mental inputs, such as visual, musical, or verbal inputs at the same time. Able to attend to two or more activities at the same time.

Sinistrality - Left-handedness.

Spatial - Able to perceive and understand the relative positions of objects in space and able to manipulate them into a desired relationship.

Spiritual - Having to do with spirit or soul as apart from the body or material things.

Symbolic - Abe to use and understand objects, marks, and signs as representative of facts and ideas.

Synapse - The microscopic gap between two adjacent nerve cells. Chemical neurotransmitters carry nerve impulses across the synapse.

Syntax - Grammar; a set of rules for arranging words into phrases and sentences in a given language.

Synthesizer - One who unites separate ideas, elements, or concepts into something new.

T

Tachistoscope - An electro-mechanical apparatus consisting of a projector, viewer, and screen by which visual stimuli can be presented to selective portions of the visual field.

Teaching/Training - Able to explain ideas and procedures in a way that people can understand and apply them.

Technical - Able to understand and apply engineering and scientific knowledge.

Temporal Lobe - The portion of the cerebrum below the Sylvian fissure.

Thalamus - A twin-lobed mass of nerve cells at the top of the brainstem containing relay centers for sensory and motor information to and from the brain.

Theta - The band of EEG brain wave patterns in the range of 4 to 8 cycles per second (Hz). A consciousness level associated with a free flow of ideas and images. A state of deep relaxation.

Triune Brain - An evolutionary model of the brain as a three-layered structure. Each layer represents a different evolutionary state developed by Paul Maclean. The oldest layer, the reptilian brain governs vital body functions. The old mammalian brain, the middle layer, is the center for instinct and feeling and maintains the body's internal equilibrium. The third and latest layer to evolve is the new mammalian brain or cerebrum, where higher thought processes arise.

V

Verbal - Having good speaking skills. Clear and effective with words.

Visual Cortex - The part of the occipital lobe of each hemisphere at the back of the cerebrum. They receive and interpret what the eye sees in each visual half-field.

Visual Half-field - A field of vision to one side of the point of fixation. The total visual field consists of a left visual half-field and a right visual half-field.

W

Wernicke's Area - Part of the left temporal lobe where language is perceived.

White Matter - Connective fibers of brain cells consisting primarily of axons and their myelin coating.

Writer - One who communicates clearly with the written word and enjoys it.

Bibliography

BOOKS

Adams, James. *Conceptual Blockbusting.* W. W. Norton, 1979.

Adizes, Ichak. *How To Solve the Mismanagement Crisis.* Adizes Institute, 1979.

Albrecht, Karl, and Steven Albrecht. *The Creative Corporation.* Dow-Jones-Irwin, 1987.

Arieti, Silvano. *Creativity.* 1976.

Asimov, Isaac. *The Human Brain.* Mentor Books, 1963.

Assagiloi, Roberto. *The Act of Will.* Penguin Books, 1973.

Austin, James H. *Chase, Change, and Creativity: The Lucky Art of Novelty.* Columbia University Press, 1978.

Bandler, Richard. *Frogs Into Princes.* Real People Press, 1979.

Bandler, R., and J. Grinder. *The Structure of Magic.* Science & Behavior, 1975.

Blakemore, Colin. *Mechanics of the Mind.* Cambridge University Press, 1977.

Blakeslee, Thomas. *Right Brain.* Doubleday, 1980.

Blofeld, John. Translated, *I Ching,* 1963.

Bloom, Tagerson, and Hofstader. *Brain, Mind, and Behavior.* W.H. Freeman & Co., 1985.

Bondi, Angelo, ed. *Have An Affair With Your Mind.* The Creative Education Foundation, 1974.

Bondi, Angelo. *The Creative Process.* 1972.

Bonny, Helen, and Louis Savary. *Music and Your Mind.* I C M Press, 1983.

Bransom, Robert, and Allen Harrison. *Styles of Thinking.* Anchor Press: Doubleday, 1982.

Brown, Barbara B. *New Mind, New Body.* Harper & Row Publishers, 1974.

————. *Supermind.* Harper & Row Publishers, 1980.

Bruner, Jerome, and others. *A Study of Thinking.* John Wiley & Sons, 1957.

Bry, Adelaide. *Visualization: Directing the Movies of Your Mind.* Barnes & Noble, 1978.

Buckley-Allen, Madelyn. *Listening: The Forgotten Skill.* John Wiley & Sons, 1982.

Buzan, Tony. *Use Both Sides of Your Brain.* Rev. and updated ed., lst ed., E. P. Dutton, 1982.

Campbell, David. *Take the Road to Creativity.* Argus Communications, 1977.

Campbell, Don G. *Introduction to the Musical Brain.* Magnamusic Baton, Inc., 1984.

Damm and Jerseld, eds. *Serious Fun.* Denmark: Inter Lego, 1979.

DeBono, Edward. *Lateral Thinking.* Harper & Row Publishing, 1970.

Deacato, Carl H. *The Treatment and Prevention of Reading Problems: The Neuropsychological Approach.* C. C. Thomas, 1971.

Diagram Group, The. *The Brain - A User's Manual.* Perigee Books: Putnam Publishing Group, 1987.

Diamond, Schakel, and Elson. *The Human Brain Coloring Book.* Barnes & Noble, 1985.

Dixon, Terence, and Tony Buzan. *The Evolving Brain.* Holt, Rhinehart, & Winston, 1978.

Eccles, Sir John, and David Robinson. *The Wonder of Being Human.* New Science Library, 1985.

Edwards, David D. *How to Be More Creative.* Occasional Productions, 1980.

Edwards, Betty. *Drawing on the Artist Within: A guide to Innovation, Invention, Imagination, and Creativity.* Simon and Schuster, 1985.

————. *Drawing on the Right Side of the Brain: A Course in*

Enhancing Creativity and Artistic Confidence. J. P. Tarcher, Inc., 1979.

Ehrenberg, Miriam, and Otto. *Optimum Brain Power.* Dodd, Mead, 1985.

Fearn, Leif, and Ursula Golesy-Benson. *72 Ways to Have Fun With Your Mind.* Kabyn Books, 1978.

Feldenkrais, Morshe. *Awareness Through Movement.* Harper & Row, 1972.

Ferguson, Marilyn. *The Aquarian Conspiracy.* J. P. Tarcher, 1980.

————. *The Brain Revolution.* Taplinger Publishing Co., 1973.

Fields, Rick, ed. *Chop Wood, Carry Water.* J. P. Tarcher Inc., 1984.

Fincher, Jack, ed. *The Brain.* U. S. News Books, 1981.

Fincher, Jack. *Human Intelligence.* Putnam, 1976.

Fisher, Richard. *Brain Games.* Schooken Books, 1982.

Flesch, Rudolph. *The Art of Clear Thinking.* Harper & Row Publishing, 1951.

Flory, Charles D., ed. *Managing Through Insight.* Mentor Books, 1968.

Flugelman, Andrew. *The New Games Book.* Doubleday/Dolphin, 1976.

Franck, Frederick. *The Zen of Seeing.* Random House, 1973.

Gabriel, Rico. *Writing the Natural Way,* J. P. Tarcher, 1983.

Gallant, Roy A. *Our Universe.* National Georgraphic, 1986.

Gallwey, W. Timothy. *The Inner Game of Tennis.* 1974.

Galyean, Beverly. *Mind Sight, Learning through Imaging.* Center for Integrative Learning, 1983.

Gardner, Howard. *The Mind's New Science.* Basic Books, 1986.

————. *Frames of Mind.* 1983

Gazzaniga, Michael S. *The Integrated Mind.* Plenum Press, 1978.

————. *The Bisected Brain.* Appleton-Century- Crofts, 1970.

Gillmy, Dick, and Robin Brightwell. *The Human Brain.* Facts on File Publishers, 1982.

Goble, Frank. *The Third Force, The Psychology of Abraham Maslow.* Pocket Books, 1971.

Goldberg, Philip. *The Intuitive Edge.* J. P. Tarcher Inc., 1983.

Goldstein, Gerald, and Michael Herser, eds. *Handbook of Psychological Assessment.* Pergamon, 1984.

Goodspeed, Bennett. *The Tao Jones Averages.* Dalton, 1983.

Gordon, J.J. *Synectics.* Harper & Row, 1961.

Green, Elmer, and Alyce Green. *Beyond Biofeedback.* Dell Publishing Co., Inc., 1977.

Grove, Andrew S. *High Output Management.* Random House, 1983.

Hall, Calvin S. *The Measuring of Dreams.* McGraw-Hill, 1966.

Hampden-Turner, Charles. *Maps of the Mind.* Collier Books, 1982.

Hanson, Peter, M.D. *The Joy of Stress.* Andrews, McMed, & Parker, 1985.

Hart, Leslie A. *How the Brain Works: A New Understanding of Human Learning, Emotion, and Thinking.* Basic Books, 1975.

Hayakawa, S.I. *The Use and Misuse of Language.* Fawcett Books, 1962.

Hendricks, Gay, and Russell Wells. *The Centering Book.* Prentice-Hall, 1975.

Hersey, Paul, and Ken Blanchard. *Management of Organizational Behavior.* Prentice-Hall, 1982.

Hobson, Robert. *Forms of Feelings.* Tavistock, 1985.

Houston, Jean. *The Possible Human.* J.P. Tarcher, 1982.

Hunt, Morton. *The Universe Within.* Simon & Schuster, 1981.

Hutchinson, Michael. *Mega Brain.* William Morrow, 1986.

Ingalls, John. *Human Energy*. Addison-Wesley, 1976.

Jamison, Kaleen. *The Nibble Theory*. Paulist Press, 1984.

Jantsch, Erich, and C. H. Waddington. *Evolution and Consciousness: Human Systems in Transition*. Addison-Wesley, 1976.

Jastrow, Robert. *The Enchanted Loom: Mind in the Universe*. Simon & Schuster, 1981.

Jaynes, Julean. *The Origin of Consciousness in the Breakdown of the Bicameral Mind*. Houghton-Mifflin, 1977.

Kanter, Rosabeth Moss. *Change Masters*. Simon & Schuster, 1983.

Keersey, David. *Please Understand Me*. Promelhan Books, 1978.

Kidd, J. R. *How Adults Learn*. Academic Press: Follet Publishing Company, 1973.

Koberg, Don, and Jim Bagnall. *The Universal Traveler*. William Kaufman, Inc., 1976.

Koestler, Arthur. *The Act of Creation*. Dell Publishing Company Inc., 1967.

Kolb, Rubin, McIntyre. *Organizational Psychology*. 2nd ed. Prentice-Hall, 1974.

Kolb, Bryan, and Ian Whishaw. *Fundamentals of Human Neuropsychology*. 2nd ed. W.H. Freeman & Co., 1985.

Kudel, J.R. *How Adults Learn*. Follett Publishing, 1973.

Laborde, Gene Z. *Influences with Integrity*. Syntony Inc., 1984.

Lawrence, Jodi. *Alpha Brain Waves*. Avon, 1972.

Lee, James A. *The Gold and Garbage in Management Theories and Descriptions*. Ohio University Press, 1980.

Leff, Herbert. *Playful Perception*. Waterfront Books, 1984.

Leonard, George B. *Education and Ecstasy*. Dell, 1968.

Lewis, David, and James Green. *Thinking Better*. Rawson-Wade, 1982.

Likert, Rensis. *The Human Organization*. McGraw-Hill, 1967.

Luria, A. R. *The Working Brain*. Basic Books, Inc., 1973.

Machado, Luis Alberto. *The Right to Be Intelligent*. Permagon Press, 1971.

Mandler, George. *Mind and Emotion*. John Wiley & Sons, 1975.

Masterson, James. *The Real Self*. Brunner/Magel, 1985.

McCarthy, Bernice. *The 4Mat in Action, Creative Lesson Plans for Teaching to Learning Styles with Right/Left Mode Techniques*. Excel, 1983.

———. *The 4Mat System, Teaching to Learning Styles Through Right/Left Mode Techniques*. Excel, 1981.

McConnell, James V. *Understanding Human Behavior*. 1974.

McKim, Robert. *Experiences in Visual Thinking*. Brooks/Cple, 1972.

Meirowitz, Marco, and Paul I. Jacobs. *Brain Muscle Builders*. Prentice-Hall, 1983.

Meyers, William. *The Image Makers*. Times Books, 1984.

Mintzberg, Henry. *The Nature of Managerial Work*. 1973.

Monroe, Robert A. *Journeys Out of Body*. Updated. Anchor Press: Doubleday, 1977.

Moore, Linda. *You're Smarter Than You Think*. Holt, Rhinehart, and Winston, 1985.

Neurenberg, Gerard. *The Art of Creative Thinking*. Simon & Schuster, 1982.

Ohmae, Kenichi. *The Mind of the Strategist*. Penguin Books, 1982.

Ornstein, Robert E. *The Psychology of Consciousness*. W. H. Freeman & Co., 1972.

———. *Mind Field*. Crossman, 1976.

———. *The Nature of Human Consciousness*. W. H. Freeman & Co., 1973.

Ornstein, Robert E., and Richard Thompson. *The Amazing*

Brain. Houghton-Mifflin Co., 1984.

Ornstein, Robert E., Philip R. Lee, David Galin, Arthur Deikman, and Charles T. Tart. *Symposium on Consciousness*. Penguin Books, 1976.

Ostrander, Sheila. *Superlearning*. Delta Publishing, 1979.

Ostrander, Sheila, and L. Schroeder. *Superlearning*. Delacorte Press & Confucian Press, 1979.

———. *Superlearning*. Pocket Books, 1975.

Paivo, Allen. *Imagery and Verbal Processes*. Holt, Rhinehart, and Winston, 1971.

Parnes, Noller and Angelo Biondi. *Guide to Creative Action*. Charles Scribner's Sons, 1977.

Pascale, Richard, and Anthony Athos. *The Art of Japanese Management*. Warner Books, 1981.

Pearce, Joseph Chilton. *Exploring the Crack in the Cosmic Egg: Split Mind and Meta Realities*. Julian Press, 1974.

———. *Magical Child*. paper, Bantam, 1980.

Peck, Scott, M.D. *The Different Drum*. Simon & Schuster, 1987.

———. *The Road Less Traveled*. Simon & Schuster, 1978.

Pelletier, Kenneth. *Mind as Healer, Mind as Slayer*. Dell Publishing, 1977.

Pelletire, K. and C. Garfield. *Consciousness East and West*. Harper & Row Publishing Co., 1976.

Penfield, Wilder. *The Mystery of the Mind*. Princeton University Press, 1975.

Penfield, Wilder, and R. Lamar. *Speech and Brain Mechanisms*. Princeton University Press, 1959.

Peters, Thomas, and Robert Waterman. *In Search of Excellence*. Warner Books, 1982.

Pinchut, Gifford. Intrapreneuring: *Why You Don't Have to Leave the Corporation to Become an Entrepreneur*. Harper & Row, 1985.

Pines, Maya. *The Brain Changers*. Signet.

Pirsig, Robert M. *Zen and the Art of Motorcycle Maintenance*. Morrow, paper 1974.

Prather, Hugh. *Notes To Myself*. Real People Press, 1979.

Pribam, Karl. *Languages of the Brain*.

Prince, George M. *The Practice of Creativity*. Macmillan Publishing, 1970. (out of print)

The Rand McNally Atlas of the Body and Mind. Rand McNally, 1976. contributing editor, Claire Raynor.

Raudsepp, Eugene. *Growth Games for the Creative Manager*. Putnam Publishing Group, 1987.

———. *Motivating and Managing Creative Individuals*. (S.L.) Princeton Creative Research, Inc. 1978.

———. *How Creative Are You*. Putham Publishing Group, 1981.

———. *Conformity vs. Innovation*. (S.I.) Princeton Creative Research Inc., 1978.

———. *Characteristics of the Creative Individual*. Princeton Creative Research Inc., 1978.

———. *Why Be Creative?* (S.I.) Princeton Creative Research Inc. [197-]

Raudsepp, Eugene, and George P. Hough, Jr. *Creative Growth Games*. Harcourt Brace Jovanovich, Inc., 1977.

Restak, Richard. *The Brain*. Bantam Books, 1984.

———. *The Brain: The Last Frontier*. Doubleday, 1979.

Rivlin, Robert, and Karen Gravelle. *Deciphering the Saises*. Simon & Schuster, 1984.

Rogers, Carl. *Carl Rogers on Personal Power*. Delta, 1977.

Rose, Steven. *The Conscious Brain*. Vintage Books, 1976.

Rowin, Roy. *The Intuitive Manager*. Little, Brown, 1986.

Russell, Peter. *The Global Brain*. J. P. Tarcher, 1983.

———. *The Brain Book*. Hawthorn Books, 1979.

Sagan, Carl. *The Dragons of Eden.* Random House, 1977.

Samples, Bob. *Open Mind/Whole Mind.* Jalmar Press, 1987.

———. *The Metaphoric Mind.* Addison-Wesley, 1979.

———. *Mind of Our Mother.* Addison-Wesley, 1981.

Samuels, Mike, and Nancy Samuels. *Seeing with the Mind's Eye.* Random House, 1975.

Segalowitz, Sid, and F. Gruber. *Language Development and Neurological Theory.* Academic Press, 1977.

———. *Two sides of the Brain.* Prentice-Hall, 1983.

Shah, Idries. *The Sufis.* 1st ed., Doubleday, 1964.

Sheehy, Gail. *Passages.* Dutton, 1976.

Shook, Robert L. *The Entrepreneurs.* Barnes & Noble. 1980.

Sin, R.G.H. *The Master Manager.* John Wiley & Sons, 1980.

Sittrock, M.C. *Changing Education.* 1973.

Smith, Adam. *Powers of the Mind.* Ballantine Books, 1975.

Sobel, Roberto, and David Sicilia. *The Entrepreneurs: An American Adventure.* Houghton-Mifflin Co., 1986.

Springer, Sally, and George Deutsch. *Left Brain, Right Brain.* W. H. Freeman & Co., 1981.

Steele, Fritz, and Stephen Jeuks. *The Feel of the Workplace.* Addison-Wesley, 1977.

Summers, George J. *Test Your Logic: 50 Puzzles in Deductive Reasoning.* Dover, 1972.

Thompson, William, M.D. *Brain and Personality.* Dodd, Mead. 1906.

Tichy, Noel and MaryAnne Devanna. *The Transformational Leader.* John Wiley & Sons 1986.

Vaughan, Frances. *Awakening Intuition.* Anchor Books, 1979.

Virshup, Evelyn. *Art and the Right Hemisphere.* Art Education, 1976.

Vitale, Barbara Meister. *Unicorns Are Real: A Right-Brained Approach to Learning.* Jalmar Press, 1982.

Von Fange, Eugene. *Professional Creativity: A New and Timely Analysis of Creative Thinking.* Prentice-Hall, 1959.

Wallas, Lee. *Stories for the Third Era.* Norton, 1985.

Whimbey, Arthur, and Jack Lockhead. *Problem Solving and Comprehension: A Short Course in Analytic Reasoning.* Philadelphia: Franklin Institute Press, 1979.

Wittrock, M.C. *Changing Education - Alternatives From Educational Research.* Prentice-Hall, 1973.

Wittrock, M.C., and others. *The Human Brain.* Prentice-Hall, 1977.

Williams, Linda. *Teaching for the Two-Sided Mind.* Prentice-Hall, 1983.

Winter, Arthur, and Ruth Winter. *Build Your Brain Power.* St. Martins, 1986.

Wolf, Fred Alan. *Star Waves.* MacMillan, 1985.

Zdenek, Marilee. *The Right Brain Experience.* McGraw-Hill, 1983.

PERIODICALS

Brain-Mind Bulletin. Editor, Marilyn Ferguson, P O Box 42211, Los Angeles, CA 90042.

Dromenon. Foundation For Mind Research (Houston & Masters), Editor, Jane Prettyman, GPO Box 2244, New York, NY 10001.

Harper's Magazine. Special Issue: The World of the Brain. December 1975.

Re-Vision. Special Edition. A Journal of Knowledge and Consciousness. Summer/Fall 1978 (Vol. No. 3/4).

Saturday Review, Special Edition. August 9, 1975.

Science News. *"Brain Hemisphere Dominance,"* May 1971, p.265

UCLA Educator. vol. 17, no. 2 Spring 1975, *Education and the*

Hemispheric Process of the Brain: I. Introduction to Research on the Brain by Harry J. Jerison. II. Recent Research on Hemisphere Lateralization of the Human Brain: "Review of the Split Brain" by Michael S. Gazzaniga; "Man's so-called 'Minor' Hemisphere" by Robert D. Nebes; "The Major Hemisphere" by Stephen D. Krashen. III. Educational Implications of Hemispheric Lateralization of the Human Brain: "Educational Aspects of Hemisphere Specialization: by Joseph E. Bogen, M.D.; "The Generative Processes of Memory" by M.C. Wittrock.

MEETINGS/DELIVERED PAPERS

6th Annual Meeting of the Biofeedback Research Society. "Biofeedback Training for Bilateral EEG Synchronization of Individuals and Subject Pairs," 1975.

Biological Foundations of Psychiatry. "Hemispheric Specialization: Implications For Psychiatry," 1976.

6th International Congress of Electroencephalography and Clinical Neurophysiology EEG Phase. "Asymmetries and Laterality Preference," 1965.

American EEG Society. "Electroencephalography and Clinical Neurophysiology," 1967.

ARTICLES

Bakan, Paul. "The Right Brain is the Dreamer." *Psychology Today,* November 1976, pp. 6-68.

———. "Hynotizability, Laterality of Eye Movements and Functional Brain Asymmetry." *Perceptual & Motor Skills* 28 (1969): 927-932.

———. "The Eyes Have It." *Psychology Today,* 11 April 1971, pp. 64-67.

Bakker, D., T. Smink, and P. Reitsma. "Early Dominance and Reading Ability." *Cortex* 9 (1973): 302-312.

Beckmanm, Lucile. "The Use of the Block Design Sub Test of the WISC as an Identifying Instrument for Spatial Children." *Gifted Child Quarterly,* Spring 1977.

Bever, T., and R. Chiarello. "Cerebral Dominance in Musicians and Non-Musicians." *Science* 185 (1974): 537-539.

Brandwein, P., and R. Ornstein. "The Duality of the Mind." *Instructor,* 86, no. 5 (January 1977): 54-58.

Brazier, M. A. "The Analysis of Brain Waves." *Scientific American,* June 1962, pp. 142-153.

Buck, Craig. "Knowing the Left from the Right." *Human Behavior,* June 1976, pp. 9-35.

Damasio, H., A. Damasio, A. Castro-Caldas, and J.M. Ferro. "Dichotic Listening Pattern in Relation to Interhemispheric Disconnexion." *Neuropsychologia,* 14 (1976): 247-250.

Foster, Suzanne. "Hemisphere Dominance and the Art Process." *Art Education,* February 1977, pp. 28-29.

Franco, L., and R.W. Sperry. "Hemisphere Lateralization for Cognitive Processing of Geometry." *Neuropsychologia* 15 (1977): 107-14.

Garret, Susan V. "Putting Our Whole Brain To Use: A Fresh Look At The Creative Process". *Journal of Creative Behavior* 10, no.4 (1976): 239-249.

Gazzaniga, Michael S. "One Brain-Two Minds?" *American Scientist,* May-June 1972, pp. 311-317.

———."The Split Brain Man." *The Brain and Consciousness,* August 1967, pp. 24-29.

———. "The Split Brain in Man." *Scientific American,* August 1967, pp. 24-29.

———. "Review of Split Brain." *J. Neurology* 209 (1975): 75-79.

Geschwind, Norman. "Language and the Brain." *Scientific American,* April, 1972.

Golt, Peggy S. "Cognitive Abilities-Following Right and Left Hemispherectomy." *Cortex* 9 (1973): 266-73.

Green, Alyce, Elmer E. Green, and E. Dale Walters. "Report: Brain Wave Training, Imagery, Creativity, and Integrative Experiences." Research Department of the Menniger Foundation, April 1973.

———. "Report: Biofeedback for Mind-Body Self Regulation." Research Department of the Menniger Foundation, October 1971.

Hammond, John. "The Roles of Manager and the Management Scientist in Successful Implementation." *Sloan Management Review.* 15 (Winter 1974): 1-24

Kimura, Doreen. "The Asymmetry of the Human Brain." *Scientific American,* March 1973, pp. 70-78.

Lamott, Kenneth. "Why Men and Women Think Differently." *Horizon Magazine,* May 1977, pp. 40-45.

McKenney, J. L., and P. G. W. Keen. "How Managers' Moods Work" *Harvard Business Review,* May 1974, pp. 79-90.

Mintzberg, Henry. "Planning on the Left Side and Managing on the Right." *Harvard Business Review,* July 1976, p. 49-58.

Regelski, Thomas A. "Who Knows Where Music Lurks in the Mind of Man: New brain research has the answer." *Music Educators Journal* 63 no.9 (May 1977): 31- 38.

Regelski, Thomas A. "Music Education and the Human Brain." *The Education Digest,* 43 (October 1977): 44-47.

Ray, W., M. Morrell, A. Frediani, and D. Tucker. "Sex Differences and Lateral Specialization of Hemispheric Functioning." *Neurophysiology* 14 (1976): 391-394.

Samples, Bob. "Are You Teaching Only One Side of the Brain?" *Learning,* February 1975, pp. 25-28.

Sperry, R. W. April 1977. "Bridging Science and Values — A Unifying view of Mind and Brain." *American Psychologist,* 32 no. 4 (April 1977): 237-245

Springer, S., and Michael Gazzaniga. "Dichotic Testing of Partial and Complete Split-Brain Subjects." *Neuropsychologia* 13 (1975): 341-46.

FILMS

Split-Brain, Indiana University, 1967.
The Mind of Man, N. E. T. 1971.
The Hidden Universe: The Brain, McGraw-Hill, 1977.
The Enchanted Loom, Thames Films Co., 1978.
The Beginning, Stephen B. Productions, 1978.
Where All Things Belong, Essential Productions, 1976.
The Human Brain, University of California at San Diego
Left Brain/Right Brain, Canadian Broadcasting

ACKNOWLEDGMENTS

In reading this book, you may have formed the impression that I did all this work myself. In fact, I have had many collaborators who helped me along the way. I feel it appropriate here to acknowledge all those who contributed directly to the book, as well as those who played such an important role in my life that I was able to write it.

THANK YOU, GE YOU'VE BROUGHT GOOD THINGS TO MY LIFE!

GE didn't recruit me. I already knew that it was the right company for me. Perhaps my own sense of inner diversity led me to seek a company with over a quarter of a million products. The decision, right at the time, is one I've never regretted.

After 35 years of preparation for my exciting new career, it was also right to initiate the process of "graduating" from GE. It was this transaction that revealed the true soul of the corporation. In recognition of its value and on conditions that I would continue to make my work available to the company on request, GE assigned to me everything regarding brain dominance that I had created during the previous seven years. In particular:

- My three standard employee patent agreements with the company were formally revoked.

- Copyright ownership of the Herrmann Brain Dominance Instrument was transferred to me for the sum of one dollar on the condition that my name be included in the title.

- The designs of the Brain Update Seminar and Applied Creative Thinking Workshop—ACT I (and ACT II, the follow-up workshop). The company agreed to sponsor both workshops by including them in the company's Professional Development Catalog for the next five years.

When people ask me, "Why didn't you leave sooner?" my answer is, "I hadn't learned enough to leave any sooner." It's the same with this book: I couldn't have written it any sooner because I hadn't learned enough until just now.

GE was the ideal company for me because it provided diverse opportunities and because it was filled with wonderful people. Some of them were especially helpful to me because they had faith in me and were willing to take a chance on my uniqueness. The key ones among many are Maynard Boring, Marion Kellogg, Warren Hutchins, Don Wright, Jerry Hoyt, David Shaw, Barbara Woods Smuland, Gil Dwyer, Lindon (Lindy) Saline, Naomi Steinberg, Christine Metzger, Bob Mills, Dave Dickson, Frank Doyle, Jim Baughman, and Reginald Jones.

Principal among these was Lindy Saline. He knew me first as a singer and actor in the early stages of my career, 20 years later as an artist. His knowledge of my work at GE was pretty general, but he did know that I was effective as a teacher and presenter. It is of special significance to me that his initial attraction came about as a result of my "non-work," right-mode activities. Many executives would have considered these activities inappropriate or, at best, only peripheral to my career. These activities were in fact the basis of being selected for the position that was to ultimately lead me to my life's work.

Lindy's acceptance and support of me as an artist was particularly important to my self-image and motivation. Having already claimed my creative space, I now flourished under his sponsorship, which allowed me to further establish myself as a creative person in a highly visible way. For example, the original art show he'd invited me to hold at the Management Development Institute evolved into an annual event and resulted in my becoming known throughout the company as a "creative person." The self-confidence this generated encouraged me to use my creativity every day in business applications. So it was largely through the understanding and support of my mentor that my creative urge, once again, became "normal" and for the first time since my joyous high school years, I was able to function as an integrated person throughout my workday and leisure hours. Through the actions I took to claim and own my space, I was able to validate myself.

While Lindy exhibited extraordinary faith and support, he also set very high performance standards and demanded results befitting a world-class company. This suited me very well, for my strategy was to excel in everything I did, but particularly those things that were generated and sponsored by corporate headquarters. Performing superbly in those areas would evoke more tolerance for self-initiated experimentation. This strategy paid off. Work done in developing a strategic planning seminar and an effective cash management seminar, each for 10,000 key managers, produced such overwhelmingly positive results that I feel my brain research was tolerated by those who might otherwise have shut me down.

We don't often get the chance during our active careers to ask our managers to consider why they supported us the way they did. I recently had that chance, five years after I left GE, when I visited Lindy Saline in his new home on the banks of the Mississippi near LaCrosse, Wisconsin. He, too, had "graduated" from GE three years after my departure. When I asked him, "Lindy, why did you support me?" he replied that his long knowledge of me as a singer, actor, and artist gave him a firm basis for trusting my creativity. He indicated that he knew from my work record that I would come through with good results. But it was his trust of my right-mode interests and capabilities that motivated him to support me the way he did. Although he has never revealed it, I am absolutely certain that he sheltered me from the disapproval of a few high-level executives who considered my ideas and research as too far out for a company like GE.

Of crucial significance to my success was the sensitivity and understanding of Reginald Jones, who was then the Chief Executive Officer of the company. Reg Jones's understanding of the potential significance of my work and his expression of personal interest in it helped establish research into left brain/right brain and triune brain theories as appropriate activity for one of the world's largest and greatest corporations. That in itself represented a major contribution to my ultimate success. He became interested and intrigued with my work, and after several years of receiving occasional progress reports, invited me to address the Corporate Policy Board in GE's boardroom in June 1977. Although I had already run 20 brain update workshops for 1,000 people, I worked hard at putting together the most professional and effective presentation possible. As a result of this session, a high-level study was commissioned to determine whether or not the company should support my continuing research and development. A month later I was visited by two senior vice presidents who delivered what they characterized as "some good news" and "some bad news." The good news was that my research could continue and even be funded at a higher level. The bad news they had to report was that the scope of my research and application work had to be confined to what they described as the relatively narrow fields of learning and creativity. Little did these two traditionally minded executives realize that for me their "bad news" opened the golden doors to heaven. I proceeded immediately to claim the creative space they made available to me, and by the work I've done, took ownership of that space for the pursuit of what has now joyously become my life's work. Thanks again, Lindy! Thanks again, Reg! Thanks again, GE!

THANKS TO MY ART COLLEAGUES

To the Stamford Art Association—its founders, officers, and members—I express my thanks and never-ending gratitude for their artistic stimulation, friendship, and especially for the creative opportunities provided me that played such an important role in my rediscovery of the brain as the source of creativity. Particularly important to my development were Bob Calrow, Vivian Reed, Faber Birren, Alice Katz, Bill Strosahl, and especially Bob Jones—an artist's artist, whose high standards, impeccable ethics, good humor, and artistic competence influenced me greatly.

To the members of the SilverMine Guild of Artists—I express my thanks and appreciation for the opportunity to be artistically and musically stimulated by my association with this enormously talented group.

THANKS TO MY KEY ASSOCIATES

To my key associates—I express my special appreciation and gratitude for their continuing interest, support, and significant personal contributions to my own understanding of the brain dominance concepts that have been developed and advanced through our mutual interaction. Special thanks to senior associates Forrest Belcher, Geil Browning, Ted Coulson, Ayn Decker, Penny Dunning, Manny Elkind, Martha Laucius, Chuck McVinney, Gene Myers, Ron Pevny, Jean Paul Plumez, Alison Strickland, Mark Wilcox, and Wendell Williams. I especially thank Alison Strickland and Ted Coulson, who as the original members of my faculty became the principal leaders of ACT. Over the years, they have contributed significantly to the design of the ACT I workshop, as well as CPS and ACTAL, and thus have enriched the lives of many hundreds of participants as well as my own.

To my business associates who are working with me to develop new applications of my work through The Whole Brain Corporation—particularly Charles Atkinson, Irving Goldberg, Andrew Farrar, and Michael Coyle—I express my appreciation for their longstanding interest and continuing commitment.

In the development of the Herrmann Brain Dominance Instrument, no collaborator deserves more thanks than C. Victor Bunderson. His continuing interest and commitment single him out amongst all colleagues. His guidance and counsel have been of inestimable value, his psychometric and computer expertise essential to my success. More than anything else, it's Vic's friendship that I truly appreciate.

Victor's past associate, James Olsen, and his current associate, Kevin Ho, also contributed substantially to the validation process.

THANK YOU EDITORS

To my editors—Sue Kidney, Nahum Stiskin, Pat Stonick, and Jacqui Bishop—I owe an enormous debt of gratitude, particularly to Jacqui Bishop, who as both the beginning and final editor, greatly influenced the concept, organization, format, and writing of the book. She not only edited it, but also translated many of my only partially verbalized thoughts into finished writing. Her contribution to the final result cannot be overstated.

Sue Kidney made a major contribution by organizing my extensive first drafts into related topic areas. Nahum Stiskin made a major contribution by bringing coherence to the book through the organization of topics and issues into discrete chapters. Pat Stonick contributed importantly to both style and grammar.

THANK YOU, STAFF
YOU SAVED MY LIFE!

To my Applied Creative Services, Ltd., office staff—my special gratitude and appreciation for their encouragement, support, and always good-humored help. This includes their understanding and affirmation of me during the writing process and especially for preparing and keeping track of numerous pieces and parts of the book over the five years of its writing. Those who have been especially involved over this period include Ann Herrmann-Nehdi, Laura Herrmann, Terry Beck, Angie Conner, Marie Crisp, Rebecca Fairer, Sylvia McDaniel, Nehdi, Linda Powell, Dorothy Roche, and Bob Geyer. Marie Crisp and Sylvia McDaniel did most of the word processing during the early draft stage. Sylvia McDaniel deserves special commendation for her major role in preparing the final manuscript, which sometimes involved as many as 20 "final" drafts of each chapter. Her patience, skill, and good humor are most appreciated.

SPECIAL THANKS TO MY
BOOK PRODUCTION STAFF

I am particularly grateful to Laura Herrmann for her contributions as Book Project Manager. Working with editors, book designers, artists, printers, distributors, promotion experts, and numerous other specialists, she brought the book into being in a timely and impressive manner. Her job called for patience and understanding beyond the norm, and I am especially pleased that our relationship as father and daughter was enhanced as a result.

Roger Merrill—graphic designer and illustrator from Orem, Utah—spent many hours to make this book into a visually coherent and unique whole. In both the format and the illustrations, Roger translated my ideas into sound graphics and illustration. As the manuscript evolved, we both learned how to grow and change with it. His expertise, creativity, responsiveness, and patience throughout the project were essential to its completion and are qualities which I admire.

MY HEARTFELT THANKS TO THESE SPECIAL PEOPLE WHO KEPT MY BODY AND SOUL TOGETHER:

Abraham Genicin, M.D. of Baltimore, Maryland who monitored my health for the past 23 years and gave me lifesaving advice on numerous occasions.

William Burch, M.D. of Lake Lure, North Carolina for keeping me healthy the past 6 years and in the process, greatly improving my chances for good health the next 5 years.

Rev. Everette Chapman of the Fairfield Mountains Chapel for reawakening my spiritual self with his inspirational ministry and warm friendship.

TO MY FAMILY

Over the course of the five years that I have been actively engaged in writing this book, I was blessed by the support and understanding of my entire family—my wife, Margy, and my three daughters, Pat, Ann, and Laura, and my 92-year-old mother, Charlotte. The star of the family show is Margy. She not only supported and affirmed me in the writing of the book, but was a constant, positive force toward the book's successful completion.

INDEX

p. 79   profiles
86-87   single/double
            dominance
               A & B dominance
91   time
163   comm
191   stages & brain
104   Entrepeneur